JOIN LOYALTY AND LIBERTY

JOIN LOYALTY AND LIBERTY

A History of the Worshipful
Company of Joiners and Ceilers

CHARLOTTE YOUNG

AMBERLEY

First published 2021

Amberley Publishing
The Hill, Stroud
Gloucestershire, GL5 4EP

www.amberley-books.com

British Library Cataloguing in Publication Data.
A catalogue record for this book is available from the British Library.

ISBN 978 1 3981 0822 6 (hardback)
ISBN 978 1 3981 0822 6 (ebook)

1 2 3 4 5 6 7 8 9 10

Typesetting by SJmagic DESIGN SERVICES, India.
Printed in the UK.

Contents

Contents

H. James de Sausmarez CC, Master of the Worshipful Company of Joiners and Ceilers.

Foreword

From the Master of the
Worshipful Company of Joiners and Ceilers

I am writing this preface at the end of an extraordinary year, not just for the Worshipful Company of Joiners and Ceilers and the City of London, but for everyone across the world as we fight the COVID-19 pandemic. Our banquets, dinners and events have all been cancelled and replaced with online meetings and activities. The annual Church service of re-dedication at St James Garlickhythe was, for the first time in living memory, moved from its traditional St James' Day date at the end of July to September, when it was live streamed to those members unable to attend. My installation as Master took place at the end of that service.

It is a great honour to serve as Master of a City Livery Company and, rather unusually, I have the honour of serving for a second time having already been Master in 2009–10. I was given this special honour by my fellow Past Masters and my brother and sister Liverymen so I could lead the celebrations of the 450th anniversary of the granting of our Royal Charter by Queen Elizabeth I in 1571. These celebrations include an exhibition of our Company, its history and its craft at the Guildhall Art Gallery; a celebration Banquet at the Mansion House in the presence of the Lord Mayor and, we hope, the Duchess of Cornwall; a special service of re-dedication; and participation in the Lord Mayor's Show in 2021. It also includes the commissioning and publication of this first full history of our Company.

In this regard, I am deeply indebted to Past Master John Skarratt, who first mooted the idea of commissioning a full history, and to Past Master Tony Stockwell, whose constant encouragement and support ensured I persevered with making it happen. I am also indebted to our Clerk and Archivist, Past Master Alastair MacQueen, for all his help and support. Of course, it would not have happened without the financial support of our sponsors who between them made sure the costs of this history were covered. These sponsors are listed below, and I offer them not only my most grateful thanks but the thanks of those Freemen and Liverymen who came before us and will come after us. All but one are members of the Company with that one exception being James Latham Timber, a close friend and supporter of our Company and a long-established firm of timber merchants.

My biggest thanks go, of course, to Dr Charlotte Young for agreeing to research and write this history. Her dedication, academic rigour and uncanny ability to read Elizabethan and Georgian handwriting has ensured that this history will not only be an important record for the Worshipful Company of Joiners and Ceilers, but also a major contribution to the history of the Livery movement of the City of London. Dr Young has brought the Company to life by making this history easy to read and also fascinating in the tale it tells of a Company dedicated to excellence in the crafts of joinery and wood carving; constant in its charitable support of its members and their dependents and of those seeking to learn the craft; justifying its nickname of the 'Jolly Joiners' in all its functions and events; and, equally importantly, playing its part in the great history of the City of London.

I am sure there are many others to thank including the London Metropolitan Archives and the Guildhall Library where the Company's minute books and records including the original Royal Charter are kept so safe and well. I apologise if I have omitted to mention you in person.

I hope you enjoy reading this history and that it causes you to take a greater interest in the Worshipful Company of Joiners and Ceilers and the Livery movement in general. Perhaps my successors as both Master and Liveryman in the years ahead will find this history as fascinating as I have and be equally proud that they are now part of it.

H. James de Sausmarez CC
Master
Worshipful Company of Joiners and Ceilers
31 December 2020

From the Author

This has been, without doubt, the most challenging, rewarding, fascinating, and at times infuriating project I have ever been involved with. I began it knowing absolutely nothing about the Worshipful Company of Joiners and Ceilers, but have grown to deeply admire their passion, their journey, and their history.

This project was handed to me by Dr Jessica Lutkin who had previously been in charge of it but was unable to continue. A semi-flippant comment to her in the common room at the Institute of Historical Research about not having enough work led to the handover, and I am eternally grateful that I bumped into her that day. I must also thank Jessica and Dr Laurie Lindey for graciously sharing their theses with me at the start of this project, both of which proved to be invaluable. Thanks are also due to Catherine for her excellent proofreading, to Christine for her constant support and encouragement, and to Andrew for keeping me sane during the final stages of preparing this text for publication.

My biggest thanks go to the Master, H. James de Sausmarez, and the whole Company for trusting me with this project. In spite of the challenges of archives and libraries being closed due to COVID-19, which caused considerable disruption to the research, I hope I have produced something you can be proud of, and that you feel I have done your Company justice.

Charlotte Young
4 January 2021

Sponsors

This history of the Worshipful Company of Joiners and Ceilers was commissioned by the Court of Assistants of the Company as a part of the celebrations of the 450th anniversary of the granting of the Royal Charter to the Company in 1571. However, this would not have been possible without the financial support of those listed below, to whom the whole Company, past, present and future, owes an enormous debt.

Master and Past Master H. James de Sausmarez CC
Past Master Tony Stockwell and the whole Stockwell family
James Latham (Timber Distributors)
Past Master David Latham
Past Master Clive Capel
Past Master and Clerk Alastair MacQueen
Liveryman John Briner
Liveryman Keith Miller
Past Master James Vickers
Liveryman Christian Steinman
Liveryman and Steward Jeremy Baldwin
Past Master Roger Poulton
Liveryman Gareth Watkins
Renter Warden Joe Parker
Liveryman Peter Ames
Liveryman Stephen Robbins
Liveryman Chris Castle
Liveryman Lester Corp
Past Master John Farrar
Liveryman Geoff Ellis
Liveryman Edward Corp
Past Master Clive Turrell
Liveryman Garry Wykes
Immediate Past Master and Upper Warden Chris Chivers
Yeoman Robert Zipfel
Liveryman Nigel Laws
Liveryman The Rt Rev Graeme Knowles CVO
Past Master John Corp
Past Master Derek Woods

Past Masters of the Worshipful Company of Joiners and Ceilers, 1571–2021

Note: An asterisk (*) indicates the holder died in office.

Name	Date	Name	Date
Lewis Stockett	1571–2	Nicholas Eales	1636–7
Edmund Chapman	1572–3	Henry Myland	1637–8
William Land	1574–5	Thomas Hardinge	1638–9
John Symons	1590–1	William Graves	1639–40
Matthew Grace	1613–4	Thomas Coe	1640–1
Lancelot Smith	1618–9	John Richmond	1641–2
William Gossen	1621–2	Robert Johnson	1642–3
Rowland Worlington/ Worthington	1622–3	Stephen Gold	1643–4
		Joseph Peake	1644–5
Roger Dalton	1623–4	William Leversidge	1645–6
Francis Atkins	1624–5	Henry Sille	1646–7
John Hamond	1625–6	George Peirson	1647–8
Henry Johnson	1626–7	Abraham Nunns	1648–9
Robert Linton	1627–8	John Burte	1649–50
Thomas Saunders	1628–9	Christopher Turner	1650–1
William Rogers	1629–30	John Johnson	1651–2
Edward Ashe	1630–1	Christopher Turner	1652–3
Leonard Tennant	1632–3	Edward Huson	1653–4
Edward Lilley	1633–4	William Lucas	1654–5
Thomas Cosen	1634–5	Robert Hage	1655–6
William Smith	1635–6	Gabriel Holland	1656–7
Mr Hardinge	1636–7*	Gabriel Townsend	1657–8

Name	Date	Name	Date
John Norris	1658–9	Thomas Poole	1693–4
William Vyner	1659–60	Thomas Sumner	1694–5
John Brown	1660–1	William Streete	1695–6
Robert Stone	1661–2	Thomas Needler	1696–7
William Leversedge	1662–3	John Smith	1697–8
John Green	1663–4	Francis Higgins	1698–9
Thomas Turner	1664–5	Edward Fuller	1699–1700
Abraham Nunns	1665–6	Abraham Harris	1700–1
Thomas Page	1666–7	Thomas Bayly	1701–2
Randall Nuns	1667–8	Abraham Harris	1702–3
Roger Weeks	1668–9	Edward Tomkins	1703–4
Henry Phillips	1671–2	Stephen Reeve	1704–5
Oliver Atkinson	1672–3	John Smallwell	1705–6
John Newland Esq.	1673–4	Joseph Helby	1706–7
Thomas Steaks	1674–5	John Murden	1707–8
Richard Cleare	1675–6	Charles Hobson Esq.	1708–9
Richard Cleare	1676–7	Leonell Sharpe	1709–10
Thomas Whiting	1677–8	Robert Reynolds	1710–1
Thomas Wratten	1678–9	James Peerman	1711–2
William Polladay	1679–80	Samuel Row	1712–3
Thomas Moore	1680–1	Samuel Lavarick	1713–4
James Goodwin	1681–2	William Wood	1714–5
Thomas Shrewsbridge	1682–3	Thomas Stone	1715–6 (resigned)
Thomas Tyre	1683–4		
John Player	1684–5	Ezekiel Cooke	1715–6
Thomas Wratten	1685–6*	Thomas Kirby	1716–7
Henry Phillips	1685–6	John Pulleday	1717–8
George Newland	1686–7	Walter Bott	1718–9
James Ball	1687–8	John Leadbeater	1719–20
John Player	1687–8	Daniel Bayly	1720–1
John Harris	1688–9*	Simon Berkley	1721–2
Robert Langridge	1688–9	John Haines	1722–3
William Reade	1689–90	Richard King	1723–4
Thomas Pistor senior	1690–1	William Astell Esq.	1724–5
Thomas Thornton	1691–2	Richard Coxell	1725–6
John Green	1692–3	William Sherborne	1726–7

Name	Date	Name	Date
William Lawrence	1727–8	William Palleday	1758–9
Samuel Robinson	1728–9	Richard Collins	1759–60
Nicholas Tomkins	1729–30	John Browne	1760–1
John Burt	1730–1	John Willis	1761–2*
John Smallwell Esq.	1731–2	William Lepard	1761–2
Edward Malin	1732–3	Somerset Phillips	1762–3
Joseph Wade	1733–4	Thomas Poultney	1763–4
John Cooper	1734–5	John Wills	1764–5
Thomas Gates	1735–6*	Captain John Furnish	1765–6
William Astell Esq.	1735–6	Giles Grendy	1766–7
John Reynolds	1736–7	William Hopkins	1767–8
Thomas Millward	1737–8	Thomas Bilcliffe	1768–9
John Bosley	1738–9	John Burnell	1769–70
Thomas Millward	1738–9	John Wilkes	1770–1
Thomas Millward	1739–40	Revd Dr Thomas Wilson	1771–2
Abel Skinner jnr	1740–1		
Robert Territt	1741–2	John Wendleborough	1772–3
Joseph Maisters	1742–3	Edward Compton	1773–4
Joseph Manning	1742–3	Edward Chandler	1774–5
John Deighton/Deeton	1743–4*	William Foard	1775–6
Joseph Manning	1743–4	Isaac Warden	1776–7
John Arnatt	1744–5	Thomas Treslove	1777–8
William Sellon	1745–6	Samuel Griffis	1778–9
James Welch	1746–7	John Jenkins	1779–80
Thomas Jones	1747–8	Peter Astie	1780–1
Robert Rampshire	1748–9	Richard Clark	1781–2
Edward Newman	1749–50	John Harrison	1782–3
Samuel Linsell	1750–1	William Nightingale	1783–4
Robert Groome	1751–2	Joseph Loder	1784–5
Edward Owen	1752–3	Humphry Webb	1785–6
John Stephens	1753–4	Samuel Hanson	1786–7
William Smith	1754–5	John Willis	1787–8
William Boyce	1755–6	Thomas Vardy	1788–9
Lancelot Dowbiggin	1756–7	Samuel Toulmin	1789–90
Thomas Cleare	1757–8	Thomas Vanhagen	1790–1
Timothy Farish	1758–9*	John Cooper	1791–2

Name	Date	Name	Date
John Jacob	1792–3	Thomas Porter	1825–6
Samuel Smith	1793–4	Thomas Agutter	1826–7
Major Edward Stone	1794–5	William Smith	1827–8
George Seddon	1795–6	Stephen Ponder	1828–9
Daniel Gee	1796–7	John Johnston Esq.	1829–30
John Priest	1797–8	Thomas Haycraft	1830–1
Robert Swannell	1798–9	William Wickings	1831–2
Thomas Tucker	1799–1800*	George Thornhill	1832–3
Edward Mann	1799–1800	George Thornhill	1833–4
Jarvis Chambers	1800–1	Timothy Greated	1834–5
George Dyson	1801–2	Press Granger Esq.	1835–6
Thomas Carltar	1802–3	Andrew George Backhoffner	1836–7
Willoughby Brewer	1803–4	William Mullins	1837–8
James Griffiths	1804–5	Samuel Gardiner	1838–9
Samuel Garnault	1805–6	Thomas Dow	1839–40
Richard Brewer	1806–7	John Balls	1840–1
Richard Budd	1807–8	Joshua Thomas Bedford	1841–2
James Brewer	1808–9	Daniel Higley Richardson	1842–3
Robert Blake	1809–10		
George Beauchamp	1810–1	William Snoxell	1843–4
Richard Clark Esq.	1811–2	James Phillips Esq.	1844–5
William Farmer	1812–3	Jabez Price	1845–6
Joseph Greated	1813–4	George Taylor	1846–7
Robert Pingston	1814–5	Thomas Holt	1847–8
Stephen Ponder	1815–6	William King	1848–9
Edward Hanson	1816–7	Brodie McGhie Willcox MP	1849–50
Charles Johnson	1817–8		
Henry Carrington Bowles Esq.	1818–9	William Thomas Bedford	1850–1
James Arding	1819–20	Thomas Ponder	1851–2
James Sanders Esq.	1820–1	Richard Mathews	1852–3
Josiah Harris	1821–2	James Johnston	1853–4
John Micklem Hanson	1822–3	Joseph Alexander Batho	1854–5
Peter Watson	1823–4*		
Samuel Garnault	1823–4	John Thomas Bedford	1855–6
Joseph Dixon	1824–5		

Name	Date	Name	Date
Samuel Thomas Wood	1856–7	Thomas Winter	1886–7
Charles Gorton	1857–8	Alfred Tozer Esq.	1887–8
James Winter	1858–9	John Watson	1888–9
Frederick Lindner	1859–60	Millner Holt	1889–90
Abraham Smith	1860–1	Alfred Bull	1890–1
Charles Edward Butler	1861–2	Thomas Francis Rider	1891–2
Stephen Ponder	1862–3	William George Howard	1892–3
Edmund William Wiginton	1863–4	George Smith Howard	1893–4
William Ponder	1864–5	Sir Albert Joseph Altman	1894–5
Thomas Illman	1865–6	George Charles Barnes	1895–6
James Barnes	1866–7	Thomas Murray Janes	1896–7
John Holt	1867–8	Roger Henry Abbott	1897–8
Samuel Gardiner	1868–9	Philip Felix R Sailland	1898–9
William Mathews Meredith	1869–70	Benjamin Turner	1899–1900
George Wilson Meredith	1870–1*	Alfred Holt	1900–1
		Thomas Baker	1901–2
William James Nutting Esq.	1870–1	Frank Milton Ponder	1902–3
James Johnston junior	1871–2	Septimus Ponder	1903–4
William Gorton	1872–3	Harry Butler	1904–5
Joshua Thomas Bedford	1873–4	Frederick Butler	1905–6
		George Evan Evans	1906–7
Charles Comfort	1874–5	Benjamin Charles Turner	1907–8
John Edwin Ponder	1875–6		
Thomas Smith	1876–7	Arthur Bedford	1908–9
James Legasick Shuter	1877–8	George Herbert	1909–10
Benjamin Phillips	1878–9	Joseph Young	1910–1
Henry Laverock Phillips	1879–80	Henry Nicholls	1911–2
William Illman	1880–1	Harry Hallifax Wells CC	1912–3
Harry Ambrose Rayner	1881–2	Henry Newson	1913–4
David William Williams	1882–3	Ernest Stanley Rider	1914–5
Henry Bull	1883–4	Frederick Lindner Wiginton	1915–6
George Tacchi	1884–5		
Henry Phillips	1885–6	John Russell Bedford	1916–7
		Charles Comber Welch	1917–8

Name	Date	Name	Date
Walter Aldridge	1918–9	Sidney Oaks Brick	1948–9
Henry Harvey Phillips	1919–20	Samuel George Lidstone	1949–50
N. P. Lardner	1920–1	L. T. Phillips	1950–1
Walter Harold Phillips	1921–2	Samuel George Lidstone	1951–2
Thomas Free	1922–3		
Edward S. Lancaster	1923–4	Jack Stratford	1952–3
Tom Alfred Newman Stephens	1924–5	W. H. Lawson	1953–4
C. G. Algar	1925–6	Walter H. Bull	1954–5
Thomas B Phillips	1926–7	G. P. Pick	1955–6
Charles Newson	1927–8	Lawrence R. Ponder	1956–7
William Alfred Herbert	1928–9	J. G. Briggs	1957–8
S. N. Hallett	1929–30	Revd W. M. Masters OBE	1958–9
Sydney J. Ross	1930–1	Sidney E. Lane	1959–60
James F. Janes	1931–2	W. E. J. Hodge	1960–1
Leonard Wells	1932–3	Clifford Holmes	1961–2
H. J. Butler	1933–4	W. J. B. Stray	1962–3
Sidney R. Baker	1934–5	H. F. A. Turner	1963–4
J. Jeffrey Baker	1935–6	William B. Farrar	1964–5
Benjamin James Turner	1936–7	Adam K. Kirk	1965–6
Arthur Norman Dove	1937–8	R. C. Scatt	1966–7
Francis B. Phillips	1938–9	Walter W. Grace	1967–8
Charles Bruce Long Filmer	1939–40	Norman A. Dove	1968–9
Frederick William Butler OBE	1940–1	Ernest A. Corp	1969–70
		Charles Meade	1970–1
Frederick William Butler OBE	1941–2	D. Scott Bayfield	1971–2
		F. W. Meade	1972–3
Frederick William Butler OBE	1942–3	Jeremy T. Lawson	1973–4
Frederick William Butler OBE	1943–4	H. E. Reed	1974–5
		David A. Knight	1975–6
Frederick William Butler OBE	1944–5	Anthony Dabbs	1976–7
		K. B. North	1977–8
Frederick Lindner Wiginton	1945–6	Ernest William Perrott	1978–9
		Ian J. R. Spofforth	1979–80
Cyril Laverock Phillips	1946–7	Frederick E. Capel	1980–1
A. Cecil Phillips	1947–8	Henry Howard	1981–2

Name	Date	Name	Date
Henry Howard	1982–3	John Brown	2001–2
John Elliott	1983–4	John Snelling	2002–3
Michael Rayner	1984–5	Harry Evans	2003–4
Alan Stevens	1985–6	John Corp	2004–5
Revd. John Cotton	1986–7	Alastair MacQueen	2005–6
A. George H. Clare	1987–8	Peter Motteram	2006–7
John H. T. Brown	1988–9	David Latham	2007–8
Roy Peppiatt	1989–90	David Spencer-Phillips	2008–9
Tony R. Stockwell	1990–1	H. James de Sausmarez	2009–10
Brian Smith	1991–2	Paul Ridout	2010–1
John Farrer	1992–3	Clive Turrell	2011–2
Eddie Gale	1993–4	James Vickers	2012–3
Anthony Young	1994–5	Anthony Bown	2013–4
Peter Hogarth	1995–6	Derek Woods	2014–5
Stewart Riddick	1996–7	Mark Snelling	2015–6
Clive Capel	1997–8	John Skarratt	2016–7
Tom Boucher	1998–9*	Roger Poulton	2017–8
Revd. John Cotton	1998–9	Clive Capel	2018–9
Richard Rogan	1999–2000	Chris Chivers	2019–20
Michael J. Chapman	2000–1	H. James de Sausmarez CC	2020–1

Introduction

What Is a Joiner?

The wording of the Company's 1571 charter described it variously as the *mistere, facultatis*, or *communitatis 'Junctorum et Celatorum Civitatis London'*; that is to say, the mystery, faculty, or community of Joiners and Ceilers of the City of London. *Junctorum* is from the Latin *junctus*, meaning joined.[1] The word also has origins in the Old French *joigner*, meaning to join, which led to the Middle English word *ioynour*. The *Oxford English Dictionary* noted the first use of the term in English was in 1386, and defined it as 'a craftsman whose occupation is to construct things by joining pieces of wood; a worker in wood who does lighter and more ornamental work than that of a carpenter, as the construction of the furniture and fittings of a house, ship, etc'.[2]

John Baret's 1574 dictionary contained several definitions for the term joiner, all of which were contemporary to the charter: 'A joyner, one that joyneth together or coupleth'; 'The joyning & setting of the timber handsomly'; and 'Joyning woorke, or seeling with waynscot'.[3] John Rider's 1589 dictionary described wainscoting as 'to cover the walles with Wainscot' and 'a seeling with wainscot', as in to seal the walls.[4] *Celatorum*, from celature, referred to the art of carving or engraving.[5] John Palsgrave's 1530 dictionary of the French language also linked the term *joyner* with *menuisier*, which traditionally translates to either joiner or carpenter. Palsgrave defined the word in a sentence as 'I carve as a carver or a joyner dothe an ymage or any suche lyke thyng of wood'.[6]

An important distinction between the trades of joinery and carpentry is that joiners are able to join two pieces of wood together securely and strongly without the assistance of metal nails or adhesives. An article in *The Furniture Gazette* in 1876 contained a description of the trade:

The joiner is generally the same person with the carpenter. However, as a joiner, he is employed in making doors, laying floors, preparing the ceilings for the plasterer to nail his laths on; in dividing the house with partitions, and wainscoting the several apartments. As a joiner's work requires a nicer hand, and a greater taste in ornament, his business requires that he should be acquainted with geometry and mensuration; and, in these respects, an accurate accountant. It requires labour in the execution, and is attended with proportional profit; the master works for so much a yard square, and pays his journeymen generally half a crown a day; but in piece or jobbing work charges three shillings to his employer. He sometimes lets out work to his journeymen

19

by the piece or yard, allowing him proportionately less than he charges himself. Of these jobs an industrious workman generally makes more by the day-wages; perhaps, because he applies closer than if working for a master. There are few joiners but pretend to be carpenters, or vice versa, but some hands excel more in one than the other, and are esteemed according as the master builder wants them.[7]

When Renter Warden Sidney Crick visited the Trades Training School in February 1939 he made a point of asking the instructors for their opinions of the differences between the trades:

The instructors say that a Carpenter works on unwrought material and his work is usually executed on the 'job' whereas a Joiner is a high class worker who makes up the finer parts of woodwork in the 'shop' and then is possibly sent out to put a finish to the fitting in a building after the Carpenters have finished, presumed to be much better work altogether.

He also noted that 'the men who are in the Carpenters class usually sign the report book in the hall of the building as Joiners', and with tongue in cheek added a 'hope [that] the Carpenters Company do not do the same thing when they sign on. I am sure they are not so jealous.'[8]

Joinery is one of the oldest crafts. The ability to utilise wood, one of the most plentiful natural resources on earth, was a necessary aspect of civilisation. Recent experimental archaeology taking place in Ergersheim in Germany based on a 7,000-year-old wooden well recovered from an excavation at Altscherbitz near Leipzig has confirmed that Neolithic craftsmen utilised the mortise and tenon joint,[9] to date the earliest example of this technique.[10] The same joint has also been observed on ships discovered in the pyramid complex of Khakaure Senusret III at Dahshur outside Cairo in Egypt. Senusret III was pharaoh of Egypt from 1878 BC to 1839 BC during the Twelfth Dynasty of the Middle Kingdom.[11] Archaeological evidence indicates that this joint was also used in the shipbuilding of Mycenaean Greece.[12] The mortise and tenon joint was common amongst the woodworkers of the Roman Empire, along with the dovetail, butt, scarf, box, half-lap, and mitre joints.[13]

In the early modern period, when explorers and missionaries were venturing into what they perceived to be new parts of the world, their reports often contained accounts of the workmanship in the communities of native peoples they encountered. For example, the Spanish missionary Cristóbal Diatristán de Acuña's account of his exploration of Peru and the Amazon River in the 1640s, first published in English in 1698, contained great praise for the joinery work he observed amongst the Peruvians:

All the Tools which they have either to make their Canoos, to build their Huts, or to do other necessary Jobs, are Axes and Hatchets, not such as have been forg'd by ingenious Smiths, but such as have been form'd in their Fancies by Necessity, which is the Mother of Invention, and has taught 'em to cut the hardest part of the Tortoise-shell (which is that under the Belly of it) into Leaves of about a hand's-breadth, and not quite so thick as ones Hand. After having dry'd it in the Smoak, they whet it upon a Stone, then fasten it to a wooden Helve, and make use of this Tool to cut every thing they fancy, as well as if it were the best Ax that can be, but with a little more pains. They make their Hatchets of the same matter, and the Handle they put to 'em is a Pegebeuy's Jaw-bone, which Nature seems to have purposely fitted to this use. With these Instruments they finish all their Works, not only their Canoos, but their Tables, their Cupboards, their Seats, and their other Houshold Goods, and that as compleatly as if they had the best Joiners Tools that are in use among us. There are some among these Nations who make their Axes of Stones, which they grind to an Edg with main Strength; these are much stronger than those of Tortoise-shell, so that they will cut down any great Tree which they have a mind to fell, with the less fear of breaking 'em, and with much more speed. Their Chizzels, Plains and Wimbles, which we use for the finest Works of Joinery (in which they work excellently well) are made of wild Hogs Teeth, and of the Horns of other Animals, which they graft in to Wooden Handles, and make use of 'em as well as we can do of the best that are made of Steel.[14]

Early settlers in America in the seventeenth century recognised the importance of joinery as a craft. An account of Pennsylvania and New Jersey published in 1685 recommended that schools should be provided in all towns and cities to teach children

... to Read and Write true English, Latine, and other useful Speeches and Languages, and fair Writing, Arithmatick and Book-keeping, and the Boys to be taught and instructed in some Mystery or Trade, as the making of Mathematical Instruments, Joynery, Turnery, the making of Clocks and Watches, Weaving, Shoe-making, or any other useful Trade or Mystery that the School is capable of teaching.[15]

As technology evolved, particularly during the nineteenth century, the art of the joiner moved away from hand tools and embraced modern machinery and technology. An anonymous article written 'By a Workman' in 1877 was full of praise for this, but cautioned young apprentices not to become complacent in their work:

Since the introduction of machinery for the working of wood, I may safely say that the necessity for great muscular exertion on the part of the joiner and cabinet-maker has decreased not less than thirty per cent; while the necessity for brain work has increased in the same ratio. Now-a-days, in consequence of the heavy labour being performed by machinery, the workman has to think more quickly. The power to see his work in his mind's eye, finished, before he begins it, is an essential qualification for a good workman, and upon this aim the apprentice should steadily concentrate his ideas ... When I see the present position of the joiner and cabinet-maker, and compare it with that of twenty-five years ago, I feel grateful to the men who have invented and perfected the planning, tenoning, morticing, and other machines which have so largely reduced the amount of excessive labour that formerly fell to the lot of the worker in wood. But the apprentice should bear in mind that each new machine, and each improvement of an existing one, tend to make it more imperative that he shall use his brains; more necessary that he shall think quickly, and he may then rest assured that it will be a long time before the man with mere muscular strength will be able to hold his own against his thoughtful intelligent fellow work-man.[16]

However, in a comment which echoes down the years as the perpetual lament of the craftsperson dissatisfied with the next generation, a joiner in 1877 lamented the reliance on machinery:

> The least labourious methods are chosen; in fact, our age is essentially one of labour-saving or labour-scamping. The demand is so great, and labour so costly, that we have to content ourselves with furniture of a kind that the old joiner and cabinet-maker of the early Georges would have been ashamed to turn out, if indeed they could have done so. We deplore the result, but what remedy is there?[17]

Chapter 1

The Origins of the Company

The Guild of St James Garlickhythe

Documentation relating to the Company's early years is scarce. Financial and administrative accounts were created from the turn of the sixteenth century onwards, but a series of fires destroyed the majority of them and the corporate archive only contains detailed records from the mid-seventeenth century onwards. The Company has its origins in the Fraternity of St James Garlickhythe, which was established in 1375,[1] but the evidence that remains suggests that it was not established as a craft guild.

Parish guilds such as this one were established as community support during life and a source of salvation after death. Jessica Lutkin described the St James fraternity as 'a caring community and a formally organised and structured group'. Their ordinances, dated 1388, do not specifically refer to joiners, but they reflect an organised system of meetings and support which would later be reflected in the Joiners' Company's own administration:

> This included the payment of quarterage by fraternity members, payment of an entry fee of 6s 8d, the wearing of a common livery, attendance at the annual feast, attendance at quarterly meetings, the maintenance of members who had fallen on hard times or suffered false imprisonment, and prayers for a dead brother or sister.[2]

Lutkin has identified that one of the first joiners to be associated with the fraternity was Adam Fullere, who bequeathed money to them in his will of 1398–9. She also identified fellow joiners Richard Mimms (d. 1405), John Wydemere junior (d. 1407), and Ralph Fuller (d. 1412), who all likewise bequeathed money to the fraternity in their wills. Lutkin concluded that 'the lack of documentation connecting joiners to St. James Garlickhithe before 1398 suggests that joiners, rather than founding the fraternity, were drawn to it after it had been established'.[3] She cited the fact that a network of joiners were already living in a close-knit community centred around St James Garlickhythe when the fraternity was founded,[4] due in no small part to the church's proximity to the river wharfs which provided easy transportation for wood used by the craftsmen. Between 1300 and 1500 the parish had the largest joiner population in London, and Lutkin argued that the sheer number of the craftsmen in the parish suggests that the 'fraternity was likely to have been dominated by them'.[5] By the fifteenth century 'the fraternity of St. James was pretty much an association of the joiners' and was the foundation of their community.[6]

Using wills proved in the Archdeaconry Court of London, Lutkin identified fifteen bequests made by joiners to St James Garlickhythe between 1351 and 1500. The nature of these varied depending on the individual; some left money to support the church fabric, whilst others provided money for the decoration of the high altar. Additionally, between 1383 and 1474 nine joiners specifically left bequests to support the fraternity of St James Garlickhythe.[7] However, from the late 1470s onwards the number of joiners living and working in the parish dropped, and only five were still living there in 1500. In 1518 a deed requested the craft of joiners to keep a solemn obit for the souls of the brothers and sisters of the fraternity.[8]

It seems probable that the Joiners' formal association with the fraternity of St James Garlickhythe was loosened in the 1540s. The dissolution of the monasteries under Henry VIII in the 1530s had seen the widespread confiscation of ecclesiastical property, but chantries largely escaped persecution until the mid-1540s. On Christmas Eve 1545 Henry VIII passed a Chantries Act which sought to investigate the endowments made to parish chantries, the nature of each foundation, and the value of the property they held. The London guilds and companies were investigated in the first two weeks of May 1546. The lack of surviving documentary evidence from the Joiners' Company from this period means that we cannot clearly reconstruct what happened to them, but something of the process is known. Chantry commissioners met at Guildhall to sign warrants ordering all city parsons, vicars, and curates to complete a Bill of Articles – a questionnaire concerning their chantry holdings. The priests, along with masters, wardens, and governors of colleges, hospitals, guilds, and fraternities, were then summoned to Guildhall to present their reports and be questioned further if necessary.[9]

In December 1547 the young Edward VI expanded this investigation in his own Chantries Act. He authorised the Court of Augmentations to carry out a nationwide survey of all chantry endowments, leading to their closure and the seizure of their assets for the Crown. Sylvia Gill has noted that

> in addition to churches, colleges and chapels, commissioners were empowered to enter all lay foundations, 'guilds, fraternities, companies and fellowship of Misteries or Crafts incorporate' and view all the evidence, 'compositions, books of accounts and other writings' to establish what money and other property was 'paid or bestowed to the finding or maintenance of any Priest or Priests, anniversary or obit, or other like thing, light or lamp'.[10]

The investigation at St James Garlickhythe itself made no mention of the guild, but a separate entry recording the City Companies noted that the Joiners had an obit in the church maintained by 'lands and tenements given by Agnes Sawmon' which yielded profits of £2 per annum.[11] This same Agnes Sawmon or Samon will appear again in this text in Chapter 5. The returns from St James Garlickhythe confirmed that the church was well endowed. There were 400 communicants served by rector Thomas Longlow, who also employed a curate. Various bequests of money and land made to the church made it possible for ten chantry priests to be employed to hold masses for the souls of the deceased, as well as for a lamp to be maintained before the high altar. However, it was noted that the money intended to maintain the lamp had been re-allocated into parish poor relief, perhaps a response to the 1538 ban on keeping lamps burning before images.[12]

Nevertheless, on 24th January 1551 joiner John Campion delivered to Lawrence Ripley and other joiners in trust his messuage and tenement in Fryer Lane, which was comprised of 'howses Edifices Gardens Shopps Sellers sillors halls chambers warehowses'. The property had been assigned to maintain a 'certen Priest to Celebrate in the parish Church of Saint James Garlickhil'.[13]

Early Joiners of London

The earliest references to potential joiners of London are those with the word as a suffix to their name. The men were often described as 'le Joynour' or a variant spelling; that is to say, the joiner. In 1222 a man named William le Joynour was elected as one of the Sheriffs of London, and Lutkin has described him as 'possibly the earliest known joiner'. In 1239 William Joynour, presumably the same man, was elected as Mayor of London. Unfortunately his suffix is the only evidence of his occupation, but if he truly was a joiner Lutkin stated that he was 'the only one of the craft to hold a civic post in the period 1200–1550'.[14] Raphael Holinshed's chronicles of England named 'William Ioyner' as the man who had arrested Ranulph Brito, canon of St Paul's, on the orders of Henry III.[15] Ranulph had been the king's treasurer but he lost his position after his patron Hubert de Burgh fell out of favour with the monarch. He was accused of misappropriating royal funds and was later falsely accused of treason, and William Joyner oversaw his incarceration in the Tower of London in 1239. The Dean and Chapter of St Paul's responded by excommunicating anyone involved with his arrest, and after the Archbishop of Canterbury joined their protest the King was obliged to release Ranulph. He was later cleared of all charges.[16]

A 1292 subsidy roll for Vintry ward, containing amongst others the parish of St James Garlickhythe, noted the residence of Stephen le Joignur, John le Joignur, and Richard le Joignur.[17] On 2nd February 1306 John le Blound, Mayor of London, ordered the sheriffs of the City to arrest Alderman Ralph de Honilane until he satisfied a debt he owed to John le Wengrave. Two joiners, Richard le Joynur and John FrAunceys, who described himself as a 'joynur', were among the twelve witnesses who confirmed that de Honilane held property worth £18 per annum 'in the Vintry in the parish of St. James', which can only be St James Garlickhythe.[18] Richard le Joynur could well be the same Richard le Joignur referred to in the 1292 subsidy. The two men appeared in another inquisition at the Guildhall in March 1317, this time investigating the property held by Ralph Gubbe, Ralph de Beverley, and Adam Wade. The twelve jurors included John Fraunceys, Richard le Joygnour, John le Joygnour, and Roger le Joygnour, and they confirmed that 'Adam Wade had a tenement in the parish of St. James de Garlekhethe [and] a house in the same parish called "le Bouisishous"'.[19]

On 6th January 1310 Richard de Burstowe, 'joignur', was freed from his apprenticeship with Stephen le Joignur. A week later, on 13th January, John Mai, 'joygnour', was freed from his apprenticeship to John atte Hoke. Both men lived in Vintry ward.[20] Ivo de Wattone, a 'joygnour', was admitted to the freedom of the city on 14th February 1312 at a cost of half a mark.[21] De Wattone was also recorded in the 1319 subsidy roll as either a handicraftsman or small dealer. He was assessed at 2s and had goods to the value of 24s.[22] Two joiners, John de Berdene and Richard le Joignour, were amongst a group of five men who provided mainprise[23] before the Mayor and Aldermen for John Pedefer de Boloygne on 14th February 1312. They gave their assurances that 'no evil or damage should arise through [John Pedefer de Boloygne] to the City this side of the sea or beyond'.[24] On 6th December 1319 Richard le Joynour de Cornhull provided mainprise for John le Fourbour of Cornhill who had been arrested and imprisoned in Newgate for bearing arms without permission.[25]

In the Common Pleas court on 12th March 1322 the moor of Haliwell and Vynesbery, part of the manor of Finsbury, was demised to Robert le Joignour and Walter le Fannere for seven years at an annual rent of four marks. The following month, on 11th April, Robert was elected as a watchman in Queenhithe 'to guard the places where corn is sold and other places in order to prevent it from being taken out of the City or removed unsold from the market'.[26]

Gilbert, son of Alan de Brauncestre and Agnes de Staines, married the daughter of joiner Richard Godefrei. In February 1325 Gilbert provided an acquittance, or a receipt acknowledging the settlement of a debt, to the executors of his mother's will for property she had left him. Gilbert appeared before the Mayor and Aldermen with his father-in-law Richard Godefrei le Joignour and the men agreed to provide another acquittance when Gilbert came of age. Later that year, on 18th October, Juliana, the widow of Richard le Joynour of Cornhill, provided herself as surety to save the Mayor, Aldermen, and Commonalty harmless in that acquittance.[27] There was clearly at least basic interaction but more likely friendship or even professional collaboration between Richard le Joynour and Juliana, and Richard Godefrei le Joignour and Gilbert de Brauncestre.

Two more joiners served as jurymen on 7th July 1341 during the trial of tailor Richard de Pembroke, who was accused of stealing a breviary worth 20s from Benedict de Fulsham of Vintry ward. Richard le Joynour and Alan le Joynour were two of the twelve men who found Richard guilty, and he was sentenced to be hanged.[28]

Early London joiners can also be glimpsed through surviving statute merchant and statute staple records, documents which ensured that a debtor would repay a creditor, usually sworn before the Lord Mayor of London. In 1340 John de Cressingham, citizen and joiner of London, became a creditor when he loaned 100s to William le Clerk of Harrow.[29] Eight years later de Cressingham agreed to lend £10 to William le Eyr of Lewisham.[30] Joiner Gilbert atte Leigh borrowed £6 from citizen and girdler Roger Huberd in 1345.[31] William de Bath, described as a joiner and fuster, loaned £10 to Surrey carpenter Simon de Beddington in 1352.[32] Roger Reigate borrowed £6 2s 4d from stockfishmonger William Brampton in 1373.[33] Joiner and fuster John French borrowed 1000 marks from Nicholas, Abbott of Westminster in 1384,[34] and joiner William Bolyfant borrowed £16 from merchant Peter Feryby in 1388.[35]

The Craft or Mystery of Joiners

In spite of uncertainty about its origins, the craft of Joiners of London was active as a guild from the late fourteenth century onwards. The earliest reference to City activities was its participation in the elections of representatives to the Common Councils in 1376, 1377, and 1381.[36] An account of the election of 9th August 1376 was preserved in the Corporation's letter books. An 'immense Commonalty' assembled at the Guildhall and presented the two people from each of the forty-two summoned mysteries who had been elected to serve on the

Common Council, and the Joiners presented Robert Louthe[37] and Nicholas Pays. The inclusion of joiners in the Common Council indicates that the mystery was rapidly rising in importance in London. All elected men were required to swear an oath, which was translated as follows:

> You swear that you will readily come when summoned for a Common Council of the City unless you have lawful and reasonable excuse, and good and lawful counsel shall you give according to your understanding and knowledge, and for no favour shall you maintain an individual benefit against the common weal of the City, preserving for each mistery its reasonable customs. And when you shall so come, you shall not depart without reasonable cause or leave of the Mayor, or before the Mayor and his fellows have departed.[38]

The 1381 election saw the Joiners present Laurence Joynour and John Wydemere as their representatives.[39] A man named as 'Laurence Joynour' also appeared on multiple lists of workmen employed towards the maintenance of London Bridge in 1420, possibly the same man or perhaps his son.[40]

On 18th March 1401 the 'good men of the Mistery of Joynours' petitioned the Mayor and Aldermen requesting 'that they may elect two Wardens to govern the mistery' and also have 'certain ordinances for regulating the mistery' approved and enrolled.[41] The confirmation of their ordinances marked the official beginning of the Company, even though the craft had been operating for some time before. There is very little evidence about who led the mystery in these early days, but a small selection of names have survived. Simon Serle and Richard Resoun were sworn in on 28th July 1415 'to rule the mistery well and truly, sparing none for love nor molesting any from hate, and to present to the Mayor and Aldermen and the Chamberlain any defects they may find'. The Corporation's letter book described them as masters of the mystery, but the title warden is a more accurate representation of their positions and is consistent with the petition from March 1401.[42] Three years later, on 27th July 1418, William Wytman and John Boylot were sworn into the same roles,[43] and in 1419 they were succeeded by John Dero and William Godfrey.[44]

Early Wardens of the Mystery of Joiners
28th July 1415 – Simon Serle and Richard Resoun.[45]
27th July 1418 – William Wytman and John Boylot.[46]
4th July 1419 – John Dero and William Godfrey.[47]
16th August 1424 – John Gay and Nicholas Gylle.[48]
21st August 1425 – John Derk and John Welles.[49]
22nd September 1427 – Simon Beld and John Lynde.[50]
27th August 1429 – Peter Attehoke and John Derk.[51]
10th August 1432 – John Stone and John Bridde.[52]
28th September 1441 – John Lynde and William Holt[53]

Lutkin has noted that six of these men – Resoun, Wytman, Godfrey, Derk, Lynde, and Attehoke – were parishioners of St James Garlickhythe, thus reinforcing the link between the mystery and the parish.[54] In particular, in his 1421 will Wytman bequeathed the residue of his estate to William Huntyngdon, rector of St James Garlickhythe, 'and the masters of the Fraternity' and their successors 'to the use and behoof of the said fraternity'.[55]

On 13th September 1427 'the Masters and good folk of the Mistery of Joynours' appeared before the Mayor and Aldermen at Guildhall to complain about the lack of regulation governing journeymen, foreigners, and aliens working as joiners in London. Their petition stated that many craftsmen were working by the day 'more for their own private gain than for public benefit'. This was causing 'the great hurt of poor folk of the said Mistery', and they requested that those craftsmen should be bound to work with freemen joiners for terms between a quarter of a year and a full year, not by the day. Their petition was granted.[56]

Another early reference to the organisation appears in the will of joiner John Lynder, who died in 1461. He instructed that his real estate in the parishes of St James Garlickhythe and St Mary Woolnooth should be sold by his executors, and the wardens of his craft of joiners were to have the option of purchasing the same for the benefit of the craft, at a discount of £20 lower than the price offered to other buyers. Lynder insisted that the proceeds of the sale should be used to maintain a chantry in St James Garlickhythe, as well as for the repairs of bridges and highways 'and other pious and charitable uses'. Fellow joiner William Lee acted as one of his executors.[57] The wording of his will and the references to 'his craft' of joiners indicates that he was an active member.

Joiners and the Early Tudor Monarchs

Bartholomew Halley, usher of the bedchamber to Henry VI, was granted the honorary position of joiner of the Tower of London in 1455. He received an allowance of 12d per day for life, in consideration of his long and faithful service to the king.[58] A memorandum of 13th March 1456 noted that Nicholas Caumbrigge held the post of 'chefe joynour of the kynges werkes'.[59]

In October 1495 Henry VII passed a statute concerning the prices which could be charged by artificers, including joiners. Between Easter and Michaelmas, when days were longer, joiners could charge 6d per day if they were not provided with meat and drink, or 4d per day if they were. Between Michaelmas and Easter, when days were shorter, they were allowed to charge 5d or 3d respectively.[60] Under Henry VII it was also specified that alien joiners were to be 'under the serch of the wardens of the occupacio[n]', and they were required to have 'a sign or a merk which they shall put uppon theyr work' so that prospective customers would be able to tell that they were not free of the City. Any alien joiners caught flouting this rule would forfeit double the value of the item.[61]

When Richmond Palace, a largely wooden construction, burned down on 23rd December 1497 Henry VII commissioned a replacement which would become known as the new Richmond Palace. Joiners were an essential part of the workforce hired to construct the palace, and craftsmen from within and without London were employed. The necessity of hiring both free and alien joiners caused tension amongst the workforce, and it became necessary for the Chamberlain of London to intervene. An agreement was reached that every householder stranger, that is to say alien craftsman, would pay into the Chamber of London 4d per quarter as surety, and journeymen strangers would pay 2d. In return the Joiners promised to 'never sue them or molest them', but by 1521 this agreement had broken down. A group of strangers petitioned Cardinal Wolsey in August to complain that 'Now the Englishmen make new acts against [us] in their hall' and were having them imprisoned. The aliens refused to submit to the Joiners without the express command of the Cardinal, and begged him to set their incarcerated colleagues free.[62]

A later letter from the Company's Clerk to the House of Commons dated February 1725 reveals that upon examination of documents in the Town Clerk's office he had been able to confirm 'that the said Company was a Livery Company in the 19th yeare of the Reigne of King Henry the Seventh', which would be 1503–4.[63] In that same year a statute was passed on 25th January 'for makynge of statutes by bodyes incorporate', which contained regulations about the ordinances guilds, fraternities, and livery companies could introduce.

Prayen the comyns in this psent plyament assembled that Where in a plyament holden at Westmynstere the xv yere of the reygne of the blessyd kynge He[n]ry the vii for that that mayster Warde[n]s & people of gyldes fraternytee & of other co[m]panyes corporate dwellynge in dyvers ptyes of the realme often tymes by colour of rule & governaunce to theym graunted & confermed by charters and letters pate[n]tes of dyvers kynges made amonge the selfe many unlawfull and unresonable ordynaunces aswell in pryses of Wares as other thynges for theyr owne synguler pfyte and to the comyn hurte and domage of the people It Was enacted that there sholde from thens forth no suche mayster Wardens nor companies make nor use none ordynaunces in dysherytance or dimynacyon of the prereogatyf of the ki[n]ge nor of other nor agenst the comyn profyte of the people nor none other ordynaunce of the charge make and use but yf it were fyrst dyscussed and approved by good and resonable aduyse by the Justycs of the peas or the chyef gouernours of cytees & before them entred of recorde And that upon payn to lese & forfeyte the force & theffecte of all the artycles in theyr sayd letters patentes & charters conteyned co[n]cernynge the same & ouer that to lose & paye [£10] to the kynge for euery ordynaunce that any of them made or use to the co[n]trary of this ordynaunce. The same ordynaunce to endure at the kynges pleasure as in the same acte it apereth Which acte is now expyred & syth the expyrynge of the same dyvers & many ordynaunces have ben made by many & dyvers priuate bodyes corporate Wythin cytees townes & borughs co[n]trary to the kynges prerogatyf his lawes & the comyn Wele of his subgetes Be it therfore ordeyned establysshed & enacted by the kynge our souerayne lorde by thaduyse of the lords spyrytuell & te[m]porell & of the comyns in this psent plyament assembled & by auctoryte of the same That no maysters Wardens & felysshyppes of craftes or maysters nor ony of them nor ony rulers of guyldes or fraternytees takes upon the[m] to make ony acte or ordynau[n]ces to execute ony actes or ordynau[n]ces by them here afore made in dysherytau[n]ce or dimynucyo[n] of the prerogatyf of the kynge nor of other nor agenste the comyn pfyte of the people but uf the same actes or ordynaunces be examined & approued by the chau[n]celer tresourer of Englonde or chefe Justyces of eyther benches or iii of theym or before bothe the Justyces of assyses in theyr cyrcyite or progresse in the shyre Where suche actes or ordynau[n]ces be made upon payne of forfeytyre of [£40] for every tyme that they do the co[n]trary.[64]

Thomas Stokton was 'the King's joiner' under Henry VIII. In January 1511 the king granted a warrant to the Archbishop of Canterbury authorising him to commission Stokton 'to employ in the works at the Tower of London, Westminster, or elsewhere, joiners, carvers and "intailers" and provide timber and other necessaries for the same'.[65] By 1514 William Heyward held the title of King's Joiner, and he provided the monarch with 'such stuff used in the joustes' as well as staves and standards for the ships *The Lyon* and the famous *Mary Rose*.[66] In 1519 alone Heyward had provided the king with 206 spears and burres, a testament to Henry's love of sport.[67] John Ripley had taken over as the king's joiner in 1526,[68] and Thomas Ware was appointed chief joiner of the king's works in England and chief joiner of the Tower of London on 25th May 1544.[69] He was not destined to hold the post for long, however, as he died in 1545, and his replacement was John Mannyng.[70] James Marcady, a joiner also described as 'the King's servant' was awarded an annuity of £12 3s 4d per year on 2nd August 1546.[71]

Joiners were also actively involved in the creation of court revels, lavish entertainments featuring masques, revels, and plays. Receipts from the early years of Henry VIII's reign reveal that joiners assisted in the construction of Harry Gyllforth's revel in 1511, which featured 'a hill summit, thereon a golden stock branched with roses and pomegranates crowned, out of which hill issued a Morryke danced by the King's young gentlemen, as hynmen, and thereto a lady'. In December 1512 the king ordered a revel to celebrate Epiphany, and Gyllforth commissioned a pageant called 'the Ryche Mount'. Amongst a wide variety of other craftsmen a team of eighteen carpenters and joiners were engaged 'for 22 days and divers nights' at a total cost of £5 18s 10d. The pageant took place at Greenwich Palace on 6th January and featured

> a rock or mountain of gold and precious stones, set with herbs of divers kinds, and planted with broom to signify Plantagenet, and also with red and white roses; on the top, a burning beacon; on the sides, fleurs de lis; at the foot, 6 lords, apparelled in crimson velvet and goldsmith's work 'of korryas kast and ingyen'; above them, 6 minstrels in blue and yellow damask; at the entrance, two armed men in green satin. It was drawn by two 'mighty woordwossys or wyld men'. After the descent of the lords, the mount opened, and showed 6 ladies in gold and rich clothes.

In May 1515 a pageant called 'the Pallys Marchallyn' featured an entire house. It was constructed 'in 4 separate parts, joined in one, and every piece of timber set together with "forlokks" and bolts of iron'. The house featured ten towers and was on a frame which enabled it 'to be borne by men'. The interior of the house was 'hyllyd with rich clothes of gold and silks'. In this case the names of the carpenters, joiners, and carvers employed on the project between 19th March and 9th May were recorded, although it is unclear which man was employed on which task. Richard Gibson was the superior craftsman, receiving 12d per day, and was assisted by Thomas Williamson, Harry Devell, Thomas Koll, Hew Hollmys, and Thomas Hamand, who were paid 8d per day.[72]

One of the most famous events of Henry VIII's reign was the meeting at the Field of the Cloth of Gold in June 1520. The king met with Francis I of France in Balinghem in northern France to strengthen the Anglo-French treaty of 1514. The meeting was a gorgeous spectacle, with each monarch constructing elaborate and decorative accommodation for themselves and their courtiers in an attempt to outdo the other. The English commissioners overseeing the king's accommodation wrote to Cardinal Wolsey on 26th March 1520 requesting him to send 250 carpenters, 150 bricklayers, 100 joiners, sixty sawyers, and forty plasterers, as well as 1,000 units of wainscot, 'for [t]here is none to buy'. William Heyward was later appointed to be one of the king's attendants accompanying him to France.[73]

In the early 1530s a series of payments to individual joiners were authorised based on their involvement in the construction of the Palace of Westminster. Roger Basyng and John Giles were paid for wainscot in July 1531. In February 1532 unnamed joiners completed the construction of the ceiling in the new gallery, and the following month joiner Clement Armystone was employed 'in garnishing the roof of the new gallery; viz, buds of timber turned and carved, leaves of lead attached to them, garnishing of jowpieces with the King's posy in letters of lead'. The leaves and buds were tacked to the ceiling using pine nails and tackets, and the ceiling was later painted and gilded. More wainscoting was completed by John Ripleye who had a workshop in the parish of St Giles without Aldersgate.[74] In a letter to Thomas Cromwell in Calais, master of works Thomas Alvard reported that the construction was progressing 'at a great forwardness with the joiners', and he was pleased to have received word of the king's satisfaction.[75]

Joiners were engaged at the Tower of London in 1532 and early 1533, and a complete schedule of their works was recorded:

> In the King's dining chamber a mantle of wainscot with antyk set over the chimney; new wainscot on ceiling, &c. In the King's closet an altar wrought round about the edges with antique, and a coffer with tills thereto for the priest to say mass on; new wainscot panel on the east and south sides, &c. Panels and crests of wainscots in various other chambers.[76]

It is not improbable that some or all of these joiners working for the early Tudor monarchs were associated with the Mystery of Joiners in some way. Indeed, the next chapter will demonstrate that one of their successors had a very close relationship with his monarch and the Company.

Chapter 2

The Company's Charters and Ordinances

Background to 1571 Charter and Lewis Stockett

The question of why the Worshipful Company of Joiners and Ceilers did not receive a royal charter until 1571 has hitherto remained unanswered. In his *Annals of the Worshipful Company of Joiners* Henry Laverock Philips simply noted 'the Charter granted', and Sidney E. Lane's *Chronological History* of the Company similarly noted its grant and that said grant is preserved at the Guildhall.[1] Certainly within the wider context of Company charters this was quite a late award. The Fishmongers, for example, received their charter in 1272, and the Goldsmiths were awarded theirs in 1327. However, the Charter itself contains a vital clue about why the grant was made in 1571. Queen Elizabeth I named a man called Lewis Stockett as the Master of the Company, and she described him as 'our welbeloved servant'. This was not just rhetoric; Stockett was her servant.

Lewis Stockett is believed to have been born in Hackington in Kent around 1530, but very little is known about his early life. He presumably moved to London as a young man and found work as a craftsman in the royal household. On 24th March 1563 Stockett was appointed as master mason of the works within the Tower of London and all castles and manors where the Queen was accustomed to dwell, with the exception of Windsor Castle. He was to hold the office for life, and would receive a salary of 1s per day.[2] However, on 11th December of that year he was promoted for life to the office of surveyor of the works in the Tower of London and all royal residences, following the death of the previous surveyor, John Revell.[3] His salary was increased to 2s per day for himself, with an allowance of 4s per day to cover his diet, boat hire, and riding charges, as well as 6d per day to pay for his clerk.[4] He surrendered his previous position of master mason on 27th March 1564. Exchequer certificates of residence for the 1560s confirm Stockett's positions and state that he was liable for taxation as a member of the royal household. In 1563 he was described as the Queen's master mason, but by 1566 and 1567 he was 'Surveyor of her Ma[jes]t[y]s workes'.[5]

As surveyor of the works Stockett submitted regular accounts to William Cecil, Lord Burghley, the chief adviser to Elizabeth I. All nineteen of his accounts survive at The National Archives, covering the period 1563 to 1578,[6] and they contain detailed information not only about the projects Stockett oversaw, but also the involvement of joiners more generally in the maintenance of royal residences in the sixteenth century. Each of the accounts began with a copy of the patent which had granted Stockett his position.

> Elizabeth by the grace of God, quene of England, ffrance, and Irelande, defender of the Faythe, &c To all and evrye to whome this prsents shall come greetings Knowe ye that we ... do gyve and grante to our welbelovyed servant Lewes Stocket the Offyce of Surveyor of our works wthin the Tower of London and in all and singular our houses, Castells, Lordeshipps, & Manors the wch we have usuallye reserved for our Repayre and abode, or in tyme to come shall appointe and ordeyne for our Repayre & abode, To have, holde, occupye, and exercyse the sayde Offyce, unto the sayde Lewes Stocket by hym selfe, or hys suffycyente deputye or deputyes ... during hys naturall lyfe together wth all and singler pfytte, comodytyes, prferyments, and Advantags, whatsoever to the sayde Offyce belonging or in anye wyse appteyning.[7]

An examination of the first of Stockett's accounts, which is dated 12th December 1563 to 29th September 1565, reveals how significant his status was in the royal household.[8] The repairs carried out under his supervision were to buildings which were then, and remain to this day, key landmarks in the history of England.

The first project Stockett oversaw was for repairs at the Tower of London to the freestone windows, floors, and wharf gate at St Katherine's by the Tower. His account lists the purchase and cost of all materials necessary for this project, including timber, bricks, tiles, lime mortar, nails, baskets, glass, and locks and keys. It also notes the hire of masons, carpenters, bricklayers, plasterers, plumbers, blacksmiths, pavers, and common labourers, who were all managed by overseer John Swythen. The combined cost of materials and workmen on this project was £153 16s 9d, and it took over four months to complete.

The repairs at the Tower of London were swiftly followed by repairs at Windsor Castle, which included mending the pastry ovens, paving the privy kitchen, adding windows to the privy larder, adding a new scullery, unspecified alterations in the great kitchen, and repairs to the stables at Eton. This was a more elaborate project than that at the Tower and required eighteen months' worth of work from teams of craftsmen which, crucially, included joiners. It is unclear how many of them were hired for this project, but each man was paid 11d per day, and the total cost for the 'greate worke' they did was £9 3s 6d. The next royal residence listed in Stockett's account was the honour of Hampton Court; that is, the manorial lands comprising the Hampton Court estate.[9] The list of materials includes timber, bricks, tiles, glass, nails, shovels, spades, and candles, which all imply that the work involved constructing or altering some sort of building. Joiners were hired once again, this time at a cost of 12d per day, but the total paid to them was only 5s, which represents five days' work for one man, so their contribution to this project was smaller than at Windsor Castle. Carpenters, on the other hand, received a payment of over £20 for their work at Hampton Court.

After Hampton Court was a long list of work carried out at Whitehall Palace, with the creation of a new hedged orchard and also some work inside the building. Joiners were hired 'for wainscote stuffe', which implies that they were panelling an internal room. In contrast, carvers were hired 'for embossing of Beasts', 'repayring of olde Beasts', and 'carvyng of poosts for the greate Gardens', so they appear to have been tasked with the decorative work on this project. Smaller-scale repairs 'upon the Standerde at Wesm[inster] Hall' were followed by fifteen days of repairs to the Parliament House. After this came the creation of 'the newe house for the Recordes of the Courte of Theschequer at Westm[inster]'. At least four joiners earning between 6d and 12d per day were employed in the creation of 'a greate wainscote dore for the newe Stores'. Wainscot was synonymous with oak at this time, and indeed the account noted the purchase of over £64 worth of 'Oken Tymbre' for this project, so presumably the joiners had been tasked with crafting an oak door for the archive.

A more unusual aspect of Stockett's role required him to travel with the Queen when she went on her progresses to ensure that the houses she stayed in were suitable to host a monarch. The first progress he was involved in was in 1564, and his account noted 'chardges of worke done aswell in & upon certeine of the quenes mats owne howses as upon other mens howses in her highnes p[ro] gresse in the Sixte yeare of her Mats Reigne'. This particular progress moved northwards from Enfield to Hertford Castle and then on to King's College, Cambridge, where Stockett oversaw the creation of some new windows at a cost of almost £40. The Queen then moved north, staying at several private houses on her way, including Hinchingbrooke House on 18th August. Hinchingbrooke was the seat of Sir Henry Williams alias Cromwell, nephew of Henry VIII's adviser Thomas Cromwell and future grandfather of Lord Protector Oliver Cromwell. From Hinchingbrooke she moved to Kimbolton Castle, where her father's first wife Catherine of Aragon had died in 1536. Boughton House, the seat of MP for Northamptonshire Sir Edward Montagu, was next on the itinerary, followed by Launde Abbey in Leicestershire, the home of another member of the Cromwell family: Henry Cromwell, 2nd Baron. This was as far north as the 1564 progress ventured, and the Queen's return journey to London took her via Northampton and St Albans. Stockett's alterations to the houses she stayed in during this tour amounted to the grand total of £248 3s 2d, roughly equivalent to £58,000 in today's money.[10] Generally speaking alterations to private houses in preparation for the visit of a monarch were paid for by the owner of the house, so Stockett's alterations were last-minute finishing touches to ensure the buildings were perfect, rather than any major structural changes. Indeed, the cost of preparing for a royal visit crippled many a landowner in this period. If Stockett had spent such a vast amount in finishing touches then the sums laid out by the owners must have been staggering.

These extracts from Stockett's first account, which do not even cover all of his first year as surveyor of works, reveal just how significant his position in the royal household was. He was responsible for ensuring that the royal residences were literally fit for a queen, and he did his work well. His role required him to move in exalted circles within the Queen's court, and it gave him the opportunity to travel across the country and stay in some of the grandest houses in the land. Subsequent years saw him carrying out additional alterations to the properties he had already worked on, as well as new projects at St James' Palace. Indeed, the remainder of 1564 and 1565 alone saw him overseeing work at Somerset House, Customs House, Greenwich, Richmond, Eltham, Hatfield House, Ashridge, Otford, Waltham, and elsewhere. The total spent by Stockett between December 1563 and the end of September 1565 was a staggering £7,226 3s 7d, which is the equivalent of approximately £1.7 million in today's money.[11]

There is also evidence of Stockett's involvement in the Queen's diplomatic duties. On 1st July 1564 the Treasurer was instructed to give Stockett £123 11s 7d 'to paye for the charges of suche workes as were made against the comminge hither and in the time of the beinge here of Monsr Gonnort of late Ambasador owte of ffraunce'.[12] This referred to Artus de Cossé, Seigneur de Gonnord, who would later return to England as an ambassador sent to negotiate a potential marriage between the Queen and the Duke of Anjou, although ultimately the union did not take place. Stockett's office of works was therefore involved in the day-to-day function of the Queen's diplomatic court, and the entertainments associated with it. Albert Feuillerat quoted an account from the years 1567 to 1570 which included the 'newe making and setting up of Scaffoldes, particions and dores and other necessaries for the Maundayes, Playes, Tragedyes, Maskes, Revelles, and Tryumphes at divers and sondry times'.[13]

The account covering the period September 1570 to September 1571, during which time the Company was granted its charter, reveals that Stockett was a busy man overseeing a variety of projects at the royal residences. Extensive work was carried out at the Tower of London, including re-planking the bridges, making new doors for the prison cells, and repairs to the lodgings of the Lieutenant, Duke of Norfolk, and porters. The crane at Custom House was repaired, and the shoreline reinforced. Major changes also took place at Somerset House, with the creation of a new kitchen, boiling house, larder, and porter's lodge, the latter at the water gate. Joiners were involved in some of this work at a rate of 12d per day, perhaps working on the decoration of the interior rooms after construction was complete.

Whitehall Palace saw the construction of a new fountain in the orchard, as well as the repair of the fountain in the great garden. Wainscot casements were installed in the hall, and a receipt for 'Joyners stuffe, viz Tables, Stoles, Cubbords, Wainscots, Casements, portulls, Sealing and other Joyners worke' was recorded at a cost of £33 3s. Intriguingly the Whitehall entry distinguished between joiners, paid 12d per day, and carvers, paid between 12d and 14d per day. Carvers' apprentices were also employed on the site at 10d per day. Stockett was personally involved in overseeing the works at Whitehall, and was paid £35 for his attendance over 175 days. Joiners were also employed at the Exchequer. Work at that site included the creation of seating, windows, and a staircase, and laying a new deal floor in one of the chambers. The account noted the commission of 'Joynrs Stuff viz Tables, Stooles, Cubberds, dores, portals, Sealing, Casements, presses, and sondry other Joynrs stuff and Joyned worke' for £51 12s 9d, with a further 48s for the hire of the craftsmen themselves. Joiners also provided tables, stools, forms, doors, portals, ceilings, tressells, and 'sondry other Joynrs worke' at Parliament House.

At Hampton Court Palace over £25 was spent on the hire of joiners and their apprentices, although this page of the account is damaged so it is unclear precisely what work they were doing. However, the general description of works noted the erection of a new barn and stables, repairs to the lodgings of the Clerk of the Kitchens and Mr Secretary, and the creation and repair of various doors and windows. Again, this was overseen by Stockett himself. At Greenwich Palace a joiner created 'A Table of deale boards wth a fframe to brusshe the Q mats Robes on' at a cost of 13s, with an additional 16d spent on some new wainscot.[14]

The impression from these entries is that Stockett was a very busy man, involved in the construction of major buildings in London, some of which are still standing. His rapid promotion from master mason to general surveyor of works indicates that Elizabeth I was pleased with the work he had done for her, and Stockett became a valued, trusted, and respected member of her household. Caring for the royal residences was an important task, and the implication in all the surviving documents is that Stockett did his work well. However, it was not just Stockett but also the joiners of London themselves who were demonstrating their skills to the royal court on a daily basis in the 1560s and 1570s.

In spite of how busy he was as surveyor of works, there was another role which Stockett took very seriously in the 1560s and 1570s; that of a member of the Company of Joiners. Due to the lack of surviving records from the sixteenth century it is unclear when or how Stockett joined the Company. However, by 1570 he was in a position of leadership; if not already the master, then perhaps a warden. On 1st August 1570 Lewis Stockett and Thomas Lovell secured a grant from the Court of Aldermen concerning freedom for joiners;

> Item at this Court it was ordered and agreed at the suyt of Lews Stockett Surveyor of the Quenes Mats works and Thomas Lovell gent one of the wardens of the Joyners that there shalbee tenne psons admitted into the freedome of the liberties of this Cyttie in the companie of Joyners by Redempcon every of them payeing unto the Chamberleyn of the Cyttie vl [£5] in the name of a ffyne to the use of the Comynaltie of this Cyttie.[15]

The following year, on 14th April 1571, Elizabeth I granted a charter to the Worshipful Company of Joiners and Ceilers of London, and she named Stockett as their Master. There seems little doubt that he was directly responsible for the charter. Whether it was a personal reward to him for the work he had done, or perhaps a combined acknowledgement that Stockett and the joiners of London were an integral part of the Office of Works, remains speculation. Nevertheless, he can be credited as the man who raised the Joiners to the rank of a full livery company. The Company's continuing gratitude to Elizabeth I for the grant of their charter can be seen in the commission of the queen's picture in glass to be added to the parlour window in 1641.[16]

Stockett died in early 1578 and was buried on 21st February in his local parish church of St Dunstan in the West.[17] His position in the royal household meant that he died a wealthy man. In his will, which was proved on 19th March 1579, he bequeathed numerous pieces of real estate to the children from his first marriage and to his second wife Lucy, including houses and grounds in Camberwell, Lambeth, Westminster, and Barking, as well as an estate called Wicklands in East Ham, and a house known as the Dolphin on Fleet Street, near Temple Bar.[18] He retained his connection with the Company until his death, and indeed his sons were named as trustees of Joiners' Hall in 1590.[19]

In the mid-seventeenth century a book of ordinances was created containing the key documents relating to the Company's governance. The first entry was a word-for-word Latin transcription of the 1571 charter, followed immediately by an English translation. The translation has been reproduced below, retaining the spellings and grammar used in 1685. The book of ordinances was regularly used during court meetings, and its contents regularly read aloud to the Court of Assistants, so the following text would have been a familiar one to the Company's early modern members. In 1957, after a consultation with the City Librarian at the Guildhall Library, this document was described as 'the most valuable Charter in the City of London and ... a priceless possession'.[20]

1571 Charter

> Elizabeth by the grace of God Queene of England Ffrance and Ireland defendor of the faith &c To all to whom theis pnte Letters shall come greeting Whereas by the humble Peticon of our welbeloved ffreemen of the Mistery or ffaculty of Joyners and Ceelers of our Citty of London, It is given us to understand, that

the Workmanship and busines in the said Mistery by default of circumspect Governmt in the Mistery and ffaculty aforesaid often tymes are insufficiently and deceiptfully made aswell to the prjudice of us as to the deceipt of our leige People and Subjects Know yee therefore that wee willing to meete with such prjudice and deceipt, of our speciall grace certeine knowledge and meer mocon Have given granted and confirmed for us our heires and Successors And by theis pnts for us our heires and Successors wee do give grant & confirm (as much as in us is) to our welbeloved servant Lewis Stockett, and to our welbeloved Thomas Lovell and John Mason ffreemen of the said Mistery or ffaculty, that they & all the ffreemen of the same Mistery or ffaculty of and in the Citty aforesaid and Suburbs of the same be in deed and name one body and Cominalty perpetuall And that the same body or Cominalty every yeare for ever may elect and make of that Cominalty one circumspect man of that Cominalty and in the same ffaculty expert Master of the said Mistery or ffaculty, and Two other men of the same ffaculty to Survey Governe Order and Correct for that yeare the Cominalty aforesaid, and all menservants & Appntices of the same ffaculty in the Citty and Suburbs of the same or by Two myles in Circuit of the same Citty exercising the same ffaculty And that the same Master Wardens and Cominalty may have Succession perpetuall and a Comon seale for to serve for the buisnes of the said Master Wardens and Cominalty for ever And that they and their successors may been for ever persons capeable, and able to purchase and possesse in ffee, & perpetuity Lands and Tenemts Rents and other possessions whatsoever Wee have also granted to them and their Successors for us and our Successors That they and their Successors may purchase to them and their Successors aswell within the said Citty as without, Lands and Tenemts whatsoever not exceeding the yearly valew of Tenne Markes, and which are not holden of us our heires or Successors imediatly in cheife The Statute of Alyenacon unto Mortmaine notwithstanding And that they by the names of Master Wardens and Cominalty of the ffaculty of Joyners and Ceelers of the Citty of London may plead and be impleaded before whatsoever Judges in whatsoever Courts and Accons And that the aforesaid Master Wardens and Cominalty and their Successors may make lawfull and honest Assemblyes and Statutes and Ordinances for the good Governmt Survey and correction of the aforesaid Cominalty and of all menservants & Appntices exercising the said Mistery or ffaculty in the same Citty or Suburbs of the same or by Two Miles in the Circuite of the said Citty as necessity shall require when and as often as need shall require lawfully unpunishable without the lett of us our heires & Successors or of the Justices Escheators Sheriffs or other Bayliffs or Ministers of us our heires or Successors whatsoever Wee have also granted for us our heires and Successors to the said Master Wardens and Cominalty and their Successors, that none exercise the said Mistery or ffaculty in the said Citty or Suburbs of the same, or within Two Myles of the same, Except hee bee thereunto admitted by the said Master and Wardens and their Successors for the tyme being Moreover wee will and grant for us our heires and Successors to the said Master Wardens and Cominalty and their Successors That the said Master and Wardens and their Successors for the tyme being may have survey governmt and serch of the Cominalty aforesaid, and of all menservants & Appntices exercising the same Mistery in the Citty aforesaid and Suburbs of the same and within Two Myles in circuit of the said Citty, and also of all works marchandize & other things whatsoever in the said Mistery occupyed used made sold or putt to sale, and the punishmt and correction of all men offending in the said Mistery when and as often as need shall require, So that the punishmt of all offenders in the prmisses by ffines amerciamts imprisonmt of their bodyes and by other ways reasonable and congruent bee executed Wee comand also by the tenor of theis presents to all and singuler Mayors Sheriffs Sargeants at Mace Bayliffs and other Officers whatsoever within the Citty aforesaid & Suburbs of the same That they to the same Masters Wardens and Cominalty and their Successors for the tyme being in the Exercise and Execucon of the prmisses at the request of the said Master and Wardens for the tyme being in all things bee comforting and assisting An'y Statute Act or Ordinance to the contrary heretofore made established ordeined or provided notwithstanding In witnes whereof wee have caused theis our Letters to bee made Patents Witnes ourselfe at Westminster the ffowerteenth day of Aprill in the Thirteenth yeare of our Reigne.[21]

1571 Grant of Arms

The grant of a charter was immediately followed by a grant of arms. This gave the Company the right to display and use a crest or coat of arms bearing a unique decoration.

> To all and singular aswell nobles and gentilmen as others whiche these presents shall see or here Robert Cooke esquier alias Clarenciaux principall herehault and kinge of armes of the sowth este and weste partes of this Realme of Englande sendith greeting forasmuch as anciently from the beginninge the valiaunte and vertuous actes of excellent persons have ben comendid to the worlde with sondry monuments and remembrance of their good desertes Emongest the whiche the chefeste and most usuall hathe ben the bearing of signes in Shildes caled Armes whiche are evident demonstracons of prowes and valoir diversly distributed accordinge to the qualitie and desert of the persons To the intent that suche as have done commendable service to their prynce or contry either in warre or peace or otherwise by the lawdable and coragious enterprises or proceeding of any person or persons in the augmentacon of the estate or comon wealthe of their Realme or contrye might thereby bothe receave deue honor in their lyves and also derive the same successively unto their posteritie and successors after them And whereas yt hath pleased the Quenes moste excellent magestye in the xiiith yere of her reigne to incorporate the company of Joyners by the name of Maister Wardens and comonaltie by vertue of whiche corporation they are allowed one comon seale to use afficiate their necessary affaires, Whereuppon they have required me the said Clarenciaux to devise ordeyne and assigne unto and for them suche armes and Creaste as theye maye lawfully beare Whereuppon considering their requeste to be resonable and also at the instant requeste of Lewis Stockett esquier surveyor generall of all her maties wourkes at this present maister, Thomas Lovell gentleman, and John Mason wardens of the saide arte or mistery I have devised ordeyned and assigned unto and for the said maister wardens and comunaltie and unto their successors in the office and place the Armes and Creaste hereafter followinge That is to saye ... gules a chevron ar betwen three scallops argent on a chief of the third apale azur betweene 2 roses gules on the pale a paire of compasses or a globe in gold And to their crest on a healme a wrethe golde & gules.[22]

The Company's shield contains four basic heraldic colours: gules (red), azure (blue), or (gold), and argent (silver). Due to the difficulty of finding pigments which will not fade or blacken with age, or and argent were usually painted using yellow and white paints respectively, rather than using gold or silver leaf. It seems likely that the original grant of arms made to the Company was decorated using gold and silver leaf because both colours have faded badly, and the silver in particular has become a dark grey. 'To begin the blazoning of any coat of arms, a mention of colour had to be made at the very outset. This was because the first word in the blazon – or description of the coat of arms – was "field", which primarily concerned the colour of the background of the shield.' Thus we know that the background of the Joiners' shield was red, because the first word in the description is 'gules'. The next piece of information is 'a chevron ar', which refers to a silver or white chevron. That shape is known as an ordinary charge. The top of the shield was divided into three sections. Those on the left and right side each contained a red rose on a white/silver background, with a touch of vert (green) for the leaves. The red rose is traditionally believed to represent the Tudor rose, the national emblem adopted as a merger of the white rose of the House of York and the red rose of the House of Lancaster following the Wars of the Roses. It is one of the most common symbols in heraldry, and its presence in the Joiners' crest would remind them that their Charter and arms had been granted by Elizabeth I. Between the two roses was a silver escallop shell on a background of blue. The choice of an escallop shell is a significant one for the Company. These shells are usually employed to represent pilgrimage, but there is a deeper meaning. The patron saint of pilgrimage was St James, so the inclusion of this symbol was a tribute to the Company's origins as a guild at St James Garlickhythe.[23]

The remaining images on the shield are also tributes to the Company, although this time in reference to their work as craftsmen of wood. Two gold compasses appeared on the red background above the chevron, a tribute to the tools used by woodworkers when drafting their designs. A similar use of compasses can be found on the coat of arms of the Worshipful Company of Carpenters, which was granted to them in 1466. The compasses appear in the same position above a chevron, but they were painted black on a background of silver, and a third pair appeared in the remaining section of the crest.[24] The final symbol on the Joiners' shield is an armillary sphere or spherical astrolabe in gold. This device consisted of rings representing lines of celestial longitude and latitude in relation to the earth and the sun. The same device appears at the top of the Worshipful Company of Clockmakers' crest.[25] Above the shield was a crest bearing the figure of a demigod 'holdinge a large golde mitre a garlande of laurel aboute his hed and waste'. The demigod was separated from the shield by a manacle of intertwined gold and blue.[26]

Eighteenth-century Alteration of the Company's Crest and Motto

It had been assumed that the alterations made to the Company's crest and motto were due to John Wilkes, the famous promoter of liberty and sometime Master of the Joiners' Company, because the motto became 'Join Loyalty and Liberty'. However, this change appears to have taken place long before Wilkes' tenure as Master. A newspaper article from 1768 reporting his admission to the livery, which is discussed in greater detail in Chapter 8, stated that the Company's motto had already been set.[27] Indeed, another article described it as 'extremely remarkable' that the Company's motto so closely echoed Wilkes' own political tagline.[28] Additional changes were also made to the Company's crest, with the introduction of supporting figures on either side of it.

About the time of the Company's removal from the Hall at the turn of the nineteenth century, their corporate seal dating from 1571 was lost. It had been previously kept in their chest, safely under three locks and three keys, and a later report noted that 'how it ever went astray no living man knows'.[29] Past Master Henry Carrington Bowles informed the Company of his intention to present them with a 'Seal of the Crest of the Company' in February 1829.[30] Unfortunately he died before the seal was ready, and it was formally presented by his son in January 1831.[31] However, in February 1842 discussions were held about ordering a new seal.[32] After carefully consulting a number of books on heraldry to determine the correct design, engraver Mr Varley attended the Company to receive a commission for a seal 'handsomly cut in Steel' at a cost of 12 guineas.[33] It appears that Bowles had omitted to include the two supporters, for which 'no cause appears ... and we think the same was done without sufficient authority'. As the supporters had appeared on various iterations of the Company's crest since they were given a grant of arms, it was decided that they must be included, and Varley was instructed to proceed according to the traditional design.[34] One interesting point to note, however, is that the motto they chose for this seal was 'Join Truth with Trust', not 'Join Loyalty with Liberty'.

Arms

Gules a cheveron ar. between two pair of Compasses in chief extended at the points, and a Sphere in base, ar: on a chief of the last, a pale az: between two Roses gules, seeded of the third, barbed virl; on the pale sa; an Escallop Shell of the second.

Crest

On a wreath a demi savage proper wreathed about the head and waist with wreath leaves vort, holding in his dexter hand over his shoulder a tilled spear, or: headed as:

Supporters

Two naked Boys proper; the dexter holding in his hand an emblematical female figure [crowned] with a mural coronet sa: the sinister hold in his hand a Square.

Motto

Join Truth with Trust

The original 1571 corporate seal was unexpectedly returned to the Company in 1900, however. Alderman Sir Joseph Dimsdale had been examining a collection of seals acquired by his father and discovered that the Joiners' seal was amongst them. He graciously returned it to the Company, and as a token of gratitude they presented him with 'an emblazoned vote of thanks' with an impression of their seal at the bottom, 'this being the first use to be made of the restored property'.[35]

In October 1934 it was brought to the Company's attention that the box containing the seal and charter was in a 'very dilapidated condition', and it was agreed 'that a new box be made to contain the old box & seal', with all expenses paid by the Company.[36] Ultimately the Master, Sidney Baker, undertook the construction of a carved oak box. He was thanked and congratulated 'on the excellence of the work he had done', and the Father of the Company, G. C. Barnes, expressed his pleasure 'that the Company had a Master who was able to execute an example of the trade of the Company'. It was agreed that the box should be offered for exhibition to the students at the Trades Training School, and the Company would pay for a plate to be attached to it stating,

This case was designed made and the medallion carved by the Master S R Baker Esq. and was presented to the Company by him 7th May 1935.[37]

1572 Ordinances

After the Joiners became a full livery company they were able to have their ordinances confirmed by the government, a process which took place on 1st October 1572 before the Lord Keeper of the Great Seal, the Chief Justice of the King's Bench, and the Chief Justice of the Common Bench. The ordinances were later ratified in 1575 by Sir Christopher Wray.[38]

The ordinances governed every aspect of the Company's business. They stipulated how each rank of the Company's officers should be elected, and from which body of men they should be chosen. There was extensive detail about how apprentices should be bound and educated, and the conditions they would have to meet to be admitted as journeymen and later as freemen. The Company also received powers to suppress and prosecute 'foreigns' and aliens working as joiners in London without being free, and to impose penalties on their freemen and liverymen for disobedience, evil speech, rule breaking, and insufficient craftsmanship.

The number and type of meetings to be held each year on the Company's business was specified, as were methods of preserving important documents. Towards the end of the ordinances were oaths to be administered at each level of Company membership, from freemen all the way up to Masters. Each person would be required to swear allegiance to the sovereign and promise to serve the Company to the best of their ability. It is noteworthy that the oaths of allegiance to be sworn by the officers are still said today to almost the exact same wording as the Elizabethan originals.

The ordinances can be read in full in the Appendix.

1614 Supplemental Ordinances

Even though the ordinances confirmed in 1572 were extremely extensive, by the turn of the seventeenth century the Company felt that there were still some gaps. In particular, they were concerned that the increased manufacture of coaches and trunks was producing 'much bad sappy & insufficient stuffe' with 'very ill false & deceiptfull workmanshippe'. The supplemental ordinances of 1614, therefore, were intended to give the Company increased power to search the premises of craftsmen not of the freedom, and to make sure that any apprentice seeking freedom had produced an acceptable proof-piece. It was hoped that these measures would keep the quality of manufactured goods at an acceptable standard.

> To all xpian people to whome this present writinge shall come Thomas Lord Ellesmere Lord Chauncellor of England Sir Edward Coke knight lord Cheife Justice of England and one of his Majesties most honourable privu Counselle and Sir Henry Hobart knight & Baronett Lord Cheife Justice of the Court of Comon pleas send greeting in one lord God everlastinge Whereas we have seene perused & examined certeine Statutes and Ordinances made by the maister wardens and Cominaltye of the ffacultye of Joyners & Ceelers of the Cittye of London for the good government survey & correction of the foresaid Cominaltye according to their Charter & lres pattent graunted unto them by our late Soveraigne Lady of famous memory Queene Elizabeth under her highnes great Seale of England bearinge date att Westmynster the ffourteenth day of Aprill in the thirteenth yere of her highnes reigne which Statutes and Ordinances were examined approved and confirmed by Sir Nicholas Bacon knight Lord keeper of the great Seale of England Robert Catlyn knight Cheife Justice of the kinges bench & James Dyer

knght cheife Justice of the Comon bench by their writinge under their handes and Seales bearinge date the first day of October in the ffowerteenth yere of the raigne of our said late soveraigne lady Queene Elizabeth according to a certeine Acte of Parliament made provided & enacted in the nynteenth yere of the raigne of our late soveraigne lord of famous memorye Kinge Henrye the seaventh And afterwards examined & approvied by Sir Cristofer Wray knight late lord cheife Justice of England by writinge under his hand and seale annexed to the said writinge of the said lord keeper & Justices of either benche bearinge date the second day of June in the Seaventeenth yere of the raigne of our late soveraigne Lady of famous memory Queene Elizabeth as by the same severall writinges may more plainlye and att large appeare And whereas sithence the makinge of the same Statute & Ordinances the makinge of Coaches wherein much carving worke & Joyninge worke is for the most part used As also the making of Trunckes is very much increased in which trades of Coach makinge & trunckemakinge much bad sappy & insufficient stuffe & very ill false & deceiptfull workmanshippe is continualy used made & wrought to the great deceipt not only of the kinges highnes his noble Consort the Queenes highnes and the Prince and the Nobility & Gentry of this kingdome But also to the deceipt of all other kinges princes and fforyeine States who usually beer & transport the same out of this kingdome for their necessarye yses whereby great disgrace resoundeth unto menne of those trades & facultyes by the use of such deceiptes in Comodityes servinge for the use of so great princes States and honorable personages And for that the search survey and Correction of the same abuses most properly belongeth to the said Company of Joyners Ceelers & Carvers as men best experienced & havinge best knowledge therein beinge buines properly ivadent and belonginge to the said ffacultye of Joyninge Ceelinge & Carvinge And whereas also sithence the makinge of the said former Ordinances divers forreine Joyners and repaired & come into the Cittye of Westmynster Burrough of Southwarke Suburbes of London and other places adioyninge within twoe myles ciruite of the said Cittye of London as also divers and sundry Joyners free of other Companyes encreased in great nombers in the same Cittye libertyes thereof and two myles circuite of the said Cittye And also certene Joyners only ymploeinge themselves to the makinge of boxes & naminge themselves boxmakers & certeine Cubbordmakers commonly called plated Cubboardes or crooked lane Cubboardes & certeine Gunstockmakers and fflaskemakers are increased in great numbers which said fforeine Joyners and Joyners free of other Companyes and the said boxemakers Cubboardmakers and Gunstocke & flaskemakers pretendinge themselves not to be subiect to the survey search goverment & Correction of the said maister & wardens whereas indeede they are and ought to be under their goverment search & survey do use much bad and insufficient stuffe and make & worke verye insufficient workmanship to the great preiudice of his Maiestyes people & Subiectes that continually buy the same and to the great discreditt hinderance of the said Company of Joyners of London As also many of the same forreane Joyners & Joyners free of other Companyes Boxemakers Cubboardemakers Gunsticke & Fflaskemakers refuse to make proofe peeces beinge a spetiall Ordinance in the said Company by which every one usinge the said misterye or facultye should make proofe of their sufficiency and become expert & cunninge therein as also to obey divers other good & laudable ordinances of the said Company meete & necessary for the said Companye and profitable to the Comon welth and do take & binde to them Apprentices in what numbers they list without stint whereas the ffreemen of the said Company are tyed and restrained to the nomber of two Apprentices only Noew forasmuch as by the said letters pattentes and Ordinances before mentioned the survey goverment and search of all Joyners aswell free as forreine and of all other person and persons usinge & makinge any thinge belonginge or in any wyse apperteyninge to the said ffacultye of Joyninge Ceelinge & Carveinge within the said Cittye of London libertyes thereof or within two myles circuite of the said Cittye is given & appointed to the said maister & wardens as a thinge incident and properly belonginge to their said ffacultye The maister & wardens of the severall Companyes of which the said free Joyners are free nor any other Corporation in London (other then the said maister & wardens of the said Company of Joyners) barringe neither power given them or skill or knowledge to survey search or trye the premisses or to finde out the faultes deceiptes and other abuses comitted by the said Coache makers Trunckmakers Boxemakers Cubboardmakers gunstock and flaskemakers or to punish the Offendors therein The maister wardens & Assistantes of the said Company of Joyners Ceelers and Carvers of London beinge verye willing & desirous to take speedy order for redresse of the severall Offences before mentioned not putt in practise at the tyme of the making of the said Charter & Ordinances before mentioned but sithence crept in used & putt in practise and for better explanation of the said former Ordinances touchinge the premisses have by their deliberate advise and by force and vertue of their said Charter and letters pattentes and of the power & authoritye thereby to them given made & added divers Actes and Ordinances and the same Actes & Ordinances so newly made & added as also the said former Ordinances so allready examyned approved & confirmed have presented unto us the said Lord Chauncellor and Justices of either bench instantly desiringe of us that att & every the said the former statutes Actes & Ordinances allready examyned & approved as also the other newe Actes Ordinances & Statutes of new made & added might be by us examyned allowed approved & confirmed according to the Acts of Parliament in that behalf The tenor of which said new Ordinances & Actes so lately made hereafter enseweth Inprimis it is ordered & established that from henceforth the said Coachmakers Trunckmakers Boxemakers Cubboardmakers fforeine Joyners & Joyners free of other Companyes and Gunstock & fflaskemakers now inhabitinge & dwelling or which hereafter shall inhabite or dwell within the said Cittye of London suburbes or libertyes of the same or in any other place or places within two myles Circuite of the said Cittye of London and all wares and stuffe made or sould and hereafter to be made or sould by them or any of them shalbe subiect to the said lres pattentes and to the former Actes & Ordinances of the said Company and to the search survey goverment & Correction of the said maister and wardens of the said Cominaltye of Joyners & Ceelers of London for the tyme beinge & of their successors forever And that it shalbe lawfull for the maister & wardens of the said Company or ffellowshipp for the tyme beinge from henceforth forevermore from tyme to tyme as often & when it shall seeme good unto them at convenyent tyme & in convenyent manner without force to enter into the howses shopps sellers sollers warehowses and booths of any pson usinge the said trades of Coachmakinge Trunckmakinge Boxemakinge Cubboardmakinge Gunstocke & fflaskemakinge & of anye person workinge usinge or sellinge any thinge or thinges made by Joyners & Ceelers or Carvers aswell free as forreine or any thinge to the said faculty of Joyninge Ceelinge or Carvinge belonginge or apperteyninge or incident thereunto aswell within the said Cittye of London & suburbes of the same or within two myles Compasse of the same aswell in places priviledged & exempt as not priviledged & exempt and aswell in ffayres & marketts within the said Cittye & two myles Compasse of the same as elsewhere within the said precinct and there without any fee reward or other thinge to be taken to viewe & search all manner of workes & wares whatsoever made by any person or persons of the trades aforesaid or of the faculty of Joyning Ceelinge & Carvinge or any thinge thereunto proper incident or belonginge whether the same be well & workmanlike wrought and of good sufficient & lawfull stuffe in manner & accordinge to the lawes & Statutes of this realme in such Cases provided And the Offenders in that behalfe to punish in such manner & forme as by their former Actes Constitutions & Ordinances and accordinge to the lawes of the realme they may lawfully do in such & the like Cases Item it is ordeined and established that the said Coachmakers Trunckmakers Boxemakers Cubboardmakers fforeine Joyners & Joyners free of other Companyes & Gunstockmakers & flaskemakers & all & every other person & persons usinge or exercisinge any thinge belonginge to the said facultye or misterye of Joyninge Ceelinge or Carvinge or incident or belonginge thereunto now inhabitinge within the said Citty of London libertyes & Suburbes thereof or within two myles Circuite of the said Cittye and all such as hereafter shall use or exercise any of the Actes aforesaid within the said Citty Suburbes & places aforesaid before their settinge upp for themselves or before they or any of them shall take any servant or Apprentices to dwell with them or any of them shall come unto the said maister & wardens of the said Company of Joyners & Seelers of London for the tyme beinge & in a workehowse appoynted in the Comon hall of the said Company for that purpose in the presence of the said maister & wardens or one of them or in the presence of any others whome the said maister & wardens or the most part of them shall appoint shall make with their owne handes some handsome peece of worke for his proofe whereby it may be knowne whether he be a good and sufficient workeman or no without takinge any thinge of any such workman therefore And whosoever setteth up or reteyneth any servant or Apprentice before he himself be allowed uppon the makinge of his said proofe peece in forme aforesaid to be a workeman shall forfeyte to the maister wardens & Cominalty of the said ffellowshipp for every moneth so offendinge Twenty six shillinges & eight pence and shall have his shopp windows shutt upp untill such tyme as he hath made his proofe peece the said money to be payed to the said maister & wardens of the same Company for the tyme being to be ymployed to the use of the said Company or ffellowship Item it is ordeined & established that no man of the trades before mentioned now inhabitinge or dwellinge or that hereafter shall dwell or inhabit within the said Cittye of London suburbes thereof or within two myles Circuite of the same Cittye shall retein or take any Journeyman to worke with him by the space of one moneth unles before the end of the said moneth he present him before the maister & wardens of the said Company or ffellowshipp for the tyme beinge or att the next Court to be houlden at the Joyners hall after such retainer To the intent the same Journeymen & anye of them may be examined whether they have served seaven yeres apprentishipp accordinge to the statute and that tyme may be given them to prove the same by lawfull certificate from the places where they served uppon which proofe made it shalbe lawfull for everye such person so takinge or retayninge such Journymen the same Journymen to reteine & keepe by the whole yeare half yere or quarter of the yere or otherwise as betweene the maister & servant shalbe agreed accordinge to the lawes and Statutes of this Realme without takinge any thinge therefore uppon payne that every one offendinge contrary to this Ordynance to pay for a ffyne to the maister & wardens of the said Company or ffellowshipp for every such offence the some of ten shillings of lawfull money of England to be by them ymployed to the use of the said Companye or ffellowshipp Item it is ordeyned that none of the said Coachmakers

Trunckemakers Boxemakers Cubboardmakers Gunstocke & fflaskemakers and Joyners free of other Companyes and usinge any of the trades aforesaid shall at any tyme or tymes hereafter at any one tyme keepe above the number of two Apprentices as ffreemen of the said Company are bound to do by vertue of their said Ordinances And that the same free Coachmakers Trunckemakers Boxemakers Cubboardmakers Gunstocke & fflaskemakers & Joyners free of other Companyes shall within one moneth next after they or any of them shall retaine or take any Apprentice or Apprentices shall prsent & shewe the same Apprentice & Apprentices togither with his & their Indenture of Apprenticehood to the maister and wardens of the said Company of Joyners of London to the intent they may understand under what forme the same Apprentices were bound And lastlye yt is ordeyned That if any person or persons usinge any of the trades before mentioned or selling any kind of wares apperteyninge to any of the said trades of whatsoever degree or condition soever he or they be that shall offend in any Act or Ordinance before expressed That then it shalbe lawfull to the maister & wardens of the said mistery or ffacultye of Joyners & Ceelers of London or any of them for the tyme beinge at their will & pleasure to enter into the howse shop or boothe of him or them so offending & there to take a distresse or distresses convenyent & meete for the same somes of money And those distresses so taken lawfully to leade drive carry & beare away & to keepe to the use of the same Maister wardens & Cominaltye untill the same penaltyes forfeytures or somes of money be payed assigning the party a tyme convenyent & reasonable within thirty dayes next after the takinge of such distresses to pay the same penaltyes somes of money & forfeytyres except he sue a replevin for the same within ten dayes after the said distresse taken All which Actes & Ordinances so formerly made & allready perused read & examined by the said lord kepper & lordes cheife Justices of either bench As also theis present newe Actes & Ordinancse conteyned in this present writinge we the said Lord Chauncellor & lords Cheife Justices of either bench have at the request of Mathewe Grace now maister of the said Company of Joyners & Ceelers Launcelott Smith & Richard Oulton nowe wardens of the said Company & of the rest of the Assistant of the said Company seene perused & examined & fully considered of and for good & lawfull Ordinances & Constitutions we by vertue of the said Act of Parliament made in the said nynteenth yere of the raigne of our late soveraigne lord of famous memory Kinge henry the Seaventh do accept allowe & admitt And by theis presents as much as in us is & resteth do ratifye allowe confirme & approve In witnes whereof to this our present writinge we the said lord Chauncellor & lord Cheife Justices have sett our handes & Seales proven the eight day of Aprill and in the yeres of the raigne of our Soveraigne lord James by the grace of God kinge of England ffrance & Ireland defender of the fayth is the twelfath and of Scottland the seaven & ffortyeth.[39]

The English Civil Wars and Background to the 1685 Charter

When James I died in 1625 his son Charles inherited the throne. Unfortunately the young king, aged just twenty-four, had ideas about governance which were not in line with those of his Parliament, and he faced great opposition from both Westminster and the general populace. He dismissed Parliament altogether in 1629 and began a period known as the personal rule, where the king's word was law. His financial policies during this time were particularly unpopular. The tax known as ship money had been levied on coastal towns and counties in times of warfare during the medieval period, and its purpose was to fund the navy. Coastal areas were expected to pay the tax because they had a vested interest in ensuring that no invasions could land. However, levying this tax was in the monarch's prerogative and it could be imposed without the authorisation of Parliament. After proroguing Parliament in the summer of 1628, Charles I made the unpopular decision to impose ship money on every county, not just those on the coast. This met with immediate and fierce resistance, but ultimately few were able to withstand an order from the king, and those who tried often found themselves imprisoned.

The Joiners' Company was not exempt from this tax. The Renter Wardens' accounts first list a payment of £6 towards ship money for the year 1633–4.[40] This is consistent with the timing of Charles' treaty with Philip IV of Spain to assist in the Thirty Years War against the Dutch. The Attorney General, William Noy, suggested that ship money should be used to finance this campaign because technically it was a tax used during times of warfare. Although in this instance it was issued in a time of peace, the King justified his decision by citing unrest in Europe and the potential danger to trade through piracy. A writ was issued in October 1634 instructing the Lord Mayor, commonalty, and citizens of London to provide ships 'no less for the honour and safety both of the King and kingdom, and the securing and clearing of commerce'.[41] London did not respond favourably. Arguments were made that the City was exempt from providing the money through its charter, but the money was collected nonetheless. The 1634 writ was followed by additional writs in 1635 and 1636, after which the King narrowly obtained judgement in the Star Chamber that imposing the tax was in his prerogative regardless of military danger, and it became a permanent policy.

Between 1634 and 1639 the Joiners contributed £18 13s 4d in ship money payments, approximately £2,300 in today's money.[42] This was in addition to the £6 13s 4d previously provided to unspecified subsidies to the King between 1621 and 1629,[43] and a further £24 in November 1638 following an order from the Lord Mayor that they must contribute towards 'the passing of books & patents to the City by the Kings Maty'.[44] However, much larger sums would soon be required because a war was coming.

The conflict which became known as the Bishops' Wars began in 1639 after Charles and his Archbishop of Canterbury William Laud attempted to impose religious innovations on the staunchly Presbyterian Scotland. In 1637 they had introduced a new Book of Common Prayer with a very Episcopalian doctrine, but this was met with widespread rioting. The following year Scotland produced the National Covenant, a document subscribed all across the country pledging resistance to innovations. The king's reaction was to resort to military force to maintain his authority, but he did not have the money to pay for this. He was forced to recall Parliament in an attempt to secure further funding, but after eleven years of enforced absence his MPs were not willing to agree to his demands. He dismissed them again on 5th May 1640 after only three weeks. However, the increasing threat of invasion from the Scottish forces compelled him to recall them once again in November.

In the year 1640–1 the Joiners' Company paid £4 in four subsidies to Parliament, as well as £5 2s on two barrels of gunpowder, which was kept in an upper garret of the Hall. The Clerk, Mr Rochdale, also acquired a copy of the grant lending £50,000 from the City to the King.[45] 1642, however, saw the greatest contribution from the Company to date. The City of London agreed to lend Parliament £100,000 ostensibly in response to the Irish rebellion which had taken place in 1641 but largely to equip a Parliamentarian army.[46] Each of the livery companies were expected to pay a proportion of this sum. The Joiners were assessed at £300, but this was far more than they could afford. After deliberation the £300 was split into three parts; the Company would pay £100, and two members, Mr Rogers and Mr Holland, would each pay £100 to make up the full amount. They lent the money on the security of the Company's seal.[47]

When relations between Charles and Parliament had deteriorated to the point of the outbreak of civil war in August 1642 the Joiners appear to have followed the general attitude of London in supporting the cause of Parliament. In 1660 Handmaid Johnson, wife of royalist-supporting cabinetmaker Aaron Johnson, complained to Charles II that during the war

> her husbands integrity and loyalty being eminently knowne some of the Company of Joyners of London prvailed soe farr wth Collonell Barksteed (the prtended Leiut of the Tower) that they got his Order for her husbands Banishmt wch to prvent hee was forc't to give Bond of 100l to the Company of Joyners never to worke at his Calling, and feareing least the said Bond should bee sued upon him hee dares not worke soe that hee & his family are like to perish.[48]

The conflict placed further financial burdens on the Company. Their contribution to Parliament's taxes was smaller in 1642 and 1643 than in previous years, totalling just £4 10s, with a further 4s given to a fund for maimed soldiers.[49] However, in 1644 they paid another £100 into the Guildhall as their portion of a further £100,000 loan raised through the City.[50] That year they received £15 back from the Guildhall 'in parte of the money dew to this Company', and using this money combined with ready cash they had accumulated they were able to repay Mr Rogers £50 of the money he had lent in 1642. They provided him with a further £11 the following year. However, from 1645 onwards the taxes imposed by Parliament grew steadily higher and more numerous. The Company was expected to pay separate taxes on their Hall and adjoining tenements, as well as contributing towards the maintenance of the army and military campaigns in Ireland. The combined total of tax payments on the Hall and tenements between 1645 and 1651 was £63 17s 2d, which is roughly the equivalent of £6,600 in today's money.[51] In addition to this property tax were smaller taxes for the support of the army. Between 1646 and 1648 there were two payments totalling £7 in the Renter Wardens' accounts explicitly described as 'taxes for Sr Tho Ffairfax Army'. That same period also saw 15s paid to 'the Collectors for the Brittish Armie in Ireland', and £5 for two more unspecified Parliamentary taxes.[52] This was one of the great ironies of the English Civil War years; both Parliament and the people had considered the ship money tax imposed by Charles I as excessive and exploitative, and yet the taxes now imposed by Parliament to fund the war were dramatically higher than the sums claimed by the King during the 1630s.

On 10th February 1649 Parliament passed an ordinance making it compulsory for every freeman of London to swear an oath of allegiance:

> You shall Swear, That you shall be true and faithful to the Commonwealth of England; and in order thereunto, you shall be obedient to the just and good Government of this City of London: You shall to the best of your power,

maintain and preserve the Peace, and all the due Franchises thereof; and according to your knowledge and ability, do and perform all such other acts and things as do belong to a Free-man of the said City.[53]

The English Civil Wars were bloody and brutal; Charles Carlton has estimated that a higher percentage of the country's population died during these conflicts than in the First World War.[54] Parliament's victory culminated in the execution of Charles I for treason on 30th January 1649, following which the monarchy was abolished. The country became a commonwealth, governed by a republican parliament.

In an attempt to suppress the publication and circulation of scandalous books and pamphlets, Parliament ordered in September 1649 that

no Joyner nor Carpenter shall make any Printing-Presse &c, nor any Smith forge any Ironworke &c, or any Founder cast any Printing Letters; nor any man let any House, Vault, or Cellar for Printing in, without notice first given to the Master or Wardens of the Company of Stationers.[55]

An entry in the accounts from 1649–50 noted the disbursement of 21s 7d 'paid at severall meetings in goeing to Westminster about the Companies Charter'. The precise cause of these journeys is unclear and there don't appear to be any corresponding records in the journals of the House of Commons. However, contrary to belief within the Joiners' Company, this was not Oliver Cromwell's doing or fault.

Unfortunately, the Renter Wardens' accounts from the summer of 1651 to the summer of 1653 do not contain detailed itemised descriptions so it is unclear what the Company's outgoings were in the first years of the Commonwealth. From the summer of 1653 onwards, however, the detail returns. It is clear that although the civil conflict had ended, the taxes exacted from the livery companies had not. Between the summer of 1653 and the end of 1659 the Joiners contributed a further £69 3s 3d in Parliamentary taxes to support the army and navy. They also contributed £1 7s to the Corporation's poor relief fund, and 8s 9d towards the repair of the City's conduits.[56]

The death of Lord Protector Oliver Cromwell in 1658 sent the Commonwealth into turmoil. He was succeeded by his son Richard Cromwell, but whereas Oliver had been a powerful leader, Richard was weak and unpopular. He was deposed on 25th May 1659, and Parliament began to make overtures to the exiled Charles Stuart to encourage a return. The newly proclaimed Charles II arrived in London a year later on 29th May 1660, and the monarchy was once again restored. His return to the capital was marked with an elaborate parade through the streets. The Joiners' accounts for that summer reveal the expense the King's return had put them to. Ahead of the parade they invested £13 in new streamers and banners, as well as £3 4s 4d for decorating them and borrowing extra cloth to decorate their Company stands. A further £14 11s 6d was spent on 29th May itself, presumably on food, drink, and entertainment for the Livery. The Company also attended a thanksgiving service at St Paul's on 28th June, which cost them £2 18s 8d, and they spent a further 9s ensuring that the membership swore the oaths of allegiance and supremacy. The highest costs, however, were the Company's contributions to the financial gifts granted to the King by the City. The Joiners paid £36 'towards the Cittyes present sent to the King by order of the Comon Councell', and £9 'towards the dynner made for his Matie by the Citty at Guildhall'.[57]

The Company's total expenses in May and June 1660 at Charles II's return, therefore, were a staggering £79 3s 2d. Compared with the £133 5d paid in Parliamentary taxes over a fourteen-year period between 1645 and 1659, having to contribute such a large sum in just a two-month period was severely challenging. The Company's total income for the period September 1659 to September 1660 was £273 18s 7d and expenditure was £262 5s 9d. The costs of the Restoration celebrations represented just under one-third of the Company's total expenditure in that twelve-month period, and was the equivalent of 60 per cent of the taxes paid to Parliament from 1645 to 1659. Through Charles II's 'Act for the speedy provision of money for disbanding and paying off the forces of this Kingdome both by Land and Sea', Past Masters of the Joiners' Company, among others, were also each obliged to pay £1, and Wardens paid 15s. However, this was significantly lower than the £10 each charged upon Past Masters and £2 upon Wardens of the great twelve companies.[58]

The Company also faced a charge of £10 19s 7d on 23rd April 1661, the day of the King's coronation. They were present in their stands to watch the parade as 'he came from the tower through the Citty'. There was a further cost of £27 paid to the Chamberlain of London 'towards the pageants', money which came out of the Clerk's own pocket and was later reimbursed to him by the Company. A thanksgiving service and dinner to celebrate the King's birthday on 29th May claimed a further £2 4s 7d.[59] The merry monarch's return was not merry for the bank account. It did, however, provide the promotion of another member of the Company. William Emmett was appointed as 'Master Sculptor and Carver in Wood to the Crown', a post he retained until 1682 when Grinling Gibbons took over.[60]

The reconstruction of London following the Great Fire of 1666 crippled the City's finances. The Corporation was forced to borrow vast sums of money on the security of future coal tax receipts. Although the building work was completed by the mid-1670s, the debts endured for many years following, and in 1683 the City defaulted on the £600,000 it owed. Charles II responded by withdrawing the City's charter and privileges through the Quo Warranto Act. The following year the king also demanded the surrender of all livery charters so that the officers of the Companies could be replaced with men loyal to the Crown. None of what followed was voluntarily done by the Joiners' Company, but there was no way they could refuse to comply.

On 6th May 1684 the Court of Assistants called a special meeting of the Livery at the Hall for the following Friday afternoon 'to consult about a peticon to his Matie about the Charter of this Company'. No record was entered in the minute book about the content of that meeting, but it can be assumed from subsequent entries that the Livery had agreed that a petition should be sent. The task of composing it and delivering it to Charles II at Windsor Castle fell to the Clerk, Joseph Burrough, and he received £5 as compensation 'for writings and his extraordinary labour and paines' on 5th August.[61] The Company recorded receipt of several requests for the surrender of their 1571 charter by the Recorder of London so a new one could be drawn up, but they did not immediately comply. The sudden and unexpected death of Charles II on 6th February 1685 and the accession of his younger Catholic brother James II complicated the process, but James proved himself determined to carry on his brother's plan of reforming the Livery Companies.[62]

On 24th February an extraordinary meeting of the Assistants was held to discuss the surrender of the charter, which Philip Burton had warned that 'if not done quickly some proceedings will be taken against the said Company'. Burton was one of the lawyers who had prosecuted the quo warranto against the City in 1683. Mark Knights has described him as 'vehemently Tory' and stated that he 'did much of the Crown's legal dirty work in the 1690s'.[63] The Company responded to Burton's threat by ordering an extraordinary meeting of the Livery for the following Friday, and they also appointed a committee to raise the finances required to pay for the new charter. Seven members of the Assistants, of whom five were a quorum, were appointed to meet with the Clerk to 'drawe up some clauses to be incerted in the new Charter', and they agreed to meet at the Half Moon Tavern in Cheapside the following afternoon.[64]

The finance committee determined that the easiest way to raise the money was to borrow it. Three days later, on 27th February, they mortgaged their tenement currently in the possession of tenant Jospeh Wells to East India Company merchant Captain Samuel Chamblett for £100, with the promise to repay him £106 in one year. The liverymen of the Company also provided their assent to surrendering the charter on the 27th, and the Wardens and the Clerk were authorised to deliver the documents to the Recorder of London. A copy of the surrender was entered into the minute book:

To all to whom these prsents shall come
   The Master Wardens and Cominalty of the mistery or facultie of Joyners and Ceelers of London send greeting Know ye That wee the said Master Wardens and Cominalty for divers good causes and consideracons us thereunto moveing Have granted surrendred and yeilded up And by these presents do grant surrender and yeild up unto our gratious Sovreigne Lord King James the Second of England Scotland ffrance and Ireland defender of the ffaith &c All the powers liberties franchises priviledges and authorities what soever & howsoever granted or to be used or exercised by the said Master Wardens & Coalty by virtue of any right title or interest vested in them by virtue of any Charter Letters Pattents or prescriptions howsoever of or concerning the electing nominateing Constituteing or appointing of any person or persons into or for the severall and respective offices of Master Wardens Coalty and Clerke of the said Companie And the said Master Wardens and Cominaltydoe hereby humbly beseech his Maty to accept of this their Surrender and doe with all submission to his Maties good pleasure implore his grace and favour to regraunt to the said Master Wardens and Cominalty the nameing and chooseing of the said officers and the said Liberties and priviledges or soe many of them and in such manner as his Maty in his great wisdome shall seeme most conduceing to the good Government of the said Company and with and under such restitucons qualificacons and reservacons as his Maty shall please to appoint In witnesse whereof Wee the said Master Wardens and Cominalty of the Art or mistery of Joyners and Ceelers of London have caused our Common Seale to be hereunto affixed this Twenty ffourth day of ffebruary In the ffirst yeare of the raigne of our Soveraigne Lord King James the second over England &c.[65]

The following day at Whitehall a 'Warrant in the usuall forme for regranting to the Master Wardens and Commonalty of the Mystery of Joyners & Ceelers all their former Powers &c' was produced.[66] On 6th March another committee meeting was held at the Half Moon Tavern to finalise the new clauses to be requested. One Warden and the Clerk were instructed to deliver them to Mr Burton, along with a copy of the 1571 charter which he had requested earlier in the week, and £60 towards the cost of the new charter.[67]

A month later the Master received a letter from Burton requesting more money. This baffled the Court of Assistants, who could not understand how the £60 could have been spent so quickly. They ordered the Renter Warden to 'attend Mr Burton and desire an accompy how the said sixtie pounds hath been expended to whom and for what'. They did authorise the payment of a further £40 but told the Warden to 'acquainte him that this Company cann pay noe more unlesse moneys come in wch this Court cannot at present foresee'. Burton had now received the full £100 which the Company had borrowed from Chamblett, and they could not afford to pay more. In spite of this, they still authorised a gift of 6 guineas to Clerk Joseph Burrough as 'encouragement' for the 'extraordinary labour and paines that [he] hath taken about the new Charter'.[68]

The next monthly court meeting was held on 5th May, by which time a draft of the new charter had been delivered to Joiners' Hall. Unfortunately, it was not met with approbation, and the minute book noted that 'at this Court the new Charter was read deliberately and upon Serious examinacon of the same it is thought that it is not soe advantagious for the good of the Company in generall as was promised and expected'.[69] However, it was too late to do anything about it, and the new charter was sealed by James II on 19th May 1685.

1685 Charter

James the second by the Grace of God of England Scotland France and Ireland King Defender of the Faith, &c. To all to whom the present Letters shall come, Greeting. Whereas the Master Wardens or guardians and commonalty of the Mystery of Joiners and Carvers of the City of London have surrendered into our hands All their Powers Franchises Liberties Privileges and authority touching or concerning the Election Nomination Constitution Being and Appointment of any Person or Persons in or to the several offices of Master Wardens or guardians Assistants and Clerk of the said Incorporation Which said surrender we have accepted and by these presents do accept. Know ye That we carefully considering the Improvement of the company aforesaid of our special grace and of our certain knowledge and mere motion Have willed ordained constituted declared and granted And by these Presents for us our Heirs and Successors Do will ordain constitute declare and grant That all and singular the Freemen of the Mystery of Joiners and carvers of our City of London and the suburbs thereof from henceforth for ever, for the better order rule and government of the men of the mystery aforesaid and of all those who now exercise and use, or hereafter shall exercise and use the mystery of Joiners and carvers of London aforesaid the works merchandizes or things whatsoever concerning the said mystery, and for the utility benefit and relief of the good and honest, and terror and correction of the wicked deceitful and dishonest; May and shall be, by the force of these Presents, One Body Corporate and Politic in deed fact and Name, by the Name of the Master Wardens or guardians and commonalty of the Mystery of Joiners and Carvers of the City of London: and them, by the Name of the Master Wardens or guardians and commonalty of the Mystery of Joiners and Carvers of the City of London, We do, for us our Heirs and successors, create make ordain constitute and declare One Body Corporate and Politic in deed fact and name, really and fully, by these Presents; And That by the same Name they may have perpetual succession. And That They and their successors, by the Name of the Master Wardens or guardians and commonalty of the Mystery of Joiners and Carvers of the City of London may and shall be at all times hereafter Persons fit and capable in law to hold purchase receive and possess Manors Messuages Lands Tenements Liberties Privileges Jurisdictions Franchises and Hereditaments whatsoever, of whatsoever sort nature or kind they may be, or of any yearly value, to them and their successors, in Fee and Perpetuity or for Term of life or lives, year or years, or in any other manner howsoever; and also Goods and Chattels and whatsoever other things of what name nature quality or kind soever they may be. And also, by the name aforesaid, to give grant demise alien assign and dispose of Manors Messuages Lands Tenements and Hereditaments and to do and execute all and singular other deeds and things by the name aforesaid. And that by the same name of the Master Wardens or guardians and commonalty of the Mystery of Joiners and Carvers of the City of London at all times hereafter may and shall plead and be impleaded answer and be answered defend and be defended in what courts and places soever and before what Judges and Justices and other Persons and Officers soever of us and our Heirs and Successors in all and singular actions Pleas suits quarrels causes matters and demands whatsoever of what sort quality or kind soever they may or shall be, in the same manner and form as any other our liege People of this our Kingdom of England, Persons fit and capable in law or any other Body corporate and politic within our Kingdom of England may and can hold purchase receive possess enjoy retain give grant demise alien and assign dispose plead and be impleaded answer and be answered defend and be defended do and permit and execute. And That the same Master Wardens or guardians and commonalty of the Mystery of Joiners and Carvers of the City of London and their successors may and shall have for ever a common seal to serve for the causes and businesses of them and their successors whatsoever to be done. And that it may and shall be lawful for the Master Wardens or guardians and commonalty of the Mystery of Joiners and Carvers of the City of London aforesaid and their successors at their pleasure from time to time to break charge and make anew such seal as to them it shall seem best to be done and to be. And Further We will and by these presents for us our Heirs and successors do grant to the aforesaid Master Wardens or guardians and commonalty of the Mystery of Joiners and Carvers of the City of London and their successors, That from henceforth for ever there may and shall be One of the Commonalty of the Mystery aforesaid in the form in these Presents hereinafter mentioned to be elected who shall be and shall be named Master of the aforesaid Mystery of Joiners and Carvers of the City of London And in like manner that there may and shall be Two of the Commonalty of the same Mystery of Joiners and Carvers of the City of London in the form hereafter in these Presents mentioned to be elected and nominated who shall be and shall be called Wardens or Guardians of the Mystery of Joiners and Carvers of the City of London aforesaid and sixteen or more of the Freemen of the same Mystery in the form in these presents hereafter likewise mentioned to be named and constituted who shall be and shall be called Assistants of the Mystery aforesaid And We do will and grant That it may and shall be lawful for the same the Master Wardens or guardians and commonalty of the Mystery of Joiners and Carvers of the City of London and their successors at all times hereafter to have retain and appoint a certain Hall or Council-house within our City of London or the Liberties thereof And That the same Master Wardens or guardians and assistants of the Mystery of the aforesaid Mystery of Joiners and Carvers for the time being and their successors or seven of them at the least (of whom the aforesaid Master and Wardens or guardians we will shall be always three, or the Master and one

Warden or Guardian for the time being shall be two) may and shall at all times hereafter from time to time as often as they shall think fit and necessary summon and hold within the same House or Hall a certain court or assembly of the same Master Wardens or guardians and assistants or seven of them at the least (of whom the aforesaid Master Wardens or Guardians we will shall be always three, or the Master and one Warden for the time being shall be two) and in the same Court or Assembly may and shall treat confer consult and determine upon the Statutes Articles and ordinances respecting touching or concerning the aforesaid Master Wardens or Guardians and Commonalty and the good Rule State and Governance of the same according to their sound Directions. And Further We Will and by these Presents for us our Heirs and successors Do Grant to the aforesaid the Master Wardens or Guardians and commonalty of the Mystery of Joiners and Carvers of the City of London and their successors That the aforesaid Master Wardens or Guardians and commonalty of the Mystery of Joiners and Carvers aforesaid for the time being or seven of them at the least (of whom the Master and Wardens or Guardians for the time being We will shall be always three, or the Master and one Warden or Guardian shall be two) upon public summons to be thereof made for that purpose assembled may and shall have full and absolute Power and Authority to frame constitute ordain and make from time to time such reasonable Laws Statutes Ordinances Decrees and Constitutions in writing as to them or seven of them at the least (of whom the Master and Wardens or Guardians for the time being We will shall be always three, or the Master and one Warden or Guardian shall be two) shall according to their sound Discretions seem good salutary useful honest and necessary for the good Rule and Government of the same Master Wardens or Guardians and commonalty of the Mystery of Joiners and Carvers aforesaid and of all other Persons for the time being exercising using or in any manner occupying the Mystery of Joiners and Carvers within our aforesaid City of London suburbs and precincts thereof and for declaring in what manner and order the same Master Wardens or Guardians and commonalty of the Mystery aforesaid and all and singular other Persons for the time being exercising using or occupying the said Mystery within the said City of London Suburbs and Precincts thereof shall hold bear and conduct themselves in the Duties of their Mystery for the more abundant public good and common utility of the same Master Wardens or Guardians and Commonalty of the Mystery aforesaid and for other matters and causes whatsoever touching or in any wise concerning the Mystery aforesaid. And That the same Master Wardens or Guardians and Assistants of the Commonalty aforesaid and their successors for the time being or seven of them at the least (of whom the Master and Wardens or Guardians for the time being We will shall be always three, or the Master and one Warden or Guardian shall be two) as often as they shall make frame ordain or establish such Laws Statutes Ordinances Provisos Decrees and Constitutions in form aforesaid may and shall have power to make limit and provide such and the like Pains Punishments and Penalties by Fine and Amercement or by either of them against and upon all Persons offending against such Laws Statutes Ordinances Provisos Decrees and Constitutions or any of them as to the same Master Wardens or Guardians and Commonalty aforesaid or seven of them (of whom the Master and Wardens or Guardians for the time being We will shall be always three, or the Master and one Warden or Guardian shall be two) shall seem necessary fitting and requisite for the observance of their Laws Statutes Ordinances Provisos Decrees and Constitutions And That the same Master Wardens or Guardians and Commonalty of the Mystery of Joiners and Carvers of the City of London for the time being and their successors from time to time shall and may have recover and levy the same Fines and Amercements by action of Debt Distress or otherwise or by any other lawful ways and means to the use of the aforesaid Master Wardens or Guardians and commonalty of the Mystery aforesaid and their successors without the impediment of us our Heirs or successors to be therefore rendered or paid. All and singular which Laws Statutes Ordinances Provisos Decrees and Constitutions so as aforesaid to be made We will shall be observed under the Pains therein contained so that they be reasonable and not contrary to the Laws of this our Kingdom of England or to the customs of our City of London. And for the better execution of our Will and Grant in this behalf We have appointed named created constituted and made and by these Presents for us our Heirs and successors Do appoint name create constitute and make our Beloved Thomas Wratton to be and remain the first and present Master of the Mystery of Joiners and Carvers of the City of London to continue in the same office of Master of the Mystery aforesaid from the date of these Presents until the twenty fifth day of July which will be in the year of our Lord One thousand six hundred and eighty six if the same Thomas Wratton shall so long live and from thence until one other Person shall in due manner be preferred and sworn into the Office of Master of the Mystery aforesaid according to the ordinance and Proviso hereafter in these Presents expressed and contained. Also We have appointed named created constituted and made and by these Presents for us our Heirs and successors Do appoint name create constitute and make our Beloved George Newland and James Ball to be and remain the first and present Wardens or Guardians of the Mystery of Joiners and Carvers of the City of London to continue in the same office of Master of the Mystery aforesaid from the date of these Presents until the twenty fifth day of July which will be in the year of our Lord One thousand six hundred and eighty six if the same George Newland and James Ball shall so long live and from thence until two other Freemen of the Mystery aforesaid shall be preferred and sworn according to the ordinances and provisos in these presents expressed and declared. And we have appointed named created constituted and made and by these Presents for us our Heirs and successors Do appoint name create constitute and make our Beloved Roger Weekes, Henry Phillips, John Markland, Samuel Spelsworth, William Cleere, Richard Kedge, Thomas Sympson, Hugh Cop, James Gonithclett, James Goodall, John Gibson and Matthew Williams to be and remain the first and present Assistants of the Mystery aforesaid to continue respectively in the said offices during their natural lives, unless in the meantime they some one or any of them shall for ill government or ill conducting themselves in that behalf or for any other reasonable cause be removed. And Further We will and by these presents for us our Heirs and successors Do Grant to the aforesaid Master Wardens or Guardians and commonalty of the Mystery aforesaid and their successors That They and their successors may and shall from henceforth for ever have a good and discreet Man to be and remain Clerk to the Master Wardens or Guardians and commonalty of the Mystery aforesaid and for the better execution of our Will in this behalf We have appointed named constituted and made and by these Presents for us our Heirs and successors Do appoint name create constitute and make our Beloved Richard Forster to be and remain Clerk to the Master Wardens or Guardians and commonalty of the Mystery of Joiners and Carvers of the City of London aforesaid And further We will and by these presents Do command and ordain That the Master and Wardens or guardians in these presents before named and constituted before they or any of them shall be respectively admitted to the execution of their offices shall take and every one of them shall take the several oaths commonly called The Oaths of Allegiance and Supremacy and the oath prescribed and mentioned in the Act of Parliament for the good Government and Regulation of Corporations made in the thirteenth year of the Reign of Charles the Second late King of England together with the several oaths of the Master and Wardens or guardians of the Mystery aforesaid for the execution of their offices respectively and shall also subscribe and every of them shall subscribe the Declaration prescribed and mentioned in the Act aforesaid before William Cleere, Samuel Spelsworth and Richard Kedge, or two of them, which said William Cleere, Samuel Spelsworth and Richard Kedge, or two of them We do by these our Letters Patent direct and require and do give and grant to them Power and Authority to tender administer and demand the several oaths and subscriptions aforesaid in the Court of Assistants of the same Commonalty according to the tenor and true intention of these Presents. And also We Will and by these Presents firmly enjoyning command That the several Assistants and Clerk in these presents before named and constituted before they or any of them shall be admitted to the execution of their offices respectively shall take and every of them shall take the aforesaid oaths of Allegiance and Supremacy and the oath prescribed and mentioned in the Act aforesaid together with the several oaths of the Assistants and Clerk of the Commonalty aforesaid for the due execution of the offices of Assistants and Clerk of the Commonalty aforesaid respectively and also subscribe the Declaration aforesaid before the said William Cleere, Samuel Spelsworth and Richard Kedge, or two of them whom We do by these our Letters Patent direct and require and do give and grant to them full Power and Authority to tender administer and demand the several oaths and subscriptions aforesaid in the Court of Assistants of the Commonalty aforesaid according to the tenor and true intention of these Presents. And Further We Will and for us our Heirs and successors do grant to the aforesaid Master Wardens or Guardians and commonalty aforesaid and their successors That whenever it shall happen That any Master Wardens or Guardians or any of the Assistants of the Commonalty aforesaid shall die or be removed or retire from his or their office or offices That then and in such case another fit Person or Persons shall in due manner be elected preferred and sworn in the place or places of the Person or Persons so dying being removed or retiring by such Person or Persons and in such manner and form as heretofore for the space of seven years now last past hath been accustomed in the same commonalty Provided always nevertheless and We will and by these Presents for us our Heirs and successors do command and order That No Person or Persons shall at any time from henceforth be elected named and preferred to the office or offices of Master Wardens or Guardians Assistants or Clerk of the Commonalty aforesaid or any of them severally and respectively who before his election shall not respectively hold or every of them shall hold communion with the Church of England and within six Months at the least after such Election receive and every of them receive the Holy Sacrament according to the form by law prescribed in the Church of England And That every Person and Persons after such election and before his admission in or to the offices or Places aforesaid shall take and every of them shall take the several Oaths of Allegiance and supremacy prescribed and mentioned in the Act of Parliament together with the oaths for the due execution of the offices of Master Wardens or Guardians Assistants and Clerk respectively of the commonalty aforesaid And also shall subscribe and every of them shall subscribe the declaration aforesaid before such Person or Persons before whom the usual oaths for the execution of their offices respectively have heretofore within the space of seven years now last past been taken and made which said several oaths and subscriptions aforesaid We do by these our Letters Patent direct and require and do by these Presents for us our Heirs and successors give and grant them Power and Authority to tender administer and demand the same in the Court of Assistants of the commonalty aforesaid according to the tenor and true intention of these Presents. Also We Will and command That every Clerk of the commonalty aforesaid to be from henceforth nominated and elected shall before his admission to such Place or office be presented to Us our Heirs or successors for the approval of Us our Heirs or successors And if we our Heirs or successors shall approve of such Clerk under our or their Royall signet or Hand That then he making the several oaths aforesaid together with the declaration and subscription aforesaid as aforesaid shall be thereupon admitted But If We our Heirs or successors shall refuse or shall not approve of such Person so elected to be Clerk Then such election shall be void and the Master Wardens or Guardians and Assistants of the commonalty aforesaid for the time being or the greater part of them in the Court of Assistants shall immediately proceed to the election of one other Person more fit to be Clerk in the manner and form aforesaid who shall be presented for such approval as aforesaid and so successively until such Person shall be elected who shall be approved of by us our Heirs or successors as aforesaid and shall take the several oaths aforesaid and make the subscription aforesaid. Provided Always and We further will and declare That every election of any Master Wardens or Guardians Assistants or Clerk of the Commonalty aforesaid contrary to the direction or Restriction in these Presents in that behalf mentioned shall be void and of no effect to all purposes and intents whatsoever Any thing in these our Letters Patent to the contrary thereof notwithstanding. Provided always and We do by these Presents Will and declare That it may and shall be lawful for us our Heirs and successors from time to time and at all times hereafter by order in the Privy Council of Us our Heirs or successors from time to time to remove and declare removed any Master Wardens or Guardians Assistants or Clerk of the Commonalty aforesaid now or for the time being and thereupon the Place or office of such Person so removed or declared to be removed shall be ipso facto void and another fit Person or other fit Persons in the Place or Places of the Person or Persons so removed or declared to be removed as aforesaid shall in due manner be elected preferred and sworn according to the Ordinance and Proviso aforesaid Which said Person or Persons so elected and every of them before Admission to such Place or Office shall take the several oaths aforesaid and make the subscription aforesaid as aforesaid and so as often as the case shall happen. And Further We Will and by these Presents for Us our Heirs and successors Do command the Master Wardens or Guardians and commonalty of the Mystery aforesaid That they and their successors from time to time and at all times hereafter may and shall in all things that appertain to the good Rule and Governance of the City of London aforesaid and the Commonalty aforesaid be subject and obedient to the Lord Mayor and Court of Aldermen of the City of London aforesaid for the time being. Provided Always and We also Will by these Presents That No Person or Persons of the commonalty aforesaid for the time being who shall not hold communion with the Church of England or who shall at any time hereafter frequent or be present at Conventicles or any other unlawful Assembly under pretext of Religious Worship shall be elected into or on the Livery of the Company aforesaid after it shall have been granted to the same Commonalty by the Mayor and Court of Aldermen of the City of London aforesaid. And Also That Every Person elected or to be elected into the Livery of the Commonalty aforesaid shall before he be

thereunto admitted be approved by the Lord Mayor and Court of Aldermen of
the City of London and take the oaths of Allegiance and Supremacy and the
oaths prescribed and mentioned in the said Act for the good Government and
Regulation of Corporations and shall make the subscription aforesaid before the
Master Wardens or Guardians of the commonalty aforesaid in the Court of
Assistants or any two or more of them for the time being Whom We do by these
presents for Us our Heirs and successors ordain authorize and require to tender
and demand the same oaths and subscriptions in the Court of Assistants
aforesaid. Provided Further and We do for us our Heirs and successors declare
That if any Person being an Assistant of the commonalty aforesaid at the time
of the surrender aforesaid and within the space of six months after the date of
these Presents shall not have surrendered his Office or Place of Assistant of the
commonalty aforesaid to the Master Wardens or Guardians and Commonalty
aforesaid and their successors and shall not submit himself to a new election at
the good pleasure of the Master Wardens or Guardians and commonalty
aforesaid That then every such Person shall not have or ought to have any
Power or Privilege in or concerning the election of any officer or officers or
members of the aforesaid commonalty but shall from thenceforth be utterly
discharged and excluded from the benefit of this our Grant Any thing in these
our Letters Patent contained to the contrary notwithstanding. And Lastly We
Will and by these Presents for Us our Heirs and successors do grant to the
aforesaid Master Wardens or Guardians and commonalty of the Mystery of
Joiners and Carvers aforesaid and their successors That They and their
successors at all times hereafter shall freely and quietly have hold possess and
enjoy all and all manner so many so great such the same and the like Letters
Patent Charters Gifts Grants Liberties Franchises Customs Custom Powers
Rights Jurisdictions Privileges and Immunities aforesaid (the alterations and
explanations in these Presents above made and expressed always excepted) as
they or their Predecessors by virtue or pretext of any Letters Patent of any or
some other of our Progenitors or Ancestors the Kings or Queens of England to
them made granted or confirmed or by reason or pretext of any lawful
prescription use or custom or by any other lawful means right or title have had
held or enjoyed or ought to have held or enjoy And all and singular such
aforesaid Letters Patent Charters Gifts Grants Liberties Franchises Customs
Custom Powers Rights Jurisdictions Privileges and Immunities and all and
singular the Premises together with all and all manner of ordinances constitutions
laws statutes decrees liberties powers gifts and determinations whatsoever by
the now or late Mayor and Citizens and commonalty or the Mayor and Court
of Aldermen of the City of London or any one or more of them in their common
council or otherwise at any time or times hereafter made published provided or
confirmed for or concerning the several Works Businesses and other matters
made or to be made by the Joiners and Carpenters of the City of London, and
of the several members of their company respectively and of the aforesaid
Joiners or their Mystery in any manner belonging or decreed given established
or exacted to them We do for us our Heirs and successors ratify and confirm to
the same Master Wardens or Guardians and commonalty of the Mystery of
Joiners and Carvers of the City of London and their successors And do will and
command them to be observed by these Presents. In witness whereof We have
caused these our Letters to be made Patent. Witness ourself at Westminster the
Nineteenth day of May in the first year of our Reign.[70]

Aftermath of 1685 Charter and Restoration of 1571 Charter

The new charter was read at the Hall on 28th May 1685. The surrender of the 1571 charter and the grant of the new charter meant that the Master, Wardens, Court of Assistants, and Clerk of the Company all lost their positions. Their authority was held through the charter, but in the new document James II had specifically appointed different members of the Company to those positions of power. The former officers were debarred from holding office in the Company again. Former Master John Player was replaced by Thomas Wratten, the new Wardens were George Newland and James Ball, and Richard Forster took over from Joseph Burrough as Clerk. Three previous members of the Court of Assistants were deputised through the Charter to administer the oaths of office to them.[71] When the Livery assembled at the Hall as usual on 25th July to celebrate St James' Day the new charter was read to them.[72]

In spite of having borrowed £100 from Captain Chamblett, acquiring the charter had cost the Company far more than they had expected. They were ultimately forced to borrow a further £250 from Richard Weston in order to repay Chamblett and cover the further unexpected expenses.[73] For example, after taking the £100, Philip Burton charged the Company a further £16 8s 6d in October as payment for his own labour, and in January he and the Clerk of the Patents both received 'several gratuities over & above the Comon Fees for their extraordinary pains in procuring the New Charter'.[74]

The Company hoped that the new charter would grant them greater flexibility for their own governance, but they found that the opposite was the case. On 25th September 1687 an Order of Council from James II's court at Windsor was dispatched to the Town Clerk, and a copy was delivered to the Joiners on 11th October. The King reserved the right to 'from time to time displace or remove the Master Wardens & Assistants of the said severall Companyes or any of them' and appoint new men in their places. Even though he had ordered the complete change of leadership through the charter only two years earlier, James once again removed the Master, Wardens, and Assistants from their positions. The men were all listed by name and were informed that they were 'hereby remov'd and displact from being any longer Master Wardens or Assistants of the said Company'.[75]

A subsequent notice from the Lord Mayor and Court of Aldermen explained what had prompted this decision. The King had received complaints from numerous Companies who had received new charters about their officers being removed from their positions and replaced with new men, which had of course happened to the Joiners. Even though he had been the one to order the replacements, James saw this as an opportunity to secure the favour of the London companies during such a turbulent period in his reign. The order explicitly stated that 'to countenance & Incourage all his Subjects of dutifull behaviour towards his Matie and his Governmt' James had ordered that

the said severall persons who at the respective times of the Surrenders of the said Charters were of the Assistants of the sd respective Companies … bee again restor'd & forthwith admitted according to their seniorities in their respective Companies … [and] shall bee forthwth readmitted & restor'd to the Injoymt of their former privileges & precedencies of being of the Assistants of the sd respective Companies as fully and effectually as they were at the time of the sd late Surrenders.

The Master, Wardens, and Asssitants who had been removed from office in 1685 were summoned to appear at Joiners' Hall on 20th October, at which time they were re-admitted as Assistants, and John Player was re-elected as Master.[76] They were sworn into their offices on 26th October,[77] and the following day James Ball, the recently elected Master for 1687-8, surrendered the new charter, the common seal, and all other Company documents in his possession to Player.[78] To celebrate their restoration, the Master, Wardens, and seven Assistants had a private meeting at the Dolphin Tavern in St Bartholomew's Lane on 24th October ostensibly to discuss the upcoming Lord Mayor's Day feast. An agreement was reached that in addition to bringing their wives, the Master and Wardens could also bring two friends apiece, which had not previously been allowed.[79]

At a court held on 29th October the first order of business was a resolution 'that an address of thanks bee made to his Matie for his late Gratious Declaracon of Indulgence', and the motion was passed unanimously by the Livery.[80] The Clerk drafted the address, which was read and approved in court on 8th November, and the Company's common seal was attached.[81] The restored officers then turned their attention to the Company's financial activities during the previous two years. A committee was appointed to 'examine what money the Company owes, & what is owing to them, & what hath been rec[eive]d & paid since the new Charter'.[82] The payments to Mr Burton were raised as an issue again on 8th May 1688, when the Clerk was asked to produce a list 'of what was paid to Mr Burton for & upon Acc[oun]t of the new Charter'. At that same court meeting they noted receipt of a Bill of £5 3s from a Mr Tindall 'for his charges in soliciting the new Charter', even though it had been three years since the document was procured, but at the next court meeting it was resolved not to pay him.[83] In July Philip Burton's Clerk submitted his own bill to the Company, who instructed their own Clerk to 'inquire of the Clerks of other Companyes if the like bills have been allow'd elsewhere'.[84] There was no obvious later reference to this bill, so it seems likely that they decided not to pay it.

The King's interference in the leadership of the Joiners' Company had not ended, however. On 10th February he issued an Order of Council from Whitehall removing Renter Warden Philip Milner and Assistant John Gibson from their places without explanation. At the same time, ten liverymen were removed from their places, and five were restored. One of the latter group was former Clerk Joseph Burrough who had lost his role in 1685 and been replaced by Richard Forster.[85] The removal of the liverymen was not well received by those displaced, and on 5th February 1689 a 'threatning' letter to the Master, Wardens, and Assistants was received from Messrs Owen, Smallwell, Murden, Hopson, and Carpenter, but the court decided to ignore it.[86] A further order was produced by the King on 7th October, and thirty-six formerly displaced liverymen were restored to their former places.[87]

James II's reign came to an abrupt end in 1688. His Catholic religion had caused increasing discomfort amongst his subjects, and even before he had succeeded his brother Charles II an attempt had been made by Parliament to exclude him from the succession. His reign was one of tension and an underlying threat of rebellion, exacerbated by his promotion of Catholicism. On 30th June 1688 seven noblemen wrote to Stadtholder William, Prince of Orange, inviting him to invade England. William's wife Mary was one of James II's Protestant daughters, and the couple were seen as far more appropriate rulers than James and his Catholic queen. William arrived in England on 5th November with an army at his back, but James did not attempt to defend himself and ultimately escaped to France on 23rd December.

Early in his reign William agreed to return all franchises to the City of London, and to restore original charters to Companies who had been forced to surrender them in 1684. A notice was sent to the Joiners on 7th October 1688:

His Matie having been gratiously pleasd to restore to this City its antient ffranchises And requir'd by his Charter lately given for that purpose That this Court should cause to bee restor'd to their respective places all such Livery Men of the severall Companies of this City as were of the Livery of the sd Companies at the time of the late Judgmt given agt this City upon the Quo Waranto It is therefore Order'd by this Court That all such Members of the respective Livery Companies now living as were of the Livery at the time of the sd Judgmt bee forthwith restor'd to their places in their respective Companies accordingly And it is Order'd That the Master Wardens and Assistents of all the sd Companies do forthwith see the same perform'd & executed And that the Clerk of every Company have Notice immediately to repair to Mr Town-Clerk & take a Copy of this Order to bee entred in their bookes & presently communicated to the Master & Wardens of their respective Companies.[88]

A Court of Livery was summoned to meet at the Hall on 10th October to gather the names of all deposed liverymen. Within another fortnight a charter of restitution was granted to all Livery Companies, which reinstated all original charters and rendered the 1685 charters null and void. The reinstation of the 1571 charter was greeted with joy by the Joiners and they pledged their loyalty to the new king. When James II attempted to recover his throne in 1689 by securing the support of Ireland William responded promptly, personally leading his army to victory at the Battle of the Boyne. The City asked for financial contributions from the livery companies towards the financing of the army, and the Joiners were only too happy to comply. They declared themselves 'hartily willing to promote so good and beneficiall worke for their ma[jes]t[ie]s the Government and the Protestant Religion', and they provided £50 for the cause, as well as two horses.[89] The sense from these entries is one of lingering resentment towards James for interfering in their governance which had been of no benefit to them and great benefit to him. He had attempted to secure the support of the livery companies by installing officers loyal to him, but it had backfired quite spectacularly.

1724 Additional Ordinances

On 14th April 1724 Master Richard King told the Court of Assistants that 'there seems to be a great necessity for the rectifying and altering of the present Rules & Orders of this Compa[ny]'. After 'a debate arising thereupon' the court agreed that a committee should be appointed to investigate the current ordinances and see where adjustments needed to be made.[90] When the committee made their report to the next Court of Assistants they recommended that 'the Master have a power to lay such new Rules Orders and Alterations as he shall think fitt before Councell'; in other words, to secure legal advice to make sure the alterations were acceptable.[91] The Master moved with speed, and by the June court he was able to confirm 'that he had attended Councell with severall new Rules Orders and alteracons necessary for the good Government of this Company'. The lawyer had suggested some changes, and when they were made the new rules were approved as acceptable. The Master laid them before the Court of Assistants, where they met with approval, but it was pointed out that any drastic change to the Company's governance had to be approved by a Court of Livery.[92] This approval was given on 24th June,[93] the new ordinances were confirmed three days later, and they were confirmed by the Lord Chancellor and Chief Justices in September.[94]

Whereas Certain Statutes and ordinances were made by the Master Wardens and Comonalty of the ffaculty of Joyners and Ceelers of the City of London for the Good Government Survey and Correction of the adoresaid Comonalty according to their Charter and Letters Patents granted unto them by our late Sovereign Lady of ffamous Memory Queen Elizabeth under her Highness's Great Seale of England bearing date att Westminster the ffourteenth day of Aprill in the Thirteenth year of her Highness's Reign which Statutes and ordinances were examined approved and confirmed by Sir Nicholas Bacon Knt Lord Keeper of the Great Seal of England Robert Catlin Knight Cheif Justice of the Queen's Bench and James Dyer Knt Cheif Justice of the Comon Bench by their writing under their hands and Seales bearing date the first day of October in the ffourteenth year of the Reign of our said late Sovereign Lady Queen Elizabeth according to a certain Act of Parliament Made Enacted and provided in the ninteenth year of the Reign of our late Sovereign Lord of ffamous Memory King Henry the Seventh and afterwards examined and approved by Sir Christopher Wray Knt Lord Cheif Justice of England by a writing under his hand and seal annexed to the said writing of the said Lord Kepper & Justices of the Bench bearing date the second day of June in the seventeenth year of the Reign of our said late sovereign Lady of ffamous Memory Queen Elizabeth as by the said severall writings may more plainly and att large appear.

And whereas since the Makeing thereof certain addiconal Statutes and ordinances were made by the Master Wardens and Comonalty of the said Company for the Good Government Survey and Correction thereof according to the said Charter and Letters Patents which Statutes and ordinances were Examined approved and Confirmed by Thomas Lord Ellsmere Lord Chancellor of England Sir Edward Coke Knt Lord Cheif Justice of England and Sir Henry Hobart Knt and Barrt Lord Cheif Justice of the Court of Comon Pleas by their writing under their hands and seals bearing date the Eighth day of Aprill in the Twelfth year of the Reign of our late Sovereign Lord of ffamous Memory King James the first over England ffrance and Ireland &c according to the aforesaid act of Parliament as by the said writing May more plainly and att large appear.

And whereas since the makeing thereof severall customs and usuages used and exercised by the Master Wardens Assistants and Colty of the said Company in the Eleccon of their Officers Makeing of orders and other things for the good Government Correccon and Survey thereof according to the said Charter Letters patents statutes and ordinances were approved ordered adjudged & decreed ratified and confirmed by ffrancis Lord Verulam Lord High Chancellor of England in a certain Cause depending in the High Court of Chancery wherein William Rogers Citizen and Joiner was plaintiff and the Master and Wardens of the said Company were defendants as by the Exemplificacon or Inrollmt of the said decree tested att Westminster the ninth day of October in the ninteenth year of the Reign of our said late Sovereign Lord King James the first over England ffrance and Ireland &c May more plainly and att large appear.

And whereas since the makeing of the said Statutes Ordinances and decrees the Comonalty of the said Company and persons exerciseing the said ffaculty and using and selling Goods and Wares belonging to the same within the Limitts aforesaid are very much increased and become more numerous than heretofore

By reason whereof the due Care Survey and Correccon of the same for the Good Government thereof according to the aforesaid Charter and Letters patents and Ordinances cannott be so duly and regularly observed and putt in force by so small a Number as twelve persons only to assist the Master and Wardens in the execucon thereof Butt the same will become so great a burthen on them that severall offenders and offences will necessarily go unknown and unpunished to the great Disceipt of his Majties good Subjects and discredit of the said Company which ought as much as possible to be prevented by choosing a greater Number of persons to assist the Master and Wardens in their said offices to putt the aforesaid Good Laws and ordinances in Execucon and effectually discover and punish all offenders against the same.

And whereas also since the makeing the aforesaid ordinances By reason of the Great Increase of the Number of the said Company a greater Burthen and Trouble lyeth on the Master and Wardens in the due Execucon of their said offices than heretofore there did and for that the ffines and forfeitures to be paid by every person neglecting or refusing to serve such offices according to the said ordinances are so small and improportonable to the trouble of serving the said offices that most persons elected thereto choose rather to pay the said ffines than serve the said offices by means whereof the good Government of the said Company and the surety and correccon of the same according to the aforesaid Charter and ordinances is in great danger of being neglected and in time to be wholly laid aside to the great deceipt and prejudice of his Majesties good subjects and discreditt and hindrance of the said Company unless the same be prevented by makeing such ffines larger.

And whereas also since the makeing the aforesaid ordinances The Livery of the said Company is very much increased in Number and thereby the Charges and Expences of the said Company are likewise very much increased and raised and the ffines which by the said ordinances are respectively payable by the said Liverymen att the time of their admission into the Livery of the said Company are in no respect pportonable to the present Expences and charges of the said Company and by reason of the smallness of the said ffines Many of the meaner sort of the said Company have got themselves admitted into the said Livery to the over great Increase of the same and Burthen charg and dishonour of the said Company and City and by means whereof great disorders and Confusion are like to grow in the Affair of the said Company all which Inconveniences May be in a great Measure redressed by raising & apportioning such Livery ffines to the aforesaid Charges & Expences of the said Company the Circumstances of the prsent time & the Custom of other well regulated companyes of the said City.

And Whereas also since the makeing the aforesaid ordinances the said Company being so increased as aforesaid and the ffine to be paid by such persons who are elected and chose to be stewards of the said Company and neglect or refuse to hold such Office of Steward are so small and unequal to the Charge of holding and performing such Office that very few or none for severall years last past have held and performed the same to the very great Burthen and dishonour of the said Company who are (upon takeing such small ffines) obliged to serve the place of such stewards and be att the Expence of treating the said Company on the day the Lord Mayor is sworn att Westminr which has for many years last past been considerably larger than itt was att the time of makeing such ordinances and ffines.

Therefore for the more speedy order and Redress of the premisses the Master Wardens and Coalty of the Company of Joiners Ceelers or Carvers of the City of London seriously takeing the said Matter into consideracon have upon Mature and deliberate advice and by force and virtue of their said Charter and Letters patents and of the power and authority thereby to them given and out of the customs and usages of the said Company made and added the following new orders acts and ordinances vizt;

Imprimis it is ordered and ordained that the present Master Wardens and Assistants of the said Company of Joiners aforesaid shall at some Court of Assistants to be held for that purpose at their Comon Hall on or before the [blank] day of [blank] choose so many able and sufficient persons of the Livery of the said Company to be added to the Number of the present assistants to the said Master and Wardens of the said Company as shall make the number of Assistants twenty four which said persons so to be chosen together with the present assistants shall be assistants to the Master and Wardens of the said Company and that from thenceforth there shall att all times be twenty four able and sufficient persons of the Livery of the said Company of Joiners Ceelers and Carvers of the City of London assistants to the Master and Wardens of the said Company who shall be from time to time elected and chose by the Master Wardens and Assistants of the said Company att their Comon Hall and in case of the death or removall of any of the said assistants The Master Warden and assistants for the time being within ffourteen days next after every such decease or Removall shall and may elect and choose att their Comon Hall one other able and sufficient person out of the Livery of the said Company in the place of him so deceased or removed so as there be continually twenty four persons Assistants to the said Master and Wardens and every person so elected shall upon due Notice to him given appear att the next Court of Assistants to be held for that purpose before the Master and Wardens of the said Compa or any one or more of them for the time being & upon his admission to the said place shall for the better support of the said Compa pay to the under or Renter warden of the said Company for the use of the said Company the sume of three pounds and to the Clerk for administring the oath [blank] and to the Beadle [blank] and if any person so elected and chosen an Assistant shall after due Notice given him Neglect or refuse to appear & take upon him the said place aforesaid and Make such payment as aforesaid not haveing a reasonable Excuse for such his Neglect or refusal such persons so neglecting or refusing shall forfeit and pay to the Master Wardens Assistants and Coalty of the said Company the sume of Tenn pounds of lawfull money of Great Britain to be employed to the use of the said Company.

Item itt is ordained and declared That the Master Waredns Assistants and Livery of the said Company of Joiners Ceelers and Carvers and their successors for ever shall & may on the ffeast day of Saint James the Apostle yearly if the same doe not happen to ffall on a Sunday and if it so happen to be on a Sunday then on the next day after assemble and Meet together at their Comon Hall and shall & May elect and choose either the last preceeding Master or one of the Assistants of the said Company to the Master of the said Company of Joiners & Ceelers or Carvers for one whole year from thence next ensueing & from thence untill one other of the Assistants of the said Company be chosen and sworn into the said office of a Master and two others out of the Livery of the said Compa to be Wardens of the said Company for one whole year from thence next ensueing and until two others of the then remaining Livery be chosen and sworn into the said Office of Wardens according to the said Charter to them granted which said persons so elected and chosen shall upon due Notice thereof appear at a Court to be held within [blank] then next and then and there take the Oath appointed for that purpose and also shall on the days hereafter menconed att each of their own proper Costs and Charges make and provide a competent and sufficient dinner for the Master Wardens and Assistants of the said Company according to the usuage and Custom of the said Company vizt The said Master to provide such dinner the first quarterly Court day after his being Sworn in Master The upper Warden on the next quarterly Court day after & The under or Renter Warden on the Next quarterly Court day after and each and every person so elected Master or Warden who shall refuse or neglect to appear att such Court and take upon him such office and find and provide such dinner respectively not having a reasonable Excuse for such his neglect or Refusal shall forfeit and pay to the Master Wardens and Coalty of the said Company the Sumes hereafter Menconed (vizt) Every Master so Neglecting or refusing the sume of tenn pounds Every upper Warden the sume of seven pounds and every Renter or under warden the sume of seven pounds of Lawfull money of Great Britain to be employed to the use of the said Company provided no one shall be compelled to be Master or Warden above twice in his life time.

Item it is ordered and ordained That the Mastr with the Wardens of the said Company or one of them for the time being and twelve assistants or the Major part of the twenty four Assistants for the time being shall and may from time to time as they shall find need and occasion elect choose and admitt such and so Many of the ffreemen of the said Company who shall have served or fined as Stewards of the said Company as they shall think fitt meet and able into the Livery of the said Company and every person so called and elected shall upon due Notice to him thereof given by the said Master and Wardens or any of them or by their Beadle or otherwise appear att the next Court of Assistants to be held for the said Company and then and there take on him the Cloathing as a Livery Man of the same and upon such his admission to the said livery shall for the better support of the said Company pay to the Renter or under warden of the said Company for the use of the said Compa the sume of ten pounds of Lawfull money of Great Britain and if any person so elected or chose after due Notice given him as aforesaid shall neglect or refuse to appear & take on him the Cloathing as aforesaid and make such payment as aforesaid not having a reasonable excuse for such his neglect or refusal shall forfeit and pay to the Master Wardens Assistants and Coialty of the said Company any sume or sumes of money not exceeding the sume of Twenty pounds of lawfull money of great Britain att the discretion of the Master Wardens and Court of Assistants for the time being or the Major part of them att their Comon Hall to be imployed to the use of the said Company.

Item it is ordered and ordained That every year yearly the Master Wardens and Assistants of the said Company for the time being shall and may elect and choose six fitt persons out of the ffreemen of the said Company (who have not served the office of Steward or paid the ffine for not serving the same) to be and to have and bear the title and office of Stewards of the said Company who shall for the honour of the said Compa att their the said Stewards own costs and charges Make and provide a competent and sufficient dinner in such manner as the same is now and for many years past has been used to be Made and provided for the said Company which shall be called the Stewards dinner and shall be so provided & kept on the day that the Lord Mayor of the said City of London shall be sworn att Westminr and shall before the Master Wardens Assistants and Livery and such of the said Company as shall be called to attend them upon that occasion and every person so elected Steward and having due Notice of the same that shall refuse to hold and execute the same place or fail to make such dinner or pay his proporcon of the charge of the same (not having a reasonable excuse for such his neglect or refusall) shall forfeit and pay to the Master Wardens and Comonalty of the said Company the sume of seven pounds of lawfull Money of Great Britain to be employed to the use of the said Company.

Finally for the more regular Recovery of the severall penalties fforfeitures and sumes of Money by the severall orders and ordinances heretofore Made for the Good Government of the said Company as also by these present orders and ordinances imposed set appointed or limitted to be paid Itt is further ordered That the Master Wardens and Coialty of the said Company for the time being shall and may att their wills and pleasure enter into the house shop warehouse or Booth of him or them so offending and there to take a distress or distresses convenient and meet for the said sumes of money and the distress so taken lawfully to lead drive carry and bear away and keep to the use of the said Master Wardens Assistant and Comonalty untill the same penalties fforfeitures or sumes of money be paid assigning the party a time convenient within thirty days Next after the takeing such distresses to pay the same and if not paid within that time to sell the said distress so made to answer such ffines penalties and fforfeitures as aforesaid rendring the overplus to the owner Except he sue Replexin for the same within ten dayes after the said distresses taken or otherwise to sue for the same in any of his Majesties Courts att Westminster or in any of the Courts held within the City of London by action of debt in the Names of the Master Wardens and Comonalty of the ffaculty of Joiners and Ceelers of the City of London according to the direccons and limitations of the said Charter and the same when recovered shall be to the use of the said Company.[95]

1740 By-Laws

However, in January 1739 these new ordinances were called into question at an extraordinary Court of Livery held 'on special Affairs of the Company'. Concern was raised that the ordinances were 'manifestly tending to place an absolute power in the hands of a few Persons over the whole Body & Comonalty'. The assembled men examined extracts from their original charter and by-laws, and ultimately concluded that the 1724 ordinances 'were in direct violation of the aforesaid Charter Antient By Laws & decree & were & are consequently ipso facto null & void'. A committee was instructed to 'prepare such new By Laws as they shall deem necessary for the good of the Company & supporting them in their lawfull Rights Immunitys & Priviledges'.[96] Although they were asked to proceed speedily, the new by-laws were not approved by a Court of Livery until 16th April 1740.[97]

These by-laws largely addressed the issue of finding men to serve the office of steward, which remained a concern. It was necessary to either hold the role or fine for it before a freeman could be elected as a liveryman. To dissuade freemen from fining for the role the fines were increased, with harsh penalties introduced for anyone failing to pay.

Whereas certain Statutes and Ordinances have been at divers times heretofore made by the Master Wardens Comonalty of the ffaculty of Joyners and Ceilers of the City of London for the good Government Survey & Correction of the aforesaid Company according to the Charter and Letters patent granted unto them by our late Sovereign Lady of ffamous memory Queen Elizabeth under her

Highness's Great Seal of England bearing date at Westminster The fourteenth day of April in the thirteenth year of her Highness's Reign.

And whereas since the making the said Ordinances by reason of the great increase of the number of the said Company the Charges & Expences thereof are very much encreased & raised and the ffine which by the said Ordinances is payable by the Livery men at the respective times of their Admission into the Livery of the said Company is in no respect proportionable to the present Expences and Charges of the said Company in their necessary support and Government which Inconvenience can only be redressed by raising and apportioning such Livery ffine to the Charges and Expences of the said Company The Circumstances of the present Times and the Custom of other well regulated Companys of the said City.

And whereas also since the making the said Ordinances the said Company being so increased as aforesaid and the ffine to be paid by each person respectively who is elected and chose to be Steward of the said Company and neglecteth or refuseth to hold such Office of Steward is so small and unequal to the Charge of holding and performing such Office that very few or none for many years last past have held and performed the same to the very great Burthen and Dishonour of the said Company who are upon Taking such small ffine obliged to serve or supply the place of such Steward and be at the Expence of treating the said Company on the day the Lord Mayor is sworn at Westminster which has for many years last past been considerably larger than it was at the time of making such former Ordinances and ffines and by reason of the great distance of time since they were made and of the several alterations in the said ffaculty of Joyners and Ceilers and in the Affaires of the Company since that time they are become obsolete not suited and adapted to the present Circumstances of the Company.

Therefore for the more speedy order and redress of the premisses the Master Wardens and Comonalty of the Company of Joyners and Ceilers of the City of London seriously taking the said matters into Consideration have upon mature and deliberate advice and by fforce and virtue of their said Charter and Letters patent and of the power and authority thereby to them give made and added the following new Orders Acts and Ordinances Vizt,

Imprimis That there may never be wanting a competent number of able skillfull and experienced persons to bear their share of the Care and Trouble in the Preservation & Government of the said Company out of whom the said Company may be furnished with persons To discharge the principal Offices therein from time to time with the greater Judgement and Knowledge It is ordered and ordained That the Master with the Wardens of the said Company or with one of them for the time being and six Assistants or the major part of the Court of Assistants for the time being shall and may from time to time as they shall find need and occasion call choose and admitt such and so many of the ffreemen of the said Company who shall have served or ffined as Stewards of the said Company as they shall think fitt meet and able thereunto into the Livery of the said Company And that every such person and persons that shall be so in form aforesaid chosen or called into the Livery of the said Company shall upon Notice To him or them given thereof by the said Master and Wardens or any of them or by their Beadle or otherwise appear at the then next Court of Assistants to be held for the said Company and then and there take on him the Cloathing as a Livery-man of the same and upon such his Admission to the said Livery shall for the better support of the said Company pay to the Renter or Under Warden of the said Company for the use of the said Company the

Sum of Twelve pounds of lawfull money of Great Britain which said sum of Twelve pounds shall be accepted and taken in full of his Livery ffine and if any person so called and chose as aforesaid after Notice given him as aforesaid shall neglect or refuse to appear and take on him the Cloathing or be of the Livery as aforesd and make such payment as aforesaid not having such reasonable excuse for such his neglect or refusal as by the Master Wardens and six Assistants or the major part of the Court of Assistants for the time being whereof the Master and one of the Wardens of the said Company for the time being to be two shall be thought and adjudged sufficient shall for such his neglect or refusal forfeit and pay within one month next after such his neglect or refusal the sum of ffive pounds of lawful money of Great Britain to and for the use of the said Company and shall therefore be excused from coming on the Livery of the said Company for the space of one year from such his Election.

Item Whereas it has been accustomed in the said Company to have an Entertainment provided for the Master Wardens Assistants and Livery of the said Company annually on the day the Lord Mayor is sworn at Westminster by Stewards from time to time chosen for that purpose It is Ordered and Ordained that every year yearly forever hereafter the Master Wardens and six Assistants or the major part of the Court of Assistants of the said Company for the time being whereof the Master and one of the Wardens for the time being to be two shall and may elect and choose four persons out of the ffreemen of the said Company such as to them shall seem fit who have not served the Office of Steward or paid the ffine for not service the same to be and to have and bear the Title and Office of Stewards of the said Company who shall for the honour of the said Company at their said Stewards own Costs and Charges make and provide a competent and sufficient Dinner in such manner as the same is now and for many years past has been used to be made and provided for the said Company which shall be called the Stewards Dinner and shall be so provided and kept on the day that the Lord Mayor of the City of London shall be sworn at Westminster and shall be for the Master Wardens Assistants and Livery and such of the said Company as shall be called to attend them upon that occasion and every person so elected Steward and having due Notice given him of the same who shall refuse or neglect to appear before the said Master and Wardens at the said Companies Hall in London at the time of their meeting there next after such Election and Notice as aforesaid and then and there undertake to provide and pay one equal fourth part of such Entertainment in such manner as hath heretofore been accustomed or in lieu thereof pay down to the said Master and Wardens or such of them as are then present for the use of the said Company and as a ffine for being discharged from the service of the said Office of Steward the sum of Eight pounds or that having made his election to provide and pay for one equal fourth part of such Entertainmt as aforesaid shall afterwards neglect so to do not having such reasonable excuse for such his neglect or refusal as by the Master Wardens & six Asssitants or the major part of the Court of Assistantts for the time being whereof the Master and one of the Wardens of the said Company for the time being to be two shall be thought and adjudged sufficient shall forfeit and pay to the Master Wardens and Comonalty of the said Company the sum of Ten pounds of lawfull Money of Great Britain to be employed to the use of the said Company.

Ffinally for the more regular recovery of the several Penalties fforfeitures and sums of money by the several Orders & Ordinances heretofore made for the good Government of the said Company as also by these present Orders and Ordinances imposed set appointed or limitted to be paid It is further Ordered

That the Master and Wardens of the said Company for the time being shall and may sue for the same ffines penalties fforfeitures and sums of Money in any of his Majesties Courts of Record at Westminster or in any of the Courts held within the City of London by Action of Debt in the name of Master Wardens and Comonalty of the ffaculty of Joyners and Ceiliers of the City of London according to the Directions and Limitations of the said Charter and the same when recovered shall be to the use of the said Company.[98]

This represented the final major change to the Company's ordinances, with later amendments concerned with smaller-scale issues such as the number of Assistants and the cost of fines. The ordinances confirmed by the Company have barely changed since they were introduced, and still form the basis of governance today.

Chapter 3

Joiners' Hall

Background to the Upper Thames Street Site

The history of the Joiners' Hall site is complex, but there can be no doubt that the Company's occupation of the site pre-dated their Charter. It is important to note that the Company never owned the land; they leased it from the landowners, but owned the buildings they constructed on it. They did not acquire the site in one transaction; it appears to have been acquired over time piecemeal from multiple landlords.

The earliest surviving deed relating to the site was a grant dated 1st February 1497 from leather seller Thomas Heyward and his wife Letitia. They granted messuages, tenements, and stables in the parish of All Hallows, then called All Saints at Hay, to Edward Cheseman, Thomas Marowe, Thomas Roberts, William Hill, and John Hurst. The site had previously been tenanted by 'John Vincent Citizen & Joiner of London now dece[ase]d'.[1] The site's association with Joiners, therefore, extends back to at least the late fifteenth century, if not earlier. Evidence of human occupation in Upper Thames Street dates back far earlier, however. For example, a fragment of a Roman glass inkwell was found on the site during building work in 1938.[2] On 28th May 1502 Cheseman, Marowe, and Roberts granted that same piece of property to Agnetus (Agnes) Plompton, Pade Sampe, Charles William Curteys, Thomas Jakys, and Thomas Dey. The accompanying deed contains more information about the precise location of the site; it was 'near the prior of the Convent of Greychurch London on the East on the West by Grenwiche Lane by the Tenement occupied by Edward Cheseman on the south & by the Kings Highway on the North'. The King's Highway referred to Thames Street.[3]

On 21st October 1517 another Heyward, this time William, perhaps a son of Thomas and Letitia, purchased a messuage, stables, lands, and tenements in Thames Street for an unspecified sum of money. The deed did, however, reveal that William was a joiner.[4] This is perhaps something of an understatement. He was the same William Heyward who had been appointed as Henry VIII's chief joiner in 1514 and who was discussed in Chapter 1.[5] On 19th October 1518 Heyward purchased another piece of property. He paid £20 to widow Agnes Samon, formerly Plompton, for

alle that her messuage with the'ppertents set and lying in the p[ar]issh of Alhallowes ate hay beside the Vyntre of London that is to say betwene the

Ten[emen]t of the priore and convent of Crichurch of London on the Est p[ar]
tie and the lane called Grenwiche La[ne] on the west p[ar]tie and the Tenement
sumtyme of Edward Cheseman Gentleman on the south p[ar]tie and the Kings
highwey there on the north p[ar]tie.[6]

This was the same Agnes Samon or Sawmon who had bequeathed land to the
church of St James Garlickhythe, enabling the Company to maintain an obit
there.[7] Agnes is discussed further in Chapter 5. Within three weeks Heyward
transferred all of this property into a trust of four Citizens of London; two
fishmongers, a barber surgeon, and a merchant tailor.[8] Three days after that,
the four men transferred the property into the care of the mystery of Joiners.[9]
This means, therefore, that the chief joiner under Henry VIII was responsible for
enabling the Company to build their Hall, and the chief joiner under his daughter
Elizabeth I granted the Company's charter.

The site was placed into another trust, this one containing a group of Joiners.
It would continue in their care until the majority of them had died, at which point
the few remaining survivors would bequeath it to a younger generation from
within the mystery. This remained the pattern of management for several hundred
years to come. The four longest surviving of that initial group of trustees were
Thomas Chapman, John Ripley, Thomas Peterborough, and William Lylley. On
21st July 1551 the four men transferred the property to a larger group of fifteen
Joiners, with the instruction for 'the wardens and other freemen of the said Crafte
or mistery of Joynrs of London for the tyme beyng peasibly to have holde and
enioye alle the said messuages tents and stables', as well as all rents and profits
issuing from it.[10] Another deed of conveyance was made on 26th February 1589
between William Typper and Robert Dawe on the one part, and joiners John
Symonds and Humfrey Baker on the other. Symonds and Baker had purchased
for an undisclosed sum the lease of

[a]ll that One messuage and Ten[emen]te wth Thapptences ... in ffreer Lane als
Grenewche Lane in the prishe of all Saynts the greate at hay besides or neare
the vintrye within the Cytty of London comonly called the Joyners Hall And
all and singler howses Edifices Buyldings Barnes stables Dovehowses Orchards
Gardens Tofts Crofts Curtulages Halls Chambers Shoppes Sellers Sollers pffitts
comodities and hereditamts whatsoever to the said bargained prmisses any ways
belongonge.

The land itself had been confirmed to Typper and Dawe by the Queen by letters
patent dated the previous day. An annual rent of 12d was due to the Crown on
the feast of St Michael the Archangel, payable to either the Exchequer or to the
Receiver of the City of London.[11]

The following summer Symonds and Baker transferred this property into
the hands of the trustees overseeing the Company's holdings. The feoffees were
ordered to 'pmytt and suffer the Mr wardens and Comaltie of the facultie of
Joyners and Celers of the Citie of London and their Successors forevrmore
hereafter to have holde and enioye the said mesuage and tenemt and all other
the premises with their apptences as of the guifte and graunte of [Symonds
and Baker]'. The rent due to the Company from the lease of other buildings
on site, such as warehouses and cellars, was to be distributed 'to and amonge
the poorest and moste aged freemen & widowes free of the same Company
for their better releife and sustynannce'. The document also stipulated that a
minimum of fifteen and maximum of twenty feoffees should be appointed to

hold the property in trust. Among the men named in this document were sons of Lewis Stockett.[12]

The First Hall

It is unclear precisely when the first Joiners' Hall building itself was erected, but it had clearly been built between the grant of land in 1518 and 1521. In the latter year a group of alien joiners petitioned Cardinal Wolsey to complain that 'the English joiners ... make new acts against them in their hall' contrary to an agreement from 1497.[13] Although the date of construction is unclear, it seems that 1521 is the earliest surviving documentary reference to the building. Consequently the year 2021 marks the 450th anniversary of the grant of the Charter, and the 500th anniversary of the earliest reference to the Hall.

Building the Hall gave the Joiners a base, and likely a degree of additional importance amongst the other Companies. The building itself became the focus of their activities and was an important piece of symbolism. In extraordinary cases Company matters occasionally took place elsewhere, such as the binding of apprentices outside of Court meetings, but as a rule all legitimate Company business had to take place within the Hall.[14]

The College of Arms holds copies of the 1571 grant of arms to the Company made by Robert Cooke, King of Arms.[15] On the back of one of these copies there is a description of a building, although this text is not referred to in any of the College's indices. The handwriting of the description is different from the copy of the grant of arms on the other side of the folio, and the text is undated and unsigned, but the style of the handwriting is consistent with the late sixteenth century so it can be assumed to be contemporary to the grant. Although slightly impeded by the volume's binding, at the left side of the list is the small description 'Joyners of London'. It seems highly unlikely, therefore, that this description is of the property of any other Company. Consequently, this can be taken as a description of Joiners' Hall from around 1570s, as it was when the Company received its charter, and appears to be the oldest surviving description of the first Joiners' Hall.

Most of the descriptions of the Hall and other rooms used the unit of paces, with the exception of the garden which was measured in feet. According to Richard Huloet or Howlet's *Abecedarium Anglico Latinum*, published in 1552, a pace 'conteyneth five fete, whereof a thousande make an Englyshe mile'.[16] Both the original description in paces and the conversion into feet have been used here, with the latter inserted in brackets.

The first room to be described was the parlour, which was six paces (30 feet) long and five (25 feet) wide. This was one of the most important rooms in the entire Hall, and served as the regular meeting place of the Court of Assistants. The parlour also contained 'A chymney', meaning a fireplace, and there was a buttery adjoining it for the storage of food and drink. The second room on the list was 'A Hale', which appears to refer to a passageway or entry hall, rather than the main space of the building. This room was described as five paces long (25 feet), but no width was provided. The only other information recorded was that it contained a fireplace and several formes, or benches, for people to sit on. The next room was 'A fayre Kechin [kitchen]', eight paces (40 feet) long by three paces (15 feet) wide. It also contained 'a faire chimney & shelves Rounde about'. There was also a cellar, but no measurements were listed for it.

The next room to be described was a gallery, nine paces (45 feet) long and three (15 feet) wide. The gallery contained a privy and closet at one end, which was described as able to serve the requirements of the Company. A 'faire great chamber' of eight paces (40 feet) by six paces (30 feet) was recorded next. This room was described as 'seled' or ceiled, which is appropriate given the Company's name of Joiners and Ceilers. The great chamber had 'another prety w[i]thdrawing place' leading off it, and there was also another closet. The room's size and its description as a great chamber indicate that this was where the Company's Courts of Livery were held, because the ever-increasing membership needed a large space in which to gather. The only other interior rooms described in the list were summarised as '2 other prety chambers & one hathe a chymney'. Moving outside, the document reveals that there was 'a litill court[yard]' measuring 12 feet square. The space was described as 'palled', which presumably means paled, indicating that it was enclosed. The courtyard had a pump in the middle, providing access to water. Finally there was a 'very fayre garden' measuring 22 feet square.[17]

1640s Inventories

During the 1640s, probably as a consequence of the outbreak of the English Civil War, two inventories of the Company's property in the Hall were entered into the Renter Wardens' accounts. The first was dated 5th September 1642, only a fortnight after Charles I had raised his standard at Nottingham, declaring the formal start of the conflict.[18] Plunder and the confiscation of property was a constant threat during the wars, so it is very likely the Company took these inventories in case they had to claim compensation at a later date. The two inventories give the impression of a well-stocked building suitable for hosting the lavish entertainments and dinners which formed such an important part of the Company's calendar.

An Inventory of all and every the Plate, Goods, ymplemts and other things remaininge and beinge in and about the Joyners Hall London, taken 5 September Anno Dmi 1642:[19]

In the greate Chest

Impr fower standinge bowles guilt without Covers, two bigger & two lesser
Item one great standinge salte, wth a little salt on the top, and a Cover
Item one lesse standinge salt wth a cover guilte
Item Nine wyne bowles pincked guilte
Item three deepe Wyne bowles, one bigger two lesser
Item three beakers parcell guilt
Item one white beaker
Item two pincked bowles white
Item three double bell Salts and Covers guilte
Item one double Bell Salte and Cover parcell guilte
Item one Trencher Salte & cover guilt
Item one pynt tankard white
Item Nine beere bowles white
Item two sugar dishes, & one shell spoone
Item three small wyne cupps white
Item three dozen and ffive spoones

Item the Seale of the howse
Item two stone potts edged wth silver
Item one peece of silver like a doller

In the uper Garrett
Item two Barrells of Gunpowder and Match answerable thereto

In the Kitchin
Item three great chargers, 12 platters 14 dishes of three sorts, 11 porringers, 44 sausers
Item fower spitts, and one paire of Racks
Item two kettles, & one fishpan of brasse
Item three drippinge pans, one longe barr of Iron before the Chymney one Trevett, one ffire forke, & one paire of tonges
Item two pottle potts & three fruit dishes
Item one Cesterne of lead & one stone Jugg

In the Parlor
Item twelve greene Cushions, six thrumed Cushions, one longe greene Carpett
Item Twelve Leather Chaires
Item one Bible, a statute booke & a Stows Cronicle
Item two paire of brasse Andirons one bigger the other lesser, one paire of Creeprs a ffyre shovell, Tonges, bellowes and a Capp pann of Brasse
Item two dozen of ould napkins, and three ould Table Clothes of diaper & one Cupbd Cloth, two longe table Clothes, & three dozen of Napkins of damaske

The second inventory was created on 4th September 1646.[20]

An Inventorie of all and every the plate goods ymplemts and other thinges remayninge and beinge in and about the Joyners Hall London taken the 4th of September 1646.

In the Kitchin
Item three great chargers 12 platters11 dishes if three sorts 10 porringers 44 sawsers & 10 pie plates
Item foure two spitts and one paire of Racks
Item two kettles and one fishpan of brasse
Item three dripping pans one longe barr of Iron beefore the Chimney One Tresell one fire forke and one paire of tongs
Item two pottle potts and three fruit dishes
Item one Cesterne of lead 2 stone Juggs
Item one Jack wth 2 iron waights

In the Parlour
Item twelve greene Cushions six thrumed Cushions one longe greene Carpett 3 dossen of vellure Cushions
Item 24 twelve leather Chayres
Item one bible a Statute booke and a Stowes Cronicle
Item two paire of brasse Andirons one bigger thither lesser one paire of Creeps a fire shovle, Tonges bellowes and Capp pan of brasse
Item two 12 dosen of old napkins and three old table Cloathes of diaper, one Cupbord Cloath two longe table Clothes and three dosen of napkins of damaske

New pewter 6 great dishes, 6 lesser dishes & 16 smale dishes, 1 doss plates &
    1 doss of sawcers
A pewter chamber pott
Two chargers
Two large dishes
Sixe pye plates
Two white potts tipte wth Silver
Two dozen and halfe of glasse bottells
1 dossen of new turkey Clothe Chaire
Close stoole & panne
2 p of Mot hangers

Later additions to this inventory recorded the purchase by Mr Hewson on 13th September 1647 of two chargers, two large dishes, and six pie plates. In 1651 the Master and Wardens also invested in two diaper tablecloths, six dozen napkins, eleven 'greate dishes of pewter', four pie plates, and one spit.

In 1655 extensive repairs were carried out on the Hall at a total cost of £138 1d. Unfortunately no court minutes survive from this period so it is impossible to tell whether these repairs were the result of the building's natural decay over time or necessitated by a fire. It is also difficult to ascertain exactly what parts of the building were being repaired because the Renter Wardens' accounts provide very minimal information. However, they record payments to a carpenter, a bricklayer, a blacksmith, an ironmonger, a painter, a plumber, a plasterer, a mason, a glazier, and numerous workmen, so whatever the work was it required the expertise of a wide range of craftsmen. One of the few detailed entries was a payment of £1 6s 8d to James Herndon 'for marble for the Parlor Chimnye', so at the very least some decorative work was taking place in that room. That year's account also noted the purchase of 'a dossen new Rushy leather Chaires for the Hall', as well as a new close stool, new trenchers, and a dresser for the kitchen.[21] The kitchen was also re-paved in 1657. The largest project, however, was the construction of 'the new Tenement' next to the Hall in 1657.[22] The lease of this building was given to John Burgesse in 1657 at an annual rent of £22.[23] There were also three brick and timber houses which were let to tenants shortly after completion to bring in some extra rent for the Company. On 5th July 1666 the middle house was let to woodmonger Ralph Watts and his wife Philippa for twenty-one years at an annual rent of £6. The Watts' lease revealed that the other houses were held by Thomas Broom and Mrs Payn.[24] Unfortunately, the tenants were not destined to enjoy their new homes for long.

The Great Fire of London

In a foreshadowing of the tragedy which was soon to strike, in the autumn of 1665 the Joiners were instructed to create a bonfire in the street near their Hall 'against the spreading of the pestilence'. This referred of course to the plague, which had been ravaging London and would ultimately cause the death of approximately 15 per cent of the city's population.[25] The plague directly impacted the Company in December 1665 because a payment of £3 1s 4d was made to Mrs Specks, the widow of their Beadle Thomas Specks, 'who togeather with one of his chilldren dyed of the pesilence'. Mrs Specks was later given the £4 in wages which her husband had been due to receive at Christmas.[26]

In late April and early May 1666 minor repair work was carried out at the Hall. The new Beadle was paid £1 4s 4d for amendments and cleaning he had overseen, and that entry was followed by payments to a bricklayer, a blacksmith, a plumber, a plasterer, and a painter, totalling a £11 4s 3d. There was a further payment of £1 7s to a glazier in August 'for worke done in the hall'. One of the final entries in the 1666 account referred to £1 given to a butcher 'for beefe for the Audit [dinner] intended to bee at the Hall', as well as another £1 12s 'for damsons Artichoaks & other things'. The audit dinner of 1666 was held in the newly cleaned and repaired Hall, for which the Company had invested a not inconsiderable sum of money. However, one week later all of that investment would be reduced to ash.

Shortly after midnight on Sunday 2nd September a fire began in the bakery belonging to Thomas Farriner of Pudding Lane. Although initially small in scale, the surrounding timber houses were quickly consumed. The most famous surviving account of the fire is found in the diary written by Samuel Pepys, whose cousin Charles Pepys was a member of the Company. Increasingly high winds as the day progressed blew the blaze to the west, closer and closer to the heart of the City. By the afternoon it had turned into a firestorm, causing even further devastation. Pepys described it as 'a most horrid malicious bloody flame, not like the fine flame of an ordinary fire ... it made me weep to see it'. Although attempts had been made to halt the fire by pulling down houses, the blaze moved faster than the people could. Pepys recorded that, travelling along the river on Sunday evening, 'all over the Thames, with one's face in the wind, you were almost burned with a shower of firedrops'.[27]

The fire was finally brought under control on Thursday 6th September, having destroyed over 13,000 buildings and eighty-seven parish churches, and made 70,000 people homeless. The proximity of Joiners' Hall to Pudding Lane, less than half a mile away, meant that the Hall would have been one of the early casualties of the blaze on 2nd September. Before the building was completely engulfed an officer of the Company had been able to enter and retrieve the 1571 charter and some of the early deeds, but the lack of surviving pre-seventeenth-century material related to the Company was the direct result of both the 1666 fire and the subsequent one in 1694 which is discussed later in this chapter.

All of the Company's important paperwork, including the Charter, leases, and all court minute books and accounts, were kept in a locked chest in the parlour. This chest had three locks, each with a different key, and these keys were divided between the Master and two Wardens. All three of the keys were required to open the chest, meaning that the three highest-ranking officers of the Company either had to be present or had to temporarily deputise possession of their key to someone else.[28] The Company's Clerk in 1725 confirmed to the House of Commons that important early documents were lost: 'I have Examined for the Grants and Constitutions of the Company of Joyners of the City of London by which they were made a Livery Company, but their Hall having been burnt in the fire of London and alsoe about Thirty yres since can't find the ptcular Grant by which they were made a Livery Compa[ny].'[29]

The Renter Wardens' account book which began in 1621 was another of the documents saved from the fire, and it contains a copy of 'an Inventory of the books in the p[ar]lo[u]r the 17th of August 1654 in the Cubbords'.[30] This is a very useful list because it reveals exactly what Company records were lost in the blaze. There were four earlier volumes of Wardens' accounts; the earliest was from 1492 to 1508, followed by a gap, but from 1540 onwards there were complete records until the time the inventory was made. The only survivor of those records was the account book started in 1621. There were also four earlier volumes of court minute books covering the period 1573 to 1593, and then 1604 to 1635. Three apprentice binding books were also noted covering the period 1604 until the date of the inventory in 1651. The third of these books, which was started in 1641, did survive the fire and is one of the volumes in the Company's archive at the Guildhall. One account book (1540 to 1545) and one court book (1620 to 1635) were noted to also contain details of apprentice bindings. The loss of these documents is a tragic part of the Company's history, as they contained irreplaceable information about the Company's activities both before and immediately after the grant of their charter and would have provided a fascinating insight into the earlier operations which can now only be speculated upon.

There is also no surviving court minute book from 1666, presumably a loss in the next fire, so it is unclear whether attempts were made to save the Hall, and at what point it became clear that it was a lost cause. The Wardens' accounts, however, can be used to piece together the aftermath. The second payment made in the account beginning 30th September 1666 was £5 7d to 'Labourers about cleansing the Hall', and a later payment of 5s was made 'to two men that helped at the ffire'. No immediate efforts were made to rebuild the property, because in December 1666 4s was spent 'at a view of the Ruins of the Hall and Tenem[en]ts'. The reason for this hesitation appears to be lack of ready money. The monthly courts were also held at a variety of different locations whilst the Hall was unusable. The disbursement list records money spent at meetings held regularly at the Dolphin without Bishopsgate, as well as at the Swan Tavern without Moorgate and at Mr Bowyers' house on 5th November.

In February the Company's plate and linen were sold. A note in the account reveals that the plate weighed 301½ ounces, and was sold at 5s 2d per ounce. The total raised through the sale was £77 10s 9d. However, the money could not be used towards the rebuilding. The previous autumn the Company had borrowed £100 from John Brown 'towards the paym[en]t of the Tenemts and Gardens at Hogsden'.[31] They had invested in purchasing new property at the wrong moment, and instead of using ready money they had borrowed from a member of the Company. The money raised through the sale of the linen and plate was given to John Brown 'towards paymt of a debt to him then owing by the Company'. However, Brown returned the money to them, and in fact rounded the total up to £80, to assist with the cost of rebuilding the tenements. Brown continued to be the Company's saving grace. He offered them a further £250 on the security of the previously purchased lands at Hogsden to enable them to rebuild the Hall. This offer was quickly accepted, and in the summer of 1667 the building work commenced, overseen by Beadle Richard Rogers. Indeed, Rogers' name regularly appears in the payments for labour work he had provided himself. The Master, Wardens, and Beadle kept a close eye on the actions of the workmen and appear to have held regular consultations with them. They also provided them with beer and occasionally dinner.

The two Wardens were responsible for paying for different parts of the building work. Renter Warden Robert Langridge concerned himself with the construction of the Hall itself, and between June and September 1667 he spent a total of £103 14s 11d. In the last week of June Langridge paid 7s 3d to a Mr Mills 'for surveying of the Hall', and 5s to Morris Emet 'for measuring the Hall and Tenemts and drawing a Plot'. From this point onwards things moved very quickly. Labourers were hired to clean away what rubble was left from the fire, and on 3rd July workmen arrived to construct the new building. On 20th July twenty baskets were purchased so that building materials could be more easily transported. Two primary craftsmen appear to have been hired to undertake the majority of the construction, along with teams of labourers. The bricklayer was Mr Simpson, and he received £15 for his services in July, August, and September. There was also a payment of £8 10s in September for 6,500 bricks, both of fine and coarse quality, and 14s for 2,000 units of lime mortar cement with which to bind them. The second primary craftsman was carpenter Mr Hilliard who was paid the grand sum of £60 for his work over the three months. Another carpenter, Mr Wratten, was paid a more modest fourteen shillings for creating the door in September.

Upper Warden Henry Man was tasked with paying for costs associated with rebuilding one of the adjoining messuages, which had previously been let to a tenant. He spent £6 14s 4d on tiles for the floor, along with a further 4s 4d for hearth tiles. He also purchased a dresser, a cupboard, an oval table, oak rafters, a gate, fire pans, charcoal, coals, and candles. Although he didn't specify exactly what work they had carried out, he made further payments to a bricklayer, a plumber, a blacksmith, a carpenter, a lime maker, a mason, a painter, a plasterer, an ironmonger, a glazier, and various labourers. Man's disbursements amounted to £154 9d. The combination of the two Wardens' accounts for rebuilding efforts in 1666–7, therefore, came to a total of £274 15s 8d.[32] This is roughly equivalent to £31,000 in today's money.[33] The succeeding Wardens for 1667–8 continued to make purchases to replace items lost in the fire. Renter Warden William Harley purchased from Mr Pufford seventy-two trenchers, round wooden plates, to facilitate dining in the Hall. Shortly afterwards he bought seventy-two 'rushia Chaires' and six joined stools from Randall Nuns at a cost of £3 5s 6d, in addition to two drawing tables, four glasses, four earthen pots, and an unspecified number of cupboards from other merchants.

The next Upper Warden, Henry Travers, was heavily engaged in continuing the rebuilding of the messuage on the east side of Fryer's Lane, although again the day-to-day oversight of the project was left to Beadle Rogers. The brickmaker associated with building this house was John Clarke, and he was paid £12 15s for 15,000 bricks, which he delivered on 30th May 1668. The bricks appear to have been transported along the Thames, because the next entry in the account noted costs for landing them and for wharfage. Another brickmaker, this one Robert Clarke and potentially a relative of John, was paid just over £10 for an additional 12,000 bricks, which he delivered on 26th June; again, these were transported by water. Robert Aldridge received over £14 for 12,500 bricks in June and July, and John Slyford provided 16,000 for just over £16. William Quynton provided 3,150 units of lime mortar to cement all of those thousands of bricks, and Oliver Matthews and his team of labourers provided nails, spikes, baskets, buckets, and scaffolding for the construction. Matthews and his labourers appear to have been doing most of the construction work, because he was paid a total of £46 15s 2d for their services, and carpenter John Goodchilde received £50 for his contributions to the building.[34] John Brown, who had originally lent the Company money to rebuild the Hall, later provided another £300 as a mortgage for this particular house.[35]

In spite of the great expense of time, money, and labour, the Worshipful Company of Joiners and Ceilers were not destined to enjoy their new Hall for long.

1694: 'the loss of our Hall, by reason of fire'

At 9pm on 28th April 1694 cries of 'Fire!' echoed through Thames Street. Startled residents rushed out onto the road and saw that Joiners' Hall was burning again. The cause of the fire is unknown, but in an age of timber-framed buildings, wooden interiors and furniture, and open flames, a single candle falling over could start a blaze. All members of the Company who were within easy reach of the Hall immediately set about attempting to save as much as they could. Joseph Burrough, the Clerk, who lived in an adjoining house, was later praised by the Court of Assistants for putting the preservation of the Hall 'before his owne concernes'. He left his home and endeavoured to prevent the flames from completely destroying the parlour and kitchen. Although both rooms did receive some damage, he successfully ensured that they were not 'totally consumed in that Conflagra[ti]on'. In the meantime, the flames had reached Burrough's home and he 'sustained a Considerable loss' of his own property while he fought to save the Hall. In consideration of his efforts his salary was later raised by £8 per annum.[36] Renter Warden Thomas Bayly and his servants also ran into the Hall whilst it was burning in order to rescue the Company's silver plate, and presumably they also removed the chest containing the Charter and other significant documents at the same time. Bayly's livery gown was scorched in the process, and he later claimed that he had felt 'in danger of his owne Life'.[37] His servants were rewarded with 10s for their efforts. Another unnamed member of the Company was 'much bruised' in the fire, and was given a temporary weekly pension of 3s 6d while he recovered.[38]

Whilst the Company members worked together to save as much as they could, a message had been sent to summon one of John Lofting's 'sucking worm' fire engines, a quite ingenious device which had been patented in 1691. The engine's leather pipes would be placed in a water source, and attached at the other end to a small engine manned by six men. With three at each side, they would operate a suction lever to pump water up the pipes. The long extension pipes would then carry the water from the engine and allow it to be sprayed onto the flames. It could even be thrown as high as 400 feet.[39] Presumably in this instance the engineers took advantage of the Thames as their water source, and fed the pipes along one of the side streets until they reached the Hall. Hiring the engine was expensive, and the Company had to pay the chief engineer £2 15s for their services.[40] Unfortunately, in spite of their best efforts the main structure of the Hall was completely destroyed, and the adjacent rooms and buildings severely damaged.

An extraordinary meeting of the Court of Assistants was called on 30th April 1694 to discuss 'the loss of our Hall, by reason of fire'. By extreme good fortune, the Hall was insured. Fire insurance was a comparatively new creation which had been introduced following the Great Fire of London in 1666, and although its popularity was steadily growing it was by no means widespread yet. London's first fire insurance company, the Insurance Office for Houses, was established in 1680 by Nicholas Barbon, Sir John Parsons, and ten other investors.[41] Joseph Burrough, the Company's Clerk, had raised the suggestion of insuring the Hall in 1693, and on 4th April of that year the Court of Assistants authorised him, the Upper Warden, and the Renter Warden to take out a policy for £1,000. The Hall was insured for £500, and the Company's houses which had been let to tenants were insured for a further £500.[42] After the fire Burrough was praised for having suggested the insurance in the first place because otherwise the blaze would have 'proved fatall' to the Company.[43]

The monthly Court meeting the following day on 1st May saw a resolution that the Company was 'unanimously resolved to rebuild' the Hall. A committee of eight men was appointed to consult with local craftsmen, but the final decision about designs and the men to hire would be made by the Master and Wardens.[44] In the meantime, court meetings and all other business would be conducted in the

Summer House in the courtyard, which had not been damaged.[45] On 18th May another extraordinary Court was called to be present at the Hall when insurer Alderman Sir John Parsons visited to inspect the damage. He confirmed that the £500 insurance money would be paid, and suggested that George Jackson should be hired as the primary builder.[46] The first articles of agreement between Jackson and the Company were duly signed on 26th June, and he was initially contracted to repair the lead roof over the parlour at a cost of £72. Any lead and iron which could be salvaged was delivered to Jackson to be re-used in the new building.[47] On 23rd August an order was made to pay him £200 of the insurance money, and this appears to be a down-payment on the work formally contracted on 4th September; Jackson was engaged 'about rebuilding the Hall and other contents therein'. A sum of £615 was agreed, and the Company's common seal was affixed to the contract.[48] Unfortunately none of the plans for the new Hall have survived so it is unclear whether they were intending to rebuild to the same design as the first Hall, or whether changes had been made to reflect a more modern style. One hint of the exterior design comes from April 1695, when it was agreed 'that there be no shash windows in the Parlour by reason of many inconveniences that may happen'.[49] They also appear to have constructed as separate building, described as a banqueting house, in the yard. In a report of 1698 it was agreed that the floor in that building would be white and red stone, with a black border.[50]

At the 4th September 1694 meeting it became clear to the Court of Assistants that the £500 insurance money was not going to be enough to cover Jackson's costs, and that was before any other craftsmen were contracted to complete the interiors. Consequently, at the next monthly Court summons were sent out to all members of the Company offering them the opportunity to take the Livery immediately at a cost of £5. The money raised through this scheme would pay for wainscoting the Hall, lobby, passage, staircase, and steward's room.[51]

Whilst Jackson was responsible for building the shell of the new Hall, a range of other craftsmen were hired to furnish and decorate the interior. Consistent with the Company's ethos, the emphasis was on wood. Thomas Poultney, a member of the Company, was engaged to repair and replace the joining and carving work in the parlour for £30.[52] Poultney was later also engaged to wainscot the Great Hall at a cost of 9s per yard. Additional decorative carving work in the Hall was contracted to Jonathan Maine, Richard Saunders, and Robert Jones for £100.[53] The decoration in that room was to include festoons, the royal coat of arms, and the Company's crest.[54] The royal arms were on a pedestal at the north end of the room, and were created by Jones.[55] Other carving was to be done in the Italian style.[56] The Hall would also feature tables 'made by the Joyners after the fashion as they are done at Chelsey Colledge'.[57] Samuel Livermore and Edward Brandon were asked to wainscot the passage, staircase, and steward's room for 7s per yard. John Mitchell and John Smallwell were hired to create the screen costing £77 which would stand at the lower end of the Hall and would divide that space from the passage and staircase.[58]

The building work had been completed by Audit Day 1695, and the Company approved Jackson's request for a written testimonial stating their satisfaction with his work.

Whereas the Comon Hall and other building belonging to the Company of Joyners in London were in the month of Aprill 1694 totally burnt downe and others much defaced And whereas the said Company did contract and agree to & with Mr George Jackson to undertake rebuild & reparie the said Hall and premises and to funde all manner of workmanshipp and materialls whatsoever for the compleat finishing the same Except Joyners and carvers worke

These are therefore to certifie and declare That the said Mr Jacson hath rebuilt repaired and finished the said Hall and all other buildings belonging to the same to the great sattisfaccon of the said Court In testimoney whereof wee have hereunto affixed our Comon Seale the day and yeare above, To the Right Worll the Gentlemen Patners in the ffire Office against the Royall Exchange London and all others whom these prsents may concerne or come.[59]

However, although the Hall itself was complete, the external surroundings had suffered damage during the building work. In the spring of 1698 a complaint was made that 'many of the stones and stepps in the yard belonging to this Company are broaken some wanting others loose many soe sunck that the water cannot have a free passage'. The gutters leading to the common sewer were also blocked, 'which causes an overfloweing into the said yard on any hasty raine'.[60] In May Robert Jones, one of the craftsmen who had assisted with the Hall, was hired to replace all of the paving, as well as to 'lay a passage of white and Black stone of seaven foot broad at the least from the yard gate to the Hall doore'.[61]

Other Uses of Joiners' Hall

The Joiners were always willing to share access to their Hall with other Livery Companies who did not have their own building. The earliest surviving Renter Wardens' account book reveals that the Gardiners' Company were renting the Hall in 1621 and continued to do so until at least 1625, paying varying amounts of between £3 and £10 10s annually.[62] They resumed their tenancy in the year 1649 to 1650 at the rent of £10 10s, although the amount they could afford each year fluctuated and by the mid-1650s it had been reduced to £8.[63] The Fruiterers' Company attended the Court of Assistants on 12th April 1681 'to desire to make use of this hall',[64] and they became regular tenants, paying an annual rent of between £5 and £7 depending on the number of meetings they held. The Company of Feltmakers were also using the Hall in October 1687.[65]

The building was also used for non-livery purposes, and not always legally. In May 1683 the Master and Wardens were prosecuted in the Court of Aldermen for allegedly allowing 'a certaine illegal Conventicle or Convencon' to take place at the Hall on 3rd December previous, and they had been fined £20. When they reported the charge to the Court of Assistants they argued that 'such meetings was not by them ordered ... but that the same was done by former Court or Courts wherein they were not of the [Assistants]', and begged to be saved harmless from all charges. The Assistants agreed to this and ordered that the fine should be paid out of the Company's stock.[66] The building had been let as a meeting place to a Mr Brag by 1687.[67]

On 29th December 1687 John Hicks and Richard Marriot appeared in person at a Court of Assistants and requested that they be allowed to rent the Hall as a meeting place every Sunday. The Company agreed that they could have access to the Hall, the Steward's Room, and the Lobby 'on every Sunday in the year & one day in every Month', as long as they gave the Beadle three days' notice for that weekday access. Their lease was backdated to 25th December 1687 and would be initially valid for one calendar year at the sum of £20, but the lease would automatically renew unless they gave six months' notice that they would vacate.[68] On 7th August 1688 one Mr Hicks paid the Renter Warden £5 for a quarter of a year's rent 'for the Meeting at the Hall'.[69]

It was ordered on 6th June 1757 that all applications for the use of the Hall which did not relate to the Company's business should be directed solely to the clerk, and not to either the Master or the Beadle.[70] This was an interesting departure from the norm, because until this point the maintenance of the Hall had been the Beadle's responsibility and it is unclear why this change was made.

Eighteenth-century Repairs and Changes

Keeping the Hall in good repair was a constant challenge for the Company. Minor maintenance work took place each year as problems arose, but by 1735 it became necessary to commission some substantial repairs. A committee was formed on 6th May 'to inspect what Repairs are now necessary & wanting to be done at the Comon Hall of this Company', and they were instructed to provide a written recommended schedule of works to the next monthly court.[71] The increasing severity of these repairs raises numerous questions about the quality of workmanship used to rebuild the Hall in 1694–5, which would have been a source of some embarrassment given the nature of the joinery craft. An alternative explanation could be that the Hall's proximity to the River Thames had caused excessive damp to set in. Some of the interior work was cosmetic, but there were significant structural repairs necessary to keep the Hall secure, dry, and stable. The list of work also reveals more information about what the Hall looked like:

The Roof of the Hall on the East side to take out the samell Tiles and putt in sound ones in the Room the West side to be new ripped the Leaden Guttar to be taken up & new laid the South End to be new rupped To repair the North West hipp

The fflatt over the Parlour to cut off the Ends of the Sheets that are slipped down & stop the Current of the Guttur and soder the Cracks To putt in Water Tables at the North and South Ends where wanting To nail the Lead upon the Coping & mend the Cracks of the same the three step from the fflatt to the Upper End to be made new

The upper fflatt over the Lobby & Beadle's Room to mend the Cracks of the Lead where wanting To make a brick parapett two ffeet & a half high & coped with Stone on the West & South sides a Rail without banisters on the North side The weather boarding to be nailed & new painted & a New door to the Stair head the Ciling to be mended over the Steward's Room the leaden Hepp thereof to be made new

In the Hall
To white wash all the plaistering of the same & the Stair Case & other Apartments

To take of all the old Plaistering of the Outside of the Hall & new do it with Stucco To make a water table at the bottom of new hard bricks six course high Grey stocks

The Summer house in the Yard to be repaired and painted the outside & the Clerk's Office the same the South window of the Kitchen & the window under it to be sett to rights

A new iron Gate to the Yard to repair & ornament the ffigures on the Peers on each side the Gate

The Clerk's house to repair the Chimney and Tyling

The North End of the Parlour the bottom part unsound & the Upper part buldged out a new Stack of leaden Pipes with a wooden water Trunk at the bottom of the North west Corner of the Hall.[72]

After reading this report the Court of Assistants ordered the work to be done 'with all convenient Speed'. The most urgent issue was to replace the tiles at the east end of the roof, but no sooner had the work begun than another problem was discovered. When the existing tiles had been removed the roof itself was found to be structurally unsound. The workmen reported to the Master that it was 'in a worse condition then was Expected', and they recommended that the entire roof should be replaced. When the Court of Assistants met in July they gave their assent to this; indeed, they could hardly do otherwise. They also took the opportunity to make some amendments to the schedule of works. Instead of the proposed brick water table outside the Hall they decided to use a deal plint sealed with Portland stone dust. The parapet wall over the parlour was likewise to be sealed with Portland stone dust. They asked for stone windowsills to be added to the windows on the west side of the Hall facing the courtyard, and wanted step-free access from the west door to the street with the ramp made from Purbeck stone.[73]

Whilst the workmen had been waiting for approval to completely replace the roof the progress inside the building had continued. Although the original plan was to re-whitewash the plastering, an examination of the plaster in the parlour and staircase found that it was 'in a very ruinous Condition & not fitt to stand', so this also had to be completely replaced. Now that alteration had to be made to the walls it was proposed that the roof over the Beadle's bedchamber should be removed and the walls raised to create a new room. This was agreed, and the walls were duly raised by 7 feet.[74] By August a problem had also been discovered in the kitchen. A survey of the room had revealed that 'the Girders & Timbers of the Kitchen ffloor are rotten & decayed'. These timbers were separating the kitchen from the cellar underneath, so there was potential for a full collapse into the room below. After consulting with the Court of Assistants the workmen were authorised to remove the timbers and create an arched brick ceiling in the cellar, and re-tile the kitchen floor on top.

This decision to make structural changes prompted a suggestion of dramatic alterations to other parts of the building. Past Master John Smallwell Esq. drafted some plans for amending the kitchen, staircase, and Beadle's apartments, as well as enlarging the steward's room by reducing the size of the Clerk's house. He offered the Company two options for the staircase: rebuild it up to the Hall as it currently stood, or add a Venetian window, a large tripartite window. The consensus was in favour of the version with the window, with the stairs made of red brick, and Smallwell was ordered to oversee the building work along with the Master and Upper Warden.[75]

At the end of August the workmen reported yet another problem to the Court of Assistants. When they had been digging down to the building's foundations in order to reinforce the walls they discovered that 'the comon sewer that runs along by the said ffoundacon is ffound so very ruinous and decayed That it is in great danger of ffalling in'. Unfortunately the sewers were under the jurisdiction of the Commissioners of Sewers, so a petition was hastily dispatched to them requesting their assistance with the repairs.[76] In the meantime the work on the walls had to stop, so part of the Hall was exposed to the elements and the Company had no idea how quickly the matter would be resolved. On 12th September the Commissioners of Sewers appointed a committee to inspect the Hall's sewer and create a report about its state. That document noted that the Comon Sewer under Joyner's Hall is ffive ffoot & an half high & two ffoot wide & that there are several Breaches in that part of the Sewer And the Sewer is in a ruinous condicon & may be the occasion of great damage to the ffoundacon of the peticoners new intended Building if not timely prevented.

The committee liaised with the Master, Wardens, and workmen when they visited the Hall to discuss the best way to repair it. They must have been entertained in some style, because the meeting cost the Company £4 17s 6d.[77] The Master emphasised that the building was in danger of further damage if left exposed for much longer, and the committee appreciated that it was a matter of urgency. After consulting with the workmen it was agreed that they would ask the Commissioners of Sewers to provide 25 guineas towards the cost of repairs, which would be to

[make] the [sewer] threefoot wide & to extend 50 ffoot in length & the walls to be a brick & an half thick & to be laid nine inches in Terras with great Stock bricks & to be ffive ffoot high from the pavement of the Sewer to the underside of the Crown of the Arch & to be Turned a little out of its present Course in such maner as shall be thought necessary by Mr Cooper the Bricklayer for the more effectual Security of the said new intended Building.

Their report was presented to the Commissioners of Sewers on 18th September, and agreed at the Guildhall the following day.[78] The Company asked member and bricklayer Samuel Hubbard to oversee this work, and he was offered £50 if it could all be completed within three weeks. In the meantime the Hall was temporarily bricked up and enclosed with boards to protect the interior, and all other building work was temporarily halted.[79] In mid-November, when the sewer had been finished, Smallwell's proposed alterations to the kitchen, parlour, lobby, and staircase were ordered to 'be prosecuted with all convenient speed', and Hubbard was assigned as the chief workman, along with Isaac Dawes. The staircase with the Venetian window was postponed until February, but not abandoned altogether.[80] The two men were instructed to

build the ffront & ends of the parlor & kitchen & staircase & part of the End of the Hall up to the ffloor thereof with the Vaulting under the Kitchen The ffront next the Courtyard to be of red stock bricks & the North ends of the parlor & Hall of Grey Stock & all the insider work of good hard burnt place bricks To every rod of the sd brickwork is to be used Two hundred of Lime & drift sand to all the outside work & they to clear & carry away at their own Expence all the rubbish made in pulling down and Building up the same & to indempnifye the Company from all costs or charges relating thereto & are to have Liberty to use in the said building such of the old bricks as are sound & good the said work is to be done with all expedicon at the rate of six pounds per rodd & to be paid for as soon as ffinished.[81]

Another unexpected problem faced by the Company was that of accidental injury. Peter Barrett was employed as one of the labourers undertaking the repairs, but unfortunately he fell and broke his leg. He was taken to St Bartholomew's Hospital to be treated by the surgeons, but he could not afford the fees. As the injury had been sustained whilst working for the Company the Hospital applied to them 'to allow something towards the charge', and it was agreed that they would provide £2 immediately.[82]

The repairs became steadily more elaborate and more expensive as time passed. As soon as one job was started the original condition of the Hall was found to be much worse than anticipated, prompting more and more work. Although these changes were necessary to ensure the structural stability of the Hall, it meant that the Company's finances were greatly depleted. By the end of February it had become necessary to implement some spending regulations in a desperate attempt to stave off bankruptcy. The Court of Livery agreed that the priority was to finish the parlour and kitchen, and that no bills for any other work would be paid until those rooms had been completed and the workmen compensated. If possible all bills were to be paid using ready cash in the Renter Warden's hands, but if necessary the Company's annuity stock invested in the South Sea Company could be sold. No other work would commence unless the plans and a detailed cost estimate had been agreed by a Court of Livery.[83]

When all of the workmen's bills had been received the Company was stunned by the total cost, and immediately appointed a committee to inspect them. That committee negotiated with each workman to see whether a discount of any sort could be obtained. They presented a report to the Court of Assistants in February 1737 in which they listed both the original and finally agreed costs.[84]

	Original			Discounted		
	£	s	d	£	s	d
Ffor Mr Smallwell Mr Cooper & Mr Singleton the Carpents & Joyners day bill amounting to	323	5	8.5	233	14	0
Ffor their measured Bill amounting to	91	0	1.75	76	5	6
Ffor their Bill for money laid out amountg	8	18	8	5	8	5
Ffor Mr Dawes the Bricklayrs day Bill amounting to	104	9	10	76	0	0
Ffor his measured Bill amounting to	262	18	9.5	242	3	9.5
Ffor Messrs Dunn & Townsend the Mason's measured & day bills amounting to	331	12	1.5	305	0	0
Ffor Mr Spencer the Glazier's Bill amountg to	16	9	8.25	15	8	0
Ffor mr Leaper the Pavior's Bill amountg to	4	5	6	4	1	0
Ffor Mr Ball the Plumbrs Bill amountg to	18	18	6	14	2	0
Ffor Mr Crane the Plumbrs Bill amountg to	51	3	0	51	0	0
Ffor Mr Wade the Carver's Bill amountg to	27	4	0	23	2	0
Ffor Mr Ffearnley the Plaisterer's measured Bill amounting to	21	1	2.5	21	1	0
Ffor his Day Bill amountg to	12	11	1	12	11	0
Ffor Mrs Soames the Smith's Bill	57	9	8	5	0	0
Ffor Mr Fford the ffounder's Bill amounting to	9	10	0	6	14	6
TOTAL	1340	18	0	1136	11	2

Even with a discount the total of £1,136 11s 2d was far more than the Company could afford, so it became necessary to sell their South Sea stock; this is discussed further in Chapter 8. The Clerk liquidated £700 of annuities at a profit of £97 2s 6d, and all the money was given to the Renter Warden to settle the accounts with the workmen.[85]

Topographer John Noorthouck's survey of London contained a brief description of the Hall in the later eighteenth century:

> In Friars-lane is situated the hall of the company of Joyners; remarkable for a magnificent screen at the entering into the hall-room, having demi-savages, and a variety of other enrichments, carved in wainscot. The great parlour is wainscotted with cedar.[86]

There appears to have been a large clock inside the Hall by the mid-eighteenth century, with silver hands on the dial. In February 1754 Joseph Hill was paid £1 16s for repairs to the dial, and Samuel Whichcote was given 6s 6d for 'Silvering the Hands'.[87] In June 1755 it was ordered that the Hall should be whitewashed again, and that 'the Picture of Queen Anne in the Hall be removed to some other part of the Hall and that the Kings Arms and Table of Benefactors which are now before the great Window be removed to that side of the Hall where the said Picture now is'.[88] Carpenter Mr Stephens took down the items in July, although not without damage done. At least one of the items, probably the table of benefactors, was within a pedimented frame decorated with scrolls. When it was being removed these were damaged, and part of Stephens' bill was for 'glewing the carved work' before fixing everything in their new places.[89]

This was done as part of an overall refurbishment of the Hall. Carpenter Mr Dowbiggin had installed a new door into the court parlour, and unspecified work had also taken place by a glazier, a plumber, a bricklayer, a plasterer, a painter, and a blacksmith.[90] The steward's room, pantry, and lobby were later re-plastered in August.[91] William Reading provided two new sets of 'Brass Work to the Water Closets' in February 1758.[92] A lead shoe scraper was purchased for 8s in November 1760 and placed near the front door,[93] and eight new cushions were bought for the parlour from Messrs Brown and Sons in August 1761.[94] In November 1763 a bill of £10 10s from Messrs Brown and Sons was passed 'for a Six Leaved Gilt Leather Screen'.[95] John Pugh cleaned, repaired, and re-varnished three paintings at the Hall in November 1771 at a cost of £10 10s.[96]

During John Wilkes' tenure as Master an order was made in May 1771 for 'the Door and Gateway in the front leading into the Hall yard and the Wall on each side and the figures upon the Piers' to be repaired before the next court.[97] A matter of more urgency, however, was another fire at the Hall on Sunday 20th June 1771. A building tenanted by cooper Mr Watts caught fire, and the devastation was described to the court as 'dreadful'. The Westminster Fire Engine was summoned to tackle the blaze, and at the next court meeting the Renter Warden was instructed to give them a gratuity of 2 guineas as a token of thanks 'for their Diligence and Activity at the Hall'.[98] Bills totalling over £32 for carpentry, plastering, and glazing at the Hall were passed in August, indicating that they were the primary repairs needed after the fire.[99] Further bills of over £68 to bricklayer John Elmes and almost £120 to carpenter Mr Burnell in September 1773,[100] and £36 to carpenter Oliver Burton in December 1773,[101] were also attributed to repairs following the fire.

An order was passed on 7th January 1772 for the purchase of a bath stone to be fixed in the Steward's room. On the same day William Hopkins proposed that 'the Arms of the Branches in the Hall', by which he seems to have meant protruding shelves and hooks, should be 'thoroughly cleaned and new lacquered'. He also recommended that the pans and serving dishes hanging on them should be replaced. This was to be done 'in a good and workmanlike manner for Five Guineas'.[102] However, when the bills for this were produced in March it appeared that further charges to John Hayes for painting and gilding the branches, and to Henry Phillips for taking them down and putting them back up, had brought the total cost of this endeavour to over £33.[103]

At the March court in 1779 it was lamented that the glazed cupola in the centre of the parlour's ceiling had caused 'Much Inconvenience' because it barely provided any light. A motion was carried that the light should be taken away altogether, the gap covered with timber and lead, and the ceiling re-plastered. The work was to be done as quickly as possible because it was 'very necessary'.[104] A bell was purchased in September 1780 and set up in the lobby to summon a porter. Both of the pulls were in the parlour.[105]

The Company's Tenants

Joiners' Hall was not the only building on the Upper Thames Street site, nor did it form the entirety of the Company's holdings. As soon as their 1571 charter gave them the right to own property in trust they began sub-letting to supplement their annual income. The earliest recorded example of this appears to date to 8th February 1574 when the Master and Wardens leased land adjoining the Hall to Thomas Cranage for 20s per annum.[106] The warehouse underneath the Hall was in the occupation of joiner Orwell or Otwell Methringham in1590 at an annual rent of £3, and he had also taken possession of the sawpit and yard for a further 33s 4d.[107]

They also benefited from bequests made to them in wills. The Bishop of London had granted joiner Simon Martyn a lease for land 'adioyninge to the southe syde of the wall of the Cathedrall Churche of Saint Paule in London, That is to saie, by Saint Katherynes Chappell wall' for the term of twenty-one years on 15th April 1583. The following February the lease was increased to grant Martyn 'All that tenement shed or litle shopp situate lyinge and beinge on theast syde of the steppes or staires leadinge up into the Cathedrall Churche of Saint Paule in London on the south syde of the same Church conteyninge in length from east to west twelve foote of assize, and in bredth from north to south sixe foote of assize'. A final addition was made by the Dean of St Paul's on 13th October 1585 granting Martyn an additional tenement in St Paul's Churchyard for forty years. He did not hold this property for long, however. In his will, dated 25th August 1586, Martyn bequeathed the property he held to his wife Katherine and stipulated that it should revert to the possession of the Joiners' Company after her death.[108] The Company released their rights to the tenement in St Paul's Churchyard back to the Dean of the Cathedral on 7th December 1619.[109]

On 6th September 1605 Lawrence Ripley transferred a building in Fenchurch Street previously lived in by his late father John Ripley to joiners Robert Kellett and Oliver Cawdwell. A later eighteenth- or possibly nineteenth-century transcription of various Company deeds placed this property at 101 Fenchurch Street.[110] It was described as 'divided into divers sevrall houses tenements or dwellings', and after Ripley's death it was all transferred 'to the use of the master, wardens & comynaltie of the facultie of Joyners & Ceelers of the Cittye of London'.[111] This became known in the Company as Ripley's Gift. The 1605 transfer deed contained a brief description of how the building had been broken down. There were dwelling houses facing the street, with additional rooms and buildings serving as workshops. There was a garden to the rear containing an office and coalhouse, and a cellar beneath the main building.

In 1670 John Eldred Esq. of Stamway in Essex had leased to the Master and Wardens

> all that peice or parcell of ground whereon severall houses lately stood which were burned and demolished by the dreadfull fire which happened in London as is now walled about with a brick wall conteininge the severall dementions hereafter menconed that is to say from North to South Sixtie ffoure foot of assize little more or less and from East to West Twenty one good of assize little more or less ... all which premises are scituate lying and being in Tennis Court Alley or Lane next adjoyninge to the hall of the said Company on the East ... now made & converted into a grass plot or garden.[112]

By 1688 the Company had built another messuage on this land and they leased it to silk dyer William Pickard for sixty-one years at a cost of £500.[113] Pickard was a relation of Thomas Pickard, one of the Court of Assistants at that time.

In 1668 the Company invested in purchasing two additional houses in Thames Street from blacksmith Robert Swift at a cost of £80. The deed granted them 'all those two Tofts and peeces or parcells of ground ... whereon lately stood two Messuages or Tenemts consumed in the late lamentable fire one of them knowne by the signe of the ffryer, and adjoining eastward to ffryer lane, and th'other of them knowne by the signe of the Rose, and next adjoining to the said other Messuage, and under which said Messuages or parte thereof runneth the Comon Sewer'.[114] After the houses had been rebuilt they were let to tenants, including haberdashers Edward Bayly and Nathaniel Beatrisse in 1677. They took one house consisting of

> One Cellar next the streete One shopp over the said Cellar One kitchin behinde the said shopp Two roomes or chambers over the said shopp & kitchin Two rooms or chambers over the last menconed rooms and over them two Garretts and also one little yard paved with ffreestone behinde the said hose with a doore into Greenwich lane als ffryer lane.[115]

Bayly renewed the lease for a further twenty-one years in 1684 at an annual rent of £16.[116] The other house appears to have been leased to Jacob Foster Esq., and he sub-let it to Edward Nicholson, who took over the lease for the house in 1686, although Foster remained in possession of a warehouse on site.[117] In a case of extraordinarily bad timing cooper John Aston took over Nicholson's lease for 'all that messuage or tenement together with the little yard behind the said messuage paved with ffreestone with a doore into Greenwich-lane als ffryer lane together with the Roome or kitchen beyond the said yard And alsoe all that their Roome or Warehouse with the Celler under the same' in 1693 for eleven years.[118] The fire of the following year caused considerable damage to this property, inflicting upon him losses of £200, but rather than give it up Aston negotiated with the Company to have it rebuilt. He appeared at a court meeting on 24th May to request that structural changes could be made to the cellar to turn it into an arched vault, and even offered to increase his rent from £25 to £50 per year. The Company found this agreeable and told him to liaise with their builder George Jackson and arrange 'for doing the same as cheape as he could'.[119] When the lease was due to expire in 1706 Aston agreed to renew for a further ten years.[120] However, he vacated in 1713 and the house was taken by fruiterer William Haddock, whose lease contains a very useful description of what the house looked like. It can be assumed that the second house had been built to the same design.[121]

In the streete
Two folding doores lock and key with wooden stepps into the Celler and Vault one shell covered with lead over the doorcase foure wooden shutters to the windowes one iron casement one doore next the streete one lock and key two bolts and a knocker with a doore into the seller with a lock and key the passage from the streete being wainscotted and painted

In the parlor
The same wainscotted and painted one mantle peice with fire stone on the harth a doore thereto

In the passage to the yard
One doore with a lock and key thereunto and a light into the same

In the yard
The same paved with freestone with a partition for beer with a door thereto and one door out of the yard into ffryer lane with a lock key and bolt two houses of office one over another covered with lead with two doores with a shash light

In the kitchen
The same paved with freestone one doore lock and key one iron casement two buteryes two doores one mantle peece of deale one large dresser two doores with drawes under it

In the Warehouse
Two doores into the same one paire of folding doores into ffryer lane ffour windows with iron boltes or wooden barres lights with eighteene iron barrs one wooden shutter the same paved or laid with brick under the warehouse and yard One large vault from end to end part paved or laid with brick

In the dineing room next the street one story high
The same wainscotted and painted with a closet and door therein one mantle peece one fire harth of Ryegate stone one door two pair of iron casements foure pair of folding shutters

On the same floor backwards to the Eastward
The same wainscotted and painted two pair of shashes with wooden shutters to the same with two doores into the same roome

One roome on the same floor to the Westward being a compting house
The same wainscotted two doores with one lock and key two shash windowes with wooden shutters to the same

In the roome two story high next the street
The same three quarters wainscotted and painted the other part wainscotted about three foote high one mantle peece fire harth of Rygate stone two closetts with one lock and key two doores two pair of iron casements foure paire of folding shutters two doors belonging to the said roome with one lock and key

Two closetts on the same floor Eastward next the yard
Two iron casements one lock and key
Two garrets next the street
Two doores
Two closetts on the same floor backwards
Two doores two casements
The staircase wainscotted and painted two story high with a shash window or light on the staires into the yard.[122]

By 1749 one of the houses had been transferred to cooper William Watts.[123] The other was taken by a Mr Elmes, whose lease expired in 1772, but he had sub-let the property to Watts so he was in possession of both houses. Watts expressed an interest in taking over Elmes' lease in 1772 for a further twenty-one years at £45 per annum. He waited upon the Company on 7th April at the quarter court, and the matter was agreed. He also suggested that the east wall of the Hall should be rebuilt, 'being in a very ruinous Condition', and proposed that he and the Company should halve the cost between them. This was not agreed to immediately, and two impartial surveyors were asked to assess the state of the wall.[124] At the next court meeting they reported that 'the Wall is in a very ruinous and bad Condition and ought forthwith to be taken down and rebuilt'. The estimated cost was £100 and would be divided between Watts and the Company as he had previously suggested. The surveyors also recommended that the wall should be built on brick arches rather than on a breast as it had previously been constructed.[125] The Hall had to be vacated whilst this work was carried out, so consequently the St James' Day elections and dinner took place at Innholders' Hall in 1772 instead.[126]

However, within months of this agreement being made Watts was declared bankrupt at a hearing at Guildhall.[127] The decision to sue Watts was made in May 1774 on the grounds that his rent was in arrears, 'and also in regard to his having almost pulled down and destroyed the Company's Houses under pretence of setting about the repairing and new fronting the same' according to the agreement made on 7th April 1772.[128] Watts was accused of deliberately intending to ruin and destroy the houses by stripping all the timber, lead, and other building materials from the frontage and selling everything, leaving the bare walls 'gutted, a very ruinous & dangerous Wreck'. After leaving them exposed to the elements Watts claimed that the frontage could now not be repaired 'but must be taken entirely down & rebuilt'. When the Company chased him for his rent arrears he instead presented them with a bill for £50 which he claimed had been spent on wall repairs.

The timing of the Company's action against Watts was certainly deliberate. The minute books record that 'Watts's Household Goods and Effects are now selling off by Auction at his dwelling House … and it is well known he is in very bad Circumstances and his Affairs much embarrassed'. It seemed an appropriate moment to claim damages from the proceeds of the sale of his personal estate. The Company consulted John Morgan of the Inner Temple, and he advised them to give Watts six months' notice to vacate the premises, to hold him on bail for his rent arrears, and to bring a special action against him for damage to the houses.[129] Watts was duly notified to leave by Christmas,[130] but he was declared bankrupt again on 17th December 1775.[131] In spite of his financial troubles and the fact that he parted with the Company on bad terms, Watts' name is one of significance. His daughter Ann Watts would later be the mother of John Constable, thus providing the Joiners with a tentative link to one of the most important English Romantic artists.[132]

After Watts had vacated the premises the Company commissioned a survey to assess the damage. This confirmed that 'the two Houses part of the said Premises are in so ruinous a state that they ought to be taken down & rebuilt'.[133] Renter Warden Humphrey Webb and his draftsman Mr Jupp presented plans for the new buildings to a committee on 21st March. The estimated cost was £930, but this was far higher than the Company's finances would allow. After some debate the committee decided that the Company would receive the best benefit and advantage by letting the ground on a building lease for sixty-one years, rather than rebuilding the houses themselves.[134] However, this decision was overturned at the April Court of Livery and a vote passed to rebuild the two houses. Renter Warden Webb was also appointed as the surveyor of works.[135] Advertisements were placed for builders to submit costed proposals, and four had been received by the May court.[136] After considerable debate Oliver Burton was engaged to undertake the work for £776, using as many of the old bricks and tiles which would be salvaged during demolition as possible.[137] On Audit Day the Clerk was authorised to sell £400 worth of the Company's annuity stock to go towards Burton's payment,[138] although this generated only £355 in cash.[139] The remaining £220 of stock was sold in June for £185 19s 6d,[140] but that still left a deficit. After his tenure as Renter Warden had ended, Thomas Browne offered to lend the Company £200 towards the remainder of Burton's bill, an offer which was gratefully accepted.[141]

The building work had been completed by November, but upon inspection by the Company's surveyor it was discovered that Burton had omitted to build any privies, and had also neglected to lime wash the walls of the cellar, glaze the cellar windows, or clear away the building rubble from the site. The Master, Wardens, and Assistants agreed to sort out these remaining issues themselves, but decided that Burton would be presented with the bill.[142]

There was plenty of interest in leases for the houses. As early as March 1775 Thomas Perkins had proposed to take one of them for either twenty-one or twenty-eight years at an annual rent of £50.[143] Two years later, in March 1777 George Smithwaite of Bush Lane, Canon Street, initially offered to take one house for thirty-one years at £60 per annum, but later attended a Court of Assistants in person and requested both houses for seventy-one years, and this was agreed.[144] Smithwaite did not prove to be an ideal tenant, however, and the Clerk gave him a written warning to pay the arrears of his rent in November 1779 on pain of legal action.[145]

The surviving deed from 1777 provides a very detailed description of what those buildings looked like and what they contained. The two houses were identical in design and contents.

Fore Garret Three Sash Windows Glazed with Crown Glass Lines Weights and Pulleys and Slide Double the Room Skirted

The Back Room Two Sash Windows Glazed and Slide as above and Room Skirted a Trap Door in the Passage to use out on the Roof a Window on the stairs as above

Two pair of stairs

Front Room three Sash Windows Glazed and Slide as above a Closet on one side the Chimney with one Shelf and row of Pins a Portland Stone Chimney Piece with fire stone Hearth and Portland Slab Moulding and the Chimney Piece and a Shelf over Ditto

The Back Room Two Windows Glazed &c as above a Closet with one shelf and Pins Portland Stone Chimney Piece and slab and fire stone Hearth with Mouldings and Shelf & ditto and the Rooms Skirted

One Pair of Stairs three Sash Windows Glazed and Hung as above the Room Wainscotted with Dado with Base and Import Mouldings Inside shutters with Mouldings round the Windows a Marble Chimney Piece and Slab with fire stone Hearth and Covings Moulding Round ditto with a frees and shelf over ditto

Kitchen Two Windows Glazed as above outside Shutters to ditto with Hinges and Bolts to each the Room Wainscotted round about four feet High with square Deal Wainscotting One Closet with three shelves a Dresser with four shelves over Ditto two Drawers and shelf at bottom for Pots &c a Sink Lined with lead Inclosed with Door a stone Chimney Piece and Slab spit racks and shelf over ditto Lead pipe from the street for water Rails and Square Bannisters to each Story of Stairs

Warehouse one side Lined to the Ceiling the other part skirted the front Inclosed with Sashes and pair of sash Doors with outside shutters Iron barr and Pin to Ditto a Lock and Two Bolts to Sash Doors the back front Inclosed with sashes and Door, outside Shutters Iron Barr and Pin two Bolts to the Door Back yard paved with Perbeck Paving a Door going into Fryer Lane and lock to ditto

Cellar one three Light Window Glazed in Lead one Iron Casement a Necessary Inclosed with Deal a Bolt and Turn Buckle to the Door the Cellar paved with Brick

Passage Lined about three feet high Lock two Bolts and fann light to front Door Iron Barrs to the Kirb of Cellar Windows in the Street, the other House the same a stack Lead Pipes to Convey the Water from the Top of House with Wood Trunks to Ditto one back and one forward.[146]

The Removal from Joiners' Hall

The Company's finances were in a very precarious state during the second half of the eighteenth century. A special public Court of Livery was held at Joiners' Hall on Friday 4th October 1799. Master Thomas Tucker informed the attendees that the Court of Assistants had concluded that the Company's finances were 'not adequate to supporting the Hall' and ensuring it remained in good repair. The Company's annual expenditure regularly exceeded their income due to increased costs, and the money they received through apprenticeship bindings and freedoms, as well as fines for various positions within the Company, did not balance out those costs. Consequently, the Assistants had reluctantly decided that the best course of action would be to let the Hall out to a tenant. They had received an offer from Mr Cookson of Thames Street on 13th September, who proposed to take a lease for forty-eight years at an annual rent of £63. The Assistants thought this 'a fair and adequate offer', considering the current state of the building. In order to convince the Livery the Master presented them with a copy of the Company's accounts for the last year, which confirmed 'that the Expenditure in that year considerably exceeded the Income'. After some debate the Livery voted that the Court of Assistants had the authority 'to lett the Companys Hall and Premises to such

Person for such Term of years at such Rent ... as shall appear to them most beneficial for the Company'.[147]

John Cookson was invited to attend a specially convened Court of Assistants on 19th November to discuss the terms of his proposed lease.[148] They agreed that he would receive a lease of the Hall and forecourt, with footway access through the yard. He was given permission to create a doorway through the south wall of the yard if needed. He was not allowed to erect any new buildings without permission from the Company, and they reserved the right to pull down any additions made by him either inside or outside the building if they did not approve. Cookson was also responsible for ensuring that the fire insurance policies were kept up to date, even though they were in the names of the Master, Wardens, and Commonalty of the Company.[149] Although this agreement was reached in November, the lease between Cookson and the Company wasn't created until 28th June 1800. This lease is one of the most significant documents to have survived in the Company's archive because it contains a very detailed description of the Hall at this pivotal moment when it changed hands:

> The Roof over the Great Hall South East Upper Room whip'd at both Ends and covered with plain Tiles Lead Gutters with flashings lead and Ridges a Stack of pipe and Cistern head with Companys Arms on ditto in front
>
> The West North and South external Wall coped with three Inch Portland blocking and Portland blocking course and block cornice to the west front and return
>
> The Court Room and the Staircase and Musick Gallery covered with lead
>
> Upper South East Room two three light Windows Window Bourds and linings with Casements and Iron Saddle bars to each whole Deal Chimney and Closet front door and two Shelves Chair Rail and Skirting all round the Room the width of a Board the floor laid with yellow whole Deal in straight joints (sixteen feet four Inches by fifteen feet) an Inch half two Pannel quarter round and square door hung with side hinges framed grounds rebated Jambs and Ogees round a seven Inch Brass three bolt Lock and Key on the door a Story of whole Deal steps risers and Carriage with plancer Rail and Ballisters from the Upper Room to the Music Gallery
>
> South East Room adjoining Music Gallery two two light Window Frames lead lights and Casements Portland Chimney piece and Hearth back broke floor laid with whole deal dolded and skirted all round (sixteen feet four Inches by fifteen feet) a two pannel Bead flush and square door to ditto and iron rim lock
>
> South West Room adjoining Music Gallery
>
> Music Gallery Wainscotted on the North side whole Deal folding floor (twenty feet three Inches by eight feet eight Inches) a Story of Stairs with whole Deal steps dwarf Wainscotting Rails and Ballusters down to Hall two two light window frames with lead lights and Casements on this Staircase and one in the Gallery with Window Board Lining
>
> Hall a large Oak Window frame on the East side a ditto on the North End with Semicircular head and two Semicircular Frames one at the South End and the other on the West side the whole of the Frames fill'd in with strong Iron work and glass in Church lead Wainscotted round three sides with right Wainscot belection moulded Wainscotting thirteen feet high and large carved Cove Cornice the South End Wainscotted to the top with right Wainscot and a Screen of fluten Corinthian Columns caps and entableteurs fully enriched and Carved figure over ditto at front of Music Gallery two

Doorways with framed Jambs enriched Architraves with circular Entablature and the Companys Arms carved to ditto Floor laid with one and half Inch deal forty eight feet by twenty three feet two right Wainscot Tablenacle Frames fixed on the East side over the Wainscotting with Pediment heads and carved Moldings

Court Room or Parlour Wainscotted with right Wainscot belection moulded Wainscotting to the top all round with base and impost Moldings fluted pilasters Corinthian caps and cornice fully enriched the Ceiling framed with right Wainscot Wainscotting in three compartments handsomely enriched two painted circular Pannels and an oval enriched plaister pattern in Center three Sash Frames with two and an half Inch Wainscot Sashes and glass double hung two two pannel right Wainscot doors hung with hinges two brass cover plate Locks and a large door Spring Chimney filled with Galley Tiles with the Companys Arms on each side and the Hearth laid with Marble Squares Inch half Deal straight joint floor thirty three feet by eighteen feet three Inches

South West small Room adjoining Wainscotted round with right Wainscot Ogee flatt Wainscotting a Sash Frame with two and an half Inch Wainscot Sashes and glass double hung a right wainscott two pannell door Ogee and frame with hinges and Lock to ditto and the floor laid with one and an half Inch deal

Stewards or South East Room Wainscotted to the top with right Wainscot belection Wainscotting and Cornice a painting of the Royal Ann over Chimney in carved and gilt frame a Portlad Slab broke a Sash Frame with two Inch Wainscot Sashes and glass and inside Shutters two one and half Inch six pannel right Wainscot Doors Lock and hinges to ditto Floor laid with whole Deal (sixteen feet by fourteen feet) a two light Window Frame and glass over Pantry door

Pantry a two light Window Frame lead lights Casement and Iron Barrs floor laid with one and quarter inch deal twelve feet by five feet eight Inches

Landing Wainscotted to the top with right Wainscot Wainscotting Cornice and two ditto Doors a two light and a Bulls Eye Window Frame and Lead lights Floor laid with one and half Inch deal (sixteen feet by eight feet seven Inches) two Flights of right Wainscot Stairs Rails Ballusters and Wainscotting both sides to ground floor five feet eight Inches going

Ground Floor Lobby a two Inch six pannel front door ovolo rais'd bead and fluted [illegible – badly faded] door next the Parlour with lock bolts and Chain floor laid with one and half Inch deal

Kitchen a large Portland Mantle [illegible – badly faded] flagstone three Sash Frames with Wainscot Sashes and Glass the greatest part paved with Purbeck paving (thirty seven feet by nineteen feet) a two Inch six pannell door Jambs and Architraves

West Front a Portland frontispiece with Doric Columns pedestals bases Caps [illegible – badly faded] and establture compleat to principal Entrance

The whole of the Yard pav'd with Portland and black Squares Brick Privy covered with Lead and Portland coppice on the Walls a Door and Doorcase Floor and Seat with flapps to ditto

Yard enclosed with a Brick and a half Wall and Portland parall coping camp'd at the North End two three Brick piers with Portland caps and square Bases

An Entrance Gate.[150]

The confirmation that an agreement had been reached with Cookson was relayed to the Livery on 12th December 1799. All future Company meetings would take place in the Guildhall. The Master also pointed out that Cookson's forty-eight-year lease would expire at the same time as the leases for numbers 80 and 81 Thames Street, and that consequently the entire site would then be available to let.

Cookson intended to convert the Hall into a warehouse, converting the high ceilings in the Great Hall into two separate stories to maximise the building's potential storage capacity.[151] Consequently, the Master considered that 'the Furniture and other property of the Company would now be of no further use'. He does not seem to have thought it possible that the Company would want to re-acquire the Hall after Cookson's lease; in his mind their possession of it had ended irrevocably. A motion was carried in the affirmative that 'all the Fixtures and Fitments the Wainscotting and Ornaments of the Hall Court Room and apartments attached thereto and Stair Case be sold by Public Auction'. Immediately after this a second motion passed stating that

> all the other property and Effects of the Company at the Hall except the Silver Cups and Cover the painting over the Fire Place in the Court Room the Colours and Standards the Masters covered Chair the poor Box the Masters Hammer the Beadles Staff and the four Spoons after mentioned vizt the twisted Seal Spoon with a Crest marked Wm Trowbridge in a Wooden Case a round bowl Spoon marked J. E. 1678 a Spoon marked Edward Bailey 1682 &c and Ditto marked Richard Cole 1634/5 be sold by Public Auction.

The items in this list which were excepted from sale are, with the exception of the documentary archive, all that remains in the Company's possession from this period as historical objects. The decision to place the Company's picture in the custody of the Guildhall also dates from this time. The Clerk informed the court that he had received a request from Richard Clark, the Chamberlain of London, concerning the Company's picture. Clark asked whether instead of selling it they would entrust it to him, with a promise that he 'would take the best possible Care of it' and return it to the Company whenever they requested. The court duly voted that 'the said Picture with the Frame and Arms over the same and the green shade which draws before it be delivered to Mr. Chamberlain Clark'.[152] The painting is discussed further in Chapter 7.

Although these motions had all passed on 12th December, they had by no means been unanimous. Five days later another court was held at the Hall at which several liverymen expressed their dissatisfaction with the decision, claiming that 'not only the Livery but the Freemen had an Interest therein' and the sale of almost all of the Company's property should not take place without their consent. Whilst this point was being raised the Beadle brought a letter into court which he had just received and handed it to the Clerk. Several unnamed members of the Company had commenced legal proceedings to halt the sale of the property and their lawyer, Matthew Dowley of Gray's Inn, had written to the Company with a cease-and-desist:

> I take the Liberty to address a Line or two to you by direction of several Members of your Company one of whom [is] a very old and respectable Client of mine concerning the order of the Court of Livery of the [19th] Instant for the Sale by Auction of the Wainscotts Partitions and Fixtures of your Hall the absolute Disposition of which I must on behalf of my Client without meaning

to shew the least disrespect to you or the Livery then met insist they were incompetent to order.

You'll please to observe no Corporation can have any power but what are given them by their Charter of Incorporation therefore no Corporation can alienate any part of their Freehold unless the Charter under which they hold gives them a special power for that purpose. I have searched for your Charter and upon reading it over it appears to me you have a power therein to purchase to a certain extent but none that I can find to alienate. Now the Wainscotts &c of your Hall having been once fixed to the Freehold have become an integral part of it and must always remain so nor can they again be separated for absolute Sale for you can't have any more Right to sell any part of the Freehold than the whole.

I don't give you this Opinion Gents wholly as my own but as the Result of a Consultation I had with one of the City Law Officers before whom a Case on the Subject has been laid nor would you have been troubled with this until I had procured his deliberate Opinion but that my Clients have given me to understand you were to meet this day to give directions for the immediate Sale of them. About which I hope you will now pause.

The receipt of this letter did pause any immediate steps to arrange an auction, but it did not stop the determination that the property should be sold at some point. The Clerk was instructed to seek counsel's opinion 'whether the Court have a Right to proceed to the sale of the said Fixtures ... of the Hall and the Companys personal property' or not.[153] He consulted Henry Dampier of the Middle Temple and the subsequent report was copied into the minute books on 21st January. After a detailed summary of the rights granted to the Master, Wardens, and Court of Assistants through the charter and various ordinances, Dampier addressed the question of the freemen:

Although the Charter mentions the Comonalty yet the Body of the Freemen never meet they being in Number perhaps five or six thousand and very unwieldy and the residences of a great part of them not known. The Livery (who are Elected by the Master Wardens and Court of Assistants) are the greatest Body who meet they consisting of about three hundred and they by practice and Custom are considered as to Represent the Freemen at large and do all the great Business of the Corporation the other Business of the Company is done by the Court of Assistants which consists of the Master Wardens and Court of Assistants.

In Dampier's opinion, therefore, the Court of Livery was deputised to act on behalf of the freemen and their decisions must be taken as valid. After summarising the steps taken by the Company to date regarding Cookson's lease and pointing out that the Hall was held in trust for the Company by feoffees, Dampier gave three opinions. To the question of whether the Assistants had the authority to lease he argued that 'if [the feoffees] execute a Lease to Mr Cookson under the Direction of the Court of Livery ... under the Common Seal of the Company, I do not apprehend that such Lease could be overthrown by any Person in any Court and I have no difficulty in advising the Feoffees and the Court of Livery to grant such a Lease'. He did concede, however, that it was 'a nice Question' whether the power to approve the lease rested with the feoffees or the commonalty of the Company at large, because although the former held the Hall it was the latter who held the power of making by-laws. His opinion concerning the Company's authority to remove and sell the wainscoting and other decorative carved work from the Hall was that the feoffees had the power to do so at the discretion of the Court of Livery. Finally, to the question of selling the Company's personal property Dampier recommended that the Court of Livery should draw up a document authorising the sale and affix the common seal to it. However, he advised holding sales by private contract rather than public auction, 'as the latter is liable to be disturbed by such Members of the Company who do not approve of the Sale coming in and forbidding it'.[154]

In an additional statement to the Company dated nine days after his first Dampier pointed out that there was a precedent for the sale of building materials when numbers 80 and 81 Thames Street were pulled down and rebuilt in the 1770s, and no complaint had been made about this. Notwithstanding his legal opinion Dampier did understand why there was unrest, however. He perceptively noted that this lease was particularly distasteful to some of the Livery because Cookson's conversion of the building into a warehouse 'will in all probability for ever dispossess the Livery of the use of it and render it wholly unfit for the Companys Meetings'.[155] This was not a temporary lease of their Hall; it would be the irrevocable alteration of the building which formed such a vital part of the Company's identity. Almost the entirety of their corporate business was enshrined within those walls, from apprenticeship bindings and court meetings to celebratory dinners. The possession of a livery hall was a mark of prestige, and having to acknowledge that they were financially unable to maintain theirs would have been very difficult for the Joiners.

Dampier was asked to expand his answer about the authority of the Livery to dispose of the personal property. On this he altered his answer and said it was his opinion that 'the Master Wardens and Court of Assistants have always exercised this power', although acknowledged that 'they have not so good a claim to be generally considered the Representative of the Body at large as the Court of Livery'. He stressed the importance of securing the consent of the feoffees as trustees of the physical body of the Hall, and concluded that the 'personal property may be sold by the Master Wardens and Court of Assistants', but warned that 'as they called in the Court of Livery upon the Question I fear that they are bound to follow the Direction of that Court and sell them by Auction' rather than by his recommended private sale.[156] At the next Court of Assistants held on 4th February they acknowledged Dampier's opinion that 'the Consent of the Feoffees was ... necessary to the Sale', but they had run into difficulties because 'several of the Feoffees are not to be found'. Ultimately the decision was taken to just proceed with the lease and the sale anyway because 'it will be impossible to procure the Consent of all the Feoffees thereto'.[157]

Although undertaken under his mastership, Thomas Tucker did not have to witness the Company's removal from the Hall due to his untimely death in late February or early March.[158] His successor was Edward Mann,[159] and he really had inherited a poisoned chalice. At his first court as Master he and the Wardens were authorised to meet with auctioneer Mr Ellis 'in order to prepare and give Directions for the Sale of the moveable property of the Company at the Hall'.[160] Ellis had visited the Hall in person and drawn up an inventory for the sale, which was approved by Master Mann and the wardens on 25th March, and a date was agreed for Thursday 3rd April. Unfortunately no copy of the sale list has survived so it is unclear exactly how much of the Company's property was disposed of, but it presumably represented the vast majority of their holdings.[161]

The Worshipful Company of Joiners and Ceilers met at Joiners' Hall for the final time on Tuesday 1st April 1800. Their meeting must have been a sombre one, everyone aware that it was the end of an era and that their Company's operations would never be the same again. Their business that day was brief. Two apprentices, John Rivers and Charles Thorogood, received the freedom of the Company, and Alexander Leary was admitted to the freedom by redemption. The Clerk was authorised to bind all apprentices at his own home for the time being, and Master Mann received 7s 6d for the poor box. It was confirmed that in future all Company business would take place at the Guildhall, and the Clerk was instructed to advertise this 'in one or more of the daily Newspapers'. Thus ended the Company's residence of Joiners' Hall. The building remained open for the auction of the moveable property on 3rd April, and was afterwards shut up until Cookson could take possession at midsummer.[162]

Although their relocation to the Guildhall had been planned, the transition did not go entirely smoothly. A notice board was placed at the steps on the day of each meeting advertising where members were to go.[163] The Company met there for the first time on 6th May, and the meeting opened with a notice that they had nowhere to deposit their essential documentation, including the charter, books of ordinances, and court minutes, so the Clerk was charged with their safekeeping at his own house. He was instructed to purchase a chest or closet with a strong lock and two keys and keep all papers inside it. One key would be retained by him, and the other given to the Master. He was also awarded an annual salary of £20, partly to compensate for the loss of the Clerk's House which was previously available for the post-holder to inhabit.

The 6th May meeting also 'experienced great interruption' by some apprentices being bound in the same room. It was ordered that in future no bindings would take place on court days, but only on alternate Tuesdays at the Clerk's residence between 9 a.m. and 11 a.m.[164] It is a simple example, but this problem of when and where to bind apprentices demonstrates how the loss of the Hall impacted the Company's business. Whilst the Hall was in their possession there were few to no logistical problems; there were established routines and precedents which could be traced back hundreds of years, and the administration of Company business was relatively straightforward. Now, however, everything had to be re-arranged.

On 10th June the Renter Warden James Griffiths presented the court with the auctioneer's account of the sale. The gross amount received was £237 7s 9d, whereof £27 17s was due to Ellis for commission. There had been additional costs of £2 2s for creating the initial inventory of property in March, and £1 for carefully removing and packing the picture before its delivery to Chamberlain Clark. The net amount delivered to the Company after the sale, therefore, was £203 8s 9d.[165]

The next administrative problem caused by the loss of the Hall was the issue of the Beadle's residence. Like the Clerk, the Beadle had previously resided on-site. He argued at their July court that he had sustained a 'very great loss' through the disposition of the Hall because it had 'reduced his Emoluments to little more than his Salary and one or two small Annual allowances'. The Company had paid him a small amount as compensation for quitting the Hall, but this 'was inadequate to the procuring him a decent apartment to reside in'. After some debate the court agreed to raise his salary from £8 per annum to £50, paid quarterly. The only caveat was that he would now be required to meet all of the costs of the Company's ordinary business, such as issuing summons to meetings, which he had previously been able to claim back as expenses.[166]

When election day arrived on 25th July the Company had difficulty in finding someone willing to serve as Master. Of the four candidates nominated by the

Assistants the first two, John Bond and Robert Hains, both requested to pay the fine of £10 rather than hold the office, and surely the loss of the Hall and resulting difficulties must have been a large factor in this. Leading the newly reduced Company into the future without a permanent base would have seemed like a daunting task, and the man willing to accept the challenge in 1800 was Jarvis Chambers.[167] The challenge facing Chambers and his Wardens was presented to him on Audit Day, when it was revealed that the Company had a balance of only £82 14s 10d, of which £66 was notes of money owed by various members rather than cash in hand.[168] The Renter Warden reported to the October Court of Assistants that 'the Balance of the Company's Monies in his Hands does not exceed £20 and there being several outstanding Debts to a Considerable Amount which the Income of the Company will be barely sufficient to pay'. The immediate response was a decision to cancel the upcoming Lord Mayor's Day dinner, the cost of which regularly fell into three figures.[169] In January 1801 it also became necessary to stop serving any refreshments at court meetings until further notice.[170]

Joiners' Hall as a Warehouse

The meeting of the Court of Assistants on 2nd June 1801 opened with the Clerk reciting a letter he had received from merchant Abraham Mann of Upper Thames Street who had leased the warehouse underneath Joiners' Hall. Mann informed the Company that John Cookson had 'overloaded' the Hall 'with a very large Quantity of Wheat'. The weight was so excessive that some of the timbers in the building had given way, and Mann warned that it was 'probable unless the Weight be lessened, the whole [building] would fall [down]' and crush his own warehouse. Cookson was, of course, a hop merchant, which explains why he needed such vast quantities of wheat. To avoid what would be 'a very serious Inconvenience' he 'thought it proper to give the Clerk Notice' of what Cookson had done, and make it clear that he would not be liable for the cost of repairs if the worst were to happen. Unsurprisingly this letter caused great concern amongst the Company members present that day. The Hall had been out of their hands for just over a year, but the change of usage had already caused significant structural damage. The Master, Wardens, and four Assistants formed themselves into a committee to inspect the Hall as quickly as possible.[171] However, the next reference to repairs at the Hall does not appear in the court minutes until April 1804, when the committee agreed to meet at noon on the 17th 'to view the State of Repair of the Company's late Hall' and other premises in Thames Street.[172] Their report, the first order of business to be discussed at the May court, stated that 80 and 81 Thames Street were 'in very substantial Repair'. Additionally, Cookson had made 'considerable Alterations' to the Hall 'which when finished the Committee were of Opinion would be a great Improvement'.

By April 1805 John Cookson had sub-let Joiners' Hall to packer George Archdale Low.[173] He appears to have been associated with the East India Company and kept a variety of items in his warehouse, including textiles and coffee.[174] Low warned the Company in August 1807 that the part of Joiners' Hall which had formerly been the Beadle's apartment was 'in a very dangerous state'. The adjacent houses in Friars Alley were being demolished, and this had caused extreme instability in the connecting wall.[175] The Renter Warden was duly dispatched to view the building but made no subsequent report to a court. The issue remained a pressing one for Low, however. On 21st December he received a letter requesting him to appoint two independent surveyors or workmen to liaise with Messrs Ezekiel Delight and Thomas Hood to view the faulty wall. They wished to ascertain whether it could be repaired or whether it should just be pulled down and rebuilt. Low forwarded the letter to the Company, but the Clerk James Fisher returned an answer that 'the Company had not any thing to do with [this]'. As far as Fisher was concerned the property was in Low's hands and was his responsibility. The Company disagreed, however, and instructed the Renter Warden to investigate. Although the building was no longer in their possession, the lingering attachment the Company still felt for it was clear.[176]

The Renter Warden secured the services of surveyor Henry Munn of King Street, Snow Hill, to accompany him on his visit to the building. Munn later confirmed to him in writing that 'Time and use' had made part of the south wall of Joiners' Hall 'become a party Wall', even though it had not been built as such. The Warden asked the Beadle to summon an extraordinary Court of Assistants, and took that opportunity to acquaint the assembled members of 'the ruinous state of the Wall'. The question was put before them as to whether they would hire surveyors to liaise with Low about repairs or not, but ultimately it was passed unanimously that they would not 'interfere at all in the Matter'.[177]

At approximately eight o'clock in the morning on Monday 16th December 1811 a fire broke out in Joiners' Hall, and caused considerable destruction before it could be brought under control. This was the final nail in the coffin of the Company's loss. The physical structure of Joiners' Hall which had been such an integral part of their identity and their business was gone. Although it was later replaced with another building of the same name, this morning in 1811 was the moment their Hall was truly lost. News of the fire quickly spread across the country and in the following days was reported in newspapers in Gloucester, Cumberland, Hampshire, Ipswich, and Stamford. All of Low's goods inside his warehouse, valued at approximately £20,000, were lost in the blaze.[178] Tragically, it became apparent within a few days that a life had also been lost.

> Yesterday [Thursday] as some labourers were digging in the ruins of the late fire at Joiners' Hall, Thames-street, they were surprised at finding the mutilated arm of a man; and on further search, they discovered the headless trunk. On enquiry, it proved that a soldier of the Guards, who had been assisting in removing coffee from a roasting office, in which the fire is now said to have commenced, was missing, supposed to have perished owing to the roof having fallen in: and from the tattered fragments of the garments, no doubt exists that the remains were those of that unfortunate man.[179]

An extraordinary meeting of the Court of Assistants was held at the Clerk's house in George Street on 20th December to discuss the fire, although no mention was made of the dead man. As far as the Company was aware the Hall was insured with Hand in Hand for £2,000, and Low had insured the new building with the Globe Fire Office for £1,500. The Company decided that they were entitled to the latter payment as well as the former, and sent a notice to the directors demanding the money.[180]

John Cookson appeared at the January quarter court and requested that 'the Company would rebuild the Premises', even though the fire had taken place during the tenure of his under-tenant. This was unacceptable to the

Company, largely because of the fact that Cookson's lease named him responsible for the maintenance of the Hall. The meeting became somewhat heated when the Assistants questioned Cookson as to his knowledge of the surviving insurance policies. Cookson 'knew nothing about it', and as far as he was concerned the responsibility for insurance rested with Low. The latter had been waiting outside and was now called in. The Chairman asked whether he had made all requested payments to Hand in Hand to ensure that the insurance policy had not lapsed. Low claimed he had, and that he had delivered a copy of the most recent policy to either the Clerk or the Renter Warden. However, both men vehemently denied receiving a copy of that document. Low then changed his story and claimed that he had given it to Cookson instead. When questioned as to why the policy was for only £2,000 Low claimed that when he had taken over the lease from Cookson the insurance had only been for £890 and he had taken the initiative to increase it. The Company dismissed the two men with a parting reprimand that 'they knew not in what Sum the Premises were Insured till after the Fire' because the policy had never been delivered to them. After the two men had left the room a committee of eight men was appointed to seek counsel's opinion as to the Company's rights following the fire.[181] They decided to lay the case before Mr Dampier, the lawyer they had consulted about the sale of the moveable property from the Hall, as well as two of his colleagues.[182]

The precise answer given by Dampier and his colleagues was not recorded, but after discussing it the Court of Assistants agreed 'that it would be most for the Interest of all parties that the Matter in difference respecting the said Fine should be submitted to Arbitration'.[183] A letter was sent to Cookson notifying him of the decision and requesting his presence at the next court meeting to discuss the matter. When the Master asked whether he agreed to arbitrators Cookson expressed his wish for a delay to enable him to consult his own counsel.[184] George Low wrote to the Company on 15th April, and Cookson added a post-script confirming his assent to its contents.

> Gentlemen
>
> As I am not aware that there can be any possible impediment to our arranging between ourselves (without any Reference whatsoever) as every thing that relates to the rebuilding of my Premises called Joiners' Hall I beg leave to submit to you the following propositions.
>
> First. That you immediately begin the re-erecting of the said Premises (with the Monies insured for that purpose in the Hand in Hand Office) the cover the same Scite of Ground and to be built in a firm and substantial manner for the purpose of the Business heretofore carried on in the same and that you be required to lay out no more than to the Extent of the Sum Insured.
>
> Secondly. That the Sum Insured by myself in the Globe Office shall be applied by me to the same purpose and even though it should not prove fully sufficient to the completion of the Premises for the purposes of my Business I engage not to call on your Company to make up any thing that may be deficient.
>
> That to this End a mutual Release of the Monies attached by each party shall be forthwith given and Security on each side if required for the due application of the same.
>
> That no Monies insured in the Names of the Master and Wardens of the Joiners Company be applied to the Rebuilding any part of their Premises but what are actually held under their Lease granted to Mr Cookson.

The Company demanded the entirety of Low's insurance pay-out, which they intended to 'appl[y]' towards rebuilding and reinstating the said Hall or Building'. However, Low refused to give them the money. The Master, Wardens, and Court of Assistants held several more meetings with Cookson and Low in an attempt to reach a resolution.[185] On 19th May a Court of Livery voted to ask the Court of Assistants 'whether any Arrangement can be made with the Undertanants for the purchase of their Interests in the Premises'; in other words, whether the Company could buy Cookson and Low out and regain full possession of the Hall. When this proposal was presented to them the two men begged for a week to consider it. However, at an extraordinary Court of Assistants on 25th May their terms for surrendering the lease would be £6,000; no lower sum would be accepted. This was far outside the Company's capabilities, and described by them as 'so exorbitant' as to be impossible.[186]

Eventually in the summer of 1812 the parties were able to agree 'several mutual and reciprocal Covenants'. Cookson and Low would rebuild the Hall and warehouses before 25th December, to the satisfaction of the Company. The Joiners' Company would contribute £205 18s 6d of the cost of rebuilding, and this sum would cover the warehouse underneath the Hall which was let to John Edkins and not part of the leases granted to Cookson or Low. They would also pay half of any legal fees incurred during the process. Any insurance money received from Hand in Hand would be given to the two men towards the cost of rebuilding, but if the total exceeded the insurance pay-outs Cookson and Low would pay the balance out of their own pockets. As soon as the buildings were finished they would be fairly appraised, valued, and insured. Cookson was still expected to pay the Company the £63 rent he owed for that year, and his previous lease of forty-eight years was confirmed to still stand. Rather than try to settle any future disputes which may arise, the parties agreed that in future they would hire four impartial arbitrators instead: two for the Company, and two for Cookson and Low.

Although the disputes between the Company and the two men must have been incredibly frustrating at the time, the necessity of going into such detail with their eventual agreement to make sure that there was no ambiguity means that the surviving documents are incredibly rich. In particular, there is a surviving schedule of exactly what work was necessary to repair the damage done by the fire.

Warehouse on the Ground Floor under Joiners' Hall now or late in the occupation of John Edkin

Bricklayer – To take down all the damaged brickwork and cart away the Rubbish belonging to the said walls – Rebuild the external wall next Coffee Room the same thickness and in every respect similar to the old wall (leaving No 11 arches to correspond) build the side wall next Friars Alley from Footings to the plate and top of joists in two bricks – Build the partition wall between the staircase and Friars Alley to the same height as other walls in ½ brick thick – To make good the damaged brick work to the old wall next the Aley and all the defects in the other and white the whole of the ceiling of Mr Edkins Warehouse and Friars Alley and washstop and white the sides.

Carpenter – To repair and make good with new of the same description as the old all the joists and sleepers that are destroyed by the fire – To make centers for arches and cut out the deptive Bond Timber and plates and make good with new of the same description in the external wall No 2 Tier of Bond Timber 4 x 2/2 in the other two walls and one wall new on each 7x5 – Refix the present door case and make all good.

Messuage or Building called Joiners' Hall demised to John Cookson

Bricklayer – To clean the Bricks and cart away all the rubbish – To take down all the Brickwork above the one pair floor (except the front walls) and make good the damaged work – To take down the front parapets and rebuild the same and make good the pointing – To rebuild the external Brickwall according to the plan and return the wall next Friars Alley and the Countinghouse walls as shown in the plans and section – Carry the chimney shafts three feet above the roofs – Bed and point all the sash and door frames and parget the flues and chimnies – Rebuild the end wall next Thames Street and put double tile creasing on each side all the walls (except the front) and brick flat on the same – To cut out and parget all the Indents for new walls Flues &c – To cover the roofs with Imperial or Welch slating all to be best perfect – To give the District Surveyor notice and pay his fees.

Mason – To repair all the damaged work as may be ordered take off and refix the front coping and find what new that may be requisite – Rubbed Yorkshire window-sills 8x3 to all the windows – Make good the damaged paving and find new where ordered – To provide one plain Portland slate mantle jaunts slips and shelf complete with rubbed York Hearth for Counting house.

Carpenter – To provide all necessary centering – To cut out all the decayed Timbers and make the same good with new of the same scantlings repair and make good the Floor and Joists over the old Kitchen – Trim for and make a proper ledged Flap hung with 20inch hooks and rides and iron rings complete in each floor – new fir roofs Rafters 6x2 Ridges 7x1/2 Rounded Kirbs 6x4 Pole plate 4x4 Gutter plates 9c6 ¼ inch Gutters and learer – provide 2 cut of wrought iron for Ties Bolts &c as may be ordered – Framed Ties for ceiling Floor 12x6 Fir framed Floors Joists 10x2/2 Trimmers 10x3/2 bridged into Girders Frame Girders in each floor 12x12 properly Trussed according to section including all the oak Iron work &c Frames story posts 10x10 with pak caps 5 feet long 11x8 and oak cases 10x4 to each post spiked to the Girders – Fix wall plates under each floor and returns 7x5 two Tier of Bond Timber in each story and six wood bricks in each opening – Fix lintiles one foot at each end longer than the opening and the whole width of soffik and six inches thick to each – Make one Trap door with linings hung complete and two bolts and a dormed door case cheeks and lop where shewn in plan make new two inch deal ovols sashes fixed in a solid fix frame 6x4 and oak sill 6x4 for all the front and side windows next Thames Street to admit air by Tin casements and put an ¼ inch window Board and Bearers to each.

The Counting House to have inch linings and ogee bead round the same new ½ inch yellow wrought ploughed and tongued floors – Two flights of ½ inch deal stairs and strong carriage ½ inch framed string-framed handrails and newels complete – new doors to warehouse to be ½ inch proper ledged hung with 2 feet hooks &c and a wood bar and iron staple to each – the new sashes and frames to be 2 inch deal ovols double hung complete with a sash fastening and window board as before to each – the water to be conveyed from the Roof by 5 inch Rain Trunks cap'd and shoed the water from the middle Gutter, to be conveyed by brick troughs on bearers the roofs to be boarded with ¾ inch rough yellow deal for slates and proper slates silletts where necessary – Fix an ½ inch 4 panel 3 reed flush on both sides door hung with 3/2 inch Bulls and a 7 inch iron an Lock ¼ inch double rebated Jambs Grounds and ogee bead on each side to Countinghouse line all round the same with ¼ inch dwarf wainscotting three feet high capt and skirted dormer windows & sides quartered and boarded the tops inch rough boarding and beams two inch deal ovols sashes double hung complete with iron Pullies common lines and iron weights and a sash fastening to each ¼ inch nosing two inches wide and find filletts for Plaisterers where necessary – Fix framed purlins and stutts 6x4 fix all the iron Ties Rings &c – Fix ceiling Joists over Counting house 4x2/4 Braces 4x3 – No foot quarter or rafter to be more than twelve inches apart – All the Timber to be Memel or the best Swedish free from sap or doat All the Deals to be perfectly dry and free from sap or shakes – the Firders over Mr Edkings warehouse are to be the same scantling but not Trussed – Half story posts 12x6 with oak Caps and bases as before – The whole of floors and stairs are to be of hearty yellow deal (not American) all wrought fair – the stair case as spacious as before – The Ceilings to be done with strong heart fir lath and two coats of good course lime and Hair – and set after.

Plumber – Line the Gutters and Troughs with cast lead 8lbs to the foot superficial to turn up on each side seven inches and lay a flashing of null'd lead into the joints of the Buckwork and two inches over the sides of the Gutter – To provide 3/2 inch rain water pipes and socket pipes cover the Dormer Tops with 5lb nill'd lead line the Ridges with 5lb nill'd lead eighteen inches wide.

Glazier – Glaze all the sashes with second Newcastle Glass the whole to be left clean and perfect.

Painter – paint all the outside wood and iron work and all the inside wood work usually painted from Oils any common colour.

Plaisterer – lath plaister set and white the ceiling of the Counting House and render set and colour the walls wash stop and line white twice over all the walls in both stories and the old kitchen Lath plaister and coat the Rafters over the two pair floor the Cheeks and Tops of Downers the same.[187]

In late 1813 the Master and Wardens discussed the possibility of purchasing the Hall's unredeemed land tax. In 1798 the Land Tax Redemption Office was created to enable the purchase of land at a cost of fifteen years' worth of tax payments, or the purchase of 3 per cent government consuls. The Master and Wardens estimated that their yearly land tax payments for the Hall, yard, and all appurtenances amounted to £31 4s 6d.[188] In February 1814 it was resolved 'that the redemption of the Companys Land Tax be paid for by one Instalment by a Transfer of a sufficiency of the Companys funded property for that purpose',[189] but the order was rescinded at the March court and postponed indefinitely.[190]

George Archdale Low died at his home in Vauxhall on 3rd August 1816 'after a painful illness, which he bore with exemplary fortitude and resignation, to the inexpressible loss of his family and friends'.[191] No reference to his death was entered into the Company's minutes over the next year. The lease of the Hall was inherited by his son, who declared his intention to surrender it in 1821. An advertisement for its sale was subsequently placed in *The Times*:

Joiners' Hall, Upper Thames-street – By Mr. ELLIS, THIS DAY, October 11, at 12, the late property of Mr. George Archdale Low deceased,

THAT capital Building known as Joiners' Hall, most desirably situate in Upper Thames-street, between London and Southwark bridges, consisting of a most substantially built extensive stack of warehouses, with four floors, capable of carrying any weight, excellent counting houses, and handsome dwelling room, with paved yard and good cellar: now in the occupation of

Mr. G. Low. These premises are held by lease for an unexpired term of 27 years, at the low rent of 105l. per annum. Printed particulars and tickets for viewing may be had, 14 days prior to the sale, of Messrs. Alliston and Hundleby, solicitors, Freeman's-court, Cornhill; of Mr. Ellis, 35 Fenchurch-street; and at Garraway's.[192]

Similar advertisements, some referring to Low and some omitting his name, appeared in numerous editions of London newspapers until April 1823. Messrs Williams & Co showed initial interest in purchasing the lease, but this ultimately came to nothing.[193] In the interim period the Company contracted to purchase a piece of land outside the Clerk's House for £210,[194] and a further piece of land in 1830 for £160.[195]

The new tenant of Joiners' Hall was packer Thomas Gandell, who owned and ran the firm Thomas Gandell & Co. He was later elected as a Common Councilman of Dowgate Ward in December 1837,[196] and held that position until December 1856.[197] He moved into the Clerk's House with his wife and children in 1824 and ran his business from the Hall. He was asked to make some repairs to the brickwork, glass, and paving at Joiners' Hall in 1831, as well as to paint the window frames.[198] His initial lease was until Lady Day 1848 at an annual rent of £103, but in 1847 he approached the Company to request an extension as a yearly tenant, rather than another fixed term. He even offered to increase his own rent, suggesting £143 per annum from henceforth.[199] Before agreeing to an extension the Company appointed a committee to inspect the premises, and their report was presented at the October monthly court. They confirmed that the Hall and Clerk's House were 'in a very satisfactory state of repair', and were 'well adapted' for Gandell's business as a packer. The main complaint Gandell had about the Hall was that the basement often flooded during spring tides due to the faulty common sewer running under the building. The report noted that due to this the cellars could barely be used, and were 'to a certain extent useless'. It was agreed that the Master and Wardens should petition the Commissioners of Sewers reporting 'the serious evil' the Hall faced by flooding, and requesting their assistance with repairs. Gandell also lamented 'a nuisance from the dissolute characters who occasionally occupy the four small Houses at the back in Friars Alley', but the Company could do nothing about that. He also mentioned the inconvenience of not being able to get a cart or carriage to fit inside the Hall's courtyard, which made loading and unloading his goods more difficult.

The report also contained an update about the two houses in Thames Street, which had been renumbered as numbers 81 and 82 and had been leased to Mr Smithwaite. No. 81 had been sub-let to salter Mr Harris, who was using the lower portion of the house as his business premises. The upstairs rooms were being let out to weekly tenants. No. 82 was occupied by Mr Waldron, 'who is by trade a dealer in Willow twigs for basket makers'. He resided in the upper part of the house, and ran his business from the lower rooms. However, both houses were 'much dilapidated, so much so as to require the aid of a professional surveyor to take a correct account of the defects'. Company liveryman Henry Phillips was suggested for this task. The only remaining piece of let property was a piece of land on the south-west side of Friars Alley, which was being used by Mr Miles as a builder's store. He had built a wood shed on it, but this was reported to be 'of a very unsubstantial character as well as subject to danger from Fire'.[200] Ultimately it was decided that this land should be annexed to Gandell's lease of the Hall, and the wood shed removed altogether.[201]

Gandell appeared again before the December 1847 court to re-negotiate the terms of his lease. He rescinded his previous request to hold the Hall on a yearly basis, and instead offered either three, six, or eight years at £150 per annum, depending on what would suit the Company best. They counter-offered by stating that Henry Phillips, their surveyor, had valued the premises at £170 per annum and they did not want to take less. Mr Gandell asked for time to consider this, and promised to return an answer in writing before the next court.[202] Ultimately he held firm to his original offer of £150, and after some debate the Company agreed.[203] Gandell later secured a lease for the vaults at a further £40 per annum.[204] Mr Miles also proposed to take a lease of both 81 and 82 Thames Street, and the current leaseholder Mr Smithwaite was given three months' notice.[205] However, Phillips recommended that the two houses should be repaired and then advertised to be let, rather than accepting Miles' offer, and the Company decided to follow his advice.[206] By August they had received an offer from sitting tenant Mr Waldron who requested permission to continue residing at No. 82 for eight years at a rent of £50 per year, along with a promise to undertake any necessary repairs and keep the building insured against fire. They also received an offer from Mr Andrews of Dowgate Hill to take No. 81 for £35 per year,[207] with an additional £5 per year for the vaults underneath it.[208]

The Company received a letter in March 1853 from the tenant of No. 80 Thames Street, adjacent to their houses. The tenant informed them that the party wall dividing the two was in need of repair or replacement, and gave notice that he intended to appoint a surveyor. The Company in turn appointed Francis Pouget to act as their own surveyor and report the state of the wall at the next court.[209] Pouget confirmed that the wall 'is in a very defective state and condition', and 'will necessarily be condemned'.[210] However, when the Master and Wardens inspected the wall themselves on 10th May they found that it 'did not look to be so much out of repair as they anticipated', but after requesting Pouget to show them the damage they were satisfied that it was in 'a very bad state' after all. They also confirmed that the wall appeared to be on their property, rather than that of No. 80.[211]

Mr Waldron declared his intention to sub-let No. 82 in February 1854 to corn merchant Thomas Styles. The Company made enquiries into the latter's character and were assured that he was 'a very respectable person'.[212] After taking possession Styles requested to 'open a communication with Friars Alley'.[213] An extraordinary court was called to discuss the matter, and after consulting the plans they already held of the property it was discovered that their tenancy of the land currently used as their courtyard was close to expiration. Rather than renew the lease they decided 'to obtain possession by purchase', and the Clerk was instructed to apply to the solicitor of landowner Baroness Von Landt to ascertain whether such a transaction would be considered.[214] However, the response was that 'she would not part with it unless at a very great benefit to herself', so ultimately no further action was taken.[215]

Both numbers 81 and 82 were available to be let in 1856, and advertisements were placed in the press. After receiving tenders for each individual house the Company began to negotiate with Gandell to see whether he would be willing to take both houses in addition to the Hall. His initial offer of £300 per annum for twenty-one years was rejected, with the Company asking for £500 per annum. Gandell countered with an offer of £400,[216] but the Company eventually accepted an offer of £450 per annum from wharfinger John Kearns, who was based at Red Lion Wharf in Upper Thames Street. This proved to be a sensible move on their part, because after Kearns and his partner Charles Messenger Major viewed the site they declared themselves well satisfied and increased their offer to £500 for a lease of twenty-eight or thirty years.[217] A lease was signed on 2nd February 1858 granting Kearns and Major the use of all the buildings on the Joiners' Hall site until 24th June 1887.[218] The lease for the courtyard was separate and was due to expire in September 1906.[219]

By the 1870s Mr Kearns had exited from the partnership and Major entered into business with Hamilton Field, creating the firm of Messrs Major and Field. In 1874 they approached the Company asking for permission to rebuild parts of the property which were 'not in accordance with the requirements of the present day'. They proposed to 'pull down the Clerks house and the Joiners' Hall and to erect on the site thereof Warehouses and buildings of good materials and to the satisfaction of the Surveyor to the Company'.[220] They anticipated that the Company would be unwilling to finance such a project, and so requested an additional forty years to their lease at £150 per annum in order to recoup the money expended on such a project. The Company was not immediately unwilling, but asked whether the gentlemen would be willing to take a lease of thirty-two-and-a-half years instead, which would provide the same expiration date as their extant lease for the courtyard.[221] Major and Field counter-offered by asking for the lease of the courtyard to be extended by seven-and-a-half years so all contracts would expire at the same time, rather than taking a shorter lease for the Hall.[222] After hiring a surveyor to assess the premises the Company was recommended to ask their tenants for rent of £650 per annum, which was an increase of £100 on the £150 extra they had offered.[223] Eventually their demand of an even higher £700 per annum was accepted, and legal opinion later declared that 'the rental is a low one'.[224]

However, by April 1882 Messrs Major and Field had failed to commence work to rebuild the deficient parts of the site, and the Company sought legal advice as to whether this constituted a breach of contract because the original terms stated that building work must be completed by 2nd March 1882. They even considered taking the action to the High Court. However, a lawyer cautioned them that the High Court would likely be 'unwilling' to come to a verdict in this case and would merely suggest settling for damages.[225] When they were notified of potential legal action Major and Field replied through their solicitors to state that proposed building work by the Commission of Sewers to widen Upper Thames Street, which had been 'in contemplation some 3 or 4 years' but had so far come to nothing, had caused them to postpone their own project. 'It would be a waste of money to rebuild a part of the premises without knowing exactly what the Commissioners of Sewers propose', and they asked for an extended period of time. This was rejected by the Company, who stated that the Commission's plans would in no way affect the Joiners' Hall site, and asked for 'substantial and satisfactory' compensation. A surveyor declared that if the Hall and Clerk's House had been replaced as intended the rental value of the site would have been at least £1,000 per year, a significant increase on the £700 paid by Major and Field. Instead, both buildings were described as dilapidated, and the Company was advised to sue for £1,000 for the breach of the lease. However, they ultimately decided to reduce the penalty to £500,[226] but Major and Field countered with an offer of £200 and all building costs to be paid by them. The Joiners insisted on 4th May that their demand for £500 in compensation was final, and if it wasn't received within fourteen days legal proceedings would be instigated.[227] This threat was successful and their lawyer responded that 'without admitting that the Company has sustained any damages or that there is any liability on the part of my Client … I am instructed on his behalf to offer to pay the sum of £500 as compensation'. Mr Major later declared this to be 'for the sake of peace and quiet'.[228]

There was continued tension in the weeks that followed concerning Major and Field reaching an agreement with the Commission of Sewers, and providing building plans acceptable to the Company. They proposed 'to erect three new buildings upon the old foundations leaving the present basement as it is', and Major and Field finally began to pull the old buildings down in September 1882.[229] The architect was Henry Stock, and the work was carried out by Messrs Rider and Sons of 181 Union Street, Bow.[230] Ultimately the Queen's Bench Division of the High Court of Justice was asked to arbitrate in the case, and all documentation was submitted there. The brick portion of Joiners' Hall had been rebuilt by the end of February 1883.[231] As a token of reconciliation Major and Field enquired whether it would be acceptable 'to affix the Joiners Company's Coat of Arms' to the front of the building, and the Company was pleased to allow this.[232] By the spring of 1885 all of the construction work had been completed and was reported to have been 'carried out satisfactorily in every way'.[233] It was re-insured for £11,000 in October,[234] and Major and Field and their successors remained the tenants of the Joiners' Hall site until the Second World War.

Chapter 4

The Company's Members

Apprentices

The traditional method of training successive generations of craftsmen was through apprenticeship. Generally speaking boys were bound as apprentices at the age of fourteen or fifteen for seven years. Girls could also be bound as apprentices, although it was rarer; a discussion of female apprentices in the Joiners' Company can be found in Chapter 5.

A great deal of the apprentice's experience during their training depended on the conduct and character of the master. The apprentice would live in their household, sometimes alone but often with another apprentice, and they would learn every aspect of the master's trade. The Company's 1572 ordinances stipulated that with the exception of their own children, no freeman could teach the trade of joinery to another person unless they were bound as an apprentice. Anyone caught breaking this rule would face a £20 fine or four days' imprisonment. Potential apprentices would live with their master for one month, and if the master decided to take on the student he had to present them to the Master and Wardens of the Company before that month was over. After three months the master paid the Company a fee of 2s 6d.

Apprentices were bound at Joiners' Hall before the Clerk, and sometimes before the entire Court of Assistants. The Clerk was responsible for making all apprenticeship indentures, and a fee of 12d would be paid by the master. A further 6d would be paid to the Clerk to register the indenture. Each apprentice was required to swear an oath of allegiance to their master promising to be diligent in their studies and sober in their habits. The oath specified in 1572, which is still sworn by apprentices today, was not particularly specific to their training, but made it clear that they were answerable to the Company:

> You shalbee true to our soveigne Lady the Queene and to hir heires and successors Kings and Queenes of England, yee shalbee obedient from tyme to tyme in all matters lawfull to the Master and Wardens of your Company for the tyme being and ready to come to their lawfull sumons, except you have a lawfull excuse or else you shall pay such penaltyes as you shall forfeite by your so disobeying according to the lawfull Ordinances of your ffellowship Which Ordinances and every of them to your power you shall observe and keep, all the lawfull Councell of the said ffellowship as at any tyme of Assembly shalbee

lawfull in communicacon amongst your ffellowship at your comon Hall yee shall keep secret and not disclose the same to any person of the same ffellowship nor to any others and especially to any such person whom the said matter doth concerne and touch So help you God and the holy contents of that Booke.

To avoid apprentices attempting to run away from their masters, it was warned that if anybody 'will intice or councell receive or take away any manner of person or persons being a Servant to one of the same ffellowship from their Master or Masters service before the end of the term of their service bee expired' they would be fined 40s.[1] By the eighteenth century apprentices were given a further set of instructions about how to conduct themselves during their training:

You shall constantly and devoutly on your Knees, every Day, serve God Morning and Evening, and make Conscience in the due Hearing of the Word preached, and endeavour the right Practice thereof in your Life and Conversation: You shall do diligent and faithful Service to your Master, for the Time of your Apprenticeship, and deal truly in what you shall be trusted: You shall often read over the Covenants of your Indenture, and see and endeavour your self to perform the same to the Utmost of your Power: You shall avoid all Evil Company, and all Occasions which may tend or draw you to the same; and make speedy Return when you shall be sent on your Master or Mistress's Errand: You shall avoid Idleness, and be ever imploy'd either for God's Service, or in your Master's Business: You shall be of fair, gentle, and lowly Speech and Behaviour to all Men, and especially to your Governors; and according to your Carriage, expect the Reward for Good or Ill from God and your Friends.[2]

The question of when and how often apprentice bindings should take place at the Hall bedevilled the Company for years. In August 1682 bindings were limited to 'evry Tuesday in the weeke from the hours of Tenn a Clock in the morning untill twelve at noone'.[3] In September 1684 the Clerk was authorised to bind apprentices at any time,[4] but in February 1687 it was agreed that 'no apprentice shall be bound upon any Court day after ten of the Clock'.[5] In November 1693 this was modified to ban bindings between nine and eleven, and no freedoms were to take place after noon. A notice to this effect was hung in the Hall.[6] In February 1716 bindings were only to take place on court days and every second Tuesday.[7]

The number of apprentices allowed to each master differed depending on their status in the Company. The Master could have four apprentices at once, Wardens could have three, and all other members of the Company were limited to two. Denizens working within the city and liberties were also restricted to just two.[8] If all parties agreed, bound apprentices could be turned over during their training to another person; this could be someone else within the Joiners' Company, or a freeman from a different Company.

The research undertaken by Laurie A. Lindey has shown that 'the Joiners bound 12,495 apprentices over the seventy-year period, 1650–1720'. She noted that this was significantly higher than four other companies during the same period: the Clothworkers bound 12,200 apprentices, the Drapers 6,462, the Mercers 2,347, and the Tallow Chandlers 3,787. It is notable that the Drapers and Mercers are two of the twelve great companies, but even the combination of their apprentice bindings don't come close to those of the Joiners during this period.[9] However, Lindey's research has also proven that 'fewer than half of all apprentices became freemen', and indeed between 1650 and 1720 only 41 per cent of apprentices became free by servitude.[10]

On 22nd August 1632 citizen and joiner Thomas Bradshew swore an affidavit before Christopher Walker, clerk of the commissioners for new buildings, concerning his former business premises, and this document contains tantalising details of what his experience had been as an apprentice. Bradshew was born in 1596, and had been apprenticed to joiner Francis Feltnes of Fullwood's Rents in Holborn for seven years beginning around 1611. During his apprenticeship Feltnes 'then had certaine shopps towards the streetes in ffulwoods rents'. The shops were on land held by Sir George Fullwood, and Feltnes paid him £8 per year in rent, in quarterly instalments. Bradshew lived in Feltnes' household and 'did serve his whole time in the shoppe'. Bradshew '& foure other apprentices did lodge together in two sevrall beds in the said shoppe ... and made fire daily in the said shoppe'.[11] Feltnes' house abutted the church of St Andrew, Holborn, and he was buried there in 1625.[12] The fact that Feltnes apparently had five apprentices at one time raises questions, because that is directly opposed to the Company's ordinances.

Not all apprentices had a positive experience during the years of their training. In 1737 George Hind petitioned the Westminster Quarter Sessions complaining of the treatment he had received from his master. On 3rd December 1735 he had been bound to joiner William Meadow for seven years, but on the same day he was turned over to John Lowrey of Westminster, also a joiner. However, Hind claimed that shortly afterwards Lowrey 'began to abridge your petitioner of comon sustenance both as to eating and drinking'. Lowrey was badly in debt, and a month before Hind submitted his petition he had absconded, shut up his shop, and disposed of his household goods. Hind was 'destitute of a master' and would 'have lain in the streets' but fortunately was relieved by an acquaintance of his father. Hind asked for his apprenticeship to be cancelled, and that Lowrey return the £20 premium he had paid for the education he had not received.[13]

By the middle of the nineteenth century, although apprenticeship was still an option, it had largely become a formality. An investigation in 1877 into the finances of the Livery Companies contained a critical statement about the Company's use of apprentices in recent years:

> The binding of an apprentice in former days implied that some working joiner undertook to teach some youth his business during seven years. Under the present management of the company it is not necessary for either master or apprentice to be a joiner, and the object of the apprenticeship is purely for the advantage of that method of entering the company. Thus a clergyman living in Essex could have as apprentice a boy living in Yorkshire, who never saw his master from one year's end to another, and at the end of seven years, the apprentice would be admissible as a skilled joiner, even though neither apprentice nor master had the smallest conception of the art of joinery![14]

Investment in the Trades Training School had largely replaced the Company's apprenticeships by the early twentieth century, but bindings did still occasionally take place. Contrary to the accusation made in 1877 the bindings did appear to be genuine. For example, Jack Stratford was bound to Samuel Henry Hallett in January 1924,[15] and Leslie Odell to the same master in 1932.[16] Although apprenticeship remains one route of entry into the Company today, the observation from 1877 is still largely accurate. Apprenticeships are now theoretical positions, rather than a period of training providing any education in the art of joinery.

Freemen

The Beadle was responsible for keeping track of when apprentices had completed their training so they could be summoned to attend the next monthly court to receive their freedom.[17] In 1703 Beadle John Rogers was reprimanded for 'the small number of Apprentices that has been summoned ... to the greate damage of this Company'. From then on the Beadle was required to provide a list of apprentices due for freedom to each monthly court, delivering one copy to the Master and one to the Clerk. This would ensure that nobody was overlooked.[18]

The oath to be taken by each freeman of the Company was copied into their 1572 ordinances:

> You shall swear that you shalbee good and true to our sovereigne Lady the Queene that now is and to hir heires and successors Kings and Queenes of England, the Queenes peace you shall keep to your powers and to the Master and Wardens of the Company of Joyners and of Ceelers or Carvers yee shalbee obedient and to their Successors and that none of your servants sett up no house nor shop of the said Craft of Joyners and of Ceelers or Carvers according to the Act of Parliamt made in the xiiiith and xvth yeare of our soveigne Lord King Henry the Eighth Also yee shall not make any Congregacon nor consent to any misdoers against the Queenes peace but that yee give knowledge thereof to some of the Queenes Officers for the tyme being Also the lawfull Councell of this house yee shall well and truly keep, and that yee shall not mainteine nor sett on worke no other mans servant untill that yee know that hee bee honestly departed from his Master in paien of Tenne shillings Also yee shalbee obedient to all sumons assigned by the Master and Wardens for the tyme being in paine of forfeiting for the first Offence six pence for the second Twelve pence for the Third Two shillings and for the next and every like after Six shillings and eight pence without a lawfull Excuse, the same to bee forfeited to the Master Wardens & Comunalty and to bee paid to the Master and Wardens for the tyme being to bee imployed to the use aforesaid All theis Articles yee shall well and truly keep to your power So helpe you God and the holy contents of that booke.[19]

After receiving the freedom each former apprentice had to serve two years as a journeyman joiner. He was required to live and work in the household of 'an approved Workman of the said Company', and a refusal to do so would result in a fine of £3 6s 8d. Journeymen were also banned from working with anyone who wasn't also free of the Company, so they could not immediately enter into business with a freeman from a different trade.[20]

Any freeman who wished to set themselves up with a shop, hire a servant, or bind an apprentice to work with them first had to present the Company with a proof piece. This had to be 'some handsome peece of worke' made with his own hands to demonstrate 'whither hee bee a good and sufficient Workman or no'. Anyone who flouted this rule and set themselves up in business anyway would be fined 26s 8d per month and have his shop windows boarded up until his proof piece was ready.[21]

Having the freedom of the Company was a status symbol in the early modern period. Evidence from surviving wills demonstrates that some joiners used it as a method of describing themselves. The majority described themselves as simply joiners, but others specifically referred to the freedom. John Chibnale described himself as a 'freeman of the feloweshippe of Joyners of this honorable Citie of

London' in 1592.[22] John Mounslowe stated he was 'free of the Companie of Joyners of London' in 1602, and he also noted that the Company owed him £6 14s 11d in an unpaid bill for work he had carried out during his life.[23] In 1603 William Clerke similarly described himself as 'free of the Companie of the Joyners in London'.[24]

A person could also be admitted to the freedom of the Joiners' Company by patrimony if their father was already a member of the Company. Admittance was not automatic, however. The consent of two citizens of London, who could be joiners but often practised other trades, was necessary to confirm that the individual was sufficiently skilled in their particular craft to deserve the freedom. By the 1920s the fine paid for admission by patrimony was £20.[25] It was proposed in 1956 that liverymen with no sons should be allowed to present their grandsons for admission by patrimony, but this caused 'divergent opinions' amongst the Court of Assistants.[26]

A third way to secure the freedom of the Company was by purchase or redemption; that is, admittance after appearing before the Lord Mayor at the Guildhall and paying a fine. This route traditionally enabled those with no background whatsoever in joinery or woodworking to nevertheless secure the freedom of the Company. One example of this is John Wilkes, who will be discussed in greater detail in Chapter 8. Wilkes was awarded the freedom by redemption on 10th March 1768. On the same day he requested admittance to the Livery and paid the £20 fine.[27] His appointment to the Company was directly related to his upcoming intended election as a Member of Parliament representing the City, a condition of which role was presence in a livery company.

The Lord Mayor wrote to the Company on 3rd February 1725 asking for the total number of freemen and liverymen as of 1699 and 1724. In 1699 there had been 1,724 freemen journeymen, and this had risen to 2,925 by 1724. Similarly, there had been 1,375 freemen householders but the figure now stood at 2,146.[28] However, by the nineteenth century the rule that any practising joiner within the limits of the City had to be a member of the Company was no longer being enforced, and consequently membership had dropped dramatically. By 1884 it was estimated that there were only 100 freemen left.[29]

Inigo Jones

In August 1887 the Company received an enquiry from the Genealogical and Historical Society of Great Britain, who were conducting some research into a family tree. They were curious to know whether the Company held any information about 'the celebrated Architect Inigo Jones who was a Freeman of the Joiners Company & born about the year 1572'.[30] This appears to be the only surviving reference to Jones in the Company's archive, and tragically there are no documents relating to his admission as a freeman or any other information about his activities with the Company because these were lost during the fires of 1666 or 1694. Biographies of Jones cite tradition stating that he had been apprenticed to a joiner in St Paul's Churchyard,[31] so subsequent admission to the Company seems extremely likely.

Stewards

The 1572 ordinances stipulated that the Master, Wardens, and Assistants should elect 'Two Three or ffower honest and meete persons' annually at the feast of St Michael the Archangel, which falls on 29th September. These stewards would be responsible for providing the Company's dinner on the evening of Lord Mayor's Day in November. The Company would provide 2s for each Master and Warden, and 1s for each liveryman, but the remainder of the costs would have to be borne entirely by the stewards. Anyone who refused to hold the office was required to pay a fine of £2,[32] and by the 1680s this had risen to £5.[33]

The process of choosing stewards was one of the least enjoyable aspects of the Company's yearly activities because it was a deeply unpopular job and nobody wanted to do it. Each September or October a committee of Assistants was appointed to summon members of the Company who were not liverymen and who had not held any office before. One meeting was rarely sufficient, and by the early 1720s it was sometimes necessary to hold up to a dozen before the necessary two to four required men willing to hold the post could be found. The vast majority chose instead to fine, which was beneficial for the Company's finances but did pose a problem for the organisation of the Lord Mayor's Day dinner. It was far cheaper to pay the fine than to hold the office and pay for the dinner, and everyone knew this. By 1724 the difficulty of electing stewards had reached such a crisis that the topic formed one of the additional ordinances passed by the Company.

> ... since the makeing the aforesaid ordinances the said Company being so increased as aforesaid and the ffine to be paid by such persons who are elected and chose to be stewards of the said Company and neglect or refuse to hold such Office of Steward are so small and unequal to the Charge of holding and performing such Office that very few or none for severall years last past have held and performed the same to the very great Burthen and dishonour of the said Company who are (upon takeing such small ffines) obliged to serve the place of such stewards and be att the Expence of treating the said Company on the day the Lord Mayor is sworn att Westminr which has for many years last past been considerably larger than itt was att the time of makeing such ordinances and ffines.

To counteract this the number of stewards to be elected each year was increased to six, and the fine of forfeiting the position was raised from £5 to £7.[34] This does not seem to have been an effective deterrent, however. In 1740 new by-laws were approved by the Company which addressed further administrative difficulties, and one of the ongoing problems was the election of stewards. The number was reduced back down to four, and anyone who agreed to hold the post would be expected to pay 'one equal fourth part of such Entertainment in such manner as hath heretofore been accustomed', or pay an increased fine of £8. Anyone who neglected the summons would forfeit £10.[35] These by-laws did not make the process of selecting stewards any easier, unfortunately. On 6th December 1763 the Clerk was instructed to seek the opinion of Serjeant-at-Law John Burland 'whether the Company are thereby Enabled to Recover by Action at Law the Penalty of £10'; in other words, whether they were entitled to sue their own freemen if they refused to pay the steward's fine.[36]

In 1813 the search for stewards was halted altogether after several meetings of the committee. It appeared that 'there are no freemen of the Company within the knowledge of the Court capable of taking on them the Office of Steward except such as are not Freemen of above two years standing'. Consequently it was voted that they would just waive the year's election altogether.[37] By 1837 the steward's fine had been raised to £13,[38] but that was still not a suitable incentive for liverymen to hold the position, and in 1841 it was agreed 'that the custom of summoning Freemen to take upon themselves the Office of Steward to the Lord Mayor day Dinner be discontinued'.[39] The post remained in the Company, but became largely theoretical. The fine remained fixed at £13, but it was just an administrative fee to be paid rather than a post with responsibilities.[40] The task of organising the dinner fell to the Master, Wardens, and Clerk instead.[41]

Liverymen

The most numerous body within the Company was its liverymen. They were full members of the Company with voting rights, as well as the ability to attend Courts of Livery and other official engagements and entertainments through the year. They were also eligible for election to higher office within the Company, including the roles of Warden and Master. Incoming liverymen would pay a fine and then be clothed in a livery gown during a court meeting. Liverymen wore woollen gowns lined with sheepskin, known as budge.[42] The 1572 ordinances were very specific concerning the process of election to the role:

> Item it is ordeined that the Master with the Wardens of the said Mistery or ffaculty or the more part of them for the tyme being and vi Assistants or the most part of the said Twelve Assistants for the tyme being as they shall need and find cause shall and may from tyme to tyme call choose and admitt into the Livery such and so many of the ffreemen of the same ffellowship as they shall thinke good meete and able thereto And that every person that shalbee so called or chosen by the aforesaid Master Wardens and Assistants or the most part of them into the Livery imediatly upon knowledge to him or them given thereof by the said Master and Wardens or any of them or by their Officer called the Beadle shall forfeite to the Master Wardens and Comunalty of the said Art or Mistery for the tyme being six shillings & eight pence of good and lawfull mony of England to bee paid to the Master and Wardens of the same Company for the tyme being to bee imployed to the use of the said Company or ffellowship And which of them soever so called or chosen that shall refuse to bee of the said Livery they shall forfeite and pay to the use of the said Company as aforesaid ffifty three shillings and fower pence of like lawfull mony of England or lesse at the discreacon of the said Master or Wardens or the more part of them for the tyme being and of the said vi Assistants or the most part of the Twelve Assistants for the tyme being.[43]

The 1834 report into the duties of officers stated that

> Liverymen shall be elected by the Court of Assistants from Freemen at any Court of Assistants having served or fined for the Office of Steward.
>
> The fine upon Admission shall be £17.
>
> They shall attend the Court of Assistants upon their Admission signing a Declaration assenting to the Company's By Laws and upon Election shall clothe themselves in the Company's Livery. Shall attend upon Summons of the Master Wardens and Court of Assistants all Public Courts of Livery.
>
> Shall attend at Guildhall upon the Election of Lord Mayor and Sheriffs of London and upon all Elections of Members of Parliament and Common Hall upon non attendance at Company's Meetings they shall be subject to a Fine in the discretion of the Court not exceeding 2s 6d.[44]

By 1708 the livery had become 'very numerous and chargeable', so it was decided that only six men would be invited to take the livery each year.[45] Six years later the livery fine was raised from £5 to £8 to compensate for the ever-increasing cost of feeding and entertaining everybody on quarter court and feast days.[46] There were 286 liverymen in 1724, a rise from 190 in 1699,[47] and the Joiners had the largest body of liverymen of any of the London companies by 1768.[48] Three years later Master Dr Wilson wrote to the Company actively encouraging freemen to take the livery:

> You are increasing Every Day in the No of your Livery, and I would recommend it to you to endeavour by your Persuasions, to prevail upon more of the <u>Freemen</u> to take up their <u>Livery</u>, as soon as possible; - that you may have more <u>Power</u> and <u>Weight</u> in all future Elections, and by your <u>Unanimity</u> and <u>Integrity</u>, shew the Enemies of our Constitution, that the <u>Livery</u> of the <u>Joiners Company</u> can neither be <u>intimidated</u>, <u>bribed</u>, or <u>corrupted</u>.[49]

When taking the livery the standard practice was for the individual to pay a promissory note to the Renter Warden, rather than paying the fine in cash straight away. Although this meant that the Company's finances were theoretically strong, it meant that they had very little cash in hand. This had grown to such a problem by 1780 that although theoretically the Company had a balance of £214, less than £5 of that was in cash; the remainder was all notes. Consequently, promissory notes were banned altogether and livery fines had to be paid immediately in an attempt to improve cash flow.[50]

During the nineteenth century the Company's membership dropped dramatically. In 1827 it was a struggle to find enough liverymen eligible to serve the offices of Renter and Upper Warden, so it was decided that in future anyone who decided to fine for Renter Warden rather than serve would be immediately nominated to the role of Upper Warden, and anyone fining for Upper Warden would be immediately nominated as Master. This would avoid liverymen slipping through the net and neglecting to serve high office at all.[51] By 1884 it was estimated that there were only ninety liverymen left,[52] and this had dropped to seventy-six by 1887.[53] By the 1920s the fee for taking the livery had been raised to £100,[54] although in 1922 this was reduced to £80. Perhaps the size of this fine, combined with the turbulence the country had experienced during the First World War, contributed to the further depletion of the livery. Only one man had become a liveryman since 1914, and the Company recognised the necessity of 'altering the fees & fines now charged for admittance'.[55] It was agreed that 'the sons of Liverymen having served their Apprenticeship to their Father shall be admitted to the Livery' with a fee of only £20.[56] The fine for livery by purchase remained fixed at £80.[57] The very few people obtaining the freedom of the Company via apprenticeship and then desiring to take the livery paid £45.[58]

Following the devastation of the Second World War, which had robbed the Company of Joiners' Hall and the income it brought in, a pressing matter was the necessity of encouraging new men to join the Company. The easiest way to do this appeared to be a reduction in fines. The livery by purchase fine was halved to £40, and the apprenticeship or servitude fine was reduced to just £15.[59] This was a successful endeavour, and the following months saw a drastic increase in the number of men taking the livery by purchase. During the 1970s, when the Company once again found themselves with higher expenditure than income, the fines for livery by servitude, including fining for steward, were raised from £102 to £112, and the fine for sons of liverymen was raised from £85 to £185.[60] Anyone seeking to become a liveryman by purchase would be required to pay £335.[61]

Apart from attendance at events and voting matters, liverymen were also entitled to claim for financial relief from the Company during times of hardship. Harkening back to their origins as a guild, the wellbeing of the members was a matter of supreme importance. Liverymen who later found themselves facing financial instability, such as through illness or age, were eligible to apply to become pensioners of the Company. They would receive a small sum of money every quarter to contribute towards their maintenance. In 1733 the maximum number of livery pensioners was set at twenty.[62] In the late seventeenth century quarterly pension payments were between 3s and 5s, depending on the individual's status within the Company and their current circumstances. By the mid-1700s this had increased to 10s per quarter.

Examples of liverymen admitted as pensioners are Joseph Cooke, 'by reason of his greate lameness by the palsie' in 1707,[63] and John Gunnell who found himself in 'extreem poverty not having a Bed to lye on' in 1749.[64] William Austin, described in the minutes as an 'Old & respected Liveryman', requested the Company's assistance in August 1849. Through 'a series of misfortunes' he had been reduced 'from comfort and affluence, to a state of destitution'. He had a large family of eleven children, two of whom suffered from epileptic fits, and the recent death of his wife 'has been a climax to his afflictions'. He begged the Company 'to afford him some assistance in his emergency', and after some discussion it was agreed that he should receive £3.[65]

Other liverymen found themselves in slightly more drastic circumstances. Temporary imprisonment for debt was a challenge faced by numerous liverymen in the seventeenth and eighteenth centuries, and they often petitioned the Company for a small financial grant for either themselves or their families. The Renter Warden gave the wife of Joseph Okey 10s in 1685 after he had been imprisoned in the King's Bench prison.[66] When John Knights was a prisoner in Ludgate the Company gave him 20s specifically 'to buy him some tools to set him on worke for his livelyhood', an action which would enable him to earn money, repay his debt, and regain his freedom.[67]

Cooks

The cost of feeding the Company was one of the most pressing demands on their purse, and the court minutes reflect a constant desire to engage the services of as good a cook as possible at a very low price. In October 1662 John Jackson the elder retired as the Company's cook, a position he had held since at least 1637,[68] and requested that his son John Jackson the younger should be appointed in his place, and this was agreed at a quarter court.[69] Edward Jones was dismissed as cook in July 1688,[70] and received his 40s salary two months later.[71] His replacement was William Russell. However, Jones' association with the Company did not end. On Westminster search days in 1689, 1690, and 1693 the searchers dined in the evening at 'Mr Jones the Cooke in Shooelane'.[72]

The Company may well have regretted the decision to let Jones go, because the court minute records imply ongoing dissatisfaction with Russell. At an extraordinary meeting held at the Dolphin Tavern on 21st October 1689 'to treate with the Cooke' the stewards for Lord Mayor's Day agreed to provide Russell with £26 10s, but on condition that he rather than they would be responsible for supplying knives, spoons, pewter, table linen, fire in the kitchen, and a butler. The stewards would be responsible for beer, ale, wine, cups, glasses, tobacco and pipes, candles, and fire above stairs.[73]

The following year a motion passed at a court that the Audit Day feast was becoming too expensive, and from henceforth costs would be limited to the same as a monthly court, which in the year 1689 to 1690 were averaging to between £2 and £3.[74] Conscious of the spending freeze, Russell attempted to ingratiate himself with the Company by offering to 'finde musicke for the Company on the 29th of this instant October at his owne charges'.[75] Three years later, on 22nd September 1692, Russell's bills for Audit Day dinner amounting to £10 10s were considered at a private court. The Court 'much blamed him for that he had not done their dinner according to the Agreement made with him'. He had also lost three large dishes, for which they deducted 18s from the amount owed to him, and added another fine of 20s which 'he owes for the use of the hall for Mr Ffincher', suggesting that he had provided access to Joiners' Hall for a friend who had then failed to pay for it.[76]

Although there does not appear to be a reference to it in the court minutes, shortly after this discussion Russell ceased to work as the Company's cook and the position was returned to former employee Edward Jones. However, in the summer of 1695 Jones left London 'to dwell in the Country' and the Company was once again without a cook. The contest for the position was between two men, John Hackett and Mr Moore. A vote took place at the monthly court meeting on 6th August, and Hackett was duly elected.[77] Hackett executed his position to the Company's satisfaction, but he was not irreplaceable. On 7th December 1697 they discussed a petition from Edward Kidder, who had been apprenticed to joiner John Hooper and received his freedom in 1691,[78] but who was a cook by trade. He had been elected as a steward for Lord Mayor's Day and was one of the rare few who actually undertook the job rather than fining. He had served as the cook to provide the dinner for the Livery and Assistants that evening and they had been pleased with him. Bolstered by this positive attitude Kidder 'made it his humble request to this Court that ... they would be pleased to admitt him Cooke to this Company in the place and roome of the said Hackett'. His request was accepted, and Hackett was dismissed from his position.[79] He had performed his duties well as cook and had not displeased them, but he was not a member of the Company and Kidder was. Ironically Kidder's request to oust Hackett provided the precedent for his own removal. On 9th September 1701 the Court of Assistants voted that notwithstanding Kidder's appointment it would be more convenient for them to 'have liberty to make use of any cooke', and from henceforth they could engage the services of 'any one whome they thought fitting for the good of the Company'.[80]

The next reference to a named cook came in 1706 when Mr Evans was engaged 'to provide dinner for my Lord Maiors day' at a cost of £27. He was allowed the use of the Company's damask and diaper table cloths and the pewter, on condition that he carefully clean all of them after use and would be fined if anything was found to be 'wanting wronged melted or defaced' after the meal.[81] In 1715 a motion passed that no cooks could be hired to provide Audit Day dinner without the consent of a committee.[82] During the 1720s the cost of dinners continued to be a pressing issue. The bill of £5 11s 7d the November 1725 monthly court was considered excessive, and a limit of £3 for food and another 30s for wine was set for successive courts.[83]

By the late 1730s Timothy Farish had been elected as the permanent cook.[84] Like his permanent predecessor Edward Kidder, Farish had been apprenticed to a joiner. He was bound to Thomas Bowles in 1708 and was awarded the freedom of the Company on 4th February 1717.[85] On the very day he obtained his freedom he took an apprentice of his own, John Lyall, and on 5th May 1719 Richard Hope was also bound to him.[86] However, Farish's ambition would see him rise to a far higher rank than just the Company's cook. On 25th July 1740 he was elected as Upper Warden, and he joined the Court of Assistants on 3rd September 1743.[87] Also in 1743 he was listed as a gentleman subscriber who had provided financial assistance for the publication of Leonard Twells' sermons.[88] He was elected as Master of the Company on 25th July 1758, also retaining the responsibilities of cook, but sadly he died in the spring of 1759 whilst in office.[89] At the time of his death he had been living in the parish of St Dunstan in the West, and his will reveals that he was a wealthy man. He described himself as a joiner, but he had also branched out into the moneylending business. The Honourable Benjamin Bathurst Esq. and his wife Lady Elizabeth were indebted to him for £1,000, and he was owed £413 14s 5d by Stephen Theodore Jansen Esq., whom he had rescued from bankruptcy. Farish transferred both of these debts to his brother-in-law John Prosser, a coffeeman, and his friend Richard Baynes and instructed them to use the interest to pay various legacies to his family members.[90]

Farish's long tenure as cook was followed by a quick succession of temporary cooks. Mr Chadwick took the post after Farish's death in 1759,[91] but by the summer of 1764 Mr Vanhagen held the post,[92] and Mr Angel had the role by 1771.[93] When Mr Angel submitted his bills to the Company in November of that year they were concerned about the cost and referred them to a committee to decide how much should be paid. Their subsequent itemised list reveals that Angel's bill was higher than those previously submitted by Mr Vanhagen because he had introduced turtle soup to the menu for Lord Mayor's Day dinner. In addition to the other charges for the dinner, amounting to over £38, the soup and dressing it cost a further £9 10s. Ultimately Past Master John Wilkes offered to pay 'for the Turtle' which reduced the Company's portion of the Bill, but the Company then decided to pay Wilkes £13 6d 'as a Compliment' so they ended up not saving any money.[94] Samuel Cannadine had taken over as cook by the end of 1779.[95] He reported in 1796 that 'the Kitchen Copper and Stoves are quite worn out' and the Court of Assistants agreed that replacements could be purchased.[96] However, the removal from Joiners' Hall in 1800 meant that the post of Company cook became redundant. All future entertainments were held at various taverns and hotels, and the landlord of those institutions was responsible for supplying refreshments and dinners.

Beadles

The Beadle was one of the most important of the Company's officers, and his tenure lasted far longer than the year-long service of a Master or Warden. After election the incumbent usually held the position for life, unless he was dismissed for misconduct. Traditionally the Beadle lived on-site at Joiners' Hall, although not gratis; in the 1680s he was required to pay the Company a rent of £3 per annum, payable quarterly.[97] The 1572 ordinances had a separate oath of office to be sworn by each incoming Beadle, which also contained details of the most important duties associated with the role:

> I A: B: doe sweare to bee faithfull and true to our soveigne Lady the Queene hir heires and successors Kings and Queenes of this Realme and to bee dilligent and attendant upon the Master and Wardens of this Company and truly and faithfully to give Sumons and Warning to every member of this Company for their appearances or for any other just cause when and as often as by the said Master and Wardens I shalbee comanded or appointed And being demaunded true and faithfull report of such my doings I shall make, and all other things apperteining to myne Office I shall duly doe and execute to the best of my power So helpe me God and the contents of this Booke.[98]

The 1834 report into the duties of officers stated that

> The Beadle shall be elected Annually by the Livery from their own Body. He shall summon the Court of Assistants Monthly or otherwise.
> Shall find sureties for £100.
> Shall take the Oath prescribed for that Office.
> Shall deliver all Notices to Court & Livery.
> Shall attend all Courts whether of the Assistants or Livery and Committees.
> Shall attend at Guildhall on all Common Halls.
> Shall wait upon the Master Wardens and Court of Assistants and Clerk when required.
> Shall prepare Room for Meetings.
> Shall receive Instructions for Bindings freedoms and Livery and give notice to Clerk.
> Shall collect and Account for Quarterage to the Renter Warden.
> Shall convey the Books from and to the Clerks house as directed.
> Shall receive no gratuitous fee from parties transacting Business with the Company under pain of suspension and shall generally execute all other orders at the discretion of the Court of Assistants and Clerk.
> Shall attend all Meetings and Banquets with his Gown and Staff.
> Shall Receive a Salary of £30 together with the fees hitherto received.[99]

The appearance of the Beadle was a matter of importance for the Company due to the visibility of his position. He had a staff or mace of office, a silver badge, and a gown which he was expected to wear at all times whilst undertaking Company business. Even in the early twentieth century the Beadle had to bring his mace of office with him to all meetings.[100] A tricorne hat was purchased for the Beadle at the end of 1927, an item somewhat out of fashion by that time and presumably a ceremonial rather than practical object.[101]

The primary function of the Beadle was to summon members of the Livery to attend Court meetings, either as a matter of form for monthly and quarterly courts and search days, for the purposes of binding or making free apprentices, or to answer charges of misconduct or rudeness. He also had the power to nominate people to the unpopular position of steward for the Lord Mayor's Day celebrations,[102] and collect quarterage money due from the members of the Company.[103] He was responsible for ensuring the safety and maintenance of all goods inside the Hall. In September 1692 a motion was passed for the Beadle to 'sweepe the yard and banqueting house' on Tuesday and Saturday mornings, 'and oftner if required'.[104] In practice the Beadle's wife often undertook the cleaning responsibilities and would sometimes be compensated for such work. An entry in the Renter Wardens' accounts dated 13th August 1782 noted £1 1s paid to 'the Beadle's Wife for Extra trouble &c in thoroughly cleaning the wainscot of the Hall Court Room &c'.[105]

On 5th October 1736 the Court of Assistants appointed a committee to investigate precisely what the ordinary and extraordinary business of the Beadle was, and to ascertain how much he should be paid for each of his duties. Their subsequent report was entered into the court minute books in full on 7th December 1736, and it is an extremely useful document for understanding the role of the Beadle within the Company. The standard duties included sending out summons, attendance at every meeting, keeping the Hall and yard clean and in good repair, and ensuring the safety of the Company's moveable goods inside the Hall. In addition to these, the committee listed the expenses he could claim at different times of the year:[106]

The ffour Publick ffeasts when the Ladys dine at the Hall			
	£	s	d
Cleaning Linnen	0	9	0
Scowring pewter &c p Quarter	0	10	0
Pipes and Candles	0	3	0
Table beer	0	5	0
Cheese and Butter	0	2	6
Two door Keepers	0	5	0
Mops Brooms Soap Sand and ffullers Earth p Quarter	0	9	0
Coals and ffaggotts	0	6	6
Cleaning knives and fforks and pewter	4	0	
Basket of ffine salt p quarter	0	1	6
Pens Ink and Paper ditto	0	1	6
Postidge of Letters for the day	0	1	0
Candles at Night p Quarter	0	8	0
Coffee and Tea &c p Quarter	1	5	0
A Comon Court			
Cleaning Linnen	0	3	6
Ditto pewter knives and fforks	0	2	6
Pipes and Candles		2	0
Table Beer	0	2	6
Coals and ffaggotts	0	2	6
Cheese and Butter	0	1	0
Postidge of Letters	0	1	0

Midsomer day Michaelmas day & St James's day			
Cleaning Linnen	0	6	0
Ditto pewter knives and fforks	0	3	0
Pipes and Candles	0	2	0
Table Beer	0	5	0
Cheese	0	1	6
Postidge	0	2	0
Lord Mayors Day			
Assistant to Sumon the Livery	0	4	0
Coals and ffaggotts	0	6	0
Tenders at the Stand	0	2	0
Postidge	0	2	0
Cords to Tye the Standard	0	1	6
Match to light pipes	0	1	6
And to be allowed for any Extraordinarys not in the above	0	17	0
Bill			
Cleaning Branches half yearly	0	15	0
Cleaning and Mending Gowns p Annum	1	1	0
Ffor Making out the Walcks on every search	0	3	6
The other Articles the same on that day as a Comon Court	0	15	0
Train bands	0	7	0

The earliest surviving reference to the Company's Beadles came in 1655 when Simon Spelsworth took over as acting Beadle after the death of William Long. His appointment was initially temporary until Michaelmas but it was later made permanent.[107] The implication in the Renter Wardens' account books is that Spelsworth initially did his job well. In the year 1658 to 1659, in addition to his wages of £8, he and his wife were awarded a bonus of £2, and the Company paid £2 14s 2d for a new cloak for him.[108] On 5th May 1662 an order was made in court that there should be an under Beadle appointed with a salary of £2 per annum.[109] This appears to have only been a temporary measure due to an investigation being carried out into the actions of Spelsworth, who presumably had been relieved of his duties whilst such investigation took place. Unfortunately the court minutes do not record exactly what Spelsworth was accused of, but on 1st December 1662 he was reprimanded in court for 'sundry misdemenors' and instructed to leave his post by Christmas 1663 '& noe more afterward meddle with the Companyes busines'.[110]

On 2nd February 1663 he was 'admonished to leave the Companyes service and his dwelling in the hall at Lady day next' unless he could demonstrate enough 'good demeaner' in the meantime to convince the court to allow him to stay.[111] When his salary of £8 was due at the April quarter court meeting the Renter Warden paid it to his wife, rather than to him, 'towards hir keeping of howse', but at the October quarter court Spelsworth's duties and salary were removed altogether and both given to Thomas Specks.[112] Finally, on 7th November 1663, the order from the previous December was repeated; Spelsworth was dismissed from his post 'for sundry misdemeanors' and instructed to 'leave the same and his dwelling in the hall, & noe longer to continue therein'.[113] In spite of Spelsworth's behaviour the Company remained willing to assist other members of his family. On 7th December 1663 the court ordered Specks to provide £4 of his salary to Mrs Spelsworth,[114] and on 15th September 1664 they provided her with an annual pension of £2.[115] The couple's son Samuel, who had gained the freedom of the Company by patrimony in 1657,[116] was also not penalised for his father's behaviour; he was admitted as a liveryman in 1667[117] and joined the Court of Assistants in 1682.[118]

The Beadle after Thomas Specks was Richard Rogers, who became an instrumental figure in the efforts to rebuild Joiners' Hall after the Great Fire of London. However, by the 1680s due to his 'greate age' he was not able to perform his duties single-handedly. In April 1684 he requested 'that his sonn John Rogers might be admitted his assistant', which was agreed in Court, and John, who had received the freedom by patrimony on 14th October 1679,[119] was granted a salary of £2 per annum.[120] When Richard Rogers died in the winter of 1692 John was the obvious successor to the post. An extraordinary court meeting was held 'on purpose in order to an eleccon of a Beadle for this Company'. John presented his petition to succeed his father, but William Pemberton also presented a petition for the post. The merits of both candidates were 'maturely & seriously debated' by the Master, Wardens, and Assistants, and when a vote was held John was elected as Beadle. He was sworn in on the same day.

Rather unusually, after the election John revealed that Mary Smith, the widow of an unnamed former member of the Company, had 'for many years lived with the former Beadle in the hall'. The capacity in which she did so is unclear; she may have been acting as a housekeeper, but equally it is possible that she and Richard Rogers were in some kind of relationship. John and the Assistants all agreed that for the duration of her life Mary would be granted 'meate drink washing and lodging at his apartment belonging to the hall', or a pension of £4 per annum paid quarterly if she 'hath a mind to goe away'. The Company even agreed to pay her medical expenses if she fell ill, saving John harmless from any such costs. There was clearly at the very least a sense of obligation to do the right thing by Mary, and perhaps even a degree of affection towards her by the Company.[121] When John reported to a monthly court in March 1701 that Mary 'lies now very week on his hands' and stated that he was 'not able to maintaine her without releife from the Company' they authorised a further £4 per annum towards her care.[122]

John's wife Betty was actively involved in the day-to-day maintenance of the Hall, and she received a salary in her own right. The first recorded payment to her was a gratuity of £2 on 7th February 1693 'towards the charge of her lying in being very bigg with childe and near her time'.[123] In 1705 Betty was paid 10s 'for cleaning the Companyes gownes', a duty which then became solely hers.[124] From the following year onwards her salary was raised to £1,[125] and she performed that task until 1722.[126] Following the death of her husband Betty was given the quarter's salary of £2 due to him at Christmas 1722, and then a pension of 10s per month.[127] The Company also appears to have been paying the Rogers' 6s per quarter towards the education of their son John, but this was stopped in April 1693.[128]

Complaint was made against Beadle Rogers at a monthly court on 10th January 1694, however, stating that 'he will not observe the order of the Clerk touching the affairs and business of the said Company'. No reason was offered for his supposed recalcitrance, but the court ordered him to obey the Clerk in future.[129] In 1712 Master James Peerman rocked the boat by suggesting that the posts of Clerk and Beadle should also be put up for nomination each year in the same manner as the posts of Master and Wardens. This suggestion was opposed by several Assistants who stated that 'it has not been the practice nor any power or custome since the Companies Incorporacon unless death or mismanagement'. They demanded to know whether the Master had any knowledge of malpractice from either the Clerk or the Beadle and he admitted that he had not, but nevertheless insisted on holding an election between two men for each role. Unsurprisingly the incumbents of both roles were re-elected, so John Rogers retained his position as Beadle.[130] On election day 1713 the Renter Warden suggested that the posts be once again up for nomination, and again this motion 'was opposed by severall members' because the only precedent for such a move was the election of 1712. The Master asked whether anyone could charge the Clerk or Beadle with crime or neglect, which nobody could, but nevertheless the Assistants voted that the posts should be put in nomination.[131] From this time forward both roles were included in the annual election day and were no longer guaranteed lifelong positions.

On 7th August 1722 the Beadle borrowed £5 from the Company, and suggested that the money could be repaid out of his salary when it became due.[132] It seems likely that this money was borrowed to pay for his medical expenses, because he died before the year was out. The Court of Assistants was informed of his death on 8th January 1723, and a list of people nominated to replace him was entered into the minute book. A public election was held on 24th January, and before the vote it was ordered that whoever was elected should provide a bond of £100 as security 'for his faithfull discharge of his Office', and it was reiterated that the elected Beadle had to be able to read or write. Ultimately cabinetmaker John Boyce was elected to the office, and he was sworn in on 5th February.[133]

The Boyces were destined to be a prominent family. John's son William would later become a famous composer and he lived at Joiners' Hall during the entire period of his father's tenure as Beadle. In 1743 he advertised the sale of his 'Soloman a Serenade' for a cost of one guinea in two instalments. He stated that 'Subscriptions are taken in by the Author, at Joiners-Hall, Thames-Street'.[134] Three years later, armed with 'his Majesty's Royal Licence and Protection' and the title of 'Composer to his Majesty', Boyce advertised the sale of twelve sonatas for violins, again giving his business premises as Joiners' Hall.[135] He was appointed as Master of the King's Music in 1755, a position which saw him composing and directing court music, and he was an organist at the Chapel Royal by 1758.[136] A William Boyce was elected as Master of the Company in 1755, and it seems very likely that it was the same person.[137] Indeed, when the Company hosted a day out for the ladies at Windsor Castle in 1999, it was arranged for some of Boyce's music to be played during Evensong.[138]

The death of Beadle John Boyce was reported to the Company at their court meeting on 5th December 1752, and a date for the election of his successor was set for 11th January at 2 p.m.[139] The Company took advantage of the temporary vacancy of the post to re-adjust the allowances given to the Beadle for various tasks.

For each of the two publick Feasts when the Ladies Dine at the Hall			
	£	s	d
Cleaning Linnen	0	10	0
Cleaning Knives Forks & Pewter	0	5	0
Pipes Wax Candles and Tobacco	0	8	0
Candles at Night	0	10	0
Table Beer (The Beadle providing three firkings of Twelve Shillings Beer)	0	9	0
Cheese and Butter	0	2	6
Coffee Tea &c for the Ladies	1	10	0
Two Door Keepers	0	5	0
Mops Brooms Soap Sand and Fullers Earth p Quarter	0	9	0
A Baskett of Fine Salt p Quarter	0	1	6
Pens Ink and Paper p Quarter	0	1	6
Postage of Letters for the Day	0	1	0
For a Common Court			
Cleaning Linnen	0	3	6
Cleaning Knives Forks & Pewter	0	2	6
Pipes Candles and Tobacco	0	5	0
Table Beer (to be Twelve Shillings Beer)	0	3	0
Cheese and Butter	0	1	6
Postage of Letters	0	1	0
For Midsummer day, Michaelmas day and Saint James's Day			
Cleaning Linnen	0	6	0
Cleaning Pewter Knives and Forks	0	4	0
Pipes Candles and Tobacco	0	5	0
Table Beer (to be Twelve Shillings Beer)	0	7	6
Cheese	0	2	0
Postage	0	3	0
For Lord Mayors Day			
Assistants to Summon the Livery	0	4	0
Tenders at the stand	0	2	0
Postage	0	2	0
Cords to tye the standards	0	1	6

He was also to be allowed 10s each time he scoured the Company's pewter, as long as he did so four times per year. A further £1 10s compensated him for caring for the Company's gowns, with 3s 6d for creating an itinerary for each search day.[140]

Seven liverymen nominated themselves for the position of Beadle on 11th January 1753, which made the election process more complex. A motion was made that the choice should be 'made by holding up of hands & Reducing the Candidates one by one untill reduced to the two who shoud have the most hands'. When the choice was reduced to two the final vote would take place by ballot. The two men left standing were John King and John Boyce, the latter the son of the deceased Beadle and the brother of composer William. Ultimately John Boyce was elected as his father's successor by 103 votes to just 32 for King.[141] The news of his election was reported in the newspapers:

> Thursday came on at Joiners-Hall, the Election of a Beadle of the said Company, in the room of John Boyce, deceased, when John Boyce, Son of the deceased, was chose by a very great Majority.[142]

He was sworn in at the next Court of Assistants on 6th February.[143] His brother William Boyce provided a bond of security for him.[144] He was not destined to hold the post for long, however. On the same day that William was elected Master of the Company for the year 1755–6, John's death was reported to the court. Four men presented themselves as potential successors: Robert Groome, Henry Branson, Joseph Cranfield, and Jeremiah Bromley. When a show of hands for each candidate took place Branson and Bromley were eliminated with the least support, leaving the choice between Groome and Cranfield. After a vote between the two the Master declared that Groome had won, but a poll was demanded by two of Cranfield's supporters. The result was incredibly close, and was even reported in the press.[145]

> Last Friday Night about Eight o'Clock the Poll ended at Joiners' Hall in Thames-street, for the Election of a Beadle of that Company, in the Room of Mr. Boyce, deceased; and, after a smart Struggle, the Numbers stood thus;
> For Mr. Cranfield   108
> Mr. Groome   104
> Whereupon Mr. Cranfield was declared duly elected.[146]

Cranfield's tenure was destined to be even shorter than Boyce's, and he died in May in the parish of All Hallows the Great.[147] The Court of Assistants was informed of his death on 7th June, and a public court was convened three days later to elect a replacement.[148] Hopeful nominee Robert Groome placed a front-page advertisement in *The Public Advertiser* on Friday 10th June 1757 addressed to his 'good Friends, the worthy Master, Wardens, Court of Assistants, and Livery, of the worshipful Company of Joiners':

> Give me Leave thus publicly to put you in Mind, your Election for the Choice of a Beadle in the room of Mr. Joseph Cranfield, deceased, will be this Day at Two in the Afternoon, at your Hall, at which Place I humbly intreat you to attend, and then am of Opinion shall have but little Reason to doubt my Election; but if too many of my good Friends, under the Idea of my having gone thro' all my Offices, and have the most equitable Right, think I am very safe, so do not

attend, the Consequence must be as it was the last Election, when I lost it by four. I hope all my Friends will excuse this Freedom, for I am very sensible a great many of you were not a little concern'd at the Loss of my Election last Time, as well as myself. I am your sincere, obedient, humble Servant,

ROBERT GROOME.

I beg the Favour of all my Acquaintance, who see any of my Friends of the Livery this Morning to refresh their Memories, for Fear of Non-Attendance.[149]

In addition to Groome, five other members of the Company put themselves forward as potential candidates: John Edwards, Robert Rutty, Richard Vanhagen, Jeremiah Bromley, and John Rea. The two most popular candidates were Groome and Edwards, and it quickly became a contest between the two. When the final show of hands was called the majority voted for Groome, and he finally secured the position he had coveted for years.[150] The *London Evening Post* noted that 'last Friday Mr. Robert Groome was elected Beadle of the Joiners Company, in the room of Mr. Cranfield, deceased'.[151]

Groome continued as Beadle until his death in April 1770.[152] Samuel Sherwin was elected as his successor,[153] and served until his own death in July 1779.[154] At the election the choice was between John Edwards and Thomas Touse.[155] The former was elected and served only a short time until his death in early 1782. Intriguingly, Edwards' death gives a glimpse of a woman playing an active role in the Company's administration. It was necessary to summon a public Court of Livery to elect his successor, and the Clerk was instructed to give a list of liverymen and summons 'to Mrs Hopkins the lately deceased Beadle's Daughter to be by her or such Person as she shall appoint delivered to the Livery'.[156]

At the extraordinary court held on 6th February to elect Edwards' successor four candidates presented themselves: Edward Burton, Thomas Harris, Thomas Touse, and Caesar Augustus West. The show of hands appeared to be in favour of Touse, but a poll was demanded by supporters of Burton. This poll opened immediately and lasted until 5.30 p.m., at which point the court adjourned until eleven o'clock the following day.[157] The poll closed finally at three o'clock on the 7th, and after counting it was clear that Touse had secured the position.[158] After a succession of short-lived Beadles, Touse's appointment marked a period of stability. He was also destined to serve through one of the most controversial periods of the Company's history: the decision to dispose of Joiners' Hall. As Beadle he would have been responsible for overseeing the sale of the Company's property, as well as for carefully preserving and transporting items retained by the Company to the Guildhall.

Thomas Touse died on 3rd February 1806, and George Biggs was elected as his successor.[159] Biggs was given a formal reprimand by the Master in May 1812 after he had failed to summon the Livery to attend an extraordinary court, and also failed to attend himself. He was warned that 'in Case he was in future guilty of similar neglects or any other Breach of his Duty he would be reported by the Court [of Assistants] to the Livery who in all probability would dismiss him from his place of Beadle'.[160] However, he redeemed himself through the 'considerable Extra Trouble' he was obliged to undertake following a fire at Joiners' Hall, for which he was given a reward of £10 in 1815.[161] Biggs remained in his post until his death in 1819,[162] following which Robert Low was elected to the office.[163] Low's tenure was a short one, however, with his own death occurring in early 1823.[164] The two nominees for the post were Richard Lambun and Robert Needham, but Lambun won the vote twenty-one to eighteen.[165] He served until his death in early 1834, and his wife was admitted as one of the Company's pensioners, along with a gratuity of £5 to assist with funeral costs.[166]

Ahead of the election of a replacement Beadle far more information about potential candidates was written in the court minutes than usual. The first named candidate was fifty-four-year-old John Tyler, who had three children and had been a liveryman for twenty-three years. The second was Thomas Bennett, also aged fifty-four. He had been a liveryman for twenty-nine years and had no children. The third candidate was John Waghorn, aged fifty-nine, who had been a liveryman for thirty years and also had no children. John Glynn Biss was the final candidate, at the age of sixty-six. He had been a liveryman for twenty-three years and had four children. It is clear from these descriptions that they were keen to elect someone who already had a deep understanding of the Company's functions and aims. After 'a full inquiry into the qualifications of each Candidate and after taking into consideration their several ages standings of character and habits' the candidates were narrowed down to Tyler and Bennett.[167] However, Biss still presented himself as a candidate when the election was held on 4th March. Tyler won the vote by a landslide, securing thirty-nine votes to three for Biss and two for Bennett.[168]

Tyler served as Beadle until his death on 12th July 1854 following 'an Apopleptic Fit of 64 hours duration without any return of consciousness', as his daughter informed the Court of Assistants. Edward Hanson was elected as his successor on St James' Day.[169] In June 1877 he tendered his resignation due to failing health,[170] but by St James' Day he declared himself sufficiently recovered to be able to continue with his duties if his son were permitted to assist him.[171] The following year, however, he announced his intention to withdraw from the position,[172] and his son Alfred Hanson was elected to the post.[173] He resigned due to ill health shortly before St James' Day 1897, and the Court of Livery voted to allow him a retiring allowance of £50 per annum in grateful recognition of his services. William Illman was appointed as his successor, with a salary of £40.[174]

On 5th March 1918 it was reported to the Court of Assistants that 'the old silver Beadles Badge', dated to approximately 1750 and containing the Company's crest, had been found in the possession of Mr Frederick Simpson of Brighton. The badge had been 'lost to the Company for many years'. Mr W. H. Newson proposed that he would acquire the badge from Mr Simpson and present it to the Company, which was met with unanimous approval and thanks.[175] At the April court, after the return of the badge, it was voted that the Beadle should wear it from henceforth.[176]

Clerks

The Clerk was one of the most important officials in the Company's hierarchy, and was one of the officers for whom a special oath of allegiance was written in the 1572 ordinances:

> I A: B: doe sweare to bee true and faithfull to our soveigne Lady the Queene hir heires and successors Kings and Queenes of England and to the Company of Joyners and of Ceelers or Carvers all heir Councells and secrets lawfull to be concealed I shall keep secret, I shall truly without addicion diminucon or abstraccon enter into their Register all such Statutes Ordinances rules and other

lawfull things as the Master Wardens and Assistants of this Company or the most part of them shall make and agree upon in open Court And in all things touching my Office I shall faithfully and truly behave my selfe towards this Company, and to the Master Wardens Officers and Rulers of the same and for the Comonwealth of the same to my power and cuning So helpe me God and the holy contents of this Booke.[177]

The 1834 report into the duties of officers stated that,

The Clerk shall be elected annually by the Livery.
Shall take the Oath prescribed for that Office.
He shall enter all Minutes and keep all the Books of the Company.
He shall draw out settle and sign all Letters and Summonses to Court, and Livery.
He shall prepare Indentures.
He shall attend at Stamp Office to get Stamps affixed to attend Monthly with the Freedom Book to have the same inspected.
He shall prepare Lists of Liverymen to be nominated to Offices and settle printed forms and Letters convening Meeting on St James day.
He shall prepare and settle printed Lists of Livery.
He shall attend all Meetings of Court and Livery and read Minutes of last Court of Livery and intervening Courts of Assistants.
He shall arrange and Copy Renter Wardens Account to enter same in Book and prepare same for Printer and cause the same to be printed and circulated amongst the Livery annually.
He shall attend with refractory Apprentices before the Lord Mayor and Chamberlain and give all necessary Information at his Chambers without fee receiving a salary of £60.
He shall attend all Committees take Minutes of their proceedings and draw up reports and transact all other Business for which he shall be allowed extra professional charges in the discretion of the Court of Assistants.[178]

The main duty of the Clerk was to be present at all Company meetings, and to keep a full and accurate record of them. The Company's surviving minute books were all created by the Clerks. They also attended any extraordinary meetings, and were responsible for the creation of apprenticeship indentures. They lived on-site at Joiners' Hall in accommodation which would become known as the Clerk's House. Along with the Beadle the Clerks were given distinctive gowns to wear, at the Company's expense.[179] By the early twentieth century the gown was supplied by Ede & Ravenscroft.[180] Although the Clerks received a salary for the work they were expected to do, £10 per annum in the 1730s, they could also receive additional compensation for what was usually described as 'extraordinary labour' or 'extraordinary paines'. Examples of this included the creation of new leases for tenants, or arranging prosecutions through the Court of Aldermen.[181]

The Clerk in office in the 1680s was joiner Joseph Burrough. He was born in 1643 and was elected to his position in 1675. When the Company's charter was surrendered to James II in 1685 Burrough was one of the officers who subsequently lost their position. The new charter appointed Richard Foster to the role instead, but when that document was repealed Master John Harris and the Court of Assistants informed Foster that his services were no longer required. At a Court of Livery, where much debate took place as to whether serving officers had been legally chosen, a query was raised 'whither Mr Burrough the old Clerke chosen by vertue of the old Charter or Mr Richard Ffoster put in by the new which of them was Clerke'.[182] After obtaining legal advice the Court of Assistants unanimously agreed on 11th December that Burrough should resume his former role, 'and ordered him to take his place as Clerke and looke after the business of this Company as he did before he was turned out'.[183] On 7th May 1689 the Master, Wardens, and Assistants signed a declaration concerning Burrough's continued appointment:

> Wee the Wardens and Assistants of the Company of Joyners Doe hereby declare That Mr Joseph Burrough hath been above ffourteene yeares Clerke of the said Company and never was put out of his said place save only by the late King James when he granted a new Charter and when the same was made void and the old Charter tooke place Wee the Wardens & Court of Assistants as in right and Justice wee ought to doe restore the said Mr Burrough to his said place as formerly wherein he hath performed the same to the sattisfaccon of this Court And wee doe and shall protest against and oppose to our power any new Eleccon or designe in order to bring in any other Clerke untill the said Mr Burrough be first displaced from his said Employ by order of the Court of Assistants that is now or hereafter shall be.[184]

When Joiners' Hall was all but destroyed by fire on the evening of 28th April 1694 Burrough was one of the first men to respond to the blaze. Without any concern for his own property he rushed to the Hall's defence, and he was later credited with preventing the total destruction of the parlour and kitchen. Whilst he was saving what he could of the Hall the flames had reached his own home, causing considerable personal losses.

In early 1696 an audit was carried out into Burrough's expenditure on the Company's account after he requested some extra compensation for extraordinary service.[185] The committee appointed to investigate produced a report which was presented to the Court of Assistants on 3rd March:

> In pursuance of an order of this Court, Wee have seriously Considered and debated the matters thereby transferred relating to Mr Joseph Burrough Clerke to this Company and perused and Examined the Account now by him produced to us with the Bookes of this Company of such moneys as have bin rec[eive] d by him as Clerke of this Company from the Twenty ffifth day of December 1694 to the Twenty ffifth day of December 1695 and do approve thereof, and have informed ourselves as near as wee can what the profitts of his place Amounts to per Ann, which wee find much less then the Beadles with respect to his living Rent ffree and other profitts accrewing to him, which to us seemes very unreasonable in regard of the inquallity of their respective Offices, and port of living and also have informed ourselves as near as we can, what belongs to the said Office of a Clerke to be performed as such for this Company, and we are of opinion that the said Clerke is onely obliged in respectof his place for the perquisites accrewing thereby to the duties ffollowing vizt To fill up all Indentures of Apprenticeship and see them Executed and Entred in the Companyes Bookes. To Enter all ffreedomes in the said Bookes. To Examine and Enter the payments of all moneys for Quarteridge. To draw the Renter Wardens Accounts and Enter them faire in the Bookes of this Company. To give Attendance at all Court of this Company, and likewise to give his Attendance on the Lord Mayor and Court of Aldermen with refractory members. And its our Opinion that for all other Negotiations for this Company (exclusive to

the perticulers aforesaid) that he ought to be allowed such consideracon as the nature thereof shall require and as any other person should deserve for the doing thereof And for as much as the said Joseph Burrough hath quitted his former habitacon & taken from this Company lying Contignous to their Hall, the better to applye himselfe to the Service of this Company, Wee Conceive that his former practice as a scrivener may be something lessened thereby, and that he as we are informed hath laid out above fffifty pounds to repaire the said Companyes house and make it fitt for his recepcon the better to ffacilitate this Companys affaires, the Improvement whereof will accrew to this Company so that we conceive it highly reasonable that the said Clerke ought to be further gratified for his service and diligence touching the premisses, especially for that wee find and are fully satisfied That at the late ffire in this Companyes Hall, that the said Joseph Burrough was an Instrument to preserve the Parlour and Kitchen belonging thereto from being totally consumed in that Conflagracon, and by his dillgence therein, which he preferred before his owne concernes, as we are informed that he sustained a Considerable loss to himselfe by that ffire, and it appears to us that he advised the Ensuring this Companies Hall against ffire, which otherwise had proved fatall to them, And therefore wee are of Opinion (the premisses considered) That the said Joseph Burrough ought to be Gratified for the Consideracons aforesaid, And its our Opinion that the said Joseph Burough ought to be allowed as an Addition to the perquisites of his place (over and besides all Sallaries and allowances accrewing to him thereby) The perticulars ffollowing vizt The summ of Eight pounds per Annum to make up his Salary now paid him by this Company Twenty Pounds per Ann during the pleasure of this Court And also six pence for every stampt paire of Indentures and scripts used in the service of this Company for his trouble and attendance to procure the same, to be increased on all bindings, which we are informed is allowed to all or most Clerks of Companyes and more their Extraordinary trouble occasioned by the late Act of Parliament for releife of the Orphans of the City of London.[186]

In addition to this, it was voted in May 1700 that he should be allowed to live in his house rent free.[187] By early 1702, shortly before he turned sixty, Burrough had taken Daniel Williams as his Clerk, and the latter received yearly gratuities of one guinea from the Company.[188] When Burrough requested the Company's permission 'to goe into the Country for the Sumer' in 1707 Williams was deputised to act as Clerk in his absence.[189] As Burrough grew older more and more of the Company's business was overseen by Williams instead.

Joseph Burrough died in Hackney in February 1725. In his will he bequeathed £20 to be distributed to the Company's poor at the discretion of the Master, Wardens, and Assistants, along with an instruction that each Assistant should receive a gold ring valued at 10s to be worn in his memory. Daniel Williams, who had served as his Clerk for over twenty years, received £15.[190] The Master informed the Court of Assistants of Burrough's death on 2nd March, and Williams was authorised to continue acting as a temporary Clerk until an election could be held for a replacement.[191] Somewhat surprisingly Williams did not offer himself as a permanent candidate, and the role was given to Lieutenant-Colonel Samuel Robinson instead.[192] Williams was nominated as a candidate for both positions of Clerk and Beadle on St James' Day in 1725, but he was not elected.[193] Robinson did not hold the post for long, however. In 1728 he was elected as Chamberlain of London and was obliged to resign as Clerk. He is discussed in greater detail later in this chapter. An election for a new Clerk was held on 10th July, which

Robinson attended, and James Fisher was appointed to the role.[194] In recognition of his new status, and by extension the positive impact this would have on the Company, Robinson was elected as Master on St James' Day.[195] Fisher's son, also named James Fisher, was admitted to the freedom of the Company by patrimony on 4th September 1750. On the same day he paid the fine for Steward and was admitted as a liveryman.[196]

Fisher appears to have become indisposed in October 1753 because the handwriting in the court minute books changed drastically.[197] At the quarter court on 8th January 1754 the Company was informed of his death, and an extraordinary court was summoned for the following week to elect a successor.[198] As with the election of a replacement Beadle which had taken place at the beginning of 1753, James Fisher junior presented himself as a replacement for his father. Nobody stood to oppose him, and he was unanimously elected to the post.[199] He would have had the advantage of an in-depth knowledge of his father's duties, and indeed he appears to have taken over when Fisher senior became ill. The handwriting in the minute books both before and after his election is identical, so it seems likely that he was already working as his father's unofficial deputy.

From St James' Day 1763 the handwriting in the minute books changed again,[200] although Fisher remained the elected Clerk until his death. It appears that, like his predecessors, he was employing at least two clerks of his own to write out the minutes. He died in 1787, and the Court of Assistants was warned that 'the vacant office of Clerk of this Company will be strongly contested'.[201] Ultimately only two candidates presented themselves for nomination: Liscomb Price, and James Fisher the third, the son of the deceased Clerk and the third generation of Fisher clerks. In keeping with tradition Fisher was elected to the post.[202] The Clerk's salary was raised by £20 per annum in 1817, and a new gown was purchased for him.[203] The younger Fisher died in 1819,[204] and Assistant Clerk Thomas Reynolds took over the duties until an election could be held on 16th February at an extraordinary Court of Livery.

John Pullen was unanimously elected to the post,[205] and would later serve as an Under Sheriff of London.[206] His son, also named John Pullen, was admitted to the Company by patrimony on 5th October 1819, and fined for Steward and took the livery on the same day.[207] Pullen the elder resigned from his post in December 1828 after an investigation into the Company's finances had discovered omissions and discrepancies in his records.[208] His resignation was accepted unanimously by the Court of Assistants, who felt that 'it is the Duty of this Court to express their Disapprobation of the Conduct of the said Clerk in the management of the affairs of the Company', noting particular the 'irregular and confused way in which the Books have been kept'.[209] However, he was later acquitted of 'any wilful intention to apply the Funds of the Company to his own use'.[210] In spite of this he was later nominated for the post of Master for the year 1831–2, but requested to fine instead.[211]

Four candidates presented themselves as potential Clerks: John Pullen the younger, Stephen Ponder the younger, James Drury, and William Webb.[212] An election was held on 15th April at an extraordinary Court of Livery, and the two favoured candidates were Pullen and Ponder. In spite of his father's conduct, Pullen the younger was victorious, securing fifty-one votes to Ponder's thirty-nine.[213] He took the oath of office on 5th May. Although he lost the vote, Ponder was asked to accept a silver cup valued at 20 guineas as a token of gratitude for his services in investigating Pullen the elder.[214]

On St James' Day 1837 the Court of Livery was informed that Pullen was unable to attend, and so Stephen Ponder the younger was asked to serve during that meeting.[215] Pullen was absent at all August meetings, which appears to have caused irritation amongst the Assistants. It was ordered on 24th August that 'in future no person be eligible to the Office of Clerk who does not possess the same Qualification as that which is required for Master and Warden'.[216] Pullen eventually wrote to the Master, Wardens, Assistants, and Livery on 5th September to explain his absences, and the letter was read out at an extraordinary Court of Livery held that day:

Gentlemen,

Nearly ten years have elapsed since I had the honor to be appointed your Clerk, during which period I have invariably received unequivocal testimonials of your approbation. Many questions of importance to the Company have during my Clerkship been submitted to the consideration of the Court, from the difficulties of which I think it will be admitted, I much relieved that body, and upon some of which occasions I was fortunate enough to receive their thanks.

From misplaced confidence, I am for the present, suffering for another, imprisonment, and am obliged to remain in the Rules of the Queens Bench, till he can exonerate me from the liabilities, under which, I am lying, and which have prevented me since the 6th of June, from attending the Meetings of the Courts of Assistants.

Immediately on my being detained, I candidly made my Case known to the Court, and requested one of its Members (Mr Ponder) who has at all times, professed himself in the most friendly manner towards me, to take the Minutes, of course furnishing him with the necessary instructions. I beg to mention, incidentally, that I was not allowed to depute my Clerk, or any one out of the Court to act for me, or I would not have troubled one of the Court.

Up to the 25th of July (St James' day) the Minutes thus taken were brought to me, by my Clerk, settled, and copied by me in the proper Books, and all such Business as I could execute, without appearing at Guildhall, including the nomination of Office, circulars and arrangements for St James' day, preparation and settlement of List under the Reform Act, in short, everything, but my personal attendance, was transacted by me. On the first Tuesday in August, after preparing for such Meeting, and taking Instructions for the Renter Wardens Bond and other matters, I was surprised to find, that the Books, without my consent, with any previous intimation to me, and before I had prepared them for the Audit, were, together with my private box and papers, all kept from me, and handed to the custody of others. Of course the Books were incomplete, for which, no doubt, I shall be unjustly censured, but I was not allowed to have them for completion athough I applied for them in writing. I am obliged to go into detail, because I fear no one will mention these facts for me, and it is only fair, as I am prevented attending personally, that you should know what has occurred. I am not making this statement to call forth your sympathies, nor to strengthen any claim I have, from long service, and attention, to my reappointment as your Clerk, because, unless I am allowed, as is the case in all other Companies, to appoint a Competent Deputy 'till November, I could not attend to all the duties of that Office, and you ought not to be without the assistance of a Clerk, but I do it, to exonerate myself from the charge of wilful neglect, or the imputation of indifference to the interests of a Company, with which, my Family has been intimately associated for nearly three hundred years.[217]

Rather than grant his request to allow a deputy, it was voted that the office of Clerk should be declared vacant. Having anticipated such a move, Pullen had authorised Antonio William Julian Harrison to tender his resignation in absentia, and this was accepted by the court. Another extraordinary Court of Livery was called on 12th September at eleven o'clock to elect a replacement. Pullen's arrest also prompted some new regulations as to the character and circumstances of potential Clerk; the candidates had to live within seven miles of the General Post Office and could never have been declared bankrupt nor compounded with creditors.[218]

Two candidates presented themselves for election on 12th September: Stephen Ponder, son of the late Past Master of the same name, and Henry F. Richardson. When the matter was put to a vote Ponder was elected by forty-five votes to twenty-nine.[219] Ponder took the oath of office at the quarter court held on 3rd October.[220] However, there was some difficulty in retrieving the Company's title deeds to all of their property, which were still in Pullen's possession. Ponder reported to the Company in April that 'he had made several applications to John Pullen the late Clerk for a tin Box containing the property of the Company' but had received no response. Past Master Ponder, his father, then reported that the box was at Pullen's lodgings at 4 Chester Place, but due to his incarceration he was in arrears for his rent to the amount of £6 5s and consequently the landlord was holding the box as ransom until the debt was paid. After some consideration the Company agreed that it was a small price to pay for retrieving their documents, and the Renter Warden Daniel Higley Richardson and Past Master Ponder were authorised to pursue the matter.[221] The two men called upon Pullen at the Queen's Bench to inform him they would be paying the debt, and after seeing his landlord at Chester Place they successfully regained possession of the box. At the next court Pullen was sharply condemned in absentia for 'his conduct in having on a former occasion declared, "That he had delivered up all property belonging to the Company", with a full knowledge that he held possession of the whole of their Title Deeds'. The court declared his conduct 'to be based on extreme ingratitude'.[222]

Stephen Ponder consistently performed the duties of the Clerk until the spring of 1841, when business unexpectedly called him overseas. He wrote to the Master, Wardens, and Assistants on 24th March offering the services of his business partner to act on his behalf during his absence, with a hope that he would not be required to resign his position altogether:

> I beg most respectfully to inform the Court that I am unexpectedly required to proceed to India upon urgent business and therefore I shall not be able to attend at the next Court and I deeply regret that my departure should be so sudden as to prevent my attendance upon that occasion in order that I might afford to the Court my personal explanation.
>
> I trust that from the manner in which I have fulfilled the duties of the Office of Clerk, that it will not be considered that I am wanting in respect to the Court or that I disregard the interests of the Joiners Company.
>
> Under these circumstances I venture to ask the indulgence of the Court to allow my Partner Mr Richard Barnes to act in my stead during my absence, he is I believe previously known to some of the Members of the Court, and I feel assured that the interests of the Company will not suffer by being intrusted to his care and attention; he will do himself the honor of attending the next Court of Assistants to receive the orders of the Court or to offer any explanation which may be required.[223]

Barnes was summoned to the next court, as Ponder had suggested. However, circumstances quickly changed. Ponder wrote to the Company again from Bombay, now known as Mumbai, on 22nd May, and his letter was read in the July court:

> In my Letter which I had the honor to address to the Court in the month of March last I stated that Business required my presence in India and I asked the indulgence that during my absence my Partner Mr Richard Barnes might be permitted to perform the duties of the Office of Clerk to your Worshipful Company, but finding that my return to England is uncertain, I am compelled therefore to tender to you my resignation of that Honorable Office and which I hereby beg most respectfully to do, and at the same time to return my warmest thanks for the kindness and courtesy which I have received from the Court, as also from the Gentlemen of the Livery. I have also to express my deep regret at being thus severed from the exercise of those duties which as your Clerk devolved upon me, the discharge of which was ever a source of pleasure and satisfaction to me. In thus retiring allow me to hope that my conduct has been such as to deserve the honor and esteem which I have enjoyed, the pleasing remembrance of which will endure to the latest period of my life.

A vote of thanks to Ponder for his previous service was recorded in the minute, and his father Past Master Ponder was elected as an interim Clerk until an election could be held.[224] However, on St James' Day Ponder senior was elected as Clerk for the ensuing year.[225] Ponder senior held the post until 2nd December 1851 when his declining health compelled him to resign. He expressed his regret at not being able to continue in the post and thanked his colleagues and friends in the Company for the kindness and support they had shown him. The Company expressed their 'extreme regret' at Ponder's ill health and offered sympathy. Stephen Ponder junior, now returned from India, temporarily took over the duties of Clerk again until an election could be held.[226] Although he was nominated as potential candidate for the post, the vote was won by Benjamin Granger by thirty-one votes to twenty-one,[227] and he was sworn into office on 13th January 1852.[228] Granger was the son of Past Master Press Granger. Following his appointment, the Clerk's duties as they stood in 1852 were copied into the court minutes:

> He is to be elected annually by the Livery on St James' day, except in case of death or resignation when he is to be elected until the following St James' day.
>
> He is to attend all Meetings of Courts of Assistants, Courts of Livery or Committees of either Body to take the minutes of their proceedings and prepare reports when required, to read the Minutes of former Meetings and to afford his advice and assistance generally.
>
> He is to keep all the Books of the Company constantly posted to prepare Letters and Summonses and annual Parliamentary and other Lists of the Liverymen causing the former to be published as required by the Act of Parliament and the latter to be circulated amongst the Livery.
>
> He is to prepare Indentures for Apprentices and to have the proper Stamps affixed thereto, and whenever occasion shall require he is to attend before the Lord Mayor or Chamberlain with refractory Apprentices.
>
> He is to assist in the preparation of the Renter Warden's Accounts previous to their Audit and to cause the same to be printed and circulated amongst

the Livery and to afford necessary information to parties seeking the same in relation to the business of the Company.

For the whole of which duties he is to receive an annual salary of sixty pounds.[229]

The death of Ponder senior in December 1853, along with that of fellow Assistant John Ashford, was noted with sorrow by the Company. The Court of Assistants paid tribute to the two men, and expressed their

> desire to bow with submission to the Great Disposer of all events, and to acknowledge with gratitude, the lengthened period to which their lives had been extended, thus furnishing them with the opportunity of carrying out plans of human action, which this Court believes have been accomplished, with credit to themselves and satisfaction to surrounding friends.
>
> While they would express their sympathy with surviving relations, they are anxious to record their deep sense of the efficient services which by their wise counsel, and active effort, they have rendered to the Worshipful Company of Joiners.[230]

The Court of Assistants

The Court of Assistants is the governing body of any livery company. The members are elected for life and have usually held office, and in the case of the Joiners they were generally required to have passed the office of Master. There was a finite number of places on the Court of Assistants, and elections were held when a sitting member died or moved outside the suburbs of the City. They were required to attend the monthly court meetings, but they did not have unilateral control over the affairs of the Company. Any major decisions, such as the election of officers or modifications of the Company's by-laws, had to be referred to the wider livery at a quarterly court. Election to the Court of Assistants implied relative prosperity on the part of the candidate. From 1716 Assistants elect had to pay a further £3 fine before assuming the office,[231] and by the 1840s this had risen to £5.[232] The fine was £10 in the early 1900s.[233]

Assistants were expected to wear foynes gowns at all times when on Company business.[234] These gowns were of higher quality than the budge gowns worn by the Livery and were lined with marten fur.[235] In 1661 Assistants were warned that they would be fined if they came to court without their gowns,[236] and in 1682 it was ordered that they would forfeit 5s if they wore a budge gown rather than a foynes gown.[237] This remained an issue, however, and in 1691 a complaint was made in court that the instructions 'hath of late been much neglected and omitted'.[238] A significant change in policy came in 1738 when Assistant John Loadman requested a special dispensation to attend court without his gown. The entry in the minutes described him as 'being one of the people called Quakers', who advocated simplicity of dress. He 'made it his request to the Court that he might be excused wearing a Gown in Court & that he might be at Liberty to sit without'. He offered to pay a voluntary fine of 10s 6d in lieu, and the court agreed to his request.[239] It seems likely that he was the John Loadman who died in 1748 at the age of eighty-five. He was described as a carpenter of St Olave's parish in Southwark, and was buried in the Friends Burial Ground in Long Lane.[240]

The very first clause in the 1572 ordinances concerned the Court of Assistants, an indication of how important they were to the Company's governance. The clause stipulated that there must be twelve members of the Court of Assistants serving at any one time, although it was not necessary for all of them to be present for meetings to be quorate. After the death or relocation of an Assistant an election had to be held at Joiners' Hall within fourteen days to elect a replacement. All Assistants were required to swear an oath of allegiance, the wording of which has not changed and is still sworn by incoming Assistants today:

> I A: B: shall to my power mainteine keep and cause to be kept all the Ordinances rules and Statutes of this Company and shall give my best assistance advice and councell for the Comonwealth of the same, and aid and helpe the Master and Wardens of the same in all due and lawfull doings and execucon of right and justice so often as I shalbee required, if the performance of such request shall not bee to my owne greate hinderance So helpe me God and the holy contents of this Booke.[241]

The 1834 report into the duties of officers contained a detailed description of what being an Assistant entailed in the nineteenth century:

> The Members of the Court of Assistants shall be Elected by the Livery of the Company from their own Body at a Court of Livery held for that purpose upon the usual Summons.
>
> No Person shall be Eligible who shall reside upwards of 7 Miles from the General Post Office, have been Bankrupt or compounded with his Creditors and not paid 20s in the pound or who shall be absent. Every Liveryman elected on the Court shall pay £5 fine upon his Entrance into Office.
>
> Each Member of the Court of Assistants on entering upon his Office shall take the Oath prescribed for that Office in the Book of Ordinances.
>
> They shall attend every Court of Assistants upon the usual Summons for which they shall receive each a fee of 10s 6d provided they be in attendance before 12 O'Clock by the Guildhall Clock. They shall together with the Master and Wardens direct and Control the Affairs of the Company and elect deserving Liverymen or their Widows as Pensioners, shall examine and direct the payment of all Bills that may be due by the Company, shall direct Investments of the surplus moneys of the Company in the purchase of Freehold Property or the purchase or Sale of Government Securities but they shall not vote away any money in any Gift or Present without the sanction of a Court of Livery excepting the proceeds of the Poors Box which shall be entirely at their disposal in charitable purposes.
>
> Shall provide a Dinner for the Livery on Lord Mayors day payable out of the Companys funds, The Court shall have power to inflict or remit fines on Freemen or Liverymen in all cases sanctioned by the amended By Laws.
>
> The Master or his Deputy one Warden and Six of the Assistants shall form a Court.[242]

However, in reality the number of Assistants soon grew above twelve. In December 1698 the Company held a serious discussion at their monthly court about 'the great number of the Assistants and the likelyhood and probabillity of its increase through the favour of some members thereof'. It was feared that the cost of maintaining them would be a great inconvenience. A vote passed confirming that in future there would be no more than twenty Assistants, in addition to the Master and Wardens. No new Assistants would be appointed until a vacancy presented itself, unless 'any member of this Company not of the Assistants be chosen Alderman or Sherriffe of London'. This notice was entered into the minute books and was read out each year on St James' Day to ensure that everyone knew the rule.[243]

On 31st July 1738 the sitting Court of Assistants was abolished altogether and two elections were held to appoint nineteen new men to the roles. Twelve additional Assistants were elected in September 1739.[244] In 1742 it was agreed that any Assistant who had been absent from meetings for twelve calendar months should be expelled.[245] By the 1770s the number of Assistants had returned to a stable twelve, and new members were only added after the death of a sitting member. However, in 1778 after two deaths in quick succession, reducing the number back to ten, the decision was made to elect six new members rather than only two.[246] This was apparently a wise decision, because by the summer of 1781 the number had once again dropped so low 'as to render the making of a Court rather difficult'.[247] At an extraordinary Court of Livery held in September 1815 the Master acquainted those present that

> several Members of the Court of Assistants from their great Age had retired to live for the most part at a Distance from London and therefore that their Attendance at the Court of Assistants had become so precarious that some Difficulties had lately arisen in procuring a sufficient Number of Members to make Courts to do the Company's Business.

It was proposed to the Livery that four additional men should be added to the Assistants, and the question carried in the affirmative. Four Past Masters were duly elected.[248] Complaint was raised in 1821 that the Assistants had 'augmented the remuneration to themselves without the sanction of the Livery from 5s to 10s 6d for their attendance on every Court day', and this was described as 'an infringement on the Rights & Privileges and if unresisted might establish a precedent highly dangerous to the Best Interests of the Company'. After discussion the Livery did agree to the higher sum of 10s 6d; it appears that it was the lack of democratic process which irked them, rather than the increased cost. They agreed that 5s was 'inadequate' and simply wanted due process to be followed.[249] This sum was raised to £1 in 1831.[250]

A committee was established in 1833 to consider the word 'suburbs' from the 1572 ordinances, and to consider 'what space is included therein' and whether any sitting Assistants were living too far away from the City to be eligible for office. It was concluded that 'a residence within a reasonable distance from the City with facility any Member could be reasonable expected to attend the various Meetings and Courts' was sufficient, and suggested that a maximum of seven miles from the Post Office would be sensible.[251]

In January 1916 it was voted that any Assistant who absented himself from twelve successive court meetings would automatically lose his seat, and a new Assistant would be elected from the Livery to take his place.[252] The number of Assistants was formally increased from twelve to seventeen in 1930 'so that some of the Old Past Masters can again associate themselves with the Management of the Company as they did during the three years they serve[d] in the office as Wardens & Master'.[253]

It was proposed in 1987 that the status of Assistant Emeritus could be offered to Past Masters who no longer felt able to continue actively serving the Company, but who did not wish to resign their post entirely. The conditions were that they would have had to serve as an Assistant for a minimum of seven years, and upon election as Emeritus they would lose voting rights. They were still entitled to attend all meetings, and would be identified by the addition of a gold ribbon to their Past Master's badge.[254]

Wardens

The Company elected two Wardens each St James' Day, and they were expected to serve for one year. Traditionally they oversaw the Company's finances, and the wardens' accounts are some of the earliest surviving documents in the archive. The lower of the two Wardens was the Renter Warden, and it was common for him to progress up to the position of Upper Warden the following year. After passing both positions it then became common for the officer to take the chair as Master. The Wardens had to provide a bond of security from two friends for £200 when taking office, and this was surrendered to them on Oath Day the following year when their successor was sworn into office. Each Warden also had to name a deputy who could serve in their place in case they had to be absent from a meeting. It was not necessary for all Assistants to attend for meetings to be quorate, but the Master and Wardens did have to be present.

The Wardens were vital officers, and the oath they were required to swear was the same as that sworn by the Master:

> You and every of you shalbee true to our sovreigne Lady the Queene and to hir heires and successors Kings and Queenes of England yee and every of you shall endeavour yourselves the best you can justly and indifferently to execute or cause to bee executed your Offices in every respect, and all the good and lawfull Ordinances in this Booke of our Ordinances expressed without sparing any person for affeccon regard meed dread or promise of reward during the tyme yee shalbee in the same Office of your Master & Wardenship, and of all and every such goods plate jewells sums of mony or any other thing or things that by reason of your said Office shall come to any of your said hands you shall according to your Ordinances aforespecifyed make a good true and plaine Actompt or else pay such ffines as yee bee ordered to pay by our Ordinances for your not so doing, yee shall not for mallice nor for love or affeccon assesse any person or persons in a greater or lesse sum then after the quallity and quantity of his Offence after your discreacon and according to your Ordinance So helpe you God and the holy contents of that Booke.[255]

The oath sworn by the Wardens and Master today has barely changed:

> I, AB, shall be true to our Sovereign Lady the Queen and her Heirs and Successors, Kings and Queens of England. I shall endeavour the best I can, justly and indifferently to execute, or cause to be executed, my Office of [Master/ Upper Warden/Renter Warden] in every respect, and all the good and lawful ordinances in the book of our ordinances expressed, without sparing any person for love, affection, reward, need, dread, or promise of reward, during the time I shall be in the said Office of your [Master/Upper Warden/Renter Warden]. All and every such goods, plate, jewels, sums of money, or any other thing or things, that by reason of my said Office shall come into my hands, I will, according to the ordinances afore specified make a good, true and plain account, or else

pay such fines as I may be ordered to pay by the ordinances, for my not doing so. After using my discretion, I will not for malice, nor for love, nor affection, assess any person, or persons, in a greater or less sum than after the quality and quantity of his offence, against our said ordinances. So help me God and the holy contents of this Book.

The 1834 report into the duties of officers stated that

[t]he Upper Warden shall be elected by the Liverymen of the Company from their own body at a Court of Livery held on Saint James day or in case of decease or vacancy at any other time upon the usual Summons and notice having been given. No person shall be Eligible who shall reside upwards of 7 Miles from the General Post Office or who shall have been Bankrupt or compounded with his Creditors and not paid 20s in the pound.

Any Liveryman chosen to this Office and declining to serve may be exempted upon payment of a fine of £5 to the general Funds of the Company and he shall be placed and remain in the List of Liverymen Past Upper Warden next in relation to the last person who shall have served, shall be then serving or fined for such Office.

The Upper Warden shall attend on St Bartholomews day next after his election or in case of emergency on any other convenient day appointed by the Court of Assistants for the purpose of being sworn into his Office and shall then and there take the Oath prescribed for that Office and upon failing to attend for that purpose on the day appointed he shall be fined the whole of the Expences of any future especial Court that shall be called for that purpose or if the Master or Renter Warden or both from the like Cause shall be sworn in then a proportionate part of such Expences.

He is next in precedence to the Master and shall attend all Courts of Assistants and Livery and shall receive a Fee of 10s 6d for each attendance at Courts of Assistants, shall present Freemen on their Admission to the Chamberlain and shall uphold and support the Master upon all occasions.

He shall Jointly with the Renter Warden whilst in Office provide a Dinner for the Master and Court of Assistants.

Any Liveryman chosen to this Office and not coming forward to serve or fine shall be fined £8 for such neglect.

The same report also explained the duties of the Renter Warden, who was subject to the same fines as the Renter Warden for non-attendance or refusal to serve. The report specified that

[o]n Entrance into Office he shall give a Bond in the sum of £500 with two Sureties for the due performance of his Office The Stamp & Expences whereof shall be borne by the Company.

He is next in relation to the Upper Warden he shall attend all Courts of Assistants and Livery and uphold and support the Master on all occasions.

He shall receive a Fee of 10s 6d at all Meetings of the Court of Assistants.

He shall receive all Rents Dividends Fines and other monies due to the Company and keep an Account and enter every receipt & disbursement in a Book to be provided and kept for that purpose.

He shall pay no monies unless directed by a Court of Assistants or Livery except the Court Fees Pensioners Rents Insurances and the Salaries of the Clerk and Beadle which latter he shall pay quarterly.

He shall prepare his Account Current within 20 days from St James day that the same may be audited and shall pay over the balance in his hands to his Successor upon order of the Court of Assistants.[256]

The Master and Wardens were each expected to provide a dinner for the Company, or money in lieu. The first surviving reference to this comes from the court minutes on 7th March 1664, when it was 'ordered that the renter warden shall provide this day a dynner for the Assistants & their wives'.[257] Thomas Thornton, who served as Renter Warden in 1684, failed to provide his dinner, and in 1689 he agreed to pay a fine of £3.[258] Complaint was raised in June 1693 by some freemen 'concerning the mean[n]es[s] of the Dinners of the Master and Wardens of late' and a committee was appointed to investigate what changes should be made.[259] Their report was presented at the next monthly court:

Whereas complaint hath been made to the Master Wardens and Court of Assistants of this Company by some of the members thereof That it hath been the custome time out of minde till within these few yeares for the Master & Wardens for the time being freely to make their particular ffeasts at their respective charge for the Court of Assistants and for some or all of their wives for the grandure & good correspondency of the said Company which used to amount considerablie above their accustomed ffines But of late yeares by some it hath been totally omitted to the great damage of this Company and by some other Masters and Wardens when they make their Dinners so very meane that it is a discredit for the Court to suffer it any longer so to continue And as touching the ffeast for Auditt day of late the Court of Assistats have been very much abused and the stock of the said Company very much lessened because formerly there was spent about Tenn or Eleaven pounds on that ffeast & had plenty enough and to spare but nothing nigh the same will now serve by reason that some of the late Masters and Wardens to save their owne money spending nothing scarsely in treating their friends at their respective publick dinners but are ready and willing to advance considerably out of the said Companyes stock to accommodate their friends & relatcons to the great disturbance & detriment of the correspondence & union of the said Company which sd complainte being at this Court heard and they taking the same into their consideracon do think fitt and order that Mr Thomas Moore Mr James Goodwin Mr Thomas Shrewsbridge Mr Thomas Wildman and Mr Thomas Pistor Senr or any three of them be a Committee to examine and finde out some wayes methods and meanes to prevent for the future the said Complaints and abuses as to the Master and Wardens for the time to come as to their dinners and likewise to the expences and charges as may hereafter be laid out on Auditt day and that they reporte the same together with such wayes and methods as they shall think most beneficiall & advantageous for the honour union good and welfare of the said Company and that they reporte the same to this Court upon the next monthly Court and that the Clerke of this Company doe attend them accordingly Which order wee the said Committee whose names are here under Subscribed in obedience thereunto having deliberately and maturely considered the same and every part thereof doe give it as our opinions for the honour and credit of the said Company That every Master shall be at the charge for his ffeast the summ of six pounds to be held and kept on the ffirst Court day of the month of October yearely for every upper Warden six pounds to be held and kept on the ffirst Court day in the month of January yearely and for every Renter Warden ffive pounds to be held and kept on the ffirst Court day in Aprill yearely and more if they or any of them the said Master and Wardens for the time being shall think fitting but not less And that no Master Wardens either or any of them at his or their respective ffeast or ffeasts as aforesaid shall bring any more then Two guests besides his wife And that such Master and Wardens shall produce the next Court day after the respective ffeasts shall be made if required by the Court of Assistants or the Major part of them an exact accompt how much they have expended and for what and if it shall not amount to the severall and respective summ and sums abovemenconed That then such person or persons shall pay what shall be wanting of the respective sum or sums above menconed according to his and their severall and respective place and places on demand to be put into the poores box to be distributed to and amongst the poore of this Company which wee think will be a meanes to prevent others to hold the said places which wee doe or may hereafter believe are neither fitt nor able to serve the said places but pay their severall ffines either before or after their eleccons for the places of Master & Wardens either or any of them according to usuall customes in such cases and wee doe conceive if any should object or gainsay against this our opinions wee cannot but imagine that such persons that shall hereafter be called to the said places or any of them are as able if not abler to hold the same as for young men to hold and pay for the places of Steward and Livery and for the Court of Assistants to give them bill or bills of fare & compel them to doe the same And our opinions are that every person or persons who hereafter shall be chosen and elected to the sevrall place and places of Master Upper Warden or Renter Warden and houlds the same either or any of them and keeps not his or their ffeast and ffeasts on the severall dayes and times before appointed and layes not out the severall sums for each place as before is limited or what is wanting thereof to pay into the poores box for the use of the poore as aforesaid that then such person or persons so offending or neglecting after his or their year or yeares shall be expired shall for his imission or refusall not to be summoned warned or sitt as one of the Court of Assistants for the future till the same be complied with And our opinions are to prevent for the future the excessive charges expended and abuses committed upon Auditt day by bringing such abundance of people by the Master Wardens and Court of Assistants and some of them Wee doe therefore think fitting for the time to come that the whole charge of the said Auditt dinner yearely shall not amount unto above Twelve or Thirteene pounds at the most and that Three of the Court of Assistants whom the Master Wardens and Court of Assistants for the time being shall appoint be a Committee to settle manage and agree with the Cooke and others for the same And that no Master shall bring or cause to be brought above Two persons besides himselfe and wife Upper Warden and wife and To persons Renter Warden wife his security and wife if his security hath one and every member of the Court of Assistants and his wife and in the absence of his wife one man or woman and no more And that no child or children whatsoever be brought to the Hall nor be permitted or suffered to sitt at the Table to prevent giving disgust to any of the Assistants under the penalty of ffive shillings for every such member that he shall bring or cause to be brought any more person or persons then what is herein and hereby limited and appointed and that the person or persons so offending shall pay or cause to be paid such ffine or ffiines as aforesaid upon the next monthly Court to be put into the poores box to be distributed to and amongst such poore of the said Company as the Master Wardens and Court of Assistants for the time being or the Major part of them shall think fitt And our opinion is that no person or persons whatsoever shall sett by or send from the Table any Victualls or other things untill the Company hath dyned and risen from the Table upon the penalty of Two shillings and six pence to be paid by such person who shall doe the same And if by any woman whose husband is of the Court of Assistants that then the husband shall pay the same the next Court day to be distributed to & amongst the poore of this Company And wee desire that these our opinions and methods may be entred into the Reportory booke of this Company And that they be constantly read by the Clerke of this Company for the time being on the ffirst Court dayes in August and September yearely All which wee submitt and referr to the consideracon of the Master Wardens and Court of Assistants Witness our hands this Twenty Nineth of June 1693'.[260]

It is still a custom within the Company that the Master and Wardens will provide a luncheon for the Court of Assistants after their meeting in May, for which they bear the full expense with no charge borne by the Company.

When the election of officers took place on St James' Day 1759 a departure from the usual nomination process occurred. Rather than the names of a select few candidates being presented to the court, it was decided that any Assistant who had not previously held a specific post would be automatically nominated for it.[261] This broadened the candidate pool drastically. Forty candidates were nominated for the position of Renter Warden, compared with thirteen the year before.[262] Ironically the Renter Warden elected in 1759, William Field, was not present in court that day and had no desire to hold the post. He requested to fine for it at the next court meeting, and another public court had to be summoned to elect a new candidate.[263] The next elected officer was also absent from court, and sent word that due to infirmity he would be unable to serve. A third court was summoned, and once again an officer was elected in absentia.[264] After he failed to present himself to the next Court of Assistants they voted to summon a fourth public court to replace him.[265] After the initial election of a member who was miraculously present but begged to fine, the election finally fell on Anthony Chapman. He was, predictably, absent from the court, but he had sent word via Past Master William Boyce that he would serve the office if chosen.[266] What should have been a brief election process on 25th July had been dragged out until 15th October.

Masters

The Master was the chief governing officer of the Livery Company for the term of his office. Masters of the Joiners' Company traditionally served for one calendar year, and elections took place each St James' Day. An exception to this took place during the Second World War, when Frederick William Butler OBE served as Master from 1940 until 1945 inclusive. Prospective officers were nominated, and those for the post of Master were expected to have served or fined the office of both Wardens first. It was not compulsory for those elected to the post to serve if they were unwilling, and the option to fine for it was available. In 1735 the fine was doubled from £5 to £10,[267] and by the 1920s it was £15.[268]

The 1834 report into the duties of officers stated that

[t]he Master shall be elected by the Liverymen of the Company from their own Body at a Court of Livery held on Saint James day or in case of decease

or Vacancy at any other time upon the usual Summons and notice having been given.

No person shall be Eligible who shall reside upwards of 7 Miles from the General Post Office or who shall have been a Bankrupt or compounded with his Creditors and not have paid 20s in the pound. A Liveryman chosen to this Office and declining to serve may be exempted upon payment of a fine of £15 to the general funds of the Company and he shall thereupon be placed and remain in the List of Liverymen past Master next in relation to the last Person who shall have served, shall be then serving or fined for that office.

The Master elect shall attend the Court on St Bartholomews day next after his election or in case of Emergency or any other convenient day appointed by the Court for the purpose of being sworn into his Office and shall then and there take the Oath prescribed for that Office and upon failing to attend for that purpose on the day appointed he shall be fined the whole of the Expences of any future especial Court that may be called for such purpose or one or both the Wardens from the same cause are sworn in at such especial Court then an equal proportion of such Expences.

He shall attend and preside at all Courts of Assistants and Livery and all Banquets attired in a Gown and in case of Absence shall have power to appoint a Deputy from the Court of Assistants.

He shall receive a fee of 10s 6d at all Meeting's of the Court of Assistants.

He shall have authority to direct the Clerk when to call especial Courts of Assistants and Courts of Livery at his discretion.

He shall provide a Dinner for the Court of Assists and Wardens at his own Expence whilst in Office.

Any Liveryman chosen to this Office and not coming forward to serve or Fine shall be fined Ten pounds for such neglect.[269]

It was agreed in 1828 that 'the Master be clothed with the Livery Gown on every occasion when presiding at the Courts of Livery and Courts of Assistants' and a gown was purchased for him accordingly.[270] In 1860 it was voted at a Court of Livery that 'in order to assimilate with other respectable livery companies Gold Medals be provided for the Master and Wardens to be used by them during their year of office and to be transferred to their successors on retirement'.[271] The Committee who met to consider the medal's design decided that

> it should be in diameter, not less than two inches, that on the obverse, should be represented the full length figure of St James Major, the Patron Saint of the Company, with his proper emblems, and the words 'Worshipful Company of Joiners London' and on the reverse side, the Armorial Bearings of the Company.[272]

Ultimately it was decided that the Wardens' medals should be in silver rather than gold. The British Museum wrote to the Company in November 1860 to ask for 'a specimen of such medal to be placed in the Cabinet of the British Museum', and it was agreed that a bronze version would be specially struck and sent to them.[273] A copy was also donated to the Guildhall Library.[274] Through an order of the Court of Livery dated 24th January 1865 each outgoing Master would receive a silver medal from the Company, as a token of appreciation.[275] The name of the Master was carved along the edge. This tradition continued until the Second World War, but was revived again in 1945. A new design created by Company member Captain W. H. Herbert was adopted from 1946 onwards.[276]

Outgoing Master Frederick Capel informed the Court of Assistants in July 1981 that 'during his year of Office he had a Brooch made for his wife which bears the Company's Arms', and they wished to present this to the Company 'for the use of future Master's Ladies, should they desire to wear it'. The gift was accepted with 'deep appreciation'.[277]

As part of the ceremony surrounding the Master taking office, it is customary for a set of keys to be presented to him and also to the Wardens. Although the significance of these keys had been lost to the collective memory of the Company, this was in reference to the traditional practice of all important charters and deeds being kept in an iron chest, which only the Master and Wardens had access to. Although the iron chests themselves are long gone, the tradition of handing the keys down to their successors has remained in the Company.

There was an underlying concern that Masters and Wardens of the Company could abuse their position. In an attempt to mitigate the risk, on 15th August 1682 an order was passed that no contracts or agreements could be made by the Master or Wardens, and no bills higher than 40s could be paid, without the consent of at least six Assistants. The minute book went on to note that several sums of money had been paid by previous Renter Wardens on the basis of bills signed by the Master out of Court, which had caused 'great dissattisfaccon and murmerings' by the Court of Assistants, so from now on bills had to be presented to the Clerk and Assistants before they could be passed.[278] The Assistants were vigilant in monitoring the Masters' financial activities, and on 8th April 1684 complaint was made in Court that Master Thomas Tyre had broken the order 'in buying goods & wainscoting a roome in mr Wells house without consent'. Mr Tyre admitted that he had done so, and agreed to a fine of 2s 6d.[279] The audit of that same year also found issue with Renter Warden Green's accounts, which the auditors passed 'unwillingly by reason of extravagant expences'.[280]

There are also indications that Past Masters did not always approve of the government of the Company by their successors. On 20th August 1691 complaint was made at a public court against John Player, who had lost his position of Master upon the surrender of the Charter in 1684 but was re-elected for the remainder of the year 1687–8:

> At this Court severall Complaints being made against Mr John Player a member of this Company under the hands of some of them and some others verbally setting forth and declareing That whereas the said John Player hath for some time past given abusive Language to severall of the Court of Assistants of the same by calling them or some of them Sarrahs [sirrahs] Knavse and Rascalls and threatning to beate and break their or some of their heads & more perticularly designing and goeing about through the pride and mallice of his spirit to bring confusion disorder disturbance and discord amongst the whole Company hath of late (to others) discourseing about Mr Reade the late Master & Mr Browne his Renter Warden passing his Accounts by the then Auditors or some of them appointed for that purpose and afterwards by the Court of Assistants most Scandalously said were there ever such a parcell of ffopps fooles knaves and Rascalls unless they had a designe to ruine the Company and at other time or times asserting the same Audit to be as made under a hedge which speeches and declaracons are contrary to his Oath and severall ordinances in the booke of ordinances belonging to the said Company.

Player was suspended from the Court of Assistants, found guilty of 'abusive language expressions & offences', and at the next court he was fined £5.

However, he refused to submit to this without a fight. He appeared in person on 6th October and 'demanded a coppie of the papers & order for which he was dismist'. The court said they would consider it, and a week later he repeated his request, but they postponed any decision until November. When they failed to provide him with the relevant documentation Player decided to counter-sue the Company, and the Master, Wardens, and Assistants were summoned to appear before the Lord Mayor. They explained that Player had been fined £5 for 'severall abuses and badd language', and was barred from sitting as an Assistant until the fine was paid. The Mayor did not reach a judgement and instead referred the case to the Court of Aldermen. At that second hearing the Master, Wardens, and Assistants attended court, 'but the said Mr Player came not'. The court ordered the Common Cryer to call out a summons, 'but he nor any for him appeared' and consequently he lost his case by default, and the Company was authorised to continue their prosecution against him.[281] Precisely what followed this is unclear, but the tensions between Player and the Company continued until January 1695 when he finally paid a greatly reduced fine of £1, was discharged from all offences, and readmitted as an Assistant. It appears that his expertise as a former Master was required for the organisation of repairs following the devastating fire at the Hall, and this necessity outweighed his former offences. In the following months he became an invaluable Assistant once more, and served on multiple committees overseeing the repairs and finances.[282]

Other Ranks of the London Corporation

The election of one of the Company's members to a post of office elsewhere within the London Corporation was always a source of immense pride. John Wilkes will be discussed in detail in Chapter 8, but other officers will be explored here.

Lieutenant-Colonel Samuel Robinson had failed to secure the post of the Company's Clerk in the elections of 1712, but was eventually elected to that role in 1725.[283] He served until the summer of 1728 when he was elected as the Chamberlain of the City of London, an office he held until his death in 1734.[284] He wrote to the Company on 2nd July to tender his resignation, and his letter was read out in court:

Gentlemen
The indispensable obligacon I have this day of attending the Lord Mayor and Court of Aldermen on an especial affair relateing to my Office of Chamberlain prevents my personally attending you.
When I consider the manner of my Eleccon as your Clerk which was without permitting or expecting any personal application to my ffellow Livery men, when I reflect on their almost unanimous appearance for me on my Advancemt to that great honour of being chosen Chamberlain of this City, I must acknowledge no man can have greater Obligacons to a Body of his ffellow Citizens than I have to this Company, and as the same shall be for ever fresh in my Mind so will I on all occasions shew a Distinguishing Affection not only to it as such but to you and the Court of Assistants and to every Livery Man of this Worshipfull Company.
Could the Honour and Dignity of my present Office of Chamberlain and the time I must needs spend in the proper Discharge of my Duty therein have permitted my due attendance on you as your Clerk I should have been pleased

to have dyed in that service, but as that is impossible I therefore must desire you to permit me to surrender, which I hereby do, reserving my service till you shall please to appoint a new Eleccon which I hope will be very soon.

I desire you and the Court of Assistants will be pleased to accept of my due Acknowledgemts for all your ffavours and of my hearty Thanks for the same and to transmit such my Acknowledgemts and Thanks to all my Bretheren of your Livery and you will thereby add to the Many Obligacons I have already to you.[285]

His resignation was accepted, but in return Robinson was offered the post of Master of the Company for the year 1728–9 and was duly elected as such on St James' Day.[286] His duties as Chamberlain meant that he was more of a Master in theory than in practice, but he did still provide the obligatory Master's dinner in September. The *London Evening Post* reported that

... the Chamberlain of the City of London, and Master of the Joiners Company (of which Company he was formerly Clerk) gave a very splendid Entertainment to the said Company at their Hall, and about 150 Tickets to his Friends.[287]

Daniel Defoe addressed a letter to Robinson at the end of his 1728 *Augusta Triumphans: Or, The Way to Make London the Most Flourishing City in the Universe*. The letter primarily concerns the Orphans' Fund, and demonstrates some of the issues Robinson would have faced as Chamberlain. The Fund had been set up by the 1694 Act for the Relief of the Orphans and Other Creditors of the City of London as one of the recovery measures following the 1666 Great Fire of London, but Defoe raised concerns that instead of being used for charitable purposes the money was being embezzled:

Sir,
I Shall congratulate you on your Election into the Chamberlainship of the City of *London*, or otherwise, as you shall acquit your self in answering candidly and impartially to the following Queries.

I. Whether there is not Money sufficient in the Chamber of *London* to pay off the Orphan's Fund? Or if not a sufficient Sum, What Sum it is, and what is the Deficiency? How long it has lain there, and what Interest has been made upon it?

II. If there are not considerable Arrears due from many Wards, and what those Arrears are?

III. Who are these poor Orphans we pay so much Money to? And whether they are not some of the richest Men in the City of *London*, who have got the Stock into their own Hands, and find it so snug a Fund, they do not care to get out of it?

IV. If it would not be much better to gather-in the Arrears, join 'em to the Money in the Office, and collect the Overplus at once, rather than suffer the Tax to become eternal, and to pay so much Interest?

This is but a reasonable Request; and if Col. Robinson is the honest Gentleman Fame reports him to be, he will make no Scruple to give a ready Answer. And indeed it will be but a handsome Return made to his Fellow Citizens, for their Choice of him, to begin his Office with such an Act of Justice, Honesty, and publick Satisfaction. For many People don't know what is meant by the Orphan's

Tax: They pay it with Remorse, and think themselves aggrieved. Even those who know the Reason of the Fund think it has been continued long enough, wish it were once paid off, suspect some Secret in the Affair, and give their Tongues the Liberty all Losers claim: *Our Fathers*, say they, *have eaten sour Grapes, and our Teeth are set on Edge, we are visited for their Transgressions, and may be to the World's End, unless we find an honest Chamberlain who will unveil this cloudy Affair, and give us a Prospect of Relief.*

Thus, Sir, it lies at your Door to gain the Applause of the whole City (a few Misers excepted) by a generous and Gentleman-like Discovery of this Affair. And you are thus publickly call'd upon, that your Discovery may be as publick and beneficial to all. If you comply, I shall think you an honest Man, above a Fellow-feeling, or being byass'd, and most worthy [of] your Office: If not, give me Leave to think, the Citizens of *London* have made but an indifferent Choice.[288]

In October 1780 Sir Watkin Lewes, a member of the Company, was elected as Lord Mayor of London for the ensuing year. He was likewise offered 'the Use of the Company's Hall and the Company's Plate for his Entertainment on the day he is presented to the Lord Chancellor'. Having two members of the Company elected as Lord Mayor within such a short amount of time was undoubtedly a boon, but it did put another strain on the already seriously depleted finances. The preparations for the Lord Mayor's Day parade and dignity again had to be adapted 'for the dignity and honour of the Company yet consistent with and agreeable to the Circumstances of the Company in a decent and frugal manner'. Fortunately having such a recent precedent as John Wilkes' parade made this a straightforward process; Wilkes had been elected as Lord Mayor in 1774. The Company hired eighteen men 'to walk and clear the Way before the Company'. They would be wearing cockades and carrying white staffs tipped with gold. There would also be standard bearers and whifflers as usual, all adorned with ribbons and cockades. The City's Marshalls would be given scarves, and the Marshalls' horses decorated with ribbons. There would also be 'the same Number and Sorts of Musick ... as were provided when John Wilkes Esq. ... was Lord Mayor'.[289] The Marshalls were later given a guinea each as thanks for their attendance,[290] and the ribbon bill delivered to the Company by Mr Sibley was a rather painful £14,[291] compared with only £5 12s the following year when their attendance at the Lord Mayor's Day parade had not needed to attract unnecessary attention or expense.[292] The question of whether a barge should be hired was raised, but it was decided that the Company was too large to fit on one boat, so to avoid 'discontent and disorder' they would march from the Hall to the Guildhall, escort Lewes down to the river, and return to their Hall. When Lewes returned to Blackfriars they would march there from the Hall, and escort him back to the Guildhall before adjourning for dinner at their Hall.[293] This dinner ended up costing £55.[294]

Lewes was not the only member of the Company to serve as Lord Mayor in the 1780s, however. Richard Clark was given the freedom of the Company by patrimony on 11th March 1776.[295] His father, also named Richard, was a joiner from the parish of St Botolph, Aldgate. Clark the younger was a lawyer by training, and became a successful attorney. On the same day he received his freedom he fined for steward and took the livery of the Company, after paying a fine of £20. He was elected as an Alderman of the Broad Street ward in 1776 and as one of the Sheriffs of London in 1777. He was offered 'the use of the Company's Hall and Plate during his Sheriffalty'.[296] He was elected as the Master of the Joiners' Company in 1781, as Lord Mayor in 1784, and as Chamberlain of London in 1798.[297] Clark's election as Lord Mayor was a particular boon for the Company, and a long account was entered into the court minutes concerning the suitable arrangements for Lord Mayor's Day. The same decisions were reached as with Lewes' appointment.

Richard Clark Esquire a Member of this Company being elected Lord Mayor of the City of London for the Year ensuing Resolved and agreed that he have the Use of this Company's Hall and Plate for his Entertainment on the Day he is presented to the Lord Chancellor for Approbation; the Plate to be cased only in the Company's Hall, he giving an Acknowledgement to the Renter Warden of the Plate being delivered for such his Use on that Day And the Court taking into Consideration what Preparations may be necessary to be made for the next Lord Mayor's Day for the Dignity and Honour of the Company but consistent with and agreeable to the Company's Circumstances in a decent and frugal manner It is Resolved and agreed that eighteen Men be provided to walk and clear the Way before the Company with white Staves tipped with Gold and Cockades – That Standard Bearers Whifflers and Boys be provided as usual and they to have Belts Ribbons and Cockades according to the Custom of the Company – That a proper Band of Musick be provided – That the City Marshalls be fitted and provided with Scarfs &c usual on the Occasion – And That the usual Ribbons &c be provided for the Marshall's Horses.

And it being considered that much Inconvenience may arise if the Company should be in a Barge for the next Lord Mayor's Day as none of the City Company's Barges is large enough to convey as many of the Livery of this Company to Westminster as may think proper to attend upon the Occasion and that much Discontent and Disorder may happen by part of the Company going on board the Barge and others being left out for want of Room – Resolved and agreed therefore That this Company do not hire any Barge but instead thereof that the Company do march from their Hall to Guildhall on the Morning of Lord Mayor's Day at the usual Hour to attend his Lordship from thence to the Water Side and after seeing him in his Barge then to return to their Hall to regale and again to march from thence to wait the Arrival of his Lordship at Blackfriers or wherever else he may happen to land And then to march before him to Guildhall and afterwards to adjourn to their own Hall to Dinner.[298]

In 1781 Clark tried to arrange for Lord Rodney to receive the freedom of the Company. George Bridges Rodney was an experienced naval commander who rose to particular fame during the Seven Years War and the American War of Independence. He had previously served as the Governor of Newfoundland and Commander-in-Chief of the Leeward Islands, and had been nominated as the MP for Saltash in the 1750s. He returned to England in August 1781 to regain his health after extensive service defending the Caribbean. He was due to receive the freedom of the Joiners' Company at an extraordinary meeting at the Paul's Head Tavern on 20th November, but was 'prevented coming by Illness'. The meeting was rearranged for the 29th of the same month, and although Clark was in attendance that day, 'Lord Rodney was prevented coming on account of his being ordered immediately abroad'. These two aborted meetings cost the Company £5 15s.[299] Rodney's sudden departure from the country was to prepare for what would be a decisive victory over the French in the Battle of the Saintes, which took place in the Caribbean between 9th and 12th April 1782.[300]

In November 1923 the Master acquainted the Company that their present Upper Warden John Baker was a candidate for the office of Sherriff of London at the next election in June:

> And as the Company had not been honored for over 100 years, by one of their Members being elected a Sheriff, he thought that he should with the consent of the Court circularize by a personal letter [to] all the Members of the Joiners Company asking them to support their Upper Warden and also to use their influence with all their Friends who are Liverymen of other Companies to secure the election of Mr John Baker.[301]

Aliens, Strangers, and Foreigns

Prosecuting those practising the trade of joinery without being free of the City was one of the Company's priorities for hundreds of years. There was a distinction between different types of non-free tradesmen. Those of English origin were known as foreigns, and those from abroad were known as aliens or strangers.[302] The document containing the earliest known reference to Joiners' Hall concerned this very topic. After Richmond Palace burned down on 23rd December 1497 Henry VII commissioned a replacement. A large number of joiners were required to contribute to this project, and both free and alien craftsmen were employed. The Chamberlain of London decreed that every householder stranger had to pay 4d quarterly to the Chamber of London as surety for their work, with journeymen strangers charged 2d. The free joiners of London in return promised to 'never sue them or molest them', but by 1521 this agreement had broken down. A group of strangers petitioned Cardinal Wolsey in August to complain that 'now the Englishmen make new acts against [us] in their hall' and were having them imprisoned. The strangers refused to submit to the Joiners without the express command of the Cardinal, and begged him to set their incarcerated colleagues free.[303]

By 1540 a group of foreign joiners were living in East Smithfield, and in 1567 there were twenty-four foreign joiners and carpenters living in the Ward of Bridge Without, now part of Southwark. The Joiners' Company became increasingly incensed by the competitors setting themselves up in and around London, and in 1582 they submitted a petition with a list of the names of 100 foreign joiners complaining that

> [t]he Master and Wardens of the Companye of Joyners never licensed nor admitted any of the persons hereunder expressed to use their said trade, yett they, dwelling somme in Westminster, somme in Sainct Katherins, and somme in Sowthworke, do use the sayd occupacion, and have joyned themselves togeather and have sued the joyners these tenne yeres in the lawe and procured to be spent above £400 only to thend to worck in London as fullye as a freeman may doe, to the utter undoing of a great number of freemen joyners, mere Englishemen, who are all sowayes ready for any service for her Majestie, this Realme and Citie of London.[304]

This was still a pressing issue in 1622, when Master William Gossen and his wardens addressed a petition to Sir Robert Heath, MP for the City of London.

Calling themselves the Company of Joyners, Ceelers and Carvers, they provided the names

> of all the straingers borne, Inhabitinge & dwelling wthin the Citty of London, and liberties thereof, and wthin the Borough of Southwarke (soe neere as theye can be collected) wch doe use the Arte or mistery of Joyninge Ceelinge and Carvinge aswell the Masters as the servants, By whome the said Corporation doe receive great detriment and losse by meanes of theire private and seacrett woorkinge.[305]

They had gathered the names of sixteen masters and fifteen apprentices operating within the limits of the City without freedom. This was a two-way street, however, and when joiners working abroad found themselves prosecuted they complained to the government. A petition signed by thirty-five English tradesmen living in Paris, including three joiners, was sent to Oliver Cromwell in 1654, complaining that they had

> had our worke & Tooles taken by violence from us, & broken, and cut to Peces; our selves reviled, with bitter names against our nation; our Bodyes beaten; and imprisoned; onely for workeing there as masters and for noe other cause: And that wee are not suffered to worke att all, but as servants & Journeymen under them.[306]

The Great Fire of London, which had destroyed vast swathes of the City in 1666, provided local tradesmen with constant employment over the following years as rebuilding efforts took place. In an attempt to ensure that no workman charged exorbitant rates legislation was introduced giving the Lord Mayor and Aldermen power to limit prices and wages. At the same time it was agreed that

> all Carpenters Brickelayers Masons Plaisterers Joyners and other Artificers Workemen and Labourers to be imployed in the said Buildings who are not Freemen of the said Citty shall for the space of seaven yeares next ensueing and for soe long time after as untill the said buildings shall be fully finished have and enjoy such and the same liberty of workeing and being sett to worke in the said building as the Freemen of the City of the same Trades and Professions have and ought to enjoy.

At the end of the seven years the workmen would all 'have and enjoy the same Liberty to worke as Freemen of the said Citty for and dureing their naturall lives'.[307] Tensions remained, however, and in May 1694 the Joiners submitted a lengthy petition to the Lord Mayor and Court of Aldermen complaining about men working as joiners without being free of, or regulated by, the Company. An incomplete copy of their petition was copied into the court minutes:

Sheweth
That by the Petrs Charter of the 13th of Elizabeth Enrolled amongst the records of this City and ordinances conformed according to 19 H 7 Cap 7 All Artists exercising their trade within the limmits of their grant are required to be subject unto and regulated by the constitucon and ordinances of the sd Company. That by reason of the dreadfull fire in the year 1666 in which your Petrs Hall and houses were burnt down, there resorted to London very great numbers of

forreigne Workmen, who having assisted at the rebuilding thereof, there passed an Act of Parliamt that such of them as were therein imployed, should for seaven yeares then following enjoy the same liberty of working in the building, as ffreemen of the same trades and professions ought to have, And that such Artificers which for seaven yeares should work in the said rebuilding, should enjoy the same liberty to work as ffreemen for their lives Provided that such Artificers should undergoe all such offices and pay and performe such duties as ffreemen of the City of their respective arts and trades are lyable to doe. By pretext of which Act a very great number of the aforesaid Artificers, who use the trade of Joyners and Carvers for very small and inconsiderable fines procured themselves to be made free of London of other Companies, as if it had beene by way of redempcon, and many others are ffreemen of other Companies not by force of the said Act, and yet are of the trade of Joyners and Carvers. All which Artificers refuse to submitt themselves to any governmt or by:laws of your Petrs Company. By meanes whereof your petrs are disappointed & discouraged in their Governmt, & the kingdom in generall and this City in particular are exceedingly abused and deceived by insufficient and all workmanship and wares. That severall of the members of your Petrs own Company have for many yeares last past privately obtained Joyners free of other Companies to bind Apprentices for them and cause them to be turned over to them, we having no penalty by our Bylaws for such offences. By meanes whereof the Joyners free of other Companies are already growne to a very great number, your Petrs defrauded of their quartridge and just dues, which should maintaine & [illegible] support their increasing poore, they having nothing settled on them but Twenty shillings p ann out of some houses in Ffanchurchstreet to defray that great charge of supplying the necessaries of so many poore and lame creatures as they doe every Court day by which the said Corporacon is reduced almost to a name without a substance.

Ffor prevencon of which great evils which threaten the ruine of your Petrs Company if not timely prevented your Petrs being in debt, are really necessitated to pray this honble Court to be pleased to order that all the Apprentices of Joyners and Carvers free of other Companies, as also such of their Sonns as shalbe bred up in the said trade be henceforth presented bound and made free of your petrs Company and that those who are allready bound and not yet made free of the said Company when their times are expired which favour hath already beene granted to severall Companies in the like necessity, the better to enable them to governe and correct offenders, and to reduce all persons using their trade to conformity

And they shall pray &c

The reasons and ground of the humble desires of the Company of Joyners in their Peticon are these

1. That the fundamentall cause of incorporating handicraft trades & manuall occupacons into distinct bodies was to the end that there might be a succession of expert and skillfull Governours, who should take the charge and care of regulating, ordering and correcting the severall Artificers in their materials and workmanshipps, whereby the Kingdom might be furnished with good and substantiall wares and commodities & the credit of the manufacturers preserved

2. That those contrary Companies of which sundry Joyners by profession are free, as they have no clause or branch in the least, to regulate & order any

part of the said trade by, neither have the Governours of the Companies any skill or knowledge to judge of or reforme any of their manufactures when they are illwrought or defective Which your Petrs are dayly sensible of upon their views or searches and upon complaints of others

3. By which meanes many unskillfull & ignorant persons setup & thereby
   a. deceive Gentlemen and others for whom they work, or to whom they sell their commodities
   b. They deceive their Apprentices not being able to teach them true and solid workmanship

4. As the case is at present the priveledges and immunities purchased by their Predecessors of late yeares are become their greatest snares, Because
   Each Joyner free of the Joyners Company is bound up by oath to the due observance of the constitucon and ordinances of the said Company
   a. In the number and qualificacon of their Apprentices and Journeymen
   b. In the nature and manner of workmanshipp
   c. In their respective services and charges which they cannot avoid &c

> And yet those Joyners which are free of other Companies, and who seldom or never beare any offices of charge in those Companies do within Two or Three yeares after they are ffreemen take more Apprentices then those who have beene Masters and Wardens of the Joyners Company And have laid out themselves for the publick good, Insoemuch
>
> That many Joyners free of the Joyners Company perceiving that these Joyners that are free of other Companies are made no penalty for any offence they commit, though enver so irregular or unreasonable, have and doe procure ffreemen of other Companies to bind the said Joyners sons and servants to the Companies they are free of and then turne them over backe to the said Joyners againe To the end their said sons and servants should not be under the government and correccon of the Petrs Company, Albeit they use the Joyners trade.
>
> By meanes whereof your Petrs are discouraged, the art almost ruined, & thereby loose their quarterage and other fees, they not binding nor making free so many as formerly which was in time past and should be now a support to their numerous and indigent poor, they having nothing settled on them to doe the same, but One Annuity of Twenty shillings p ann which they are forced to relieve monthly and quarterly Upon these and like inconveniences which might be enumerated, upon due applicacon made to this honble Court, it hath been the prudence and wisdom of this Court ...
> [Nothing else written].[308]

Their petition was successful and resulted in the Act of Common Council for Regulating the Company of Joyners and Ceilers, London.

Whereas the Company of Joyners and Ceilers is and hath beene an antient Brotherhood and long since incorporated and their Charter inrolled amongst others of like nature in this City but of late yeares is much lessened & decayed by reason that divers unskillfull in the said arts do dayly practise and use the same not being subject or liable to any governmt correccon or controll, and for that such as are free of other Companies and thereby obtaining the freedom of the City do use and practise the trades of Joyners Carvers and Ceilers and other imployments pertaining thereunto, & are not under any regulacon or restriccon either as to the number of their Apprentices, seasons of timber, or goodness of work whereby much deceiptfull work is dayly made and exposed to sale, within this City and libties thereof to the great injury fraud and deceipt of unskillfull buyers as well within this City and the liberties thereof as without.

Ffor remedy and reformacon whereof and to the intent all freemen of this City and libties thereof using the trades and acts aforesaid or any of them may for time to come be obliged to be free of the said Company of Joyners and Ceilers and thereby become subject to the good lawes and ordinances of the same and be brought under their search view and regulacon, whereby all frauds defaults unskillfull workmanshipp and other offences in the said trades arts & misteries may be discovered corrected and punished.

Bee it therefore enacted ordained and established by the right honble the Lord Mayor Aldermen & Comons in this prsent Comon Councill assembled and by the authority of the same That from henceforth all & every person or persons hereafter using or exercising the said trades arts or misteries of Joynery Carving or Ceiling or any of them and other imploymts pertaining thereunto within the said City or libties thereof, who hath or shall have right or priviledge to be made free by Patrimony or otherwise by vertue of his fathers freedome in any other Company whereof his father was is or shalbe free or by service with any freeman of any other Company, shall at the next Court of Assistants of the said Company of Joyners and Ceilers after notice thereof to him given by the Clerk or Beadle of the said Company by order of the Master & Wardens of the said Company for the time being accept and take upon himselfe the freedome and be made a free man of the said Company of Joyners & Ceilers in like manner and forme as he might or could have been in such the Company whereof his father or Master was so free as abovesaid Any custome or usage to the contrary in any wise notwithstanding.

And that for the future noe person or persons who shall use or exercise the said trades misteries or occupacons of Joyning carving or cieling within this City or the libties thereof shalbe made free of this City by redempcon in any other Company save only the said Company of Joyners and Ceilers.

And be it further enacted and ordained by the authority aforesaid That if any person or persons using or exercising or which shall use or exercise the trades arts or misteries of a Joyner Carver and Ceiler or any of them within this City of Lno or libties thereof who hath already served his Apprenticeshipp or shall hereafter serve his Apprenticeshipp in the said trades arts & misteries or any of them and is not yet made free of this City or who shall procure his freedome by redempcon service or Patrimony of any other Company then of the said Company of Joyners and Ceilers and shall exercise the said trades arts or misteries or any of them not being free of the said Company That then all and every such person and persons so doing and offending shall forfeit and pay for every such offence the summ of Tenn pounds of lawfull money of England to be recovered by accon of debt bill or plaint to be commenced and prosecuted in the name of the Chamblein of the said City of London for the time being in their Mats Court of Lord Mayor & Aldren to be holden in the Chamber of the Guildhall of the said City of London And that the Chamblen of the said City for the time being in all suites to be prosecuted by vertue of this present Act against any offender shall recover his ordinary costs of suites to be expended in and about the prosecucon of the same.

And be it further enacted by the authority aforesaid That one Moyety of all such forfeitures to be recovered by vertue of this present Act (the costs of suits for recovery of the same being first deducted and allowed) after recovery and receipt thereof shalbe from time to time paid into the Chamber of the said City to the use of the Mayor Coalty and Citizens of the said City of London And the other Moyety to the Master Wardens and Assistants of the said Company of Joyners and Ceilers for the time being for the use of the poore of the said Company

And that incase the said Chamblen for the time being shalbe nonsuited or a Verdict or Judgemt shalbe given against the said Chamblen in any such accon to be brought by vertue of this Act, atht athen the costs of such Nonsuite Verdict or Judgemt shalbe paid and borne by the Master Wardens and Assistants of the Company of Joyners and Ceilers for the time being, and the said Chamblen to be fully indemnified & saved harmless by the said Master Wardens and Assistants of and from the same Any law usage or custome to the contrary notwithstanding.

And be it further enacted by the authority aforesaid That noe person or persons using or exerciseing the said trades arts or misteries of Joyners Carvers or Ceilers or any of them shall from henceforth be admitted by the Chamblen of this City for the time being into the freedom or libties of this City in any other Company then the said Company of Joyners and Ceilers And law or custome of this City to the contrary notwithstanding.[309]

Edmund and Clement Chapman

The contribution made by the first Master, Lewis Stockett, to the history of the Company has already been explored in Chapter 2. However, he was not the only joiner associated with the Company who found himself working in the royal household.

Edmund Chapman was named as one of the first members of the Court of Assistants in the ordinances of 1572, and he was Stockett's successor as Master of the Company for the year 1572–3. He was responsible for securing the confirmation of the ordinances from the Lord Keeper of the Great Seal and Lords Chief Justices. Chapman had also served as a churchwarden at St James Garlickhythe since at least 1562.[310] He died in 1588, and in his will he described himself as 'maister Joyner to the quenes maiestie'. He requested burial in St James Garlickhythe 'wheare I was borne close under the monument whiche I have sett upp in the quier of the same churche'. He also instructed that the date of his death should be added to that monument, which was in alabaster, immediately under the Queen's coat of arms, along with a statement recording that 'I was ... Joyner to her maiestie And also yeoman of her maiesties armorie of East Grenewiche'. He also bequeathed £5 to be distributed to the parish poor on the day of his funeral, and £20 to pay for a house for the parson to live in.

His will also contained a reference to the Company: 'Item I give to the company of Joyners for their recreation they goinge to churche withe me on the day of my buriall five poundes.' A further £2 was bequeathed to the Worshipful Company of Armourers, who were also expected to attend the funeral. His association with them was no doubt due to his role of Yeoman of the Armoury at Greenwich. There is a suggestion that Chapman may have been in business with fellow Company member Lawrence Ripley, because he instructed his servant William Brookeman to help his widow Margaret Chapman 'to sell all suche of my wares as shalbe in the hands of Lawrence Ripley and Richard Pynfolde'. Some of the property was in his own shop and some was still in the hands of the two men.

The individual legacies specified in his will included the sum of £6 13s 4d to be paid to Richard Chapman of Tottenham within six weeks of his death, and £5 to Richard's brother John. It is unclear what the relation between Edmund and the two brothers was, but their inclusion in his will implies that they were family. There was also a bequest to a Peter Chapman of £6 13s 4d 'to buy him tooles withall' which was to be paid 'when he shalbe made a freman of the cittie of London'. Edmund also gave Peter 'twoe of the best Staplers that are in my howse', suggesting that he was also in the woodworking trade and indeed may have been a joiner.[311]

Clement Chapman was born in Tottenham in May 1572, the son of the same Richard Chapman referred to in Edmund Chapman's will. Richard was a husbandman and Clement was the fourth of his seven children. There are no surviving records for the supposed period of his apprenticeship or freedom, so it is unclear precisely when he joined the Company. He was certainly a member by 1614 when he was appointed as one of the trustees overseeing the Joiners' Hall site, and he may well have been a member of the Court of Assistants at this time too.[312] Due to the lack of records it is unclear whether Chapman ever served as a Warden or Master of the Company, but it seems probable. He had married Anne Sparks at St Margaret's, Westminster on 9th January 1599.[313] The couple set up home in the Long Ditch district of Westminster.[314]

On 29th February 1604 Chapman was appointed as chief joiner of the Tower of London.[315] By 1607 he was listed as a member of James I's royal household and liable for taxation as such.[316] Chapman's duties were varied. One of his responsibilities was constructing barges for the royal family. He received a warrant on 31st March 1609 to construct two boats for Prince Henry and Princess Elizabeth,[317] and two years later he was paid £86 9s 6d 'for works done by him about his Majesty's, the Queen's, the Prince's, the Duke of York's, and the Lady Elizabeth's barges'. He was one of four craftsmen involved in the creation of another royal barge for the King in 1620.[318]

However, Chapman also occasionally found himself on the wrong side of the law. He was issued with a recognisance on 27th March 1614 instructing him to appear at the next Middlesex Quarter Sessions Court. He had been accused of receiving a stolen cloak belonging to merchant tailor Thomas Estowe or Easter of the Strand.[319] Three years later he was fined by the same court for refusing to serve as a watchman in Westminster.[320]

Chapman is also known to have been involved in the construction of Inigo Jones' Banqueting House between 1619 and 1622. He completed 614 yards of wainscoting in the building, working alongside fellow joiner Samuel Jeniver. The two men received £312 for their work, and Jeniver later received a further £642 13s 8d for joinery work at Whitehall Palace.[321] An undated list of payments to King James' servants reveals that Chapman received 1s per day as chief joiner of the Tower of London, and another shilling per day as chief joiner of all the King's works. He had also received a robe as a demonstration of his status, paid for by the Crown, at a cost of £16 2s 6d.[322] He is believed to have continued in his role in the royal household until his death in 1626, after which he was buried at St Margaret's, Westminster.[323]

Butcher, Baker, Cabinetmaker

The Company's quarterage accounts reveal that membership was incredibly diverse, and those enjoying the freedom practiced more trades than just those relating to woodworking. At first glance many of these occupations wouldn't be relevant to joinery, but the Company made good use of its members. Diversity enabled them to be self-sufficient. If they needed builders, they had them. If they needed printers and stationers, they had them. If they needed orange merchants, they had them.

Some occupations were consistent with the larger craft of joinery, including box makers, cabinetmakers, carpenters, cartwrights, carvers, chair makers, coach joiners, coffin makers, coopers, gunstock makers, pictureframe makers, sawyers, table makers, timber merchants, and turners. There was also a large group who identified themselves simply as joiners. Other occupations were completely unrelated to joinery, including but not limited to attorneys, bookbinders, breeches makers, brokers, butchers, cheesemongers, chemists, coal merchants, cordwainers, distillers, engravers, gardeners, gingerbread bakers, grocers, hair merchants, hoop petticoat makers, jewellers, mathematical instrument makers, mustard grinders, orange merchants, pastry cooks, peruke makers, plumbers, publicans, schoolmasters, silversmiths, stationers, stockbrokers, tobacconists, watch engravers, watermen, wine merchants, and workhouse masters.

Chapter 5

The Women of the Joiners' Company

Agnes Samon

Perhaps the earliest surviving reference to a woman actively involved in the Company's business is Agnes Samon or Sawmon. Her exact relationship with the Joiners is unclear, but she may have been a joiner herself. Certainly she was an important person within their hierarchy in the early sixteenth century. The earliest reference to her in the Company's records comes on 28th May 1502 when Edward Cheseman, Thomas Marowe, and Thomas Roberts conveyed a messuage bounded by Greenwich Lane to the west and Thames Street to the north to five trustees: Agnetus Plompton, Pade Sampe, Charles William Curteys, Thomas Jakys, and Thomas Dey. Interestingly, and perhaps unusually given her status as a woman, Agnes was the first of the trustees to be named in this deed, precedence which could well indicate her relative importance to the Company.[1] However, exploration of documents outside the Company's archive reveals more information about her life, and paints a picture of a determined woman who outlived many husbands and who was not afraid to stand up for herself.

Agnes' maiden name is unknown, but her first husband had been John Cossale or Cossall, a citizen and butcher of London. He was an active member of the Worshipful Company of Butchers, serving as a warden for the St Nicholas Shambles market for the year 1475–6.[2] Agnes was presumably significantly younger than her husband because she was his second wife; his first wife, also named Agnes, had died in 1493,[3] and the second marriage took place shortly afterwards. John Cossale died in 1496, and apart from bequests to form a chantry to pray for his soul in the church of St Nicholas Shambles, Agnes was the chief beneficiary of his will.[4] Within a short time she remarried to Edward Plompton, about whom little is known. The couple were parties in a Chancery dispute concerning land in the Bermondsey parish of St Mary Magdalen in the late fifteenth century.[5] Their marriage was not a successful one, however, and Agnes had abandoned her husband by the turn of the century. Plompton claimed that 'without cause reasonable [she] willfully departed' his household,[6] but a husband's explanation for being abandoned could differ greatly from that provided by the wife who had left him. A wife removing herself from her husband's household was a very rare and brave thing to do, and implies deep difficulties in their marriage. In 1500 Agnes was prosecuted through an action on the obligation of marriage; in other words, her husband claimed that she was bound by religion and law to live with him as his wife. A surviving document in Chancery names witnesses who appeared as defendants in the case, one of whom was Edward Cheseman.[7] This name should already be familiar, as he was also involved in the 1502 land transaction along with Agnes. Another witness to the case was William Curtas, perhaps a relation of the Charles William Curteys of the deed.

The precise outcome of this case is unclear, but Agnes' ability to be party to a land transaction in her own right in 1502 implies that the marriage may have been dissolved altogether, or more likely that Edward had died in the interim. A married woman had no property rights in the early modern period; she was a legal chattel of her husband. For Agnes to be involved with the 1502 transaction, then, means that something dramatic must have changed in her life. Between 1502 and 1518 she had remarried to a man named Samon, but she outlived him. She retained her connection to the Joiners during this period, however, and on 19th October 1518, by then known as widow Agnes Samon, she sold a piece of land which would later be the site of Joiners' Hall to William Heyward, the king's joiner, for £20.[8] The following day the land was conveyed in trust to the Joiners, and this transaction was a crucial step enabling the Company to build their first Hall. Within the month Agnes was named in another deed dated 7th November, this time stipulating that the land could remain in trust to the Joiners provided that

> the same Wardeyns and free men of the said craft of mystre of Joyners of London for the tyme being evry yre forevr shall kepe a solempne Obite or Annvrsary in the pishe Churche of Seint James of Garlikhyth of London aswell for the soules of alle the brethren and sisters of the ffraternite of Seint Jams founded on the said Churche of Seint Jame as of and for alle the soules of the ffremen of the said Craft or mystere of Joyners and of their wyves and Children in the forme folowing that is to say placebo and dirige to be song on the Sonday at after noon next after the ffest of Seint James and masse of Requiem by Note on the morn folowing and spende ate and for the same obite or Annvsary yerely evry yere forevr so to be kept [6s 8d in various sums to be distributed to the parson, Clerk, and sexton, as well as for poor relief and keeping the chantry in good repair].[9]

Agnes' death is not listed in any surviving records, but in her life she became an integral figure in the Company's history. Precisely when and why she became involved with the Joiners is unclear, but she played a vital role in the process which enabled the construction of the first Hall. Her legacy was not forgotten by the Company in subsequent years. The 1548 investigation into the chantries supported by livery companies recorded that the Joiners still maintained an obit at St James Garlickhythe supported by 'lands and tenements given by Agnes Sawmon'.[10]

Charity

Pensions

The widows of deceased liverymen were entitled to submit petitions to the Company asking for relief if they found themselves in reduced circumstances.

Although there was no guarantee of success and a small number of petitions were rejected, the majority of the widows were awarded annual pensions for life. Invariably if the widows were not admitted as pensioners they were given a gratuity payment of several shillings for their immediate relief.[11] Those admitted as pensioners would be paid quarterly, which required them to attend the quarter courts in person or send representatives on their behalf. In the 1680s there was no standard pension amount; widows admitted between 1681 and 1688 received between 3s and 9s depending on their late husbands' previous contributions to the Company and their own individual circumstances.[12] However, by 1690 the quarterly payment had been fixed at 4s.[13] By 1756 the Company faced a considerable financial burden in maintaining the pensioners, and it was feared that 'great Inconveniencies may Arise' if their number continued to rise. A cap of thirty pensioners was agreed, and no additional petitions for admission would be considered until the death of a current pensioner.[14]

In 1813 widows were to receive either 10s or 20s per quarter, depending on status and circumstances.[15] The Clerk advertised in the press in January 1815 that there were four vacancies in the Company's pension list for the widows of liverymen, and that applications would be considered at the April quarter court.[16] Although no names of new pensioners were entered in the minute book following that meeting, there was a resolution passed that the widows of Past Masters should receive £2 per quarter, and everyone else would receive £1. The increase would take place from Lady Day.[17] A minimum age of fifty for any future pensioners was set in April 1844,[18] and the following year it was agreed that no charity money, either gratuities or pensions, would be assigned without enquiry into the appellant's circumstances first.[19] The quarterly payments were raised from £1 to £1 10s in July 1850,[20] and in 1856 it was agreed that the widows of liverymen would receive £15 per annum.[21]

By the turn of the twentieth century any woman wishing to be admitted as a pensioner after the death of her husband was obliged to provide the Company with copies of her birth and marriage certificates. When Sarah Illman wrote to the Company following the death of her husband Henry she told them that she did not have her certificates and could not afford to request copies. Rather than dismissing her case, the court provided her with £2 from the poor box so she could acquire the necessary documents and promised to consider her application further.[22] When she was able send the certificates the August court agreed to admit her as a pensioner, and sent a cheque of £7 10s backdated to 5th July.[23]

In 1927, after a number of long-term pensioners had passed away, it was agreed that the Company could afford to raise the annual pension by a further £20, half each to be paid as Midsummer and Christmas gifts.[24]

Other Financial Support

There were also slightly more unusual requests for financial support. In 1704 Elizabeth Wright attended the March court. Her husband Robert had been chosen as one of the Company's stewards for the previous Lord Mayor's Day dinner, but he had chosen to pay the £5 fine rather than hold the role. His brother Thomas Wright had previously delivered 50s to the Company as half of the fine, and the remaining half was still due. Mrs Wright informed the court that she was in a 'deplorable condicon haveing herselfe and three small children to maintaine by her owne industry and her said husband haveing little regard of her and them and being by badd company'. The court ordered that she should receive the 50s previously delivered by Thomas Wright to contribute towards her maintenance, and the remainder of the fine was written off.[25] Similarly, Christopher Coney had fined for the role of steward in 1722 and had presented a promissory note for the £5 payable in December. However, at the January court the news of his death was presented to the Assistants, and as he 'hath left a Wife & several Children very poor' it was ordered that the note should be given up and his wife released from the debt.[26]

In November 1705 Edward Hancock petitioned the Company on behalf of his wife. He had been imprisoned in Ludgate for debt, leaving a wife and four children at home unprovided for. He 'beggs your charity', and the Renter Warden was ordered to give Mrs Hancock 5s.[27]

Pensioner Ann Hewitt appears to have made two separate appeals to the Company for financial support towards the cost of emigration. In August 1834 she wrote 'praying relief in assisting her to make a Voyage to Sydney to remain with her daughter who is settled there'. The Company agreed to pay her £4 and removed her from the list of pensioners.[28] However, she applied again in April 1846 with the request that they would advance her the sum of £5 'to enable her to proceed to join her Daughter who is resid[ing] at New York America', in exchange for her forfeiting any future claims for a pension. The Court agreed and she was paid the money accordingly.[29] She was likely the sixty-nine-year-old Ann Hewitt who sailed from London on the 'Prince Albert', arriving in New York on 25th June.[30]

Mary Ann Lowthorp approached the Company in June 1849 asking whether they would immediately advance her next two quarterly pension payments, totalling £2, 'to enable her to go to the sea bathing Infirmory for the benefit of her health'.[31] She repeated this request in June 1853 when she wished to return 'to the sea side for the benefit of her health'.[32]

Education for Children

A rarer way for women to claim support from the Company was to request money for the education of their children. The earliest surviving example of this was from a monthly court meeting on 7th January 1662 when Mary Payne, widow of liveryman George Payne, claimed that Past Master William Vyner[33] had promised 'something towards putting forth one of hir Children appr[enticed]'. However, at the next court she was paid £2 'toward inabling her to keepe a Chandlers shop towards the maintenance of hirself and her 6 Children', so the Court of Assistants seem to have judged it more sensible to provide her with a livelihood, which would in turn support the whole family, rather than paying the cost of binding a child.[34]

On 1st April 1735 a quarterly court ordered that Constance Hallam should be allowed £2 'to teach her son who is blind to play upon the Musick'. The Warden and Beadle were instructed to pay 5s per quarter to 'such person as shall teach him', and they were to stay in close contact with Mrs Hallam 'to see that he is taught' and the money not squandered. Unfortunately, on 9th September of that same year another entry in the court minute book recorded that the order to Mrs Hallam was discharged, 'her son being dead', but they allowed her a final 10s as a gratuity.[35] She retained a connection with the Company, however, and on 12th November 1745 the court ordered the Renter Warden to pay her another 2s 6d because she was 'a poor Woman'.[36]

1. The charter granted to the Mystery or Faculty of Joiners and Ceilers of London by Elizabeth I in 1571.

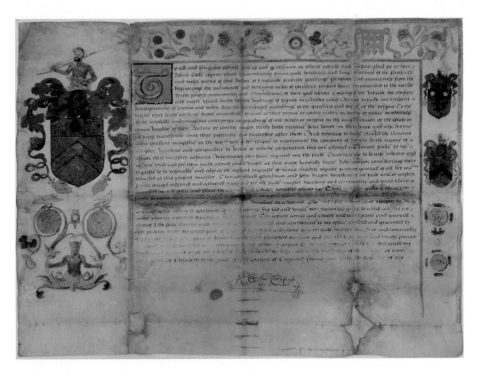

2. The 1571 grant of arms which gave the Company the right to display and use a crest or coat of arms bearing a unique decoration. Their coat of arms can be seen in the top-left corner of the document.

Above left: 3. The Company's coat of arms has undergone many changes since the first iteration. This image is believed to date from 1677.

Above right: 4. The coat of arms in 1774.

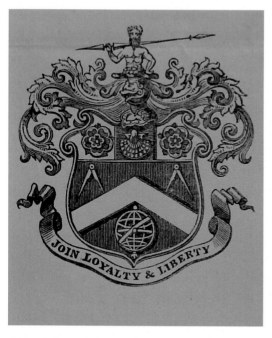

Above left: 5. The coat of arms in 1838.

Above right: 6. Arms of the Joiners and Ceilers' Company, *c*. 1880, artist unknown. (© London Metropolitan Archives, City of London)

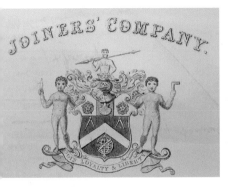

Above: 7. The coat of arms in 1913.

Right: 8. This is a copy of the instructions issued to apprentices when they began their training. Although this is a twentieth-century copy, the wording had changed very little from the instructions issued during the early modern period.

INSTRUCTIONS

For the Apprentices of the Company of JOINERS, CEILERS, or CARVERS, of the City of *London*.

YOU shall constantly and devoutly on your Knees, every Day, serve GOD Morning and Evening, and make Conscience in the due Hearing of the Word preached, and endeavour the right Practice thereof in your Life and Conversation: You shall do diligent and faithful Service to your Master, for the Time of your Apprenticeship, and deal truly in what you shall be trusted: You shall often read over the Covenants of your Indenture, and see and endeavour yourself to perform the same to the utmost of your Power: You shall avoid all evil Company, and all Occasions which may tend to draw you to the same; and make speedy Return when you shall be sent on your Master's or Mistress's Errand: You shall avoid Idleness, and be ever employed either for GOD's Service, or in your Master's Business: You shall be of fair, gentle, and lowly Speech and Behaviour to all Men, and especially to your Governors; and according to your Carriage, expect the Reward for Good or Ill from GOD and your Friends.

GOD SAVE THE KING.

9. The oil painting dated 1670 showing the Master and Wardens of the Joiners' Company inspecting the design for their new Hall after it had been destroyed during the Great Fire of London. The painting now hangs in the Guildhall.

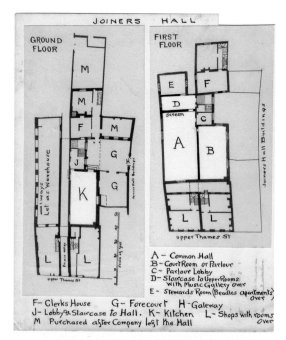

JOINERS HALL

GROUND FLOOR

FIRST FLOOR

Joiners Hall Buildings

upper Thames St

A – Common Hall
B – Court Room or Parlour
C – Parlour Lobby
D – Staircase to Upper Rooms with Music Gallery over
E – Stewards Room (Beadles apartments over)
F – Clerks House   G – Forecourt   H – Gateway
J – Lobby & Staircase to Hall.   K – Kitchen   L – Shops with rooms over
M Purchased after Company left the Hall

10. This is a supposition of how the rooms inside Joiners' Hall were organised before the building was let as a warehouse in 1800.

11. This illustration shows the plan for rebuilding Joiners' Hall after the fire of 1811. Although it was being used as a warehouse, the building was re-built on the same blueprint as the Livery Hall.

12. However, the internal design of the building had changed drastically and had been completely re-organised to function as a multi-storey warehouse.

Above left: 13. Joiners' Hall *c.* 1880 by John Philipps Emslie. (© London Metropolitan Archives, City of London)

Above right: 14. An illustration of Joiners' Hall by Thomas Hosmer Shepherd.

15. The demigods decorating the gateway into Joiners' Hall, *c.* 1908. (© London Metropolitan Archives, City of London)

16. The tradition of the Company attending a service at St James Garlickhythe continues to this day.

17. Although fewer in number than during the Company's heyday, banquets remain an important part of their calendar.

18. The Master's Chair created by Past Master Edward Newman in 1754. In preparation for the 450th anniversary celebrations extensive restoration work has been carried out on this chair by Clunie Fretton. (© V&A Museum)

Right: 19 & 20. These are two twentieth-century surviving examples of the silver spoons presented to liverymen in lieu of the July dinner.

Below: 21. The plaque placed on the former site of Joiners' Hall in Upper Thames Street in 1965. The dates have since been found to be incorrect.

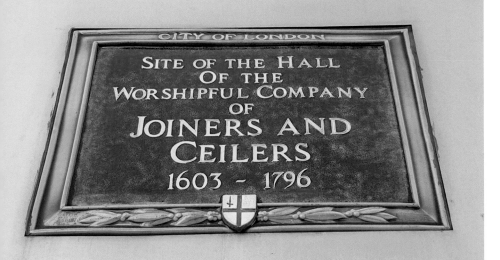

CITY OF LONDON
SITE OF THE HALL
OF THE
WORSHIPFUL COMPANY
OF
JOINERS AND
CEILERS
1603 – 1796

22. The Company still actively promotes education in the joinery trade, and regularly provides sponsorships and competitions for young craftsmen seeking to improve their skills.

23. Her Royal Highness the Duchess of Cornwall becoming an Honorary Liveryman of the Company on Wednesday 19 October 2011, seen here with the Master for 2011–2, Clive Turrell.

Joinery Mistresses and Apprentices

A largely overlooked aspect of women's involvement in the Worshipful Company of Joiners and Ceilers is the role of the mistresses of apprentices. Women were far more actively involved in the training of joinery apprentices than previously believed. Although traditionally the original indentures have been used to study apprenticeships, when it comes to tracing the involvement of women in the Joiners' Company a clearer picture can be gained using the freedom admissions recorded in the court minute books. The indentures will reveal who an apprentice was originally bound to, but these records of freedom provide a very different picture of female involvement.

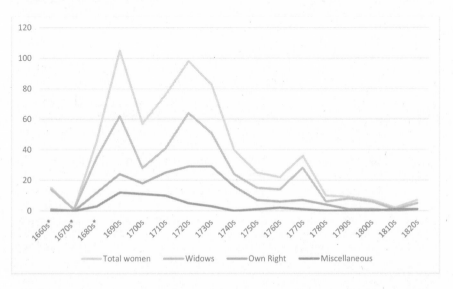

This graph plots the visibility of women in freedom admissions records from the 1660s to the end of the 1820s. There are 639 entries concerning female mistresses or widows during that time. It must be noted that, due to the destruction of the records, the figures from the 1660s, 1670s and 1680s are incomplete and therefore probably do not reflect the true scope of female involvement in apprenticeships during those decades. In 1831 the method of recording admissions changed, and instead of stating that the freedom was granted by the consent of the master or mistress the entries simply said that the person had been made free by servitude or purchase.

The graph first shows the total level of female involvement, followed by that figure broken down into three separate categories: widows who took over from their late husbands, women who had apprentices bound to them in their own right, and miscellaneous. Generally speaking the latter category captures women who had been sent to approve a freedom on behalf of their still living husbands, or women who acted as executrices but without specifying their precise relation to the apprentice master.

There were three main ways a woman could become involved in the training of an apprentice. The first was through the apprentice being bound to her husband. The terms of the indentures specified that the apprentice had to live in their master's household, and by default the wife would be as involved in the training as their husbands. It is impossible to quantify how many women assisted with training because their contributions were not officially recorded if the husband was alive. This largely hidden involvement of women implies that the daughters of joiners probably grew up learning enough of the trade too, but without being bound in a formal apprenticeship the extent of this can never be known. However, a joiner's daughter is likely to have made a very attractive proposition for a future joiner's wife.

In rare cases husbands entrusted the task of providing consent for an apprentice's freedom at Joiners' Hall to their wives. This appears to have been acceptable to both the husbands and the Company, and there was never any indication that the wife's consent was any less valid than that of the husband. Some women, such as Ann Barber in October 1690 and Thomasin Collins in December 1693, were described simply as the wives of the masters and appearing on their behalf,[37] but other cases provided more detail. Elinor Evans appeared on behalf of her husband Joseph in March 1693 because he was incarcerated in the Fleet Prison, and Elizabeth Thomas' husband David was 'a Lunatique' in 1718.[38] Hannah Hart's husband Joseph was in Plymouth in April 1698, Mary Williams' husband Rowland was 'gone to Virginia' in July 1704, and Eleanor Haddon's husband Mark had been 'gone some y[ea]res beyond sea' in 1720, which implies that she had of necessity overseen their apprentice's education.[39]

The second way a woman could be involved in training apprentices is further evidence for the first. Apprentices receiving the freedom of the Company were always recorded in the court minutes. The Clerk wrote their name, the date of their original indenture, the name of their Master, and by whose consent they received their freedom. He also specified whether the Master had died during the apprentice's training. In the vast majority of such cases the training was taken over by the widow of the joiner, and this was recorded by the Clerk. It is very rare to find an example of an apprentice turned over to another man after the death of the master. Widows represented 403 of the 639 instances of female involvement in apprenticeship, which is 63 per cent of the total. It was standard practice for widows to take over, because in the vast majority of cases they would already have been playing an active role in the apprentice's education anyway, and it was assumed that they had the requisite skills to oversee the remainder of the training. This was stated explicitly in the freedom of John Mills on 4th March 1788. He had been bound to joiner William Kay on 6th February 1781, and was made free with the consent of William's widow Alice Kay 'with whom the said Apprentice served the remainder of his Term from the said William Kay's decease'.[40] Another example is Joan Grace. After the death of her husband Thomas she oversaw the remainder of his apprentice William Lovell's training. Although she did not appear in person at Joiners' Hall in 1691 to confirm the freedom, which was granted on report of two other citizens, they told the court that Joan had asked that 'they should reporte to this Company of the servants honesty'.[41] Anomalous cases are those where the apprentice is admitted by patrimony despite the father having died before the training could be completed. For example, Sampson Shakemaple was admitted on 5th May 1696 'on the Report of Rachell Shakemaple the late Widdow of the said Stephen'.[42]

The third, and most significant, way was for women to have apprentices bound to them directly. Although this only represents 181 of the 639 entries, or 28 per cent, it raises numerous questions about the status of female joiners. The majority of these women were still recorded as the widows of joiners, but after they were widowed they had taken apprentices in their own right in addition to completing any remaining training for previously bound apprentices. However, a small number of women, particularly in the 1690s, were recorded as citizens and joiners in their own right, which implies that they had also undergone a period of apprenticeship and received the freedom of the Company. Unfortunately the lack of surviving documents before this time means that this cannot be verified.

Girls being bound as apprentices to joiners was much more uncommon than boys, but not unheard of. The earliest female apprentice identifiable in the surviving records was Elizabeth Towgood or Toogood, who was bound for seven years on 13th June 1682. Her freedom entry is unusual because it revealed that she had been bound to 'John Blinckoe Citizen and Joyner of London and Mary his wife', which implies that they were jointly responsible for her education. Six months after Elizabeth was bound to the Blinkoes, another young girl named Susan Oldfield was bound to 'Daniel Hayward Citizen and Joyner of Lno and Elizabeth his wife'. Both girls were made free of the Company within two months of each other in 1690. Edward and Rebecca Barber also shared the responsibility of their female apprentices. Their first was Eleanor Chamberlaine, bound in July 1686, but she was later turned over to innholder John Welling. Their second female apprentice, Mary Vickars, was bound in February 1688 and remained with them until she received her freedom on 3rd July 1694.[43] There do not appear to be any examples in the Joiners' Company records of male apprentices bound to both a husband and wife at once, so this must be seen as a uniquely female circumstance.

Ann Dryden was bound to Elizabeth Rand, 'citizen and Joyner of London' in her own right, on 5th September 1693. Elizabeth was the daughter of Walter Rand, who in turn was the son of Oxfordshire yeoman Christopher Rand. Walter had been apprenticed to Gabriel Holland on 27th July 1647, and received his freedom on 7th August 1654.[44] He had married Margaret Perrin at St Michael's, Cornhill on 18th September 1653.[45] Although technically still an apprentice, the parish register listed his occupation as a joiner.[46] Walter died at Bedlam and was buried in their burial ground on 23rd May 1660. Elizabeth was a posthumous child, and her baptism entry named her as 'the daughter of Walter Rand deceased & of Margaret his wife'. She was born on 30th December 1660 and was baptised on 1st January.[47] Elizabeth was admitted to the Company by patrimony on 1st August 1682,[48] and her apprentice Ann received the freedom of the Company on 5th March 1706.[49]

There is an example in the Company's records of multi-generational female apprentices bound to mistresses. Elizabeth Storey was initially bound to joiner Robert Boorne on 1st December 1724. She was later turned over to Margaret Morrice, citizen and cutler of London, on 25th May 1725 and remained with her until 14th October 1729 when she was turned over again to citizen and clothworker Richard Browne. In spite of all these changes, she was admitted into the freedom of the Joiners' Company on 3rd September 1734.[50] The Company's quarterage books reveal that she set herself up in business in Lombard Street.[51] The British Museum holds two trade cards – a cross between a business card and a flyer – advertising Elizabeth's business, and it appears that she had gone into a partnership. The two trade cards are identical, except that one lists her business partner as Sibbella Lloyd, and the other lists two partners: Sibbella Lloyd and Martha Williams. The latter card has an estimated date of 1740. The ladies' business was based at the sign of the Three Angels against George Yard, Lombard Street. The business was an eclectic one and appears to have combined the trades of furniture making with haberdashery, millinery, dressmaking, and tailoring. The ladies advertised that they sold all sorts of Baskets, Pincushions, Chimney Lines, Blankets, Rollers, Mantles, Cradles, & Linings, Bed Chairs & Tables, Childrens Dimity Coats, Holland Frocks, Flannel Pettycoats, Stockings & Shoes, Quilted Gowns & Bed Gowns, Wastcoats and Holland half Shifts, Sattin & Callicoe quilted Bed Quilts, Toilots for Tables, Damask & Diaper Clouting Hollands & Callicoes, India & French Quilting, Dimitys strip'd & figur'd, best Bone & Cane Hoops, Sattin, Sarcenet, Persian, Callicoe, Russell, & Callimanco Quilted Pettycoats, Velvet and Silk Scarves, Manteels, Mantilets, Pilgrims & Hoods, silk, scarlet & light colour'd Cloth Cloaks, double & colour'd Velvets of all sorts … Likewise Makes & Sells all sorts of Riding Dresses, Widows Weeds, Mens mourning Gowns & Bannyans Vests & Tunicks, Jocky Caps silk & Leghorn Hatts.[52]

The year after gaining her freedom, and perhaps in recognition of her time with Margaret Morrice, Elizabeth took an apprentice in her position of 'Citizen and Joiner of London' in her own right. On 2nd December 1735 Mary Horne was bound to her for a premium of £60,[53] and remained with her for the entire duration of her apprenticeship, eventually receiving the freedom of the Company on 2nd December 1746.[54] Elizabeth took a second apprentice on 19th July 1738. Her next pupil was Mary Wyan, and her premium was higher at £80.[55] Mary had been born on 1st April 1720, the daughter of Quaker parents. Her father was draper and mercer Jacob Wyan of Gracechurch Street, and her mother was his second wife Anne Markes.[56] Jacob's first wife, Sarah Quare, had died of a fever at the age of twenty-seven on 17th July 1717,[57] only five days after their fifth wedding anniversary.[58] He had remarried to Anne in Hammersmith on 14th July 1719.[59] Mary was their first child, followed swiftly by another daughter named Anne born on 17th April 1721.[60] Unfortunately, little Anne's birth claimed the life of their mother only a few weeks later, on 9th May 1721. She was only twenty-six years old.[61]

Although he was a relatively successful businessman, Jacob's life was a difficult one. He had lost two young wives and was left to care for two young daughters. He had also been the victim of highway robbery on Christmas Eve 1720 whilst travelling by coach from Hampstead back to the city with friend James Pitt. The men were robbed of a guinea's worth of silver, and a newspaper report noted that 'they had their Watches about them, but by good Management saved them'. The servant travelling on the coach tried to stop the robbers and they attempted to shoot him in the head, so the experience must have been very traumatic for Jacob.[62] Tragedy followed tragedy and on 20th August 1730, when his daughters were only nine and ten years old, Jacob died of a fever at the age of forty-two.[63] An obituary appeared in the *Daily Journal* the following day:

> Yesterday Morning died, after 17 Days Illness, of a Fever, at his House the Corner of Little Eastcheap, Mr. Jacob Wyan, an eminent Mercer, and Trader to the West-Indies: 'Tis thought that tho' he was in very good Circumstances, his being bound at the Custom-house for a Virginia Merchant, who died Insolvent a few Years since, made him uneasy, and did not a little contribute to his Illness.[64]

In his will he entrusted the care and education of his girls to his mother Mary Field with the request that she would 'lay out and expend such sumes of money in the maintenance and Education of my said Children as she shall think proper'.[65] Unfortunately, little Anne also died of a fever on 24th May 1736, aged fifteen.[66] Two years later, Mary was bound to Elizabeth Storey and would have relocated to her household for the duration of her education. Her grandmother

Mary Field appears to have also passed away in 1742, whilst young Mary was still an apprentice.[67]

After her training had ended it is unclear whether Mary set herself up in business or not. The next trace of her comes on 14th September 1752, when she married merchant William Thomas at the Quaker meeting house on Gracechurch Street, close to her childhood home. The record of their marriage described him as 'William Thomas of West River in the Province of Maryland Merchant Son of Philip Thomas Esqr of the same Place and of Frances his Wife, she being deceased'.[68] Philip Thomas of Maryland was actually, at this time, a senator in the upper chamber of the United States Congress. He owned plantations in Anne Arundel, Cecil, and Calvert counties. However, with this history there comes a far graver and less honourable side, because when he died he was known to have owned eighty slaves. Philip Thomas came from a prominent Quaker family, with both Philip and his wife Anne recorded as ministers.[69] This was a remarkable match for Mary to have made, and the couple divided their time between Maryland and London later in life. Ultimately her knowledge of joinery is unlikely to have been necessary, but this demonstrates how the life of a humble orphaned apprentice could take such a drastic turn.

Unfortunately little is known about Elizabeth Storey's later life. She took a third apprentice, Mary Merry, on 19th June 1739. She received her freedom on the same day as Mary Horne in 1746.[70] Elizabeth was listed as a householder in the second quarterage book, which covers the period 1757 to 1777, but she is absent from the third.[71]

Freedom by Patrimony

A more common way for women to receive the freedom of the Company was to be admitted through patrimony; that is, they were admitted because their fathers had already secured the freedom. Generally speaking a daughter was only admitted after her father had died, a double standard not applicable to men, who could be admitted during their fathers' lifetimes. Between 1683 and 1812 there were twenty-six women admitted by patrimony. Interestingly there were two widows who were admitted because of their fathers' status, rather than through any claim of a husband's position in the Company. Mary Polley, the widow of William Polley and daughter of William Kendall was admitted by patrimony on 4th May 1773,[72] and Ann Larken, the daughter of Thomas Ellis, was admitted on 1st December 1812.[73]

Sarah Munt, daughter of the late Humphrey Munt, requested freedom by patrimony in July 1691 because she had 'taken a shopp within this City for a Livelyhood and subsistance' and needed the freedom to enable her to trade.[74] Humphrey Munt was the son of yeoman Samuel Munt of Peldon in Essex. He was apprenticed to joiner Anthony King in 1654, and received the freedom of the Company on 2nd February 1663.[75] He was an ironmonger by trade, and set himself up in the Clare Market district of St Clement Danes. A halfpenny trade token bearing his name and business location has survived from 1666.[76] That year he also married Elizabeth Porter in Isleworth.[77] Munt's business appears to have been a successful one, and he took numerous apprentices through the Joiners' Company over the course of his career; Lionel Cork in 1663, John Pemberton in 1666, Samuel Boawre and Richard Southernwood in 1669, Thomas Farrington in 1670, Henry Harris in 1680, and Thomas Edgar in 1682.[78] However, he also found himself involved in two lengthy legal disputes which drained his finances and did not leave his children well provided for. After his death in 1689 his property was placed in trust for his children until they reached adulthood.[79] Not all of the children followed their father into the Joiners' Company, however; Robert Munt was apprenticed to ironmonger Lawrence Stevenson on 10th September 1690.[80]

There are two examples of sisters receiving their freedom by patrimony together. The first was the Kidder sisters, Elizabeth and Susannah, who were made free on 5th February 1735.[81] Their father Edward Kidder had previously served as the Company's cook from 1697 to 1701. Mary and Ann Allmond, daughters of William Allmond, were both admitted by patrimony on 4th October 1803.[82] The Company's quarterage records list them as journeymen householders of 69 Queen Street, Cheapside, and reveal that they were dealers in oil.[83] A Post Office directory from 1814 described them as M & A Allmond, Oilmen & Grocers.[84]

Women in the Quarterage Books

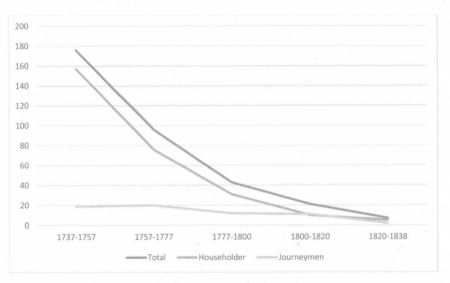

Another way to study the women of the Joiners' Company is by looking at the quarterage books, which contain alphabetical lists of Company members, both male and female. The earliest surviving book covers the period 1737 to 1757;[85] all earlier records were destroyed by fire. This chart shows all of the women recorded in the quarterage books over a 101-year period from 1737 to 1838, split into three categories: the total in each book, the number of women householders, and the number of women journeymen. It is clear from this data that there was a steady decline through the middle of the eighteenth century, and by the early nineteenth century the number of women was in the single figures.

During the period covered by the first book there were 157 female householders who paid 6d per quarter, and nineteen female journeymen who paid 3d. Unfortunately the first of the Beadles who created this book listing the women who were already members of the Company in 1737 decided that recording more information about them, such as their addresses or occupations, was unnecessary in most cases, even though such information was recorded for men. From the 1740s onwards it was more likely for this information to be captured, but still not guaranteed. Consequently it is difficult to identify many of the women listed in this book. Of the 176 women only two had recorded occupations, and they were both journeymen. Spinster Mary Norris, who was first listed in the year 1751–2, was a cork cutter in Lothbury, and Sarah Wright, who joined the Company in 1753–4, was a hoop petticoat maker in Bishopsgate Street.

Another 117 of the 176 women, two-thirds of the total, were recorded as widows. The implication is that their husbands had been joiners, and upon their deaths the women carried on their businesses. Twenty-eight of the widows also had the names of their late husbands noted in their entries, which corroborates the theory that they may have previously been members of the Company.

One example of that is Ann Seagood, widow of Henry. He was the son of waterman Thomas Seagood of Mortlake, and had been apprenticed to joiner Edward Ford on 21st June 1709.[86] After securing his freedom on 4th March 1718[87] he settled in the parish of St Bartholomew the Great and began trading as a carpenter. He married Ann Goddard of Twickenham at St Michael, Queenhithe on 26th March 1722,[88] and the couple went on to have three children: Sarah, Thomas, and Henry. On 27th July 1732 one Mary Tomlin broke into the Seagoods' home in Bartholomew Close and stole some items of clothing, including four gowns, three head-cloths, and a hat. She was arrested and tried at the local Quarter Sessions, before the case was referred to the Old Bailey. Henry was summoned to give a deposition:

> I live in Little Bartholomew-Close. On the 27th of July, between 11 and 12 at Noon, I left the Sash of my Ground-room next the Yard shut, and my Goods lock'd up in my Drawers; but returning in a Quarter of an Hour, I found my Sash pull'd down, my locks broke, the Drawers upon the Floor, and that Apparel and Linen had been taken away, to the value of 15l. A Girl told me that she saw a Creature in the Yard with a Bundle, and asked her what she did there? And the Creature said, What's that to you, ye Bitch, or some such Words. The Girl shew'd us which Way she went, and we follow'd, and found her in Long-Lane.[89]

Tomlin was found guilty and sentenced to transportation.[90]

When Henry died in 1744 he bequeathed to their son Thomas 'All my Working Tools in the Way of Trade and desire he may have the Offer and Refusal of All my Stock in Trade at the price and Value it shall be Appraised at after my demise'.[91] Thomas accepted the offer and took over his father's business in Bartholomew Street. He does not appear to have been a consummate businessman because he was declared bankrupt in 1751.[92] Ann was appointed as one of his assignees, along with Joseph Pearse, and they jointly oversaw the legalities of Thomas' case.[93]

In spite of her husband's death and her son's financial troubles, Ann oversaw the remaining training of her husband's two apprentices, who received their freedoms in 1744 and 1747.[94] The fact that she was named in the quarterage book indicates that she remained actively involved in the family business, perhaps as a manager but maybe as an artisan herself. Ann died at the age of seventy-three and was buried at St Bartholomew the Great on 4th October 1769. In her will she bequeathed the lease of three properties in Chiswick to her brother Richard Goddard, a tenant of one of the houses, and the residue of her estate was left entirely to her daughter Sarah. Neither of her sons were named in the will.[95] Sarah had not joined the family business but was nevertheless operating as a mantua maker in her own right in the parish of St Bartholomew the Great. On 26th July 1753 Rebecca Parnham was bound to her,[96] and in 1775 her uncle

Richard Goddard bequeathed the whole of his estate, including the property he inherited from Ann, to her.[97]

Another interesting family from the quarterage books are the Inces. Mary Ince of Bow Street, Covent Garden, was listed as a householder from 1746 onwards.[98] She was the widow of glass grinder John Ince, who was born in Stone, Warwickshire in 1699. On 26th July 1720 he was bound to joiner James Welch. John died in September 1745 and was buried in his hometown of Stone.[99] In his will,[100] which was written on 3rd September 1745 and proved on 4th October of that same year, he left very clear instructions that he wanted Mary to continue the family business. John specifically requested 'that my Loving Wife Mary during the Minority of my Eldest Son John shall with the same Stock and Effects solely Manage and carry on my Trade and Business of a Glassgrinder'. When the younger John reached the age of twenty-one he was to be admitted as a partner in the business, and if their younger son William also wanted to join the trade he was to be 'bound Apprentice with his said Mother for the Term of seven years'. However, if he wanted to follow a different trade John bequeathed £20 to bind him as an apprentice to someone else instead. He also bequeathed £10 apiece to his daughters Elizabeth and Mary to enable them to be apprenticed 'to a Milliner or some such like Business'.

The will did, however, contain the caveat that his household goods and business stock should be sold to pay his debts and funeral costs if necessary, and that does seem to have happened. A notice in the *General Advertiser* on 24th March 1748 announced the sale at the beginning of April of 'The Entire Houshold Goods Stock and Implements in Trade, of Mr. JOHN INCE, Glass-Grinder, deceas'd; by express Direction of his Will, at his late Dwelling House the Upper-End of Bow-street, Covent-Garden'. The notice also stated that the house was to be let at the same time, so the Ince family were having to relocate.[101]

William Ince, who had been born in 1737, was apprenticed to cabinetmaker John West of King Street, Covent Garden, on 10th August 1752. West died in 1758 before William's training had been completed, and his business was taken over by Samuel Norman, James Whittle, and John Mayhew. The latter of these three men was destined to play an important role in William's life. Together they created the partnership of Ince and Mayhew by December 1758, and became hugely important furniture makers during the eighteenth century. In addition to elaborately decorated furniture, the partnership also produced a number of publications containing designs for other joiners to copy. These included *The Universal System of Household Furniture*, published between 1759 and 1763, and *Household Furniture in Genteel Taste for the year 1760*.[102] Their clientele grew to include members of the peerage, including the Duchesses of Northumberland and Devonshire.

The Ladies' Banquet

The wives of Assistants enjoyed the privilege of attending the Livery dinners at Joiners' Hall on Audit Day and Lord Mayor's Day.[103] In addition to these, during the nineteenth century a banquet was held in honour of the Company's ladies every spring, followed by a ball. These entertainments were available to the wives of liverymen as well as Assistants,[104] and were largely financed through the Company's Irish investments through the Salters' Company, which in the 1850s had left their bank account in 'a most flourishing condition'.[105] These entertainments could be quite lavish in scale; in 1859, for example, the Company hired a steamboat to convey the Livery and their ladies upriver to the Castle Hotel in Richmond. Refreshments of cake, biscuits, sherry, and lemonade were served on board, before dinner at the hotel and a return journey back down the Thames.[106] In 1880 the Company ventured out of London, providing a day trip to Brighton Aquarium followed by dinner and a ball.[107]

The ladies were entertained with music and singing, and were presented with a gift. These were usually items made of silver to compliment the silver spoons and other items of crockery presented to the liverymen each St James' Day. However, the Ladies' Banquet was one of the events which drew criticism when the press investigated the Company's finances in 1877:

> But the art and mystery of joinery, as practised in the City of London, is not confined to men, and so accordingly we find that the lady Joiners enjoyed the benefits of the trust in the shape of an entertainment given at Cannon Street Hotel on May 30 [1876]. The Worshipful Company expended 174l 2s on this entertainment, and when it is found that 13l 1s 9d was expended in 'scent-bottles' alone, it will be understood under what pleasant auspices technical education proceeds in the City of London.[108]

In spite of this criticism the banquets continued. The banquet in 1927 was a joint celebration of the Company's successful re-negotiation of the lease for Joiners' Hall with their tenants Messrs Major and Field.[109] It was held at Carpenters' Hall on 6th July.[110] The Lord Mayor, Lady Mayoress, the Sheriffs of London, and their ladies were all invited to the 1928 banquet, again held at Carpenters' Hall on 15th March 1928.[111] Gifts were given to all ladies in attendance at the banquets.[112] In 1929 they received a silver tea strainer weighing 2oz with the Company's crest serving as the handle.[113] 1930 saw a gift of a silver sweet dish,[114] and in 1931 it was a powder compact with the crest embossed on the front and the year engraved under it.[115] The latter cost the Company 15s each. In 1932 and 1933 the ladies received a bag,[116] and a glass powder bowl with a silver top in 1935.[117] The cost of the banquet was a significant charge on the Company's finances, however. In 1936 the banquet itself cost £241 18s 6d, with a further £19 8s 6d for the hire of Carpenters' Hall and a pianist, and £52 10s spent on presents for the ladies.[118]

During the Second World War all Company events, including the Ladies' Banquet, were cancelled. However, at the end of the 1940s it became possible to reinstate some of the old customs. The Ladies' Banquet was one of the things to return in 1950, although it was combined with a general livery dinner to become 'a dinner for the Livery and their Ladies'.[119] The Lord Mayor accepted an invitation to attend, and a budget of £150 was set, higher than the £100 allocated to the November banquet.[120] The event was a success and the same pattern was followed in 1951, although the cost of tickets had dramatically increased from the pre-war prices. The cost for liverymen and their wives would be 3 guineas, with additional guest tickets at 6 guineas.[121] Even so, the total cost to the Company for the 1951 banquet ended up being £309 14s 10d.[122]

Women as Merchants or Vendors

Money

In 1693 Mary Youle became one of the Company's creditors. On Audit Day on 23rd August the Company was informed that the Lord Mayor was requesting contributions towards the 4s in the pound tax levied by King William and Queen Mary to fund the war with France. This was a 20 per cent tax on the rental value of real estate, which raised over £296,000 in the City of London.[123] The Joiners' Company's contribution to this tax was £150. However, the audit which had taken place earlier that day revealed that they only had £68 12s 8d in ready cash. Assistant Mr Atkinson volunteered to lend the Company £100 on the security of the common seal for six months at 6 per cent, but stipulated that the bond should be in the name of his widowed daughter Mary Youle. This loan, combined with the ready cash, allowed them to pay the tax at the Chamber of London the following day.[124] They found themselves unable to repay the debt after the appointed six months, so it was extended further. However, after the Hall was seriously damaged by fire in 1694 the already precarious finances were drained. Rather than demanding immediate repayment, in April 1695 Atkinson increased his original loan by another £100 to contribute towards paying the workmen, 'which this Court takes very kindly'.[125] However, Mary Youle's second husband, coachmaker Robert Robins, called in the original debt of £100 in 1696, which with interest came to £106. After some debate the Company agreed to pay him £93 17s 1d, of which they had £86 in cash, and the Master agreed to advance a further £20 to cover the deficit.[126]

At the same time as this, widow Mary Worley also offered to advance the Company some money. She was a good friend of the Company's Clerk, Joseph Burrough, and he presented her offer to a monthly court in December 1694. In return for an annuity payable during her life on good security, she offered the Company £200.[127] Her offer was gratefully accepted, and the Clerk reported to the January court that she would receive a tax free annuity of £18 each year, secured against their real estate and insurance policy.[128] When a lease was agreed the Company also gave Mrs Worley a peppercorn.[129] She received her annuity until her death in July 1700.[130] Her sister Elizabeth Hagger was her executrix and the chief beneficiary of her will.[131] Mrs Hagger attended the August court to inform them of Mrs Worley's death and to collect the arrears which had been due. The annuity was not transferred to Mrs Hagger, so the Company was able to keep the remainder of the money.[132]

Refreshments

In 1743, whilst Joseph Manning was deputy Master, a wine seller named Sarah Holly provided refreshments for the Company on at least three occasions, including Lord Mayor's Day when her bill was rather high at £17 8s.[133] The reason for her involvement with the Company that year was because Manning was her brother-in-law.[134] He appears to have been directly responsible for the decision to purchase wine from her, but she did not have the monopoly on wine that year because the court minutes list purchases from multiple other vendors too. After Manning's term as deputy Master ended Mrs Holly was not patronised by the Company again, so her brief involvement can perhaps be attributed to nepotism.

Other examples of women providing refreshments for the Company include Mrs Cockupp who provided wine on Lord Mayor's Day 1694 at a cost of 10s.[135] Mrs Mary Sparrows provided wine for the 1746 Lord Mayor's Day dinner at a higher price of £5 8s,[136] and Mrs Elizabeth Marshall provided £5 worth of wine at the Hall for Lord Mayor's Day dinner 1750.[137] Mrs Hannah Hurd provided five dozen bottles of red port wine in the spring of 1760, at a cost of £1 per dozen.[138]

Decorations

During the eighteenth century the Company regularly purchased the ribbons to adorn their stands and whifflers on Lord Mayor's Day from female vendors. Examples include Susannah Pirks in 1742,[139] Mrs Joyce Fisher in 1743,[140] and a lady described simply as Mrs Lidia in 1746.[141]

Services

Although construction work has generally been associated with men, there are hints in the Company's court minutes that some female artisans were hired at various times. During the 1690s the Company used the services of the Pigg family of bricklayers on at least three occasions. The first reference was a payment of £2 10s 'to Mr Pigg the Bricklayer' on 4th August 1691.[142] On 10th November 1692 'Mrs Pigg the Bricklayers wife' was paid £6.[143] The following August she was paid a further £5, but this time was described as 'Mrs Pigg the Bricklayer', which suggests that she was perhaps active in the business and not just gathering the money due to her husband.[144]

In the 1730s there appears to have been a female blacksmith named Mrs Soames working for the Company, although whether she undertook the smith's work herself or had workers doing her bidding is unclear. She was the widow of Mr Soames, who had been the Company's blacksmith from at least 1713 until the last reference to him in February 1729.[145] He presumably died shortly after this, and his wife took over his business. Her bill for work undertaken in 1733 amounted to 8s 4d,[146] but on 4th March 1735 she attended a monthly court with her bill of £6 7s 9d 'for Smith's Work about the Stands'. Because she was present the Company was able to negotiate a 15s 6d reduction in her bill.[147]

Women in the Twentieth and Twenty-first Centuries

During the first two-thirds of the twentieth century the involvement of women in the Company was largely confined to the attendance of the wives of liverymen at banquets. However, towards the end of the century that began to change and women were once again admitted as freemen, with an additional change making the wives and daughters of Masters eligible for the freedom. Attempts were made in the 1990s to change the Company's ordinances and allow women to take the livery, but this was only finally achieved in 2006. This change was initially met with resistance, in spite of the fact that Amanda Jackson had served as the Company's Clerk for many years. Indeed, a questionably-worded report from 2001 noted, 'We have a Lady clerk who blends in well to our male only functions', but 'the admission of females to the Livery is not ... a prime cause for concern'.[148] A questionnaire was circulated to the Livery in the summer of 2002 concerning the admission of women, which returned results of 42.9 per cent in favour, 12.4 per cent against, and 44.6 per cent not responding at all.[149] When a secret ballot was held for the Livery to vote on the matter in 2003 it was defeated 'by a very narrow majority',[150] which prompted another attempt the following year when it was noted as 'imperative for the Company to admit women ... as soon as possible'.[151] Another vote was held at the Livery meeting in July 2006, and the motion carried.

The best way to study the experiences of women in the Company in the twenty-first century is to let them tell their own stories. The first comes from Katharine Dallas, only the second lady to be appointed as a liveryman of the Company.

Everyone has always been very kind and accepting of a lady, in what was very much a man's world, but I think, even in this short time, things are changing.

I became a Court Assistant on 3/2/2015. It takes me nearly two hours, by train, to get to the Guildhall, which was one of the reasons I declined the very real honour of being asked to consider being Master of the Company. I felt the journey to London, my age and responsibilities were of concern as one needs to devote three years to this high office and I didn't feel I could do this properly. It was a difficult decision.

I was delighted to be presented to the Duchess of Cornwall when she was clothed. No one told me whether I should curtesy or not so in the end I decided to copy the others and bowed! I have greatly enjoyed the many banquets and visiting the other Livery Halls. Our first was at the Apothecary's and our local taxi driver, although he had the post code, couldn't find the Hall and we drove round for a long time and only just arrived in time.

I am looking forward to the celebrations for the 450 years. Let us hope we can enjoy some of the planned events.

The second story belongs to Clunie Fretton:

I became a Freeman of the Company on December 3rd 2014, after I won the first Carving Competition run by the Company earlier that year. Winners of the carving and joinery competitions are considered to have produced an adequate 'test piece', as I think the custom was in the past when a carver or joiner wanted to become a member of the livery, and freedom of the company is offered as an optional part of the prize for the competition. I was touched by how supportive and welcoming members had been during the awards dinner - it seemed like a good thing to become part of!

My experience has been very positive as a female craftsman. I'd honestly expected to encounter some resistance or lack of credit as a woman in a manual trade, and have been (very happily) surprised by the level of support and interest in my work regardless of my gender. In some respects, I think it's even been an asset. People often have an impression of carving as a very male-dominated profession, and are interested to discover the balance is often closer to fifty-fifty than expected.

There are an increasing number of women in the Company, and I hope that women continue to be interested in joining. But, more specifically, I hope that more craftspeople in general continue to join. The Company supports and sponsors education in craft, and greater involvement in the Company by craftspeople rewards that support by increasing awareness of the value of the craft and the Company in the first place – both feed back into one another. With regards to female craftsmen in particular, I think it's encouraging for young people thinking of undertaking carving or joinery as a profession to see people like themselves doing it – the more people interested in entering the trade, the better!

The first commission I made for the Company was very exciting, as it was my first commission after graduating in 2015. The Company's support in commissioning the coat of arms really helped me during a time when most recent graduates are feeling rather lost. More recently, being able to work on the Old Master's Chair (2019) as well as the New Master's Chair (2020) has been really lovely. They're both beautiful objects, and there's a great sense of continuity between these commissions, both from working on three different iterations of the Company's heraldry, as well as knowing that, in the case of the

Old Master's Chair, it had been made 265 years earlier by Edward Newman (a Past Master of the Company) and that it was being restored in the present day by myself as a current member of the company. Being part of that unbroken tradition and upholding of the craft felt very special.

Past Master John Skarratt brought up during his year that the Master's Chair was missing some key heraldic elements, and in 2019 I was able to go to the V&A furniture conservation workshops and restore the pieces that had been damaged over the years. I remodelled the missing pieces first in wax, with reference to the style of the chair and other work with similar motifs from the period. I was lucky enough to be given some Honduran mahogany from the V&A's stores (the same species of timber as the chair), and working from the models I recarved the missing elements and matched them to the breaks without removing any material from the chair. This was a really exciting project to work on – when restoring a carving you really have to efface yourself and try to be as true as possible to the original carver's decisions, so you spend a lot of time looking at their work and getting to know the decisions they made and the way they worked. The tools I use haven't changed a bit since the chair was carved, so it is very like treading in someone long gone's footsteps!

Chapter 6

The Company's Calendar

Monthly Court

The Company's 1572 ordinances stipulated that 'there shalbee holden monethly one Assembly or Court of this Company by the Master Wardens and Assistants of this Company there to sitt hear and determine all controversyes and debates of the same Company'.[1] These monthly Courts of Assistants were held at Joiners' Hall, usually on the first Tuesday of the month. The Master generally took the chair at eleven o'clock, and Assistants were expected to have arrived at the Hall before that time.[2] As an incentive breakfast, drink, and tobacco were all served before the meetings. However, in June 1698 the breakfast was scrapped, and anyone wanting tobacco had to provide it at his own cost.[3] At the start of each court meeting the minutes from the previous court were re-read and agreed, and the Assistants would then proceed to any pressing matters of governance.[4] The most common order of business was to deal with freedom admissions, and the names of masters and apprentices are the majority of entries in the court minutes.[5]

The earliest surviving rough court minute book contains an order dated 2nd December 1661 stipulating that 'if from henceforth either the Mr wardens or Assistants shall sit in Court wthout their Gownes' they would be fined, although the precise amount was not listed.[6] In September 1705 the Upper Warden John Voughton begged the court's permission to sit without his gown 'for reasons best knowne to himselfe'. The court did not press him to reveal his reason, and agreed that he could do so after paying a fine of 5s.[7] Another fine was introduced in 1693 to punish tardiness. Assistants who arrived to meetings late were deemed 'a very great hindrance to the affaires of the sd Company'. Anybody arriving after eleven o'clock without a satisfactory excuse would forfeit 6d.[8] By October 1750 that fine had risen to 1s.[9]

During the early modern period dinner was often offered after the meetings. However, on 30th August 1757 it was voted that dinners would only be provided after quarterly Courts of Livery.[10] To compensate for this, every Assistant who arrived at court before noon would receive an allowance of 4s.[11] This order was reversed in 1770, when it was agreed that the 4s per head would be used to provide a dinner instead, as long as the total cost to the Company did not exceed £5.[12] In 1779 it became necessary to cancel the monthly and quarterly court dinners again, and each Assistant arriving before noon would receive 5s in lieu.[13]

The final meeting of the Court of Assistants at Joiners' Hall took place on Tuesday 1ˢᵗ April 1800. Following this the Hall was let to a tenant, and all Company meetings took place at the Guildhall instead. The Company was able to secure the use of Committee Room 2, where the seventeenth-century oil painting of the Master and Assistants was also hung. This remained their meeting venue until the mid-twentieth century. Shortly after the outbreak of the Second World War the Guildhall announced that no meetings could be held in the building until further notice, and consequently the Joiners were obliged to find a new location for their monthly courts. This was a matter of difficulty, because numerous livery halls were destroyed in the Blitz. This also included Joiners' Hall, which was destroyed almost entirely on the night of 15ᵗʰ May 1941 when a V2 bomb landed nearby. Although the building was by then a warehouse and served no function for the Company, it was their main source of income and without it they faced bankruptcy. An immediate spending freeze was implemented and all regularly scheduled meetings were cancelled, with the exception of the St James' Day election and the August audit.

Monthly Courts of Assistants resumed with regularity in February 1946, with Cutlers' Hall as their regular venue until the end of 1949 when they removed to Guildhall House on Gresham Street.[14] The meetings took place there until 1974, at which time the Company returned to Guildhall.[15]

In the spring of 2020 the world was brought to a sudden halt by the arrival of the COVID-19 pandemic. Everybody experienced drastic changes to their daily lives, education, and mode of working, and the Worshipful Company of Joiners and Ceilers was no exception. As the lockdown and ban on public gatherings meant that their mandated monthly meetings of the Court of Assistants could not take place in person at the Guildhall, the Company found a way to adapt, joining thousands of people around the world who turned to the online video communication tool Zoom to conduct their business. This historic first meeting took place on 29ᵗʰ April 2020.

Quarterly Court

Although the monthly court meetings dealt with the day-to-day governance of the Company, arguably of greater importance were the quarterly Courts of Livery. The Court of Assistants had power up to a point, but any decisions concerning the election of officers or changes to ordinances had to be approved by the wider livery. The 1572 ordinances went to great length to explain when these meetings should be called:

And it is also ordained that ffower tymes in the yeare (that is to say) on the ffirst Tuesday next after the Epiphany of our Lord God called Twelfth day also the next workeday after Lowsunday the next workeday after the feast day of St John Baptist and the next workeday after the feast day of St Michaell the Archangell there shalbee holden in this Company ffower generall Assemblyes or Courts comonly called the ffower quarter dayes unto the which shalbee sumoned the whole body of this Company aswell forraines as others dwelling in the Suburbs of the said Citty or within Two Myles compasse of the same Citty To the intent they may have specially read unto them the Ordinances of this Company that they may the better learne to observe and keep the same, and whosoever maketh default in appearance at any of theis Quarterdays without lawfull excuse shall forfeite to the use of this Company such reasonable ffine as shalbee assessed by the Master Wardens and their Assistants or the more part of them so that it exceed not the sum of tenne shillings.[16]

There were four mandated quarterly courts each year, but extraordinary courts could also be held concerning issues such as the election of replacement officers after the death of an incumbent. Assistant James Phillips moved in 1852 that the quarterly courts should always be held on the second Tuesday in January, and the first Tuesday in April, July, and October.[17] On 8th July 1688 it was agreed that 'any Member that shall for the future depart the Court without leave' would face a fine.[18]

Dinner was also provided to the Livery following these meetings, and the meal was more elaborate than that offered to the Assistants after monthly courts. At the April 1750 quarter court the Master passed a bill provided by the Renter Warden for 'Sugar Lemons Oranges Onions Rum and Brandy', at a cost of £1 15s 10½d. It is unclear whether these items formed part of the meal that day, but they certainly indicate a varied menu.[19]

Search Day

Clauses 12 and 13 of the 1572 ordinances related to the Company's search days. The Master and Wardens were authorised to enter the 'houses shops sollers cellors warehouses and booths' of every person working as a joiner three or four times per year, or as often as necessary. They would examine all the wares made and sold by each person to ensure that everything 'bee well and workmanly wrought and of good sufficient and lawfull stuffe, and in manner and according to the Statutes of the Realme in such cases provided'. The joiner was required to pay 1d to the searchers when they arrived. If any products were discovered to be deficient the Master and Wardens would transport them back to Joiners' Hall and present them to the Court of Assistants. They would then be valued and sold, and the money put towards the maintenance of the Company's poor. The offending craftsman would later be summoned to appear before the Assistants and fined the same amount as the value of the products. The search would apply to every householder within a two-mile radius of the City of London, and fairs and markets would also be monitored. If the Master and Wardens failed to conduct a search at least once per quarter they would each forfeit 10s.[20]

In 1614 the Company introduced a supplemental ordinance addressing the increasing number of tradesmen working as joiners without being free of the Company. Their particular grievances were with coach makers, trunk makers, box makers, cupboard makers, gunstock makers, and flask makers. The foreign craftsmen were operating contrary to the Company's ordinance, which stipulated that joiners had to be free of the City. The lack of freedom meant that they were not subject to the Company's ordinances, including the search. Consequently they 'do use much bad and insufficient stuffe and make & worke verye insufficient workmanship to the great preiudice of his Maiestyes people & Subiectes that continually buy the same and to the great discreditt hinderance of the said Company of Joyners of London'. They presented a petition to the Lord Chancellor and Chief Justices asking for all the offending craftsmen to be subject to the Company's ordinances,

[a]nd that it shalbe lawfull for the maister & wardens of the said Company or ffellowshipp for the tyme beinge from henceforth forevermore from tyme to tyme as often & when it shall seeme good unto them at convenyent tyme & in convenyent manner without force to enter into the howses shopps sellers sollers warehowses and booths of any pson usinge the said trades of Coachmakinge Trunckmakinge Boxemakinge Cubboardmakinge Gunstocke & fflaskemakinge & of anye person workinge usinge or sellinge any thinge or thinges made by Joyners & Ceelers or Carvers ... to viewe & search all manner of workes & wares whatsoever made by any person or persons of the trades aforesaid or of the faculty of Joyning Ceelinge & Carvinge or any thinge thereunto proper incident or belonginge whether the same be well & workmanlike wrought and of good sufficient & lawfull stuffe in manner & accordinge to the lawes & Statutes of this realme in such Cases provided And the Offenders in that behalfe to punish in such manner & forme as by their former Actes Constitutions & Ordinances and accordinge to the lawes of the realme.[21]

Maintaining the standards of craftsmanship was taken very seriously by the Company. The earliest surviving Renter Wardens' accounts from 1621–2 reveal that during that year twenty-nine joiners were fined sums between 7d and 11s 'for faulty stuffe'.[22]

The Company didn't have a fixed set of dates for their search days, as they did with other regular events in their calendar. During the seventeenth century they tended to pick dates in January/February, April/May, July/August, and November/December. Due to the large geographical area of their jurisdiction each search day focussed on a different part of London and its environs: one for the City itself, one for Westminster, one for Southwark, and one for Ratcliffe. The searchers always met at eight o'clock in the morning, but at a variety of locations depending on where their search would be that day. Venues included the Exchange for London search days, and a variety of coffeehouses or alehouses for the others.[23] After the search was completed they would return to Joiners' Hall for dinner.[24]

By the turn of the eighteenth century the process of conducting searches had changed so that Assistants and liverymen could be appointed to join the search team. In June 1726 the search was divided into six divisions, although ultimately only four were searched on that occasion. When the searchers arrived at the Hall in the morning they were each given a division with a list of the names and addresses of the joiners, and appear to have undertaken the searches alone. After they reconvened at the Hall later that evening they all paid the fee money they had gathered to the Renter Warden.[25] By the 1740s the four searches had been replaced by one general search in either June or July.[26] The final search took place on 14th July 1747, although it is unclear why none were held after this.[27]

Most of the searches were completed without any problems, but occasionally a recalcitrant joiner would be discovered. John Oldfield and Thomas Blinckoe were both fined in 1688 and 1690 respectively for refusing to pay the penny search fee and for using bad language against the searchers.[28] Lazarus Styles was similarly prosecuted in January 1707 for refusing to pay the fee and then writing 'two severall scurrilous false and malicious letters' to the Clerk.[29] Christopher Sibthorpe also refused to pay the fee, and was reprimanded in court 'for his obstinacy and disobediency against the Master and Wardens and for his refractory and saucy behaviour'.[30] On 21st July 1732 during the Westminster search the goods of Thomas Perrey of Drury Lane were found to be defective. The searchers confiscated three small deal boxes from his shop and transported them to the Hall, where they were deemed to be 'made of insufficient & unlawfull stuff'. They were valued at 1s 6d and sold 'for the use of this Company'.[31]

James Bull had a shop in St Paul's Churchyard which was searched by the Master in April 1735. He seized one chair 'for being made of bad unsound & unserviceable stuff', and it was later condemned by the Court of Assistants 'for being wrought of bad insufficient & unlawfull Stuff'. Bull was given the option of paying a 1s fine and having the chair returned to him to be altered using acceptable materials, or the Company would sell it and keep the money. Bull said 'he would have nothing to do with it now' but said he would settle the matter with the Master privately.[32] In this particular instance Bull's unacceptable chair does not appear to have been a deliberate attempt by him to sell products which did not meet the Company's standards. By September of that same year he was receiving charity from the Company and was listed in the court minutes as 'a poor member'.[33] It seems very likely that Bull had already been in financial distress when the search took place and had been unable to afford better-quality wood. He had not been attempting to deceive the Company; he simply couldn't afford anything else.

The final recorded search took place on 14th July 1747.[34] Nothing was entered into the court minutes explaining why the searches had stopped so it is unclear whether it was just an oversight which became permanent, or a deliberate decision. However, in the nineteenth century it was attributed to the Company moving away from maintaining a monopoly of the trade where all joiners were required to be members.[35]

St James' Day and the Election of Officers

As previously discussed in Chapter 2, the Company had its origins as a guild attached to the church of St James Garlickhythe. An early reference to the Company's attendance at St James Garlickhythe can be found in a property agreement made on 7th November 1518. Agnes Samon made a grant of property to the Company conditional on their agreement that

> the same Wardeyns and free men of the said craft of mystre of Joyners of London for the tyme being evry yre forevr shall kepe a solempne Obite or Annvrsary in the pishe Churche of Seint James of Garlikhyth of London aswell for the soules of alle the brethren and sisters of the ffraternite of Seint Jams founded on the said Churche of Seint Jame as of and for alle the soules of the ffremen of the said Craft or mystere of Joyners and of their wyves and Children.

She requested that *placebo* and *dirige* would be sung at noon on the Sunday after St James' Day, and a requiem mass the following morning.[36]

The churchwardens' accounts from St James Garlickhythe confirm that there was a St James' Day service taking place at the church each year by 1558, but there was no specific reference to the Joiners.[37] A deed of conveyance dated 1590 contains the earliest recorded details about the Company's actions on St James' Day.[38] After the election of the new officers at the Hall the sum of 4d was distributed to each of the twenty poorest members of the Company. On the next Tuesday after St James' Day the Master, Wardens, and Livery were ordered to assemble and mete together att the Comon hall belonginge to the saide Company and from thence shall decentlie goe two and two together in their lyveries into the Churche of St James at Garleke hyve in London and there shall have and heare a Sermon preached by some godlie and learned Preacher to the praise and thancks of God for all his blessings shewed upon that Company and all others that afterwards shall or may do any good to that Company.

Varying sums of money would be paid to the parish officers of St James Garlickhythe, ranging from 6s 8d to the preacher to 4d to the sexton. However, the Company's attendance at St James Garlickhythe on St James' Day had ended by the early seventeenth century. The churchwardens' accounts of All Hallows the Great reveal that by 1617 the Company was holding their annual service at that church instead.[39] There are no surviving court minutes to explain when or why this change had taken place. The church also benefited from the service, because a collection was taken at the church door as the Joiners left and the money was distributed to the parish poor.[40] The Company also contributed towards re-pewing the church in 1686, regular payments of poor relief, and money towards the maintenance of the minister.[41]

Finally, on 26th March 1930 a resolution passed at a Court of Livery that 'the Court of Assistants take into Consideration, the desirability of the Master, Wardens & the Livery attending at St James Church Galicke Hythe City on St James Day as carried out by our Forefathers'. Thirty-two votes were in favour, with two against and two abstaining.[42] The Master arranged a short service to take place on Tuesday 28th July 1931, which 'he hoped the Members would attend'.[43] This was followed by a cold luncheon for members and their ladies at Painters' Hall.[44] The Livery's attendance at the service was entered into the court minutes as a matter of particular note due to the Company's long-standing association with the church dating back to 'as long ago as 1590', presumably an indication that the Clerk had seen the deed from that year. In addition to the Master, Wardens, Clerk, and Father of the Company, there were twenty-nine members of the Company present.[45] This marked the beginning of the Company's annual return to St James', which continued until the partial destruction of the· church during the Blitz of 1941.[46]

Irrespective of which church they had attended, after the service the Company would 'repaire to their Comon Hall agayne in decent order to the dynner then to be provided for them and then and there att their dynner in their Comon Hall according to the olde Custome in that behalfe used the whole lyvery of the same Company and their wyves sittinge att dynner there'.

Although this is the earliest recorded reference, the annual dinner was clearly a well-established practice by 1590. The cost of the dinner would be borne by the Company, rather than by any of the officers, and it was regularly one of the most expensive feasts in the annual accounts.[47]

Another important aspect of St James' Day was the election of officers for the following year. The 1572 ordinances instructed that

on the feast day of St James the Apostle next ensuing the date hereof and so yearely from thenceforth continually for ever on the said ffesst day of St James the Apostle the body or Comunalty of the said Mistery or ffaculty of Joyners and of Ceelers or Carvers for the tyme being or the more part of them from tyme to tyme and oftner if need shall so require shall at their Comon Hall elect and choose amongst the ffellowship of the said Mistery or ffaculty of Joyners and of Ceelers or Carvers one circumspect man of that Comunalty and in the same ffaculty expert Master of the said Mistery or ffaculty, and Two other men of the same ffaculty Wardens of the same Mistery or ffaculty to survey governe order and correct the same ffellowship for one yeare only then next ensuing.[48]

The 1590 document also revealed that during the dinner the outgoing Master and Wardens would place a garland upon the heads of their incoming successors 'according to the olde mannr and custome before used in the same hall'.[49]

The tradition of attending a church service before returning to the Hall for the election and dinner continued for hundreds of years, and it was arguably the most important day in the Company's calendar. However, with their changing fortunes came changing traditions. Due to financial difficulties following the lease of their Hall, on 25th July 1800 it was voted that in future all St James' Day dinners should be held 'in the Country'.[50] They did not intend to venture out of the environs of London, however. The 1801 dinner was arranged at the Canonbury Tavern in Islington,[51] and that quickly became their preferred venue.[52] When the 1806 dinner was being organised it was estimated that the cost per head would be 5s 6d, assuming a party of ninety liverymen, and each man present would be given a ticket for a bottle of wine.[53] An account of the 1860 dinner appeared in the *London City Press*:

> The Worshipful Company of Joiners' dinner took place at the Brunswick, Blackwall, on Wednesday week, Mr. Linder, the Master, presiding. Nearly 100 of the Company and their friends were present. The vocalists were Miss Ransford, Messrs. W. Dawson, W.E. Ransford, and Smythson, who greatly enlivened the evening by their performance of a well-selected programme under the direction of Mr. Ransford.[54]

The Ransfords referred to in the article were a well-known musical family. Mr Ransford was retired opera singer Edwin Ransford, who had performed at Drury Lane, the Lyceum, and Covent Garden before retiring in 1838. Music ran in the family, however, and he became the manager for his children William and Mary, two of the vocalists who entertained the Joiners on St James' Day.[55] The family were so popular with the Company that they were re-engaged to provide the entertainment at the Audit Day dinner in August, at which Edwin Ransford also performed. Miss Ransford gave a 'highly successful' rendition of 'Within a Mile', and duetted with a Miss Wells in Glover's duet 'From our merry Swiss Home'. Mr Ransford sang 'with his accustomed ability', and entertained the Company with renditions of 'The Brave Volunteers' and Dibbin's 'Blow High, Blow Low'.[56] Edwin Ransford also directed the musical entertainment at the Company's Lord Mayor's Day dinner in November, although his children did not perform on that occasion. The festivities were described as being 'of a more than usually agreeable and brilliant kind, and gave the greatest satisfaction to all who partook of it'.[57]

The celebration of St James' Day remains an integral part of the Company's calendar. A Court of Livery will be held for the election of the next year's officers, ahead of a service of re-dedication for the Company at St James Garlickhythe and a dinner for the Livery afterwards.

Audit and Oath Day

The 1572 Company ordinances stipulated that within thirty days of the election of the new Master and Wardens an audit of the previous year's accounts should be carried out. The preferred date to hold the audit was 24th August, unless that date fell on a Sunday. At least two auditors would be elected 'to take and receive such Accompts and Reckonings as shalbee made or offered to bee made for or concerning any mony plate jewells goods or other things touching belonging concerning or appteining to the said Mistery or ffaculty'. The outgoing Master and Wardens were supposed to deliver the accounts and property to the auditors 'in the Comon Hall of the said ffellowship of Joyners and of Ceelers or Carvers in the p[rese] nce of the new Master and Wardens' and at least six Assistants.[58] Although the minimum number of auditors was two, the Company's early records from the 1660s and 1680s show that they regularly appointed between five and eight.[59] All of the financial transactions were examined to ensure no irregularities, and if all was acceptable the auditors would enter a note of acceptance in the account book and sign their names. In 1780 it was agreed that in future the outgoing Renter Warden's accounts could be read first on St James' Day instead, rather than just once on Audit Day.[60] The audit was always presented at a public Court of Livery because the officers had to be accountable to the commonalty.

In the majority of cases the accounts were passed by the auditors without comment, but occasionally issues were raised. Following debate about the expenses Renter Wardens could claim in their accounts, on Audit Day 1726 it was agreed

> that noe Renter Warden shall be allowed any expences whatsoever on the Account of this Company unless such expences be in company of the Master or his Deputy, and the Bills of Expences be signed by such master or his deputy, or be allowed and signed by the Master in the next Court of Assistants after such respective Expences shall be made.[61]

An investigation into the Company's finances was launched in late 1828 which unfortunately identified a number of discrepancies and omissions in the records. One of the concluding paragraphs stated that

> [i]t may be thought extraordinary that any error should occur in so small an account and which is regularly audited every year and occupying in all not more than two pages But when it is considered that Gentlemen come to the Audit totally imprepared by any previous knowledge of the Affairs of the Company this result is not to be wondered at.

The committee recommended that all audits should take place in open court, and that the Clerk should not be allowed to handle any financial matters in future.[62] All auditors would receive £1 as a token of gratitude for their services, and would be invited to dine with the Master and Wardens.[63] The 1834 report into the duties of officers contained further details about the annual audit:

> Two Auditors of the Accounts of the Renter Warden shall be chosen by the Liverymen on St James day from the Livery who together with the last past Renter Warden shall audit such Accounts. Each Auditor shall receive a fee of 10s 6d if present.
>
> Audit shall be made before a Court of Assistants when the Books of the Company shall be compared with the Schedule and the Plate of the Company produced.[64]

In the 1950s complaint was raised that 'it was difficult for the Auditors to have to go through the whole of the books of the Renter Warden and check all the silver and other chattels of the Company in the short space of an hour and a half before the Court Meeting'. It was agreed that in future the auditors could meet privately with the Renter Warden on any convenient day and go through the documents at their leisure, providing a formal report to the Company at the August Court of Assistants as usual.[65]

After the accounts had been authorised the next item of business was for the incoming officers to swear their oaths of office for the coming year. The outgoing officers were relieved of their duties and handed over any items in their possession, such as documents and keys, to their successors. By the early twentieth century the outgoing Masters would be presented with a silver medal as a token of the Company's gratitude.

Dinner was also provided on Audit and Oath Day, but attendance was generally limited to the Master, Wardens, and Court of Assistants. The Assistants were permitted to bring either their wives or one friend with them to the dinner, but no more than one; anyone bringing extra guests would forfeit 5s.[66] The dinner in 1749 included Westmorland hams, which had been purchased from Thomas Beedham for £2 16s 2d.[67] Traditionally there was dancing after the meal, but this portion of the event was cancelled in 1755.[68] Rather than just serving the usual selection of wine, brandy, and rum at the Audit Day dinner, in 1763 the Company experimented by adding coffee and tea to their refreshments menu as well.[69] They also took advantage of the orange merchants in their Livery and purchased six dishes of fruit from Mr Shuttleworth for £2 2s.[70] After the removal from the Hall in 1800 the audit dinner became a private rather than general affair, with drastically lower costs. In 1806 the cost to the Company was just £5 15s.[71] Attendance was strictly by invitation only, and the Company was most perturbed in 1860 to find that 'Gentlemen were present at the last Audit Dinner who were not authorised to be there not having received any official invitation'. It was proposed that nobody should be allowed into the room without a card of invitation, but ultimately this was declined.[72]

In recent years the tradition of installing the new Master and Wardens was postponed from an August meeting until September, as holding meetings over the summer holidays proved increasingly inconvenient. A Court of Livery dinner traditionally held in October was brought forward into September and the installation of the officers was moved to that day. The incoming Master is installed by taking the formal oath of office, as his predecessors have done for hundreds of years. The most senior Past Master will present the Master with his badge of office and ceremonial keys.

Lord Mayor's Day

Even though the Joiners were not one of the leading livery companies it is clear from the surviving records that the appearance and reputation of the Company on public occasions was very important. The Lord Mayor's Day parade was an important event in the Company's calendar. It takes place every year to celebrate the election of the new Lord Mayor of the City of London. The parade included a formal procession from the Guildhall to Westminster, with London's inhabitants and members of all the livery companies lining the streets, and from 1453 onwards there was a flotilla down the River Thames. Between 1751 and 1959 the parade was held on 9th November, and since 1959 it has been held on the second Saturday in November.

Before the parade the Assistants and liverymen would gather at Joiners' Hall. It was compulsory for them to wear their gowns on this occasion, and anyone not properly dressed would be banned from the festivities. This was reiterated in an order on 14th October 1702 that 'noe Assistants or Liverie men shall walke with the Company to or sett in their stands or dine att their Hall on my Lord Maiors day next unless they come in their gownes'.[73] By 1761 the gathered men were also provided with breakfast at the Hall.[74] From 1706 onwards 'to prevent any disorders' all liverymen were given 6d to ensure that their servants did not linger outside the Hall during the parade, but would instead 'goe cleare away from the Hall'.[75] The Company would then process in pairs from the Hall to Cheapside, where their stands had been set up for them. Wine and tobacco would be served to them there as sustenance during the entertainments.[76]

There was always a carpenter – and a member of the Company – on hand who was responsible for transporting the stands to and from Cheapside, and for keeping them in good repair. An early surviving reference to this in the minute books is a payment of £3 5s to Mr Jermin 'for the stands' on 6th November 1688, followed by another £3 15s the following year 'for the stands at my Lord Majors'.[77] Jermin appears to have been responsible for any necessary repairs during the year too, because he was paid 10s for additional work done on 3rd June 1690.[78] Jermin's successor as the Company's carpenter was William Shrewsbridge, and he became the guardian of the stands from 1691 until his death in 1698.[79] He met an unexpected end and was 'killed by a fall', and the Company paid his widow Susanna £3 due to him in arrears.[80] The role of guardian of the stands became quite hotly contested. On 1st October 1728 two Company members, Stephen Golding and John Battle, both presented petitions for the job to the quarterly court and ultimately a vote had to take place before Battle was elected.[81]

In August 1708 an agreement was reached at a monthly court that the Company should purchase new stands and decorations. They asked current carpenter Thomas Brandon to construct them, and the Renter Warden agreed to oversee the purchase of new cloths and the donation of the old ones after they had been pressed and mended.[82] In October 1719 the stands were 'repaired where defective' and the cloths were replaced.[83] More new cloths were purchased in November 1731, and this time the court minute books recorded that they acquired 25¼ yards of blue cloth at a cost of £6 19s.[84] A further £6 8s worth of blue cloth was purchased in December 1734.[85]

When not in use the stands were stored in a cellar under the Hall. This made them susceptible to destruction in the various fires which took place on site. In the winter of 1734 it was debated whether the Summer House in the yard should be pulled down and replaced with a purpose-built storage facility for the stands, but ultimately the decision was made to leave them in the cellar.[86]

Between 1741 and 1748 the Company purchased between £3 and £5 worth of ribbons from different vendors ahead of each Lord Mayor's Day.[87] In preparation for the 1747 Lord Mayor's Day the Company made a substantial investment in some new silk streamers and banners. The fabric cost £12 12s, with a further £34 10s paid to John Coleman for painting and gilding them and 13s for a new 'Long Pole for the Streamer'. It was also necessary for the standard bearers to be equally as smart as the new streamers they would be carrying, so new 'Strip't Cotton Holland' was bought 'for Frocks for the Standerd bearers' at a cost of £1 14s 6d, with another £1 3s 6d spent on making the outfits.[88] It became tradition to purchase new ribbons each year to ensure the Company's display was always clean and presentable. The receipt to Mrs Chapman from 1753 reveals that they had not only purchased ribbons, but also bells, so that year the stands would have been a delight for the eyes and the ears.[89] For the 1754 parade they also purchased cockades in addition to the ribbons, adding another level of decoration.[90] A bill of £22 2s for 110½ yards of broad cloth for the stand was passed in November 1755.[91] The stand was decorated with 116 turned columns, and William Butler was tasked with re-painting all of them.[92] Another large piece of blue cloth for the stands was purchased ahead of the 1761 parade.[93]

In 1768 it became necessary to replace the backs of the stands. Henry Phillips, the carpenter, was engaged to make the adjustments. Master Thomas Bilcliffe generously donated 'One hundred and fifty feet of the said Backs' at a cost of £7 1s 8d, which reduced the total bill to £26 4s 7d. This was still a considerable sum, but any reduction was welcome.[94] In 1769 Phillips was also compensated for making four new trestle tables, which were used at the Hall for the Lord Mayor's Day dinner.[95] Towards the end of the eighteenth century, when the Company found themselves in financial difficulties, one of the earliest things they disposed of were the stands, which were sold in 1787.[96]

After the parade was over the Assistants and livery would return to the Hall and enjoy a dinner provided by specially elected stewards.[97] This was one of the most important feasts in the Company's annual calendar. The Company's best plate and linen were brought out of storage,[98] and the bills for the meal regularly exceeded £80. Occasionally the day ended on a foul note. In 1719 a report appeared in the *Weekly Journal* concerning a member of the Company who appears to have got into a spot of bother on his way home:

> Last week one Mr. Tompkins, a Broker in Moor-Fields, a Livery Man belonging to the Joiners Company, went to the Feast at their Hall in Tower-Street, and at Night, instead of returning home went for the Tower, and falling into the Ditch, was stilted in the Mud.[99]

Poor Mr Tompkins presumably overindulged in drink – an understandable occurrence given the quantities available. The Company had ordered forty-two gallons of red port and nine gallons of sherry for their 1755 feast, which converts to 231 litres.[100] They were somewhat more reserved at the 1762 feast, ordering only ten dozen bottles of port.[101]

Master John Smallwell complained in court on 7th December 1731 that 'he had been grossly abused by severall of the Members of the Company on the last Lord Mayor's Day', and the three men described as 'the principal Agressors' were summoned to the next court to explain themselves.[102] On 7th November 1732 Company member William Merryman appeared on summons before the monthly court to answer an accusation that he had assaulted the doorkeepers at the Hall on Lord Mayor's Day and forced his way inside 'in a violent & riotous manner'. The Clerk was ordered to prefer an indictment against him for trespass and assault.[103] In an attempt to halt the prosecution against him Merryman appeared again at the next monthly court meeting in December to beg the Company's pardon. He agreed to pay 15s as compensation to the doorkeepers, and following a debate the charges against him were dropped.[104]

A change to the regular schedule of Lord Mayor's Day festivities occurred in 1760.[105] Due to the death of King George II on 25th October the City of London was still in mourning on 10th November when the parade was scheduled. Beadle Robert Groome took out an advertisement in *The Daily Register* informing the liverymen that the dinner would take place at Joiners' Hall as planned at 2 p.m., but 'By Reason of the Death of his late Majesty, the Stand will not be out, nor will there be any Public Processions'.[106]

In 1814, at the height of the Napoleonic Wars, ten liverymen wrote to the Master expressing their concern as to 'the propriety of dining together on the ninth of November next' and requesting that a special Court of Livery might be summoned to discuss the matter. That extraordinary court was held on 22nd September, and although it was agreed that the Company's finances would support a dinner it was decided that the cost would be met by 'the Indviduals who shall then dine and not from the Companys Fund'.[107] A resolution was passed on 25th July 1823 confirming that the November banquet would be a livery banquet and would always take place on 9th November. The cost of tickets would be 5s, and the event would be held at Mr Lovegrove's Horn Tavern in Doctors Commons.[108]

Another postponement took place in 1837 'in consequence of Her Majesty's visit to the City'. The eighteen-year-old Queen Victoria had ascended the throne on 20th June that year, and in celebration it was decided that she would participate in the Lord Mayor's Day parade on 9th November. The parade was always a spectacle, but the presence of the new monarch made it even more so. It was the first time an unmarried Queen of England had participated in the parade since the reign of Elizabeth I.[109] The Joiners decided to postpone their annual dinner until 11th November so they could fully appreciate the splendour of the parade without being distracted.[110] The Dean and Chapter of St Paul's wrote to the Town Clerk offering 'the use of a portion of the Church Yard to such of the Livery Companies of the City as may feel inclined to erect Booths or Standings to witness her Majesty's Procession', and the Joiners took them up on this offer, applying for sufficient ground for '160 persons'.[111] However, by 2nd November the Clerk had received a response that 'the whole [yard] had now been disposed of'.[112]

When invitations were sent out for the 1854 dinner the Company received two strongly worded negative responses, both of which were copied into the minutes. The first was from George Payne, writing from the Guildhall:

> Mr George Payne presents his compliments to the Master and Wardens of the Worshipful Company of Joiners and begs to say he does not intend to again subject himself to an attack from hired ruffians such as occurred after the later Joiners dinner and therefore he respectfully declines the honor of their invitation for the 9th instant.[113]

The second refusal was from Mr Richardson, who presented his compliments and

> ... begs to decline dining with the Joiners Company. The insolence of the Court beggars all, not only are men excluded from office who may have been unfortunate, an unheard of piece of audacity, but Mr R finds on looking at the accounts that whilst £63 is given to the poor £489.0.2 is expended in feast Salaries and fees to the Court.[114]

At some point during the nineteenth century a song was composed which would be sung by all attendees at their November dinners. The rights to this song were acquired by the Master in 1963 and presented to the Company as a gift.[115]

The Joiners' Song

Twas good Queen Bess our Charter gave
To Joiners skilled and wise
And though three hundred years have passed
Their deeds we'll not despise.
Though years have passed and sped away,
But still our tree has root,
New branches grafted on its stem
Bring forth more glorious fruit.

Let Brother Joiners hand in hand
Their friendship never sever,
But drink the toast 'Our Brotherhood'
And may it last for ever.

We strive with others to keep pace
And have not been behind,
The student in our Joiners' craft
A helping hand will find;
And those admitted to our ranks
Will ne'er regret the day,
But heart and voice join in the toast
Our Master gives, and say –

Let Brother Joiners hand in hand
Their friendship never sever,
But drink the toast 'Our Brotherhood'
And may it last for ever.[116]

On 25th July 1903 it was agreed that the cost of tickets to bring additional guests to the banquet would be 30s.[117] In the 1950s, when the Company's finances remained in a somewhat precarious state following the Second World War, it was lamented that the 1955 banquet had cost £407 12s 11d. Although tickets purchased by the Livery offset this by £183 15s, the Company still faced a bill of £223 17s 11d. It was agreed that the Court of Assistants 'should carefully watch the expenditure on Livery and other dinners in the future so that we do not exceed our income over these dinners', and 'it might be necessary to ask the liverymen to pay more for their own ticket rather than there should be too much expense falling on the Company'.[118]

The Joiners' Company still participates in the Lord Mayor's show from time to time with a specially made float. Members of the Company watch the show but don't participate in the parade unless the Company has a float. It is hoped that they will be able to participate in the 2021 parade as part of the 450th anniversary celebrations.

Chapter 7

The Company's Goods

A succession of fires and periods of financial instability have meant that the Company's strongroom contains far fewer treasures now than in the past. Nevertheless, those which remain tell some interesting stories about the Company and its members.

The Painting

The most enigmatic of all the Company's possessions is the oil painting which hangs in the Guildhall. An inscription on the frame which was noted down in 1886 described it as 'The Master and Wardens of the Joiners Company receiving the design for their New Hall Temps 1670'.[1] This would refer to the rebuilding of Joiners' Hall after the Great Fire of London in 1666. There is no clue in the surviving documentation as to precisely when it was painted, or who the artist was. There are no surviving court minutes from the 1670s, and although there are Renter Wardens' accounts this period represents an anomalous time when financial transactions were not itemised and described as they previously and subsequently were; the only records were lump sums of money spent and received.

The painting is not referred to in the Company's documents until 1799, when the decision was made to let Joiners' Hall to a tenant and remove to the Guildhall. At that time the painting was hung 'over the Fire Place in the Court Room', which means it would have been a familiar sight to the Court of Assistants when they met in that room for their monthly meetings. There is little reason to suppose that it had ever been hung anywhere else in the Hall, because the Court Room is an appropriate place for it. The painting was one of the few items retained by the Company after the rest of their moveable goods were sold. Richard Clark, the Chamberlain of London who was also a member of the Company, wrote to ask whether they would entrust it to his care. The court duly voted that 'the said Picture with the Frame and Arms over the same and the green shade which draws before it be delivered to Mr. Chamberlain Clark'.[2] Clark sent a written receipt to the Company, and a copy of this was also pasted on to the back of the painting:

> This Picture painted by Cornelius Janssens representing the Court of Assistants of the Company of Joiners of London assembled in their Court Room on Business is the property of the said Company and was confided by them to my

care when the Company's Meetings at their Hall discontinued and their Hall let and is to be returned by me to them whenever required by and conformably to any order which shall be made by the Court of Assistance for that purpose.[3]

However, Karen Hearn, an expert in the work of Cornelius Janssens or Johnson, doubts this attribution. During the nineteenth century it was common for miscellaneous seventeenth-century work to be attributed to Johnson without any evidence. Consequently, the artist remains unknown at the present time.

On 3rd October 1826 it was resolved that the painting should be 'removed from the Custody of the Chamberlain and delivered to the Clerk in order to be preserved and to be at all times open for the inspection and disposal of the company'.[4] It appears to have remained in the safekeeping of the Clerk.[5] Discussion took place in February 1868 concerning the preservation of the painting, and the Clerk corresponded with Edward Bentley, who wrote to say,

> It is hardly possible to say what the Picture will cost to put in perfect condition as it is in such a dirty state and so obscure I can hardly see it, but if you will allow it to come to my home I will then try it and let you know. It might come to £4 or £5 or perhaps considerably less according to its condition.[6]

It was sent to Bentley for cleaning, and he wrote with a progress update in April:

> I have received the picture and have made an experiment with one of the heads and also other parts. I think it will turn out exceedingly well although difficult. I also wish to know if you would like the frame reguilt as having a Brother a Guilder we can do it at a reasonable rate.[7]

The picture and frame were returned to the Company in November,[8] and was brought to the December Court of Assistants to be examined, where 'it gave great satisfaction'. It was resolved 'that the Companys Picture ... be submitted to the care of the Corporation of the City of London & placed in one of the Committee Rooms of the Guildhall'. At this same meeting the description of the painting as 'representing the Architect exhibiting to the Court of Assistants a plan for rebuilding their Hall' first appeared in the Company's documentation, and this explanation is the one which was passed down to the present day.[9]

The painting was initially hung in Committee Room 2 of the Guildhall. This is the room the Company rented each month for their courts, so having the painting there would have been a bittersweet yet familiar reminder of their own Hall. In 1880 it was reported to be 'in good condition'.[10] It was temporarily placed on display in an exhibition of works of art held at the Guildhall in 1886.[11] In 1893 the Company once again investigated the possibility of getting it cleaned and restored, and an estimate of £20 was received from Mr Knowles.[12] They asked for the opinion of Mr Temple from the Guildhall School of Art, who wrote, 'I am of opinion that it should be, in the first place, secured at the back, all the old varnish should then be removed from it & the picture cleaned & re-varnished.' He estimated that this work, with the addition of cleaning the glass and frame, should cost no more than £12.[13] The restored painting was returned to the Guildhall in August 1894.[14]

When the First World War began the painting was 'taken down & stored', and was safely in the custody of the Guildhall authorities.[15] The Company appears to have also had property in storage in the Guildhall's vault because in August 1917 the Clerk was instructed to thank the City surveyor 'for improving the accommodation for the Company's boxes in the vault'.[16] It was returned to Committee Room 2 in 1918, but by the summer of 1919 concerns were raised about the picture 'getting very dusty and dirty behind the glass'.[17] The Clerk was instructed to negotiate with one of the curators about having it cleaned,[18] and in November he returned a cost estimate of £2, which was agreed by the court.[19] By 1921 the picture was back on display, and in December 1937 after close scrutiny the Clerk was instructed 'to see the responsible Authority in charge of the picture with a view to the possibility of its being better lighted', as it was not appearing to its best advantage.[20] He had a meeting with Mr Douthwaite, the Guildhall's librarian, who was also in charge of pictures. Mr Douthwaite informed him

> that it is his considered opinion, though such must not be taken as that of an expert, that the Company's picture in the No 2 Committee Room, has been badly used at some time or other, and has either been restored, or the painting was finished by some other artist, other than that of the original painter.
>
> He is further of the opinion that although it could be further illuminated by a concealed light at the top (which would have to be supplied at the cost of the Company) it would be unwise to carry this out, as it would accentuate the blemishes, and that it would be preferable to let the present lighting remain as it is now.[21]

The outbreak of the Second World War once again placed the picture in jeopardy. The Guildhall Art Gallery wrote to the Company on 4th October 1939 asking whether they would consent to the picture being removed 'to a place of greater safety than Guildhall', although it emphasised that they could not guarantee its ultimate survival. The Clerk returned a reply that the Company 'very much appreciated' the offer and accepted it.[22] Although the roof of the Guildhall was destroyed on the night of 29th to 30th December 1940 during a Luftwaffe raid, the main structure of the building escaped unscathed, and the painting was safe.

In 1960 the Guildhall Art Gallery informed the Company that the painting 'was in need of attention, the panel on which it is painted having warped'.[23] It was sent to Mr Lucas to be repaired at a cost of £25.[24] There appears to have been discussion in 1991 about hanging the Company's painting in the church of St James Garlickhythe, but ultimately this came to nothing.[25] In recent years it has been hanging on the third floor of the Guildhall but is not accessible to the public and can only be viewed with the Corporation's permission.

The Master's Chair

The earliest reference to the chair appears in the court minute book dated 1st October 1754, when it was 'Ordered that a Proper Handsome Master's Chair, and a Set of New Window Curtains, for the Court Parlour be Provided under the Direction of the present Master'.[26] The drapery was easy to commission, and William Ridgeway provided three pairs of crimson damask curtains at a cost of £11 8s 4d by the November court. The Company had also acquired a set of twelve dozen Spanish wine glasses from merchant Richard Farver and the bill was passed at the same time as the bill for the curtains.[27] The chair, however, was a more lengthy undertaking. The commission was given to Edward Newman, Past Master of the Company for 1749–50. The Renter Warden's accounts note a payment of £27 6s to Newman 'for the Carved Mahogany Chair in the Court

Parlour ... & for a Case for it'.[28] When the Master was recorded as taking the chair at the beginning of every meeting it was both literal and symbolic; he took control of the meeting, but also sat in the ceremonial chair.

The chair is on permanent loan to the Victoria & Albert Museum, and their catalogue describes it, before the recent restoration, as

[a] large ceremonial armchair in carved mahogany, the back elaborately carved with leafy Gothic arches, surmounted by the coat of arms of the Joiners' Company. The square legs and stretchers carved with blind tracery, and with a leather-upholstered seat. The serpentine arms, with out-turned lion-head arm-ends, have inverse cabriole supports, set back from the front of the seat.

The chair-back is pierced and carved with a symmetrical composition of leafy arched C-scrolls and gothic pinnacles, arising from a central pierced splat flanked by pair of columns. The side uprights are surmounted in a cruciform finial of acanthus leaves (the right finial missing). The chair back was carved as a single scheme after construction, as the side uprights are carved as an integral part of the overall scheme, so that their apparent juncture with the back splat does not match the actual joints. The cresting incorporates the coat of arms of the Joiners' Company. The flatter background areas of the chair-back are given texture with both punching and a chip-carved diaper pattern.

The outward-curving arms, carved in relief on the upper surface with rocaille and acanthus leaves, terminate in lion's heads with deeply undercut jaws. The arms rest on supports arising in an S-scroll from the side seat rails. In contrast to the chair back and arms, the lower part of the chair-frame is severely rectilinear, with square-section legs joined by an H-stretcher and rectangular seat rails. The back legs and uprights are raked. The outer faces of the legs, rails and stretchers are carved in relief with strapwork of interlaced C-scrolls, the carving being in deeper relief on the seat rails

The chair frame is entirely made in mahogany. The principal elements are of mortise and tenon construction. The central splat of the chair-back is carved in one piece, tenoned into the seat rail and cresting rail. The extremities of the carved decoration, such as the boys' arms, were extended with pieces dowelled in place; a dowel-hole is visible on the left-hand boy where the arm has become detached. A dowel-hole can also be seen in the top of the figure surmounting the cresting rail which has lost its head. The carving is extremely finely executed throughout, but especially evident in the figures of the boy supporters in the cresting.[29]

After the Company removed from Joiners' Hall the chair was placed in the custody of Samuel Lovegrove of the Horn Tavern in Doctors Commons, where the Company was to regularly hold its Lord Mayor's Day banquet in November. Lovegrove returned the chair to Master William Smith in the autumn of 1827, and Smith informed the Company that he would personally take care of it.[30] In 1852, following the death of Clerk Stephen Ponder senior, his newly appointed successor Benjamin Granger was instructed to write to Ponder's son, Stephen Ponder junior, asking him to provide all of the Company's deeds and documents so an inventory could be made before they were all locked up in a safe. At the same time the Renter Warden Charles Butler was instructed to 'apply to Mr Ponder for the Ancient Chair of the Company and deliver it into the Custody of the Clerk'.[31] It appears, therefore, that the chair was entrusted to the care of the Clerk and was either stored at his personal or business premises, or in a safe place of his choosing.

It was ordered in January 1868 that the chair, 'now in possession of the Clerk', should be 'entrusted to the care of the Corporation of London and placed in the Committee Room of the City of London Freemans Orphan School at Brixton'.[32] A brass plate was added to the back of the chair stating that it was the property of the Company. The chair remained in Brixton until March 1880, when it was sent for in order to be displayed along with the Company's painting at a temporary exhibition at Mansion House, after which it was returned to the school.[33]

At the turn of the twentieth century the chair was removed from the school and was temporarily housed at Carpenters' Hall until a permanent home could be found for it. In late 1903 the Joiners offered it to the Guildhall Library and Museum for display, but they returned a reply in November stating that 'they greatly regret the space at their disposal does not permit of the acceptance'.[34] In August 1905 the Company offered it instead to the Bethnal Green Museum, a branch of the Victora & Albert Museum. The museum accepted the offer almost immediately,[35] and the Carpenters' Company praised the Joiners for their wisdom in 'allowing such a work of art to be more readily seen'.[36]

The chair was on display by January 1906, and it was described as an item of particular interest. After crediting the chair to the handiwork of Edward Newman, a newspaper report described it as follows: 'The open-work back, crowned with the shield of arms of the company, is decorated in the rococo and pseudo-Gothic style which characterised the art of the period.'[37] The chair appears to have remained with the museum on permanent loan from henceforth. Following the outbreak of the First World War in 1914 the chair remained safely stored there. The museum remained open until early 1916, and when the closure was planned the curators wrote asking whether the Company wanted the chair returned. However, they agreed that they 'would be Glad for them to continue to hold the Chair'.[38] In the summer of 1919 the chair was noted to be 'well cared for' at the museum,[39] and in 1921 it was 'in good keeping & condition'.[40]

The Director of the Victoria & Albert Museum wrote in June 1922 'asking that the Company's Master's Chair be allowed to remain on view at the Bethnal Green Museum for another year', to which the court agreed.[41] The curator assured Assistant Mr Barnes that 'every care is taken to watch for worm &c + if it should show any signs, they were prepared to put it in a lethal chamber to protect it'.[42] In a speech given to Coventry's Rotary Club in January 1925 Past Master Edward Lancaster described the chair in slight hyperbole as 'the finest example of joinery in the world', and said that 'it was visited by officers of the Company each year' at the museum.[43]

The chair was transferred from the Bethnal Green Museum to the main Victoria & Albert Museum in June 1926 so it could be featured in an exhibition of livery company artefacts. A confirmation of the transfer was sent to the Company by the curator:

I beg to inform you that under your authority of the 4th ult. to the Director of the Victoria & Albert Museum (of which this Museum is a branch) we have today handed over the Master's Chair which we hold on loan from your Worshipful Company to the representatives of the Victoria and Albert Museum for exhibition with the works of Art belonging to the City Companies now in course of arrangement.

The Chair will be returned here, at the close of the Exhibition and I will in due course acquaint you with its safe arrival back.[44]

The chair was to remain at the Victoria & Albert Museum until 2nd October when the exhibition closed,[45] and the Company purchased a copy of the exhibition catalogue for their own reference.[46]

The chair was insured for £2,000 in 1936.[47] During the Second World War it remained at the Bethnal Green Museum and was carefully stored in the basement.[48] Assistant T. B. Phillips visited the museum in December 1949 to inspect the chair, and was able to report that it was in good condition. The Master returned thanks and expressed himself 'glad to know that the chair was in a good state of preservation'.[49] In 1951 the Renter Warden stated his belief that 'the Master's chair will, no doubt, be on view to the public during the Festival of Britain where it is now housed in the Bethnal Green Museum'.[50] By 1960 it had been placed in the Victoria & Albert Museum, where it remains to this day, having been moved to a new gallery in 2001.[51]

The Breeches Bible

One of the Company's oldest possessions is a Bible dating to 1578. It is bound in leather, with brass corner decorations and clasps attached to the cover along with the Company's crest. These are believed to date from 1655–6.[52] It is known as the Breeches Bible due to a small error in the text. The Bible is still in use and is carried by the most junior liveryman in the procession to St James Garlickhythe when the Company celebrates St James' Day.

At the front of the Bible there is a description written in pencil in 1903.

> Among the treasures belonging to the Worsh' Compy of Joiners London is their Bible. It is what is commonly called the Genevan version but is better known b another title the 'Breeches Bible' from its rendering of the last clause of Genesis II.7v.
>
> It has lately been rebound and elegantly restored by Thomas Baker Esq. immediate past Master of the Compy and presented back to the Court of Assistants on Nov 4 last when a hearty vote of thanks was passed to Mr Baker for the service so handsomely rendered a letter was read from Mr Baker informing the Court that although it had cost him both time and money in the restoration he had done it <u>con amore</u>.
>
> ...
>
> We may look back with pleasure upon this Old Bible and think of the many old Joiners that have been sworn upon it. The Tudors The Stuarts and the Hanoverians have all been acknowledged as sovereigns in their turn and in past times doubtless the attention of the new freemen was drawn to the text in Ezekiel 'And thou shall joyne them one to another into one tree and they shall be as one in thine hand' or probably when a former Master had not met the approval of the Court his successor was directed to Ecclesiasticus thus
>
> 'If thou be made the Master of the feast lift not thy selfe up but be among them as one of the rest take diligent care for them and so sit downe'
>
> 'And when thou hast done all thy <u>duetie</u> sit downe that thou mayest be merry with them and receive a crowne for thy good behaviour.'

The earliest surviving reference to the Company's Bible appears to be the inventory of their property which was taken on 5th September 1642 and stated that the Bible was stored in the parlour.[53] A second inventory created in 1647 described it as 'One great bible wth bosses'.[54] An inscription was added in 1704 recording it as the property of the Joiners' Company, along with the names of the Master and Wardens in office at that time. It was also included in an inventory of the Company's property created in 1852, but was simply recorded as 'The Ancient Bible'.[55] The Bible was deposited at the Guildhall when the Company removed there in 1800.[56] Thomas Butler carried out repairs in 1902, taking it 'from its former dilapidated state restored & made more perfect'. It was placed in the care of the Guildhall Library in 1905,[57] and in 1938 it was re-backed, the spine strengthened, and new joints added. Further repairs took place in 1988.[58] A second Bible, described as 'very beautiful', was donated to the Company by Mr J. Wheldon Grace in 1970.[59]

William Frisbe's Tankard

In 1646 joiner William Frisbe presented the Company with a white tin-glazed earthenware tankard. The central decoration was the Company's coat of arms painted with blue, ochre, and yellow pigments. His name was written on either side of the arms and decorated with black flourishes, and the year 1646 appeared above his surname. Any remaining space on the tankard, including the handle, was decorated with leaf vines of blue and ochre.

Precisely when and how the tankard left the Company's possession remains a mystery.[60] This item is now in the collection of the Museum of London. They have speculated that it was presented to the Company when Frisbe was elected to a senior position.[61] Unfortunately there are no surviving court minutes from this period so there are no official records of the tankard's acceptance by the Company. The Renter Wardens' accounts do survive, however. Examination of the entries from the 1640s reveals that Frisbe never held the post of either Wardens or Master, so the Museum's theory is unlikely to be correct. There are also no references to the receipt of the tankard in the Company's accounts between 1645 and 1647. An alternative theory could be that the tankard was presented to the Company as a proof piece, but this cannot be verified due to the lack of surviving records.[62]

Boyd's Inhabitants of London lists a joiner named William Frisby, to whom the Museum of London attributes the tankard. He lived in the parish of St Mary Magdalen, Old Fish Street, and married Elizabeth Lamborne on 10th June 1620.[63] There was also a William Frisbe who married Ann Aris at St Mary Magdalen in 1638, possibly a son of the first William Frisby.[64] However, another Frisby family, that of William and Christian Frisby, lived in the parish of St Peter, Paul's Wharf in the 1620s and 1630s.[65] The Company's records confirm that a joiner named William Frisbe took Richard Smith of Berkshire as his apprentice on 30th March 1647, and he was made free on 9th July 1655.[66] The Company's accounts for 1647 record a receipt of 2s 6d from 'William Freeseby' when Smith was bound to him.[67]

Silver Plate

During the late seventeenth century inventories of the Company's plate used regularly at court meetings and dinners were copied into the court minute books. This property was looked after by successive Beadles, who were liable for any losses. Due to their regular use the Company was constantly obliged to replace and re-stock their plate. In 1662 the holdings included four dozen spoons, one great bowl, one smaller bowl, three Spanish cups, sixteen small wine cups, five other cups, three silver salts, four cups with feet, two flat cups, and two beer bowls.[68] At a quarter court on 2nd October 1750 it was brought to the attention of the members present that 'the Company have lost three Pewter Dishes two Dozen and four Pewter Plates and fourteen new Napkins'. All items had been marked with the Company's coat of arms and would therefore be quite distinctive. Suspecting deliberate theft, the court ordered that the loss should 'be Publickly Advertised with such Reward for a discovery thereof or any part thereof'. As the safekeeping of the Company's moveable goods was the responsibility of the Beadle, this order was immediately followed by a suggestion that in future incoming Beadles should provide a bond of security and 'be answerable for losses'.[69]

When the Company removed from Joiners' Hall in 1800 an auction was held to sell almost all of their plate, with only a few exceptions. Some silver cups and their covers, and five silver spoons were saved, but all other pieces of crockery were sold.[70] By August 1838 the Company's store of plate consisted merely one 'one Silver Cup and Cover and five silver Spoons'.[71] Henry Phillips, whilst Renter Warden, made a donation of 'thirteen ancient Silver Spoons' to the Company in March 1880, for which 'handsome present' the thanks of the Company were returned to him.[72]

In 1914 Past Master Henry Phillips died at the age of eighty-five. His will included several bequests of plate to the Company:

> Mr. Henry Phillips, of Worcester Park, Surrey, a Past Master of the Joiners' Company of London, left estate of which the net personalty has been sworn at £2,959. He bequeathed to the Worshipful Company of Joiners a pair of antique silver candlesticks with plated snuffers and tray, and also a silver-gilt snuff-box, with the request that the Renter Warden will take this round with him to members and guests at each of the Company's dinners, and with fresh snuff therein on each occasion.[73]

Phillips also bequeathed some of his personal collection to Lambeth Central Library and Museum, including multiple books on the history of London, a cabinet of shells and minerals, and intriguingly 'fine oak carvings of the Tudor and Stuart periods'.[74] An inventory was made of the Company's plate stored at the Guildhall on 7th February 1933, valued by a licensed appraiser. Phillips' bequests form the basis of their holdings at that time:

Silver Mace head (probably Georgian)	35oz	£50
The Ponder Cup & Cover (date 1882)	71oz	£71
The Dr Wilson Cup & Cover (date 1770)	47½ oz	£95
Octagon Rose Dish (Mr Barne gift, date 1906)	66oz	£49 10s
Silver gilt Snuffbox (date 1833)	11oz	£16 10s
Pair of George III Candlesticks (made in Sheffield about 1800)	45oz	£30
Antique Sheffield plate Snuffers and Tray		£3 10s

The total valuation was £335 10s, and the Clerk was advised to insure each item against theft at a premium of £1 13s 6d per annum.[75] The inventory of property taken on Audit Day 1935 stated that the Company's plate consisted of 'three loving cups and covers, a rose water dish, silver plated snuffers and tray, two silver candlesticks, and the silver gilt snuff box', along with the five antique spoons which had been loaned to the Guildhall in 1904.[76]

Assistant Guy Barrett presented the Company with a silver chain on 28th March 1952. He was about to depart the country for Tasmania, and offered the gift in memory of his father Oscar Barrett.[77] Master Walter Bull presented the Company with a silver fruit dish in October 1954.[78] In 1963 the Father of the Company Thomas Bartholomew Phillips presented a silver cigarette box in commemoration of his sixty years as a liveryman and thirty years as an Assistant.[79] After Phillips' death the following year the Company considered purchasing another piece of silver in his memory, but ultimately decided that 'he would be better remembered in the Company by this gift which he had personally presented'.[80] Past Master Ernest Corp presented a silver porringer in 1976, one of 900 which had been produced by the Dean and Chapter of St Paul's Cathedral to commemorate the 300th anniversary of the laying of their foundation stone.[81]

The Company also held a collection of silver goblets for use by officers. Past Master Alfred Norman Dove asked for permission to present the Company with a silver goblet in 1969 to commemorate the fact that he and his son Norman had both held the office of Master. He wished for it to be known as 'The Master's Cup' and to be used by the Master at all livery dinners to toast the Livery and their guests.[82] The following year Past Master R. C. Scutt presented another silver goblet to the Company which he intended to be known as the 'Upper Warden's Cup', and to be used exclusively by Upper Wardens at dinners.[83] A 'Clerk's Cup' was donated by Past Master H. E. Reed in 1976.[84] A mahogany casket was designed by Past Master David Knight and commissioned from liveryman Donald Gaskell 'for the purpose of storing the three special cups'.[85] The wood had been salvaged from a City bank, and was presented as a gift at no cost to the Company; a 'veritable labour of love', recorded the Clerk. The Company's crest was later added to the lid.[86] The casket was displayed in an exhibition at the Guildhall Library in 1977 as an example of modern joinery.[87] A fourth goblet was presented by Past Master David Knight in 1978 for the use of the Father of the Company.[88]

A further collection of the Company's silver was offered by Miss Baker in 1979 in exchange for a reasonable sum of money. An independent valuation suggested that the items were worth £350, but the recent rise in the value of gold and silver meant that their true worth was more likely £500. It was agreed that the Company would provide an offer of £400 for the items, which was accepted by Miss Baker, and the items were added to the Company's vault in Carpenters' Hall.[89]

An inventory from 1969 revealed that the stock of crockery was once again up to pre-1800 standards, with eighteen silver forks, fifty-nine silver dessert spoons, and sixty-four silver teaspoons, in addition to five coronation spoons.[90] In 1980 it was agreed unanimously by the Court of Assistants that a portion of the Company's silver collection should be offered for sale to the liverymen. After some discussion it was agreed that four silver rosewater bowls, five coronation spoons, eight bonbon dishes, sixty-eight teaspoons, one silver tea strainer, and one silver and glass powder pot would be offered.[91] Prices would range from £15 per teaspoon to £75 per rosewater bowl.[92] Demand for the silver 'exceeded availability', and the items were allocated by ballot.[93] A further sale of silver forks took place in 1982, with each item valued at £75.[94] Another collection of silver was offered to the Company by Mrs Blackbourn in 1980 for £225, consisting of nine dessert spoons, one coronation spoon, one tea strainer, one brooch, and one medal dated 1879,[95] and Mr Richards presented the Company with a silver goblet in 1982, which was later engraved.[96]

The Loving Cups

A loving cup is a drinking container designed to be passed around at celebrations, and it forms a central part of all livery company entertainments. They are usually made of silver and contain two handles. There are records of seven loving cups held by the Company at various times through their history. In a booklet printed and distributed to guests at their November 1956 livery dinner, the Company provided some instructions as to how the cups should be used:

> Immediately after the dinner and grace, the Master and Wardens drink to their visitors a 'Hearty Welcome': the cup is then passed round the table and each guest, after he has drink, applies his napkin to the mouth of the cup before he passes it to his neighbour.

The first of these cups was presented by Master Dr Wilson in 1770. It was distinctly ecclesiastical in appearance, bearing no small resemblance to a chalice. This can perhaps be attributed to Wilson also being a prebend of Westminster Abbey. The Company's coat of arms was embossed on the front, and the demigod protruded from the top of the cover. A new case was purchased for the cup in 1876.[97]

The Company's second loving cup was presented as a gift in 1883 following the death of William Ponder, who had been the Master during the year 1864–5 and who was also the father of the Clerk John Edwin Ponder. Mrs Ponder communicated through her son that 'it would afford her great satisfaction if the Court would allow her to present to the Company a Silver Loving Cup in memory of her late husband, he having been for so many years associated with the Company, and having so many valued friends in it'.[98] Thanks were returned to Mrs Ponder 'for the valuable and beautiful work of art given by her to the Company as a Memorial of her late husband'.[99]

A third silver loving cup was purchased in 1935 in celebration of the silver jubilee of King George V.[100] It weighed 97oz and featured a cover and mahogany pedestal. It was engraved with the Company's coat of arms and an inscription stating that it had been 'purchased by the Joiners Company May 1935 to commemorate the silver Jubilee of their Majesties'. The total cost was £40 8s 11d,[101] and a further 25 guineas was donated to King George's Jubilee Trust Fund.[102] The cup was entrusted to the Renter Warden for safe keeping, and was intended to be used at all Company banquets.[103]

The fourth loving cup was presented by outgoing Master Adam Kirk in 1966.[104] Upon presenting it he stated 'that he had great pleasure in making the gift as he had received much happiness during the time he had been a liveryman of the Company and especially during his office as Master'. He also noted that he was the first Australian to occupy the Chair of the Company.[105]

The fifth cup was purchased in 1991 as the gift of the MacQueen family in memory of Past Master Benjamin Turner, who had been a member of the Company for over seventy years.[106] It was presented by his daughter, Freeman Jean MacQueen, at the luncheon following the church service at St James Garlickhythe on 30th July 1991.[107] Shortly after this another cup was purchased in memory of Past Master Scott Bayfield with the assistance of the Worshipful

Company of Upholders, and another presented to the Company as a gift by Past Master John Elliott.[108]

Silver Spoons

The Company has an extremely long and close relationship with silver spoons. Traditionally a condition of being admitted to the freedom was that the apprentice had to present the Company with a silver spoon, in addition to a payment of 3s 4d. As the Renter Wardens' accounts do not survive from earlier than 1621 it is unclear when this practice had begun, but it was clearly well established by this date. This was not unique to the Joiners; the Tylers and Bricklayers and Weavers also noted the similar practice in their Companies.[109] The Joiners were very particular about their spoons, however; each one had to be a standard quality and weight, and fines were imposed on apprentices who submitted sub-standard articles. For example, the 1650–1 Renter Wardens' account records a fine of 2s from an unnamed apprentice 'for a spoone that was too little'.[110]

The high turnover of freedoms each year meant that the Company quickly amassed a large collection of silver spoons. In the year 1621–2 they collected twenty-eight spoons, and in 1640–1 they acquired thirty-nine. Instead of keeping them to use as dinners, the collection was treated as stock which could be liquidated to provide the Company with some extra money. For example, in the 1639–40 account there is an entry recording the sale of 'eight dozen and six' silver spoons weighing 132½oz for £34 10s.[111] In the 1655–6 account it is noted that 64oz of silver spoons had been sold for £16 5s 4d by order of the Court of Assistants 'to buy the great Bole and wyne Cupps'. The account later described it as 'a large silver bowle' weighing 32oz, and it had cost £9 7s 8d. The Master ordered the Company's crest to be engraved on both the bowl and the eight silver wine cups.[112] In spite of the regular sale, and against the odds, one of the early freedom spoons has survived in the Company's custody. The spoon was provided by Edward Bayley in 1632, but sadly the Renter Wardens' accounts for the year 1631–2 are missing, and Bayley's admission is not recorded in the 1632–3 list.

The practice of presenting spoons appears to have declined during the Interregnum and Restoration periods. The accounts for 1658–9 recorded the receipt of £7 16s 1d for 47 admissions at a fine of 3s 4d, with a further £16 15s received 'in lieu of spoones and for those that wanted waight'. It appears that the vast majority of apprentices had chosen to pay the fine rather than provide a spoon.[113] In the year 1661–2 those figures had doubled to £15 received for ninety admissions, and £40 12s 2d 'in lieu of spoones' and 3s 3d 'for those that wanted weight'.[114] In 1662–3 they received only fourteen spoons out of 116 admissions, and only three out of eighty-four admissions the following year.[115] The loss of the Hall in the Great Fire of 1666 appears to have signalled the end of silver spoons. During the year 1667–8 some sixty-six freedoms were granted at raised fines of 13s 4d, and from that time on most apprentices paid the higher fine rather than having the option of a spoon.[116] There were occasional exceptions, such as the spoon presented by 'I. E.' in 1678 and from Richard Cole in 1684–5, which remain in the Company's vault today.

For 150 years spoons took a minimal role in the Company, but they were revived at the start of the nineteenth century. Following the removal from the Hall in 1800 and the subsequent complication of organising a dinner at another Hall to celebrate St James' Day, the decision was made that in lieu of a July dinner each liveryman would be presented with a silver dessert spoon in a box. Each year they sought cost estimates from at least two suppliers, but almost always chose Elkington & Co. because their estimate was the most competitive. After making the first set of dies the costs could be lower in later years if the same designs were used again. This company's head office and manufactory were based in Birmingham, but there was a London office in Regent Street. In the 1920s the one silver dessert spoon was replaced by two silver teaspoons, a decision which initially cost the Company more money because a new die had to be created. In 1929, to mix things up a bit, the teaspoons were replaced by one silver dessert spoon and one silver dessert fork.[117]

When not using Elkington & Co. the next preferred supplier was silversmith Francis Cook of Love Lane, from whom the Masters' medals and jewel were regularly ordered.[118] Cook was requested to provide some sample silver ash trays in March 1927; they were plain and circular, with the Company's arms stamped into the surface. Upon favourable inspection a choice was offered to the Livery whether they wanted to receive another traditional spoon or an ash tray,[119] but surprisingly they wanted the spoons.[120] Elkington lost their contract altogether in 1929 when a die they had previously produced was found to be 'so unsatisfactory', and Francis Cook became the Company's preferred manufacturer.[121] In 1933 another different item was offered, this time a silver tazza dish with the Company's arms embossed inside.

Some additional spoons were acquired in 1960, following the death of Past Master Roger Abbott. His daughter offered silver tea and dessert spoons, along with her father's Past Master's medal.[122] This brought the Company's stock up to twenty-four dessert spoons and twenty teaspoons.[123] A further thirteen desert spoons dated 1905 were offered by a jeweller in 1961,[124] and fifteen dessert spoons and seventeen teaspoons from a private collection in 1962.[125] Unsure what to do with this sudden influx of spoons, it was decided in 1964 that all Past Masters who had joined the Livery since 1940 would be presented with one upon leaving office, rather than the usual medal.[126] A further thirty-two teaspoons, sixteen dessert forks, twenty-three dessert spoons, six bonbon dishes, and one rosewater bowl were offered to the Company by liveryman Mr J. O. Wiginton and his mother in 1967.[127]

Stained-glass Windows

On St James' Day 1866 it was proposed that the Assistants should 'take the necessary steps to have one of the Windows in Guildhall illuminated with stained Glass containing the arms of the Company and some incident in its history'. The Company's motto was to be engraved in stone above the window, and a cost limit of £150 was suggested. This was voted down, however, and the issue was not revived until early 1870 when the Assistants were 'requested to apply for permission to fill one of the windows of the Guildhall with stained Glass as a memorial of the good taste and public spirit of the Worshipful Company of Joiners'.[128] However, this was voted down by the next Court of Livery because the estimated cost of £160 was considered too high.[129] Instead it was proposed that the cost 'should be defrayed by Private subscription'.[130] The Company agreed to contribute 50 guineas, and the Livery were asked to contribute the rest.[131] However, in September 1871 the London and Middlesex Archaeological Society declared their intention to sponsor the armorial bearings of livery companies to be added to the large window in the south end of the Library and Museum building at the Guildhall, with a much lower cost of only

10 guineas to be borne by each of the Companies. This seemed like a much more financially astute move than sponsoring a full window of their own, and the Joiners agreed to send the money.[132]

In November 1881 the Company agreed to contribute 10 guineas towards the cost of having their coat of arms included in a new stained-glass window in St Albans Abbey.[133] This was installed in the Lady Chapel in 1883.[134] Another stained-glass window containing the Company's arms was installed in St James' Church, Southampton Dock, in the 1950s,[135] and one in Guildford Cathedral in the 1960s.[136]

History Books

Past Master Henry Laverock Phillips began composing a history of the Company in 1899. This was the first corporate history of the Joiners, and was the work of many years. The text was finally ready to be presented to the Company on 1st September 1914 under the title *The Annals of the Worshipful Company of Joiners*. Phillips, 'in a few words', asked the court to 'accept for the information & benefit of the Company the Book he had written after much research'.

It is with much pleasure I present to you the Annals of the Joiners Company.

They seem, these old World Joiners, to have met their losses by fire with undaunted courage, raising subscriptions and rebuilding their Hall several times.

The part they played in London History is shown in these records, and whether Tudor, Stuart or Hanoverians were in power, they looked after their apprentices, numbering in 1668 as many as 361.

They searched for bad workmanship and punished delinquents. They even obtained the power to enforce their penalties in the Court of His Highness the Lord Protector; but they no doubt acted up to the motto on their early seal and used 'Justice with Mercie'.

These Junctors and Celators as they were anciently called duly dined on festive occasions. Their Bacon, Candlemas and Venison feasts are all spoken of and when the monarch proceeded to St Pauls after a victory to return thanks, they duly attended with their Banners.

The victory of Ramilies is spoken of; the Lord Mayors day was always celebrated by them, and at their stand in Cheapside they were able to give the coming Lord Mayor an ovation.

The Joiners frequently abused their Masters and apologised.

I can assure you, I had much pleasure in perusing the volumes, giving an account of their doings, how they subscribed for the Pageants, gave money for setting out the fleet and for maintaining the Army and subscribed for the ship called 'Loyal London'.

In conclusion I have to thank, very much the many friends that have assisted me in the Compilation of this book, particularly Dr Reginald Sharpe, who drew my attention to the Many documents to be found in the Town Clerks' office.

In return the Master expressed 'the great pleasure it gave him in receiving such a treasure for the Livery, & he also thanked him for the time and labour he must have devoted to the work & was sure that not only the Court but the Livery would be most gratified with his gift'. A committee was established to 'go into the matter of Cost, as to having the book printed & bound'.[137] Copies were donated to the Guildhall, other livery companies, the Institute of Historical Research,[138] and the City Library of Birmingham.[139] The book was even sent as a gift to Harvard University in 1921, for which librarian William Coolidge Lane returned grateful thanks.[140] The High Commissioner of New Zealand also requested a copy for the General Assembly Library in Wellington in 1936.[141] From 1930 onwards anyone joining the Company's livery by purchase was given a copy of the Annals as a gift after paying their £93 fee.[142] Phillips' archive of material was donated to the Company after his death.[143]

In the 1960s discussion turned to the possibility of getting Phillips' annals reprinted, but concern was raised that there were numerous errors in the text. Consequently the task of editing it with the view of producing a revised and updated version fell to Past Master Sidney E. Lane.[144] The first full draft was presented to the Master and Wardens for inspection in April 1968, and they provided authorisation for it to be published in May.[145] The book was published by Page & Thomas at a cost of £1 6s 6d per copy, and was offered for sale to the Livery at £3 3s.[146] Each new liveryman would be presented with a copy upon their admission to the Company.[147]

Additional shorter brochures were produced in 1971 for the 400th anniversary of the charter, and in 1987 by a specially formed Archives and History Committee.[148]

Miscellaneous Items

The sale of the Company's property in 1800 means that it is impossible to recreate a full inventory of their previous possessions. However, sporadic references to other items do appear in some records.

In April 1838 the Company purchased an iron safe and received permission to install it in the Irish Chamber in the Guildhall so they could store their documents safely. This safe replaced an old chest which was no longer fit for purpose, and the Beadle was ordered to destroy it along with the 'useless Hags and Emblems of the Company' engraved on it.[149] By 1876 the Company's iron chest was being stored in the Muniment Chamber underneath the Guildhall.[150]

On 6th September 1859 William Snoxell Esq., at that time the Father of the Company, presented a flag containing the Company's arms as a token of respect for 'the long duration my Family have been honored Members of the Joiners Company and in acknowledgement of the great kindness always received from the Gentlemen of your Worshipful Company'. The flag was gratefully accepted and 'warm and sincere thanks' were returned to Snoxell 'for the very handsome present'.[151] In 1863 it was ordered that the flag should be displayed 'at all banquets in future', as well as at the first Court of Assistants meeting each September.[152] There was also a seventeenth-century fireback made of Sussex iron and bearing the Company's coat of arms, which had found its way into the Guildhall museum by 1913.[153]

In addition to William Frisbe's tankard, the Museum of London holds two other items of particular interest to the Company. One is a bronze medal dated to *circa* 1880, presumably a medal awarded to an officer at the end of their tenure. The Company's coat of arms is on one side, along with the dates of incorporation. The reverse features an image of the Company's patron St James, flanked by two shells and with the words 'Worshipful Company of Joiners London' around the edge.[154] The second, more curious, item is an embroidered badge bearing the date 3rd July 1884. This badge was shaped into a twelve-pointed gold star, with the Company's crest inside it on a blue background. This is a very intricate piece of work and was clearly created to commemorate a specific event. The initials M. C. are above the star, perhaps giving an indication as to the owner's identity.[155]

In 1967 the Company decided to invest in ties containing their crest which could be purchased by existing liverymen,[156] and presented to all new liverymen upon their admission.[157] These were redesigned in 1978 due to the style being 'a little old fashioned'.[158]

Chapter 8

Eighteenth- and Nineteenth-century Finance and Politics

William Astell and the South Sea Company

The Astell family's association with the Joiners' Company can be traced back to 25th July 1659, when John Astell was apprenticed to Richard Gardiner. John was not a native of London; he was the son of Clerk John Astell of Church Brampton in Northamptonshire.[1] He was admitted to the freedom of the Company on 3rd December 1666,[2] shortly after the Great Fire of London had caused the loss of their beloved Hall. He remained both geographically and occupationally close to the Joiners' Company in his future career. He began trading as a timber merchant and acquired premises on what is now Castle Baynard, leading directly onto Thames Street.[3]

In the following years he trained a number of apprentices, including John Furnis (apprenticed 1668–75), Thomas Randolph (1669–76), Stephen Jones (1670–77, turned over to him from Clement Dighton), relation Roger Astell (1670–77), Joseph Kilbey (1675–82), William Halford (1676–85), Richard Coe (1677–85), Richard King (bound in 1683 but later turned over to William Holford), and Thomas Goodlad (bound in 1685 but later turned over to Charles Taylor). The apprentice of most significance, however, was his own son William, who was bound to him on 3rd April 1688, and appears to have been the last apprentice he trained.[4] William received the freedom of the Company on 4th June 1695,[5] and like his father before him he would go on to train apprentices of his own, including James Small (apprenticed 1714–21), and Ralph Field (1719–26).

On 8th October 1697 William Astell appeared at a private court at Joiners' Hall to pay the fine of £5 instead of holding the office of steward for the upcoming Lord Mayor's Day. He took the opportunity to also request that the Court 'would be pleased to accept of his ffine of £5 more for Livery which this Court did graunt and soe admitted him and [he] tooke his Clothing accordingly' after paying a total of £10.[6] The 1710 *Poll of the Livery-Men of the City of London* listed him as a joiner.[7]

John Astell died in the winter of 1697 at the approximate age of fifty-two. William was the sole executor and chief beneficiary of his father's will. John provided an annuity of £40 per year to support his widow Margaret, and left £500 to purchase real estate to be placed in trust to support the family of their daughter Elizabeth, now the wife of Shadrach Brice. Apart from some smaller bequests to his siblings and their children, John left 'all and every my moneys Stock plate Lynnen household goods debts chattels and all other my Estate and substance whatsoever and wheresoever both reall and personall' to his 'loveing sonne William Astell'.[8]

The inheritance William received following his father's death appears to have been the catalyst for him expanding his business. By November 1698 he was in negotiations with the Navy to supply timber to the dockyard at Deptford.[9] In October 1701 he was described in Admiralty papers as a 'merchant and shipper', and in July 1702 was a 'Timber Supplier'.[10] Notwithstanding his future questionable financial dealings, which are discussed below, his contract with the Navy continued until his death in 1741 and made him a very wealthy man.[11] In addition to Deptford, by 1737 he was also supplying to the naval yards at Chatham, Portsmouth, and Plymouth.[12] He provided timber from Norway, Russia, Danzig (now Gdańsk), and America,[13] as well as hemp and tar.[14] Astell's fleet of ships included the *Sea Adventure*, the *Two Twins*, the *Lucy*, the *Friendly Society*, the *James and Matthew*, and the *Merry Jacks*.[15]

In spite of his success in business, Astell's private life was less stable. His first wife Anne died at the family's London home on 26th August 1707 and was buried at St Benet's, Paul's Wharf. It is possible that she died due to complications in childbirth, because the following month on 11th September 1707 the couple's infant daughter Mary was also buried at the same church. On 17th May 1708, at the age of thirty-five, he obtained a marriage licence enabling him to remarry. His bride was twenty-three-year-old Mary Bagnall of the parish of St Stephen's, Coleman Street.[16] The couple had a large family of at least eight children, but only three appear to have survived infancy. Astell purchased the estate of Everton in Bedfordshire from William Carey in 1713. This gave him the right to be known as Lord of the Manor of Everton.[17] By 1716 he had secured himself the position of a Common Councilman of Broad Street ward, which he held as a Whig representative.

The most significant of Astell's appointments for the future affairs of the Joiners' Company was to the Board of Directors of the South Sea Company, which had taken place by 1720. The South Sea Company had been founded in 1711 to consolidate and reduce the national debt, which had risen sharply due to the costs of the War of the Spanish Succession and the Great Northern War, and by 1713 the Company had a monopoly to supply African slaves to South America. They acquired more government debt in 1719, and in 1720 the Board of Directors began to artificially inflate share prices in the hope of attracting more investors and generating larger returns.

On 15th July 1720 Astell secured a private meeting at Joiners' Hall with Master John Leadbeater, the two Wardens, and eleven members of the Court of Assistants. The Company had previously invested £200 in an annuity with the Bank of England which returned interest at 5 per cent. However, Astell presented them with an opportunity to transfer that investment to the South Sea Company instead. The terms he offered them were not recorded in the minute book, but it must be remembered that this was at the height of the South Sea bubble, which would not burst until September. People were investing in the company in their hundreds; it appeared to be a lucrative opportunity, and the Joiners took it. Indeed, being approached by one of the directors must have made it seem all the more appealing, and they had no reason to doubt Astell's trustworthiness. Consequently, at the end of that meeting an order was made to transfer the Bank of England investment 'into the South Sea Company for the use of the Company of Joyners as Wm Astell Esq. a member of this Compa[ny] & one of the Directors of the said [South Sea] Compa[ny] shall think fit for the good of this Compa[ny]'.[18] At a meeting at the Hall on 13th September for the election of stewards for Lord

Mayor's Day Master Leadbeater and Warden Bird provided a declaration which they had signed and sealed confirming at the Company's £200 annuities had been transferred from the Bank of England to the South Sea Company in trust.[19] What makes this investment particularly controversial is the fact that the South Sea Company was directly involved in the slave trade, which means that the Joiners' Company had knowingly invested in, and were set to profit from, slavery. This is something which must be acknowledged, and consideration given to what this means for the Company's reputation in the future.

The price of South Sea Stock reached its peak in August 1720, but large-scale selling meant that the price soon fell from £1,000 per share to only £100. Those who had purchased on credit faced bankruptcy, and debts were defaulted on. Parliament was recalled in December to investigate what had happened, and the Act 'For Inlarging the Capital Stock of the South-Sea Company' estimated that redeemable debts amounted to £16,564,482 7s 1d.[20] A petition to the House of Commons by a group of disgruntled investors complained that they had been 'betrayed and drawn into this Gulph of Misery and Destruction' by the directors, who had deliberately inflated the stock prices. Another petition noted the notorious 'false Insinuations and vile Practices of the late Directors', which were 'designedly to impose upon innocent and credulous Persons'.[21]

The real and personal estates and assets of the Board of Directors, including William Astell, were seized by the government, and a commission of nine trustees was appointed to examine the Company's accounts and ascertain exactly how much money had been lost. They subsequently presented two reports to the House of Commons, the first on 10th February 1721 and the second on 25th January 1722. The trustees had made complete inventories of the directors' property, which could be claimed upon by those who had lost money in the crash. The second report noted that they had received seventy-two claims from abroad, in addition to 1,031 domestic claims from residents of the United Kingdom. The trustees were staggered by the 'Multiplicity and Perplexity of the Business ... but especially the Number of Claims on the said Estates'. In spite of constant attendance to the business, by January 1722 they had only been able to investigate 327 of the claims and requested further time to examine the rest. Their third report, dated 20th March 1723, stated that they had been able to investigate 'upwards of Six hundred Claims', and had confiscated and in many cases sold over £1,400,000 worth of real and personal property from the directors towards compensation. By 1725 this had risen to almost £1,800,000.[22] This is the approximate equivalent of £209,000,000 in modern money, which shows how enormous in scale this situation was.[23] The Joiners' Company's investment at this point was minor compared with some; they had invested only £200, so any losses would be relatively low.

By 1726 almost £25,000 of Astell's real estate had been sold, along with £7,500 of personal goods and debts. A report confirmed that he had fully complied with the trustees' investigations, and as such he was entitled to an allowance out of the residue of his property. By April 1728 the value of his confiscated personal goods and debts had risen to almost £22,000, so the combination of his real and personal losses was approximately £47,000, and the total raised by the trustees was over £3,200,000.[24] The statement that Astell made in his own defence shortly after the crash has survived. In spite of his position as a director he claimed total ignorance of any illegal behaviour, and attempted to secure sympathy by referring to personal tragedy.

During the time of the Dependence of the South-Sea Bill for the Scheme, I was Two Months in my Lodgings, or out of Town, under the Pressure of that Heavy Affliction that befell me and my Family, by the Fire in Austin-Friars, and was no ways concerned in the Scheme, nor assisted in soliciting the same; not of the Committee appointed for that purpose, and wholly ignorant of the taking in, selling, or holding Stock for any Person whatsoever: I acted in the Committee of Accompts, and knew not of the Excesses of the Loans, or selling any of the Stock or Subscriptions that were pledged as Security, till it was declared by the Committee of Secrecy; nor was it possible I could, those books never coming under my Inspection; and having sate in that Court many Years, and never observed or heard of any ill Practices, had no mistrust thereof.

The Increase of the First and Second Money Subscriptions, and Decrease of the Third and Fourth, after the Declarations, were unknown to me till after they were done.

What I agreed to in the Court of Directors, I did believe was for the Interest of the Company, and the Publick, and had no particular Views to any private Interest of my own, as may appear by my acting in my own private Affairs, wherein it appears by my Account of Stock and Subscriptions delivered in, that I have not been a Negotiator therein, nor sold at High Prices.

What third Subscription I sold, I agreed to re-pay the Money upon the Reduction, and by the Stock and Subscription which I have reduced to 150l. per Cent. I am a Looser upon the Account, and by the many great Losses I have sustained, my Estate is much lessened, since this unhappy Scheme, as my Accompts make appear.

NB. I have Three small Children.[25]

The inventory of his property as it stood in June 1720 was published in 1721 amongst volume one of *The Particulars and Inventories of the Estates Of the Late Sub-Governor, Deputy-Governor, and Directors of the South-Sea Company.* The only items not included in the inventory were clothes belonging to him and his children.[26]

In spite of the enormous controversy surrounding the South Sea Company, which the Joiners could not possibly have been unaware of, they did not withdraw their investment; on the contrary, over the coming years they expanded it. The reason for this is unclear. Certainly they had received some small dividends payments after the crash, so were receiving returns on their investments. It is also possible that Astell's position in the Company made any suggestion of selling the stock awkward. On the other hand, they may have believed his declarations that he was unaware of the illegal transactions and that he had advised them to place the investment in good faith. The initial investment in 1720 was £200 in annuities. At a monthly court on 1st May 1722 it was agreed that a further £50 would be invested with South Sea, and Warden Lawrence confirmed at the next court that he had purchased warrant number 1,669 for £43 13s 6d.[27] The following February an order was made for a further £150 of stock to be purchased in trust for the Company, which brought the total investment up to £400.[28]

Even more remarkable was Astell's career within the Joiners' Company. Although there is no evidence in the court minute books that he made any kind of public statement at a court meeting concerning what was happening with the South Sea Company, it is possible that these conversations had taken place privately. Nevertheless, he retained his position on the Court of Assistants. On 14th April 1724 he was named as one of thirteen committee members charged with assessing whether the Company's ordinances were meeting their current needs.

Only three months later, on 14th July, he was elected as Master of the Company for the year 1724 to 1725.[29] He was re-elected as Master on 26th January 1736 to serve out the remainder of that year after Master Thomas Gates died in office.[30]

Whether or not this was just a coincidence or a deliberate attempt to avoid accusations of a conflict of interest is unclear, but when it was decided in court on 1st September 1724 to purchase another £150 of annuities the deputy Master was in the chair, and Astell was absent. This purchase was made by transferring what was currently held in stock into annuities, and after this transaction was completed a report was made at the October quarterly court that the Company then held annuities worth £450. Also at that quarterly court it was confirmed that the annuities had been transferred into the names of the Master and Renter Warden in trust for the Company, so ironically former South Sea director William Astell, who had previously been so deeply involved in the management of South Sea stock, now held investments in his name again.[31]

Initially when stock was acquired the transaction was done in the name of the person who had paid the money, in trust for the Company. When the new Master and Wardens were sworn in each year the stock was transferred into their names in trust. This remained the practice until 12th January 1731, when Master John Burt decided that this was inconvenient and instead ordered all stock 'to be transferred in the South Sea Company's Books in the Name of the Company of Joyners Cielers and Carvers of London'.[32] A further £150 of annuity stock was purchased on 7th September 1725 at a cost of £163 10s, bringing the Company's investment up to £600.[33] Exactly six years later, on 7th September 1731, the purchase of another £100 annuity was authorised by a monthly court, and the transaction was completed by former Master Burt by the time of the November court. At this point in time the dividends stood at 6 per cent.[34] Another £100 annuity was purchased in September 1733 from South Sea's joint stock, with a further £100 annuity acquired in November.[35] These two transactions brought the Joiners' Company's investment in South Sea up to £900, the peak it would reach.[36] This sum is roughly equivalent to £106,000 in modern money.[37]

In the autumn of 1735, when the expenses of making the necessary repairs to the Hall became much higher than the Company had anticipated, it was agreed at a quarterly court that £200 worth of annuities should be sold 'with all convenient speed'. The Clerk reported on 12th November that he had sold the stock at a profit of £17 5s.[38] It is probable that this was against the wishes of William Astell, because when he resumed the position of Master on 26th February 1736 one of his first actions was to propose to the Livery that

> no part of the Company's Anuity Stock or other Stock be Transferred or sold or money borrowed on the Company's Seal till the money in the Warden's hands be paid And if money be absolutely wanted Then so much only of the Anuitys shall be sold & Transferred as shall be needful to pay & discharge the said Bills.[39]

After his second term as Master had ended Astell was one of the committee appointed to examine all workmen's bills. When they made their final report on 10th February 1737 they reluctantly revealed that they owed £1,136 11s 2d for the repair of the Hall, although they had negotiated that down from an initial charge of £1,340 18s. To meet this cost a motion was carried unanimously that all of the South Sea stock should be sold to meet the majority of these costs.[40] The Clerk liquidated the remaining £700 annuities at a profit of £97 2s 6d, and all the money was given to the Renter Warden to settle the accounts with the workmen.[41] However, when the audit took place on 24th August it was discovered that the

Company was £393 18s 7d in profit for the year, and the Master decided that the money should be used to re-purchase £350 worth of annuities.[42] These were not held for long, however. On 7th February 1738 it was agreed at a monthly court that the annuities should be sold and the money used once again to pay a debt of £315 7s 11d due to John Smallwell, John Cooper, and Thomas Singleton for necessary repairs at the Hall.[43] This marked the end of the Company's investment in the South Sea Company.

William Astell served on the Court of Assistants of the Joiners' Company for the final time in the year of 1737–8.[44] One of his final actions was an attempt on 7th February 1738 to get his friend and fellow timber merchant Matthew Enderup of Thames Street admitted as a liveryman of the Company through payment of a £20 fine. However, when the question was put as to whether this should be debated it passed in the negative.[45] Astell died in his home in Everton on 15th October 1741, and was buried at St Mary's church on the 22nd of that month.

Later Eighteenth-century Finance

The Company's finances steadily recovered in the years following the sale of their South Sea annuities, and there was a short period of relative prosperity. Under the tenure of Renter Warden John Wills the year 1751–2 was particularly bountiful, and they cleared a profit of over £292, compared with £114 the previous year[46] and just £74 in 1745.[47] Rather than just leave the whole sum as ready cash, the Renter Warden was instructed to invest £150 of it in 3 per cent bank annuities in the Company's corporate capacity.[48] Assistant George Turner died at the beginning of 1755 and in his will he bequeathed £20 to be distributed to the Company's poor at the discretion of the Master, Wardens, and Assistants.[49] At the March court it was decided to invest this money in the 3 per cent stock, and use the interest for the benefit of the poor.[50] After a particularly successful year in 1758–9 the Company had cleared over £289 in their annual audit. The Clerk was instructed to take £150 of this sum and make a further investment in the 3 per cent annuities.[51]

The first hint that the Company was heading towards trouble came on 7th February 1764 when the Master, Wardens, Clerk, and seven Assistants were appointed as 'a Committee to Inspect into the State of the Company's Accounts'. They were authorised to meet as often as they felt necessary, with the first meeting on Wednesday sevennight.[52] This was a departure from the standard practice, which had been to only assess the finances once per year ahead of Audit Day. On 4th December the committee was instructed to present their report at the next court meeting,[53] and it didn't make for pleasant reading. They discovered that the Company was £321 9s 2½d in debt 'to several Persons', and that there were multiple tax and tradesmen's bills still unpaid to the sum of £72 18s. The combination of these two sums was almost £400. The Company did, however, hold promissory notes and security bonds worth £262, but even deducting that sum they remained in debt for £132 6s 2d. This was 'more than the Monies and Securities in the Renter Wardens hands will satisfy'. The decision was made to call in all money owed to the Company, and implement an immediate spending freeze. Instead of dining at the Hall after monthly court meetings the Master would instead 'fix on some Tavern to entertain such of the Court who attend the Business thereof', and this must cost no more than half a crown per person. Any expenses above this amount must be met by the attendee, rather than the Company.[54]

Attention quickly turned to the Company's stock investments, and in April the decision was made to sell £150 of annuities 'in order to pay off and discharge as many of the Companys Debts as the Money arising by such Sale will amount to'.[55] This transaction took place on 12th April, and the Master reported to the next court that it had produced £131 16s 3d in ready money.[56] When the next audit took place in August it was recorded that the Company's income for the previous year had been £812 13s 6¼d, and expenditure was £707 18s ¾d. In theory this left a balance of £104 15s 5½, but only 12s 5½d of this was cash in hand. The rest was accounted for by promissory notes.[57]

The following March several tradesmen presented themselves at the court meeting and complained that although their bills had been approved and signed by the Master, they were as yet unpaid. They stated that they had applied several times to the current Renter Warden, George Hoare, but he told them he had no ready money to pay them with. Hoare was accused of 'having neglected to attend the Duties of his Office' by failing to attend the last few meetings, and a new committee was appointed to enquire into the state of the finances again.[58] The committee met twice in the month leading up to the next court, but as the Renter Warden failed to attend either meeting they were unable to inspect his accounts. However, they were 'of Opinion that there is at this time a considerable Sum of Money in the Renter Wardens hands'. The deputy Renter Warden, Captain Furnish, agreed to advance the Company some money to enable them to pay their pensioners, as nothing was forthcoming from Hoare. The recalcitrant officer was summoned to attend another meeting on 14th April, and warned that if he did not an extraordinary Court of Livery would be summoned to decide on a suitable punishment. In the meantime the decision was made to cancel both the audit dinner and Lord Mayor's Day dinner.[59] In spite of the warning, Hoare did not attend the meeting on 14th April. The Clerk subsequently wrote to him to express the committee's annoyance:

> The Committee of the Company of Joyners London met at the said Company's Hall this Afternoon at 3 O'Clock in Expectation that you would have attended at such Meeting with your Wardenship Accounts, and are much surprized at your not attending, either at this, or their several former Meetings, notwithstanding the repeated Notices given you occasioned by the frequent Complaints made by several of the Company's Creditors and your non Attendance to pay them. I am therefore directed by the Committee to inform you that at the last Court of Assistants, there was a Minute made in their Book for calling a Court of Livery to lay your Conduct before them, which must certainly be done very shortly and without further Notice to you, unless you prevent the same by desiring me to call the Committee together once more in order to receive your Accounts.

Hoare did not respond to this in writing, but finally called upon the Clerk on the morning of 5th May when the next court meeting was scheduled. He claimed that he was unable to attend the meeting itself, but would present his accounts in a fortnight. The committee agreed to a meeting on that date, but its members were nevertheless doubtful that Hoare would attend because they were authorised to immediately summon a Court of Livery if he did not.[60]

Their instincts were correct, and they reported to the June court that Hoare had not attended and had not sent his accounts. As the next court meeting was already scheduled to be a livery court the decision of how to proceed against Hoare was deferred until then. He was not the only officer proving less than satisfactory, however. The June court closed with a reprimand to the current Master, Giles Grendey, who was accused of 'not having duly attended the Duties of his Office'. He was warned in writing that 'his Better Attendance hereafter on the Duties of his Office is expected', otherwise 'such Methods will be taken as shall be adjudged proper which 'tis hoped he will prevent as the same will be equally disagreeable to the Court as to himself'.[61]

Neither Grendey nor Hoare appeared at the July quarter court, nor at the election on St James' Day.[62] In the period between St James' Day and Audit Day all financial matters were dealt with severally by the deputy Master, deputy Renter Warden, and the Upper Warden, rather than relying on the two men. They nevertheless optimistically instructed that Hoare's accounts should be examined on Audit Day, as usual.[63] A member of the Hoare family did attend on 24th August, but it was William Hoare rather than George. He informed the court that George had been in the country 'for some time past' and was unable to attend in person. Unwilling to negotiate further, the court ordered Hoare to attend a meeting to close his accounts on 15th September,[64] or else the security bond he had provided at the beginning of his tenure would be called in and the money used to settle any outstanding bills he had not addressed.[65]

A quarter court was informed on 6th October that Hoare's accounts had finally been delivered to the auditors. The Company's outgoings had been lower than in previous years, but that can be attributed to Hoare's refusal to pay the tradesmen rather than any genuine financial stability. Hoare was instructed to pay the £43 remaining in his hands before the next court or forfeit his security bond. On the same day a letter was sent to Past Master Giles Grendey instructing him to also attend the next court 'to shew cause why the Penalty according to the Company's By Law incurred by him for Neglect of Duty should not be put in force against him'.[66]

Hoare did not attend the November court or provide the money remaining in his hands, so the Clerk was authorised to sue him for his security bond.[67] The bondsman was George Richard Hoare, the son of the former Renter Warden. When the Clerk had delivered notice of the intended action George Richard Hoare 'requested to be indulged a little time longer from paying', and promised to provide the money in February. The Clerk was authorised to enter into a joint note with Hoare the younger for payment,[68] but the January court was informed that the latter had not in fact entered into an agreement. Consequently the Clerk was once again authorised to commence a suit against the two Hoares.[69] After several months of silence Hoare the younger called upon the Clerk at the Hall, accompanied by his attorney. He requested that his father's accounts should be revised because he believed 'that there is some trifling Mistake therein in disfavour of the said late Renter Warden'. This request was granted, and Hoare's account was revised down to £40 16s. The younger Hoare was satisfied and paid this amount to the Clerk, plus costs. Any further proceedings against them were stopped.[70] In spite of the turmoil the Hoares had caused to the Company's finances, after the 1768 audit it was decided to invest £100 back into the 3 per cent annuity stock.[71] This would replace part of the stock sold in 1765. The Renter Warden confirmed in October that this purchase had been made.[72]

The problem of unsuitable officers sadly continued through the year 1768–9. At the November court the conduct of Upper Warden John Haines was remarked upon. He was accused of 'not having attended the Companys Business' since 6th September, even though he had taken the oath of office. He was fined 40s in absentia, and the Clerk was instructed to summon him to attend the next court to answer for his neglect.[73] Haines returned his compliments to the Master, Wardens, and Assistants, and pleaded that 'his ill State of Health had been the Occasion of such Neglect'. Notwithstanding his previous acceptance of the post, he begged permission to fine for it instead and the Court agreed.[74]

At the beginning of April 1770 the Company experienced theft. Approximately 70 feet of lead was stolen from the roof of an outbuilding in the yard, where the stands used on Lord Mayor's Day were currently kept. An advertisement was placed offering a reward of 2 guineas for the apprehension of the thieves.[75] Henry Holland later re-slated the roof at a cost of £3 1d.[76]

John Wilkes

Perhaps the most well-known member of the Joiners' Company was John Wilkes. He was the son of a Clerkenwell malt distiller, but showed early signs of promise and enjoyed an extensive education in Hertford and later at the University of Leiden. He entered Parliament through a rotten borough in 1757, and bribed his constituents to re-elect him in the 1761 election. Although not praised as an orator, Wilkes' strength was the written word and he wrote numerous tracts and articles commentating on the politics of the day. This placed him in opposition to George Grenville, who became Prime Minister in April 1763, and Wilkes was arrested on his orders for seditious libel. Wilkes secured a release on the grounds of parliamentary privilege, and the first of many 'Wilkite mobs' took to the streets of London in support of both him and liberty. Although he launched legal proceedings to defend himself Wilkes was forced to flee to Paris at the end of 1763 to avoid further imprisonment and was expelled from the House of Commons on 19th January 1764. He made brief return trips to London under an assumed name to petition for pardon, but was ignored, and in early 1768 he returned as himself and attempted to secure another parliamentary seat.[77]

Wilkes was awarded the freedom of the Joiners' Company by Redemption on 10th March 1768. On the same day he requested admittance to the Livery, and paid the £20 fine.[78] His appointment to the Company was directly related to his upcoming intended election as a Member of Parliament representing the City, a condition of which role was presence in a livery company. At first glance there is no apparent reason for his decision to associate himself with the Joiners rather than any of the other companies. He certainly did not have a background in woodworking, and nor did he come from a joinery family. His motivation for doing so, however, was revealed in a newspaper advertisement placed by an anonymous source known as Truth: 'John Wilkes, Esq.; we hear, is of the Joiners Company, the largest body of liverymen of the Livery Companies.'[79] There, then, was his reason. He had joined the company with the largest body of liverymen in the hope of securing enough votes to win himself the seat in Parliament. The same newspaper report noted that he had support amongst the Fishmongers' Company, and was dining with the Grocers the following day to promote his cause with them.

Two long advertisements in Wilkes' favour were placed in the *Gazetteer and New Daily Advertiser* on 14th March. The first was addressed to the liverymen of the City of London:

Gentlemen,

You were never called upon to give your votes for representatives in parliament, at any one time in which so many important consequences depended upon your choice as at present. The City of London has been justly considered, and often honourably dreaded by corrupt Ministers, as giving the lead to the nation; any by the political characters of the members which you return, will the world judge your political principles, and of the measures which you wish to see adopted. Thus, were you to return as one of your representatives, 'any man who has voted in favour of General Warrants, to search your house? merely at the discretion of the minister for the time being,' were you to vote for a man 'who has meanly submitted to the tyranny of favouritism, or who has bargained away his independency for a place or a contract,' what idea must the world entertain of the degeneracy of this great, this once independent city.

If there are in Britain any of these unnatural monsters who exert their utmost power and influence to enslave their native country, who delight in tyranny and arbitrary power, who wish to corrupt the guardians of our Liberties, and bid high for the representatives that they may the more readily sell their constituents? if there are any such monsters, how would they triumph to have it sonded[sic] throughout the nation, 'that the city of London approves of corruption, electing the corrupted.'

Whereas on the other hand, if you set the just mark of contempt, on every man who has at all favoured or countenanced any of the measures which are injurious to the cause of constitutional Liberty, you will by this means give the most glorious check to the destructive views of every despotic Minister, and will powerfully enforce this important lesson to every future candidate, 'that the only way to obtain your favours, is to deserve them.'

You have now gentlemen, an opportunity put into your hands, 'of making a grand and solemn determination in favour of Liberty,' you have it in your power to return a man to parliament, who, by appearing there as your representative, will give such a strong proof of your detestation to every tyrannical and unconstitutional measure, as must necessarily confound every enemy to the Liberties and Privileges of free born Englishmen.

Mr. Wilkes, Gentlemen, stood forth as the undaunted champion for your liberties, at a time, 'When you doubted how far they were to be defended:' He was committed to prison by an authority which was afterwards adjudged in the Courts of Law, to be an illegal one. He has powerful lawyers engaged against him, who for the same fee would have been ready to prove, 'That any Secretary of State might by his warrant, send his State Myrmidons to enter all your houses, break open all your most secret repositories, family or private concerns, and even hale you to some detested gaol, leaving your distracted wives, surrounded by their weeping offspring, to lament their wretched widowed state.'

Had Wilkes tamely submitted to the vile indignity with which he was treated; had he suffered this atrocious stretch of power to pass uncensured, uncontrouled, tell me, my fellow Citizens, tell me, on what foundation would your liberty; and that of your posterity, have rested? At best, you would meanly have held (under some future detested minion) as a matter of grace and favour, the continuance of these native rights which your revered forefathers purchased for you by the most noble sacrifice of their blood and treasure, and have handed down to you, as guardians and trustees for posterity, you would have been reduced to the condition of Frenchmen, but with this aggravating curse, 'that your fathers and grandfathers were British.'

Since then it is to Wilkes that you are indebted for this constitutional opposition to General Warrants, let us eagerly embrace the golden opportunity now offered to us, of manifesting to the world the just sense we entertain of those liberties for which he has so steadily exerted himself.

Embrace them, my fellow Liverymen, this precious opportunity of patronizing a genuine Son of Liberty – Return Him to Parliament, and, by your Returning Him, you will make the most awful, the most spirited protest against a measure, which, as free-born Britons, we should abhor.

The second was addressed to the public:

Mr. Wilkes declaring himself a candidate for the City of London, is an event that deserves a very serious attention: it is a very singular event, and in all probability will be attended with very singular consequences.

The question is not whether Mr. W- has any merit or not? Whether his private character be good or bad? But the question is, in what manner is it that he has been treated? Has he been treated fairly or not?

Let it be granted Mr. Wilkes is not a good man: Let it be granted he has no private nor public virtue: Let it be granted that even his political conduct was not the result of principle, but revenge: the question still returns, whether, guilty as he was, he had fair treatment? This is the only question that concerns the public.

If Mr. Wilkes was not in the least ill used, and no measures were taken against him but such as were perfectly legal, the dispute is at an end. But if Mr. Wilkes, though an Englishman, and a Senator, without any information being taken against him, was arrested by a General Warrant, in which he is not named: if, by virtue of this warrant, illegal in itself, his house was broken open; his most private papers seized; his person imprisoned; and all his privileges and liberty as an Englishman taken from him; who is there that is safe either in his person or property, however innocent and harmless he may be, whilst all this can be remembered, and be remembered without resentment?

It is not the cause of Mr. Wilkes that should be pleaded: it is the cause of the public.

Every friend to Liberty is bound to oppose and counter-act every attempt made against it; and if Mr. Wilkes, whatever may be his faults, has been unjustly treated, the treatment he received certainly ought to be publicly resented.

The Livery of London have now a glorious opportunity given them, by Mr. Wilkes's offering himself one of their candidates, to express their sense and their resentment to every arbitrary and oppressive measure exerted against any man.

The election of Mr. Wilkes will speak this language infinitely plainer, and infinitely stronger than it can be said in words.

If Mr. Wilkes has no fault and no enemies, his election would then be ascribed to his merit as a man: But, with the imperfections we are cleaving him, and the many and strong prejudices imbibed against him, if he be elected, it must be ascribed not to his merits, but to the virtue of the public, in generously resenting public injuries.

And in this view of it, how glorious would be his election for London! It would be one of the best and noblest triumphs of Liberty over oppression that was ever exhibited to the world; and would hand down to all future administrations, this great, this useful admonition, that of such value in the estimation of Britons is the cause of Liberty, that they reverence its champions, and will ever protect and honour them, be their characters in other respects what ever they will.

NO GENERAL WARRANTS. LIBERTY and WILKES.[80]

The tone of the second piece made no secret of the fact that Wilkes was not a perfect candidate, but his selling point was that he stood for liberty. The election took place on Wednesday 16th March at the Guildhall. There were four available positions, and seven candidates. Each of them gave a short speech to the assembled liverymen, and Wilkes' was transcribed in a newspaper report:

> Gentlemen, I am happy to find myself once more amongst the friends and patrons of liberty. This day makes me glorious amends for the rigour of a long unmerited exile; in which the only consolation remaining to me was, that from my sufferings you had an uninterrupted enjoyment of your most invaluable rights and privileges. Since the exertion of my firmess in an important moment, no minister has once dared to issue a general warrant against your persons, or to sign an order for the seizure of your papers; and I trust that such despotism will never be again exercised over the free subjects of this country.
>
> I stand here, Gentlemen, a private man, unconnected with the great, and unsupported by any party. I have no support but you: I wish no other support: I can have none more certain, none more honourable. If I have the happiness, Gentlemen, of being returned to parliament by your favour, I shall be ready to pay the greatest deference to the sentiments of my constituents on every occasion, and shall dedicate myself to their service, by promotion to the utmost of my abilities the trade and commerce of this great metropolis, by which alone it can maintain the first rank it now enjoys, and I hope, with its liberties, will ever enjoy.

The report noted that 'the majority of hands was declared to be for the Lord Mayor, Sir Robert Ladbroke, and Mesrs. Beckford and Wilkes.' However, a poll was demanded for the other three gentlemen and this revealed that Wilkes had in fact come last, with 1,247 votes. The contest during this poll was described as 'very warm'. Wilkes 'seemed to be the darling of the mob', and upon the revelation that he had not been elected 'some indecencies were committed by those gentry in and about the hall'. In his speech admitting defeat Wilkes stated that the result 'has not in the least abated my zeal' and he was 'not in the least dispirited'. The following week Wilkes presented himself as a potential parliamentary candidate in Brentford instead. The election took place on Monday 29th March, where three candidates competed for two posts. Although the poll revealed that Wilkes had received the highest number of votes, the other two candidates were declared the winners.

Nevertheless, Wilkes continued in his campaign to return to politics. He was elected as an Alderman for the ward of Farringdon Without in January 1769, and later that year he secured the post of Alderman of the City of London.[81] The Joiners saw Wilkes' appointment as an opportunity to raise the Company's profile. In spite of the fact that he was only a liveryman and had not served the offices of either Warden, on St James' Day 1770 a motion was made

> that John Wilkes Esquire one of the Aldermen of the City of London who has been admitted on the Livery of the Company some time past be put in Nomination for Master of this Company for the Year ensuing and that he be

put first on the list of Persons in Nomination for the said Office, And on the Question being put It was Voted and Ordered accordingly for he said Mr Wilkes first paying his Fines for both Offices of Wardens.[82]

In something of a rigged election Wilkes was duly elected as Master for the coming year, beating eleven other candidates. He was present in court during the vote and declared that he would serve the office. His mastership was more ceremonial than practical, however. Although it was the custom of the Company for the new Master and Wardens to be sworn in on Audit Day, Wilkes did not appear in court on 24th August.[83] He was similarly absent from the next Court of Assistants on 4th September,[84] and although he was elected to the committee for appointing Stewards ahead of Lord Mayor's Day he did not appear at a single one of those meetings. Instead, John Burnell appeared in his place, even though he was not officially a deputy. The Clerk was careful to note Wilkes' absence on each occasion, recording 'Mr John Burnell in the Chair the Master being absent'.[85]

Wilkes finally presented himself at the quarter court on 2nd October, and took the oath of office that day. In a thinly veiled rebuke, the meeting closed with a resolution that as he had not named a deputy, if Wilkes happened to be absent from any future meetings any member of the Assistants could be appointed to take the Chair for that particular day.[86] Wilkes continued to neglect the Steward meetings in the following weeks, with John Burnell and Joseph Baker acting as deputies in his place. He was absent from the November court, where Thomas Jones was voted as the temporary Chairman for that meeting.[87] Joseph Baker sat in his place in December,[88] and Somerset Phillips in January.[89] Baker took the Chair again in February, March, and April.[90] Wilkes finally appeared in person at the May court,[91] but Baker served again in June and July.[92] He did, however, attend a private court on 9th July when Revd Thomas Wilson was admitted into the freedom and the livery of the Company.[93] This appears to have been a strategic appointment, as Wilkes' had been, because on 25th July Wilson was elected as the next Master. Wilkes was, predictably, absent from court that day, and from the August court.[94] He did, however, attend on Audit Day when Wilson was sworn in as the new Master. As a matter of course Wilkes was thanked for his service to the Company over the previous year, although by no stretch of the imagination could he have been described as a dedicated Master.[95] Wilkes had, therefore, passed the entire year of his mastership by only attending the regular courts three times, and one extraordinary court.

Shortly after ending his tenure as Master Wilkes was elected as one of the Sheriffs of London. When he was sworn into office he travelled to Westminster Hall in a new carriage with the mottos '*Libertas*' and '*Arcui meo non confido*' painted on the side panels. Dr Wilson held a breakfast at the Hall in the morning of cold roast beef and old hock. A celebratory dinner was also held that evening at the Hall, at Wilkes' expense, attended by the Recorder of London and multiple Aldermen in addition to the Company. The dinner was 'much applauded', and the menu included turtle soup and venison, which 'had particular compliments paid to them', and a choice of four wines. A newspaper report noted,

After Mr. Wilkes had taken the oaths, and the proper officer had put on the gold chain, he turned to the Livery, and made them a very low and respectful bow, upon which he was clapped for some minutes by the whole Hall.[96]

The following day Dr Wilson led seventy-six liverymen of the Company to Guildhall:

... he was received in King Street with joyful acclamations, by thousands of spectators, and at his coming into Guildhall, there hardly ever was a more general clap from hundreds of people. The Doctor entertained his Livery at Joiners' Hall, with ten tureens of excellent soup, fourteen surloins and chumps of hot roast beef, and plenty of porter and wine at his own expence.[97]

After Wilkes was elected Mayor of London for the year 1774–5 the Company hoped to capitalise on the connection with him to raise their position. Wilkes was immediately offered 'the use of the Hall & Company's Plate for his Entertainment on the day he is Presented to the Lord Chancellor for Approbation'. Although less than a month away, it was also decided to step up the Company's preparations for the Lord Mayor's Day parade to suit 'the Dignity & honour of the Company', but 'in a frugal & decent manner' because the Company's finances were not strong. Five new silk banners were purchased for the occasion: the standard of England, the City's arms, the Lord Mayor's arms, the Company's arms, and the figure of the Company's patron St James.[98] Robert Morris, the herald painter, was engaged to make and decorate the same for £56 15s 6d.[99] A new press for storing and preserving these new banners was later purchased and placed in the Steward's Room.[100] The Company also engaged to provide the City Marshals with new scarves and ribbons, and the standard bearers, whifflers, and musicians would receive new bells, ribbons, and cockades. In a display of pomp and ceremony, eighteen men were to be hired 'to walk before & clear the way for the Company, with white Staves & Cockades'.[101]

The Grocers' Company offered the Joiners the use of their barge for the flotilla down the Thames, and this was initially accepted.[102] However, it was quickly established that 'no one of the Company's Barges is large enough to Convey as many of the Livery of this Company to Westminster as may think proper to Attend', and it was feared that this would cause 'much discontent and disorder'. Instead of hiring multiple barges, the decision was made that

the Company [will] march from their Hall to the Guildhall on the Morning of Lord Mayor's day at the usual Hour to Attend his Lordship from thence to the Waterside & see him take Water, then to return to their Hall to regale, & then again to march from their Hall, & wait his Arrival at Blackfryars, & thence proceed before him to Guildhall.[103]

Wilkes appeared before the Lord Chancellor at quarter-past two on Thursday 3rd November 1774, accompanied by the Recorder of London, and his appointment was approved. He travelled in a black coach drawn by a pair of cream long-tailed geldings, decorated with blue and silver tassels. The blue was perhaps a nod to the Joiners' Company. In the evening he dined at Joiners' Hall.[104] The Company also invested in twelve dozen new glasses and three dozen new mugs ahead of the Lord Mayor's Day dinner, along with 150 bottles of wine. Mr Beaumont provided music during the feast at a cost of £6 16s 6d, and the staffmen and whifflers were treated to a beef dinner with port wine.[105] The cook's bill for the Livery dinner amounted to £65 3s.[106]

In spite of his non-existent connection with the woodworking trade and the fact that he had entered for political purposes, Wilkes remained closely connected with the Company. On 21st November 1781 he attended an extraordinary Court of Assistants held at the Paul's Head Tavern in Catcorn Street to request that the Vice Admiral of Great Britain, Sir George Brydges Rodney, could be admitted into the freedom of the Company. His request was agreed unanimously, and Wilkes was given permission to inform the Admiral of the good news.[107]

The Company also remained proud of its connection to Wilkes, and in 1985 the Court of Assistants approved a contribution of £1,000 towards an obelisk being erected in his honour, on condition that the Company was referred to on it in some way.[108] The statue faced considerable delays in creation, and the Master was informed in 1988 that 'the inscription ... will not include any reference to his service either in the City or to the Joiners' Company'.[109]

Dr Thomas Wilson

Although Wilson's appointment to the Company appears to have been a politically motivated orchestration by Wilkes, he was far more hands-on during his tenure than his predecessor had been, but the end of his year saw considerable controversy. Wilson's background was as a prebend of Westminster Abbey, where he also lived in private quarters. He is best remembered for presenting the Company with a loving cup, which is described in greater detail in Chapter 7.

When he unfortunately found himself indisposed in November and unable to attend the Lord Mayor's Day celebrations he sent a formal letter to the Company to be read aloud to the Livery during dinner, and begged that a copy be entered into the court minutes as an official record. The letter is extremely revealing and confirms that Wilkes' motivation in becoming free of the Joiners was to hopefully secure a large livery vote in his favour:

> Gentlemen,
> I have unfortunately been Confined, by an Inflamation in my Eyes, for 3 Weekes past, and am not able to stir out of my room or else, I should have had the Pleasure of dining with you this Day.
>
> It will always be my Ambition to see you the most flourishing Company in the Citty, and if you preserve your <u>Integrity</u> and <u>Independancy</u>, & be <u>united</u> in the great Cause of Liberty, you may be the happy Means of recovering the violated Lawes and <u>Franchises</u> of our great City the Metropolis of Europe.
>
> You are increasing Every Day in the No of your Livery, and I would recommend it to you to endeavour by your Persuasions, to prevail upon more of the <u>Freemen</u> to take up their <u>Livery</u>, as soon as possible; - that you may have more <u>Power</u> and <u>Weight</u> in all future Elections, and by your <u>Unanimity</u> and <u>Integrity</u>, shew the Enemies of our Constitution, that the <u>Livery</u> of the <u>Joiners Company</u> can neither be <u>intimidated</u>, <u>bribed</u>, or <u>corrupted</u>.
>
> In this glorious Cause I will Join with you, Heart & Hand, and shall think it the highest Honour to have been unanimously Elected Your Master, by the Voice of the Livery to whom I am accountable, for the honest Discharge of my <u>Duty</u> to You, if it please God to spare my Life 'till next St James's Day; when I shall have many things of Moment to communicate to you.

After describing himself as their most faithful and affectionate friend and brother, Wilson ended his letter with a postscript that 'To Morrow being <u>Sunday</u>, I recommend to you to break up before 12 a Clock this Evening'.[110] In other words, get an early night, sleep off all the alcohol they undoubtedly consumed at the dinner, and get themselves to church in the morning. It is doubtful that they all followed this advice.

At the January court, from which Wilson was absent, liverymen Messrs Cook and Banner presented the Company with a draft address intended to be presented to the Lord Mayor in protest against several acts of Parliament which were hindering the building trade. They were eager for the Joiners to consent to the Company being added to the petition, and those present in court that day agreed in principle as long as no financial expenses would result. The final decision was postponed until the next court, but the petition was copied into the minute book.

To the Right Honourable the Lord Mayor and the Aldermen and Commons of the City of London in Common Council assembled.

The Memorial of the Master and Wardens of the several Companies of Carpenters Joiners Bricklayers and Masons of the said City in behalf of themselves and other the Builders and Workmen within the Cities of London and Westminster and the Suburbs and Liberties thereof and other the several parishes Precincts and place within the weekly Bills of Mortality the several parishes of Saint Mary Le Bone and Paddington Saint Pancras and Saint Luke at Chelsea in the County of Middlesex.

Humbly represents

That there are eight several Acts of Parliament now in force for regulating Buildings and Party Walls and preventing Mischiefs by Fire within the said Cities Suburbs and Liberties Parishes Precincts and Places some of which are in many respects contradictory and repugnant to each other in many respects very difficult to understand and insufficient for the purpose thereby intended and greatly in want of Amendments.

That it would tend to the Safety and Convenience not only of Builders but also of the Inhabitants within the Limits aforesaid if some of the said Acts were wholly repealed and instead thereof contain further Regulations Amendments and Provisions in relation to such Buildings and preventing Mischiefs by Fire together with all such Regulations by Law established as are now fit and proper to be observed were reduced into one Law.

And to that End your Memorialists intend to apply to Parliament early in the ensuing Session and are now preparing and are in great Forwardness with a Bill for the purposes aforesaid wherein it is their most earnest Request to be countenanced and encouraged by the Corporation of the ancient opulent and honorable City of London.

Your Memorialists therefore humbly request this Honorable Court will be pleased to give them such Assistance in such their Application as they shall judge meet and that the Remembrancer may be directed to give your Memorialists his Advice and Assistance therein.[111]

Luke Ideson, the solicitor employed to oversee this matter, wrote to the Company on 4th February assuring them that there would be no financial burden for the Joiners if they agreed to put their name to this address. This was satisfactory, and acting Master Joseph Baker and the two Wardens agreed to meet Ideson at the Guildhall the following day to discuss the matter.[112]

Wilson's attendance remained sporadic due to ill health through 1772. On St James' Day there had been insufficient time to proceed to the election of the Beadle and Clerk, and the court was adjourned for a fortnight. When Wilson knew he would be unable to attend that meeting he wrote to his Renter Warden Liscomb Price and asked him to act as deputy. However, this was not accepted by the court, who instead preferred to follow the precedent set during Wilkes' tenure of appointing a deputy Master for the meeting on a majority vote. Following such a vote Joseph Baker was once again voted into the Chair. However, liveryman Benjamin Crook protested this decision, in spite of Baker's repeated service as acting Master over the last two years. Crook delivered a written objection to the Clerk claiming that the meeting was illegal because Baker was a Roman Catholic and had refused to take the oaths of allegiance. As such he could not oversee the election of Company officers. The document was also signed by Henry Banner, John Horne, and William Stone. In spite of this objection, business proceeded as scheduled and the elections took place.[113]

However, on Audit Day neither the Master nor Wardens appeared in court. The Master elect, John Wendleborough, informed the Assistants that he had received a letter from Wilson in 15th August, in which the latter had 'insist[ed] upon his not issuing any Summonses in his Name for a Court to meet on this day'. However, holding an Audit and Oath Day within thirty days of St James' Day was a condition of the Company's charter. After receiving this letter the advice of Mr Eyre, the Recorder of London, was sought, and Eyre ordered the Beadle to summon a court as usual. Upon receiving notice of the intended court the Master and Wardens 'had severally declared that they should not attend'. When the rest of the Assistants had assembled in the Hall the Beadle made three loud proclamations for them to attend. However, they all remained absent. Past Master Captain Furnish was voted to take the Chair for the day so that business would not be further delayed. The Renter Warden's absence, however, meant that the Company's accounts could not be audited as usual. Ultimately the court had to content themselves with swearing in the new officers, and contemplate what steps should be taken against the recalcitrant offenders.[114]

The immediate response was to seek legal advice, and replies to their queries were received before the end of August. The Clerk first consulted Alexander Wedderburn, the Solicitor General and one of the most highly regarded lawyers of his day. Wedderburn confirmed that Baker's Roman Catholic faith was no hindrance to him holding the post of Assistant or acting as an interim Master, and that Assistants could only be removed from their office by death, relocating away from London, or by committing an offence contrary to the by-laws. The Recorder of London, James Eyre, was also consulted and his advice was the same as Wedderburn's. Eyre was also asked for his opinion on protocol if the old Master and Wardens refused to swear in their elected successors. He confirmed that an Assistant was entitled to take the Chair in such cases and swear in the new officers, and recommended that for 'greater Caution' a notice of this should be sent to the Court of Aldermen with a request for their oaths to be re-administered in that court.[115] The Master, Wardens, Clerk, and Beadle immediately followed this advice. They presented a petition to the Lord Mayor and Court of Aldermen explaining the circumstances in which they had taken their oaths. The absence of the outgoing Master and Wardens on Audit Day was unprecedented, and it was hoped that the oaths being re-administered in the Court of Aldermen would prevent any future disputes about their right to hold their positions.

The Clerk was summoned back to attend the Court of Aldermen on Tuesday 17th November, when a petition submitted by Wilson and his Wardens was discussed. Wilson claimed that his decision to deputise Liscombe Price to act as Master in his place on 8th August should have stood, and Baker should not have taken the Chair, but did admit refusing to summon a court on 24th August in contradiction of the guidelines in the Company's charter. He argued that this was justified because the business done on 8[116] August was illegal.[116] After reading the petition the Court of Aldermen were 'of Opinion that many Allegations and Assertions ... are false and groundless'.[117] When Liscombe Price was one of seven choices in nomination for a position on the Court of Assistants in 1773 he was the only person not appointed.[118]

Nineteenth-century Finance

In the early nineteenth century the Company focussed on putting consistent investments in the 3 per cent consolidated bank annuities. A portion of each year's revenue was deposited for that purpose, and by 1817 the Company's investments totalled £3,900.[119] In spite of this, the Company's finances continued to struggle for a time. In August 1838 Assistant James Mountague proposed 'that it is expedient and necessary that the Dinner usually provided on Saint James' day be discontinued as well as the Audit Dinner'. He suggested that some of the money saved through these cancellations could be used on 'an allowance to an Additional number of Poor Pensioners or in increasing the allowance to the present Pensioners'.[120] However, the idea was not popular amongst the Company and the St James' Day dinner was organised in 1839 as usual. The venue that year was the Brunswick Hotel in Blackwall Wharf, run by Samuel Lovegrove. The hotel and tavern had been opened in 1834, and under Lovegrove's supervision it was lavishly decorated and had a good reputation as a gourmet establishment, particularly famous for its whitebait.[121]

Mountague tried again the following year, but the court was deliberately adjourned before a vote could be held.[122] Indeed, Mountague took such offence to the dismissal of his idea that he appears to have voluntarily severed all ties between himself and the Company. When he was invited to attend the Audit dinner in 1843 he wrote to the Clerk stating that 'the treatment which I have received from the Company prevents my associating with them', and a note was entered into the minutes that he should not be invited to future events.[123]

The directors of the British Orphan Asylum wrote to the Company in April 1840 soliciting a charitable donation for their cause, but the Clerk was instructed to state that the Company had no funds at their disposal.[124] The cost of maintaining their own pensioners was high enough without adding additional requirements to their purse. In February another request was received, this time from the committee overseeing the construction of a new schoolhouse for Vintry Ward Charity School, but once again the Company had no funds available for such a request.[125] The directors of the General Annuity Society also made a plea for donations in June 1845, but received the same reply.[126] The Company did, however, contribute 5 guineas towards the 120[127] anniversary celebrations of the London Hospital in May 1860.[127] When an outbreak of smallpox forced the Plough Court Ragged School to close in February 1866 they donated another 5 guineas to the institution, notably a slightly higher sum than the £5 given by the Goldsmiths' Company.[128]

In January 1844 the Renter Warden warned the Court of Assistants that they were already £35 1s 6d out of pocket, and it was only halfway through the Company's financial year. £100 worth of 3 per cent stock was sold to clear this deficit and provide some ready money, but this was only a temporary solution.[129] William Williams, who also happened to be a member of the Common Council of the City of London and MP for Coventry, was elected as the Renter Warden for the year 1844–5, but he categorically refused to either serve or fine for the role. After the Clerk pressed him for a response, he declared that

> he had long since made up his mind on the subject not to serve the office or to pay the fine to be excused, unless he could be compeled to do so by a cource of Law, and that if he could be so compeled to serve, he would endeavour to effect a complete alteration in the management of their affairs. He disapproved particularly of the sums spent in dinners and entertainments &c he would take care that all the surplus finds after payment of the necessary expences &c should be devolved to relieving the wants of necessitous Members, Widows, &c, but having little or no time to spare from his many other avocations to attend to the affairs of the Company, he should not interfere with them, if they did not interfere with him.

He added, however, that he meant no personal offense to the Master or Court of Assistants through these remarks.[130] Master James Phillips was asked to write to him, and that letter and Williams' response were both copied into the court minutes. After summarising the events which led to Williams' election on 25th July, the Master wrote,

> I can bear testimony that the whole proceeding was fairly conducted, there being no desire to elect you for the sake of the fine, as the Compy would unanimously prefer to have your personal services, had it suited your convenience to afford them, nor were they at a loss for Candidates desirous, & ambitious to fill the Office, but whome they considered as being your junior, it would have been disrespectful to elect in preference. What I have stated I believe to have been the sole motives, which dictated the feelings of the Livery in electing you to what they consider one of the highest & most honorable Offices in their Corporation, & as the Court are conscious that the mode of election persued in your case, has been the uninterrupted practice of the Compy ever since its foundation, with but one instance, on which the legality was questioned, namely in the year 1729 when a Liveryman who had been similarly elected objected to serve the said Office, & who after considerable Litigation, yielded the point, at the same time paying the fine, together with the whole of the Law & other Costs incured. They feel therefore that without good cause shewn to the contrary, it is their duty to vindicate the By Laws of the Compy, which you, as well as themselves have sworn to abide by & obey, both as Freemen, & Liverymen. It appears to them therefore, the best cource to persue in case of your continued refusal to serve the Office, or pay the fine, to convene a meeting of the Livery to consider what steps shall be taken in the matter, & to authorize them to proceed as may be them be deemed advisable & proper.
>
> Having been led to make the foregoing observations as the Master of the Compy, allow me now as a brother Liveryman candidly to state my sincere wish that while I continue to serve the above Office, I hope I shall never be called upon to enter into a Litigation with any member of the Compy. I feel almost assured in your case that there has been some misunderstanding in the matter, & as there is the sincerest opposition on the part of the Court to afford every explanation that might be required & to meet the wishes of such individuals as may be elected to Office, as far as compatible with the interests of the Compy, I trust that the records of the Joiners Compy will never be handed down to future ages, with any statement of a circumstance derogatory to the honor of so respectable & esteemed a member of the Compy as yourself,

but upon reflection & after observing any information as explanation you may think requisite, you will give your consent to serve the Office or pay the trifling fine imposed as a substitute.

Williams wrote back on 1st February, and his reply contains a greater explanation about his motives for refusing to pay the fine than those previously presented to the Court by Ponder. Williams had no objection to paying the money if its use was guaranteed to be the maintenance of the Company's poor, but he knew only too well that it would be spent on providing refreshments for the Court of Assistants, men of comfortable means who did not need such excesses when so many people were living in poverty. One of the primary historic purposes of a guild, after all, was to support its poorer members in times of hardship, and not to provide lavish dinners for its officers.

On my return to Town I received your letter the contents of which has much surprised me. You are right in your conjecture that there has been a misunderstanding in the matter. About Mids[umme]r last I recd a letter from Mr Ponder informing me that I had been elected to the Office named by you & without giving me any option requested me to pay give pounds for fine & two pounds for quarterage. I wrote to him in reply that I would not pay either the demands for the latter being illegal, but if <u>legally</u> liable to serve the Office I was ready to do so & requested him to inform me what were its duties that I should be required to perform & I now repeat the same to you & I request you particularly to ask Mr Ponder to produce my letter to him refered to in order that you may be satisfied that your threat of resorting to proceedings of Law, has not been the cause of my now expressing my willingness to serve the Office (<u>if legally liable to do so</u>). Mr Ponder sent no reply but call'd upon me soon after & appeared to have no other object in doing so but then to prevail on me to pay him the five pounds. I stated to him that if the money was applied to relieve poor Freemen, or poor Widows of Freemen, or to the education of their Children, instead of being expended upon dinners, paying members of the Court of Assistants, for what they called their services, & such frivolous objects, I would readily pay it, but not for such purposes. I further stated that having already so much to do for the public I thought it unresonable to call on me who take no interest whatever in the offices of the Compy to serve an Office, for which I know as you say, there [are] so many candidates, ambitious to obtain it. He has made a most incorrect representation, of the conversation I had with him, which ended in his assuring me that I should never again be applied to serve that, or any other Office of the Company, & he even asked if I wished to have my name withdrawn from the Livery List. I replied that I was quite indifferent about it, but as I had paid for it, for the express purpose of obtaining the elective Franchise it may as well be retained. Some time afterward Mr Ponder called on me again for what object I could not discover, but he gave me no intimation that I should be called upon to serve the Office. I received several years ago a communication that I was elected, or about to be elected to this Office, & did not then refuse to serve, but declined paying any fine for the reasons before stated, since that time I believe many who came on the Livery long after me have served the Office, & even that of Master, of which probably you are an example. The Liveryman to whome you refer, who shewed such anxiety about my fine, is no doubt one of the fraternity who manifested this discontent at ceasing to get champagne at the dinners & resort to these disreputable means to obtain it, you may inform him & those like him, that they will never get money from me to pay for their Champagne, & that I hope it will come within my reach to give a helping hand to bring to amend those relicts of by gone years, so useless at the present time, & cherished only by men of childish minds. In repeating my readiness to serve the Office if <u>legally liable</u> you may acquaint the Court of Assts that I will not imitate their Conduct by accepting a few shillings of meat & drink, for performing its duties. I have already consumed more time (which is my only consideration) in reading letters, answering them & giving interviews to your Clerk, respecting these Trumperies [of] Office than would be required to discharge its duties. I cannot help pitying the spitefulness of your Court of Assts, or Fraternity, in not gratifying the ambition of these numerous Candidates, who you say are so anxious to serve the office.[131]

Master Phillips' reply to Williams was largely one of relief at having cleared up the misunderstanding, and he assured Williams that he was unlikely to be called upon to serve office again. He was also very careful to address Williams' concerns about the misuse of the Company's finances by claiming that as pensions were regularly paid, and ad hoc requests for gratuities were granted to those in need, there was no harm in spending the rest of the Company's money on champagne.

I beg to acknowledge the receipt of your letter dated the 1st instant and am happy thereby to be enabled to relieve Members of the Court of the Joiners Company from the wrong impressions under which they had been led to conclude you had altogether refused to serve the Office of Rentr Warden of the Compy to which you were elected in July last. I am personally obliged to you for the full explanation afforded me in regard to the above matter, & shall avail myself of the earliest opportunity afforded me of laying your letter before the Livery, when I feel assured that they, having elected you to the Office from misinformation conveyed to them, will readily make the amends honorable by declaring your said election to be null & void: which course I trust will be quite satisfactory to your own wishes. It will of course remain for the Livery in any future election to do as they may think expedient & proper, as to whether they will reelect you or not, but I am strongly of opinion, that as you state it to be your purpose if so elected, to bring some new lights to bear, upon the future government of the Compy which might not be palatable to them, that they will be disposed of to dispence with your proffered services, which I presume will be quite as agreeable to yourself.

I much regret that you should have been led to cast any reflection on the Court of Assistants for the part they have taken in the matter. These appear to me to be quite uncalled for. I can say as far as I have had the honor to be associated with them, I think those Gentn are actuated by quite as disinterested motives & feelings in their conduct as those on which you lay so much stress as performing for the Public, and any one acquainted with the Constitution of the Company must be aware that a Liveryman before he becomes qualified to be elected on the Court is required to pass through certain Offices, which intail upon him a heavy expence, & considering that at the period of life at which they arrive at that honor, it is but a rare instance where any individual survives long enough to reimburse his primary outlay by the fees & dinners to which you allude, to say nothing of the valuable time bestowed on the service of the Company and which in your own case, you estimate at so high a rate.

In reference to the subject of the applycation of the Funds of the Company entirely to charitable purposes I am quite of opinion, that altho' it was founded for other than such purposes, yet a due proportion ought to be so applied, and as far as my experience has gone, I have ever found, that in addition to the regular pensions of the Company, no application from a deserving poor Liveryman, Freeman, or their Widows, have ever been made in vain to the Court, but on the contrary, have been responded to with alacrity & liberality, and I think while such conduct is persued, the Company are fully justified in using a reasonable portion of the Funds in convivial injoyment amongst themselves, as tending much to the promotion of the public good, as well as the general welfare of the Company.

Williams' final letter on the subject was succinct:

I beg to acknowledge the receipt of your letter of the 4th inst. When I last address'd you I was not aware that I had the pleasure of your personal acquaintance when formerly I was connected with the City. I annually received a statement of the Company's accounts, and occasionally a list of its Members but for many years past I have not received either. I therefore thought they considered me as no longer belonging to their body. Impress'd with this belief I was the more surprised at their forcing upon me an Office for which there are so many candidates anxious to obtain it who have more leisure than I have to attend to its duties. For this I thought I was indebted to the Court of Assistants but your letter has satisfied me that I was in error. I therefore withdraw most unequivocally any expression I may have used in my former letter which may by them be deemed objectionable.

When out of the 75 City Companies I selected the Joiners to be a member of, I did so because its Members were then Men of liberal opinions. I trust they are so still and ever will remain unchanged.[132]

On St James' Day 1845 Williams was discussed in Court, and the official line taken by the Company was that 'owing to his public duty as a member of Parliament' he would not be able to hold any office.[133]

The objections raised by both Mountague and Williams about needless spending at dinners were well founded. When the 1845 Lord Mayor's Day dinner was being planned and an engagement made at the Crown and Anchor in the Strand, the Clerk was instructed to sell a further £100 worth of 3 per cent consuls to cover the costs. They weren't spending ready money; they were having to liquidate assets to pay for the dinner.[134] A further £100 of stock was liquidated in April 1847.[135] A raise to charitable spending did occur in July 1850, however, when the quarterly amount paid to the Company's pensioners was raised from £1 to £1 10s.[136] However, this was followed by the liquidation of a further £100 of stock to pay for the next Lord Mayor's Day dinner,[137] and the same again in the following years.[138]

The Company's finances showed dramatic improvement from the 1850s onwards, and they basked in handsome returns from their investments in Ireland through the Salters' Company. This investment dated back to the 1610s, when James I settled the province of Ulster. He asked the twelve principal livery companies to raise money to finance plantations, and they were each allowed to incorporate smaller livery companies into their subscriptions.[139] The Salters added the Joiners and the Dyers to theirs, and this investment brought the Joiners varying annual returns. These were particularly high during the nineteenth century when portions of the land were sold.

From the early 1860s it was voted that the sum of £50 per annum should be placed at the disposal of the Court of Assistants 'for the purposes of

Charity Benevolence or Patriotism',[140] and this was raised to £100 in 1880.[141] Early examples of charities provided with donations include the Royal General Dispensary, the London Fever Hospital, and the High Court Ragged School.[142]

In 1859 the Lord Mayor expressed his intention to commission the London Rifle Brigade, a volunteer regiment of the British Army. He sought financial contributions from London's residents, as well as from the livery companies. The Joiners were amongst the first companies to heed the call, and the Lord Mayor thanked them for their 'liberal contributions, an example he was sure other worshipful companies would follow'.[143] The Company kept a close association with the Brigade after its formation, and often stood as a sponsor at their annual prize-giving ceremonies. In 1868, for example, they presented the Challenge Cup for the best marksman for five shots at 200, 500, and 700 yards to Quartermaster Sergeant Jenkins. The prize was awarded by the Upper Warden, who attended as the Company's representative.[144] The following year their Challenge Cup was decorated with a gold jewel.[145]

In spite of the Company's previous determination that paying the salaries of Assistants and providing lavish feasts was an appropriate way to spend their money, an 1877 investigation into the finances of the livery companies was highly critical of the Joiners. A report published in *The Examiner* noted that during the year 1875–6 their total income had been £1,691 6s 6d, of which £360 14s 7d had been invested in consuls. Of the remaining sum, £204 15s had been paid to the Court of Assistants for their attendance at meetings. Each member received a guinea for each attendance at court, of which there had been sixteen in that year. The report stated that

> [t]he whole work of the company, however, consists in arranging the periods of its festivities, and looking after the quarterly payments of the one City tenant of the company, so the arrangement is purely a device for dividing the money.

In comparison, £137 10s had been spent in providing pensions, and a further £46 5s in ad hoc charitable payments. After the salaries of officers and various insurance payments had been deducted, the Company's remaining income for 1875–6 had been £664 15s 7d. The report said that in theory this money was 'available for purposes of technical instruction, and otherwise for the benefit of joinery'.

> But no one who knows anything of City companies can have any doubt where this sum – one half of the company's income – went to. With the almsgiving less than [£50], and with applications on behalf of art schools and other similar institutions declined, the rulers of the Joiners' Company spent one half of their income in feasting … It will thus be seen that the rulers of the company spent no money in teaching the trade they were formed to benefit; they aided no poor artisans; they refused money to objects in any way germane to those of their foundation, they utterly disregarded the purposes of their chartered existence. And yet a high City authority informs us that this is 'in exact accordance with the wishes of the livery.' If the statement were true, it would be a melancholy example of the degradation of judgement which City life induces in City men. It is, however, to a certain extent satisfactory to know that efforts have been constantly made – though hitherto unsuccessfully – to divert the expenditure into different channels.[146]

In spite of this criticism of the Joiners the report acknowledged that it was one of the smaller companies, and that such expenditure was 'far surpassed in many'. The article was not referred to in subsequent Company meetings.

The Trades Training School

The accusation in the article that the Joiners were investing almost nothing in promoting their trade is somewhat unfair, because in the early 1870s the Company voted to invest an annual sum towards what was referred to as technical education in the City. At a Court of Livery on 29th March 1870 William Purdy suggested that 25 guineas should be sent 'to Schools of design in the City of London with the view of encouraging the application of Art to the trades of Joiners Carvers and Ceilers'.[147] The following week the Company was approached by the secretary of the Workmen's International Exhibition of 1870 asking whether they would sponsor prizes 'for any work connected with the trade of Joiners'.[148] In November the Arts Secretary from the Museum of Art in South Kensington wrote to express their willingness to collaborate with the Company in promoting joinery classes, and the headmaster of Spitalfields School of Art also wrote to enquire whether students at his establishment would also be eligible.[149] It was agreed that £8 of the 25 guineas would be sent to the Spitalfields School for prizes,[150] with further sums of £8 going to the Charterhouse School of Design, and £4 each to the City of London Ladies' College and the Birkbeck School.[151] On St James' Day 1871 the Company's usual election of officers was followed by a prize-giving for the students of these institutions, which was reported in the *London City Press*:

> The successful students of the various schools of art connected with the City of London, and to whom prizes have been awarded by this company, for their designs of joinery then entered the room, and the prizes (which consisted of boxes of drawing instruments and various books upon joinery) were handed to them by Mr. Renter-warden Phillips, who, throughout his year of office, has taken the liveliest interest in the matter. In presenting them, Mr. Phillips advised the students to persevere in the course of study they had consumed, and to spend their evenings in Schools of Art such as these, which this company was encouraging, rather than in places of questionable character. He further admonished them to beware of being led away by stump orators, whose only object was their own aggrandizement, and who would lead them against their own interests, remarking that by studying in the way they had commenced they would become skilled workmen. After cautioning them against bringing odium upon the trade of joiners by bad workmanship, &c, he concluded by wishing them every success and God-speed in their journey through life.[152]

The same schools were sponsored again in the following years, with further prize-giving taking place on St James' Day.[153] On St James' Day 1874 the Clerk confirmed to the Livery that the Joiners had established prizes of 5 guineas and 3 guineas for building construction, 5 guineas for wood carving, 3 guineas for carving design, and 3 guineas for ceiling.[154] The Spitalfields School of Art wrote to the Company on 3rd December 1878 to report that they had awarded their prize to two students, Alfred Shorman and George C. Banks, who had both designed ornamental balustrades.[155]

In 1872 the Lord Mayor had chaired a meeting at Mansion House which was attended by representatives of a variety of livery companies to consider 'how Technical Education can be best provided' in the City, and the trades of the companies promoted.[156] The Joiners were not alone, therefore, in their desire to promote the preservation of their craft. In 1873 the Prince of Wales declared his willingness to support technical education in the City by hosting a meeting at Mansion House, which was to be attended by representatives of the companies.[157] This eventually led to the establishment of the City and Guilds of London Institute on 11th November 1878, under the patronage of the Prince of Wales. The Institute's purpose was to develop and promote technical education in the City, and the Joiners provided regular financial contributions.[158] Although it had made considerable progress in promoting education, the Institute regularly found itself 'greatly in need of funds for the equipment and maintenance of the Central Institution' and relied on donations from many livery companies to supply this shortfall.[159]

In 1881 the Company hosted a turnery exhibition at Mansion House, and the distinguished guest invited to its opening was freeman and Prime Minister William Gladstone. The items on display were

> ... varied in character, consisting in general of candlesticks, cigar cases, Gothic columns, balusters, ebony vases, inkstands, flower-pots, jewel caskets, clock cases, mirrors, &c. The work is all hand turning, processed in the lathe without special rest or tool apparatus, and the carving is in every instance done by the exhibitor. Many of these objects are remarkable for beauty of design and delicacy of workmanship.[160]

In 1883 the Carpenters approached the Joiners with the intention of holding a joint exhibition at Carpenters' Hall the following year, with preliminary dates of 26th May until 14th June. The Turners' Company were approached and asked to join too but they were planning to hold their own exhibition in October. The Joiners agreed to assign 100 guineas towards 'money and medals of the Company for award as prizes to English Working Joiners exhibiting in the Joiners department of the Exhibition'.[161] Craftsmen of all levels, from masters to apprentices, were welcome to exhibit, with the proviso that everything had to be 'hand work and not machine work'. Proposed categories included window frames and casements, shutters, handrails, and ornamental carving, with prizes ranging from £2 to £7.[162] A description of the 1884 exhibition published in *The British Architect* noted that 'we hear so much about the unapplied or misapplied funds of the City Companies ... that it is always refreshing to have a glimpse of the reverse side of the picture'. The exhibition had been held at Carpenters' Hall for three weeks and had attracted over 12,000 visitors.[163] It was such a successful enterprise that it became a regular event held every four years. The exhibition that opened on Monday 25th October 1896 was highly praised in *St James' Gazette*, which published a detailed description of some notable pieces which had been borrowed from collections around the country to serve as inspiration for craftsmen:

> It is a good thing to see two prosperous City companies taking up a matter of handicraftsmanship in the serious and practical temper in which the Worshipful Company of Carpenters and the Worshipful Company of Joiners have undertaken their series of exhibitions of works in wood at Carpenters' Hall, London-wall. It is not merely skill in the more obviously attractive craft

of wood-working that they elect to foster; but also thoughtful and thorough workmanship in constructive carpentry in its various branches. A large room in the hall is almost filled with models of carpentry arranged in different classes; and in these models considerations of the production of the maximum of strength with the greatest economy of material and such like practical merits are esteemed and rewarded, whilst the tendency merely to make a pretty little model is by no means regarded with favour. And in the department of carving the same rightness of aim is observable in the work selected for reward and encouragement; the industry that is rewarded is that which is applied in producing effects not only worthy of production in themselves but appropriate to the material in which they are to be executed. Labour thrown away upon conquering needless difficulties is not encouraged; sound, intelligent, thorough workmanship is.

As examples to the competitors, and to lend an additional interest to the exhibition itself as a whole, a collection of wood-carving has been brought together: inlaid sporting guns of the sixteenth and seventeenth centuries, carved chests and cabinets, and the like. Rarely have we seen a more fascinating collection of this art. Not only are the things beautiful in themselves, but all more or less have the further ineffable charm of association. There is, for instance, a pair of bellows, patterned with strings and curved corners like a lyre, carved by Demontreuil for Marie Antoinette. They became afterwards the property of Warren Hastings. A carved miniature frame of most exquisitely fine workmanship adorns a likeness of the Princess of Soubise by Pierre Mignard, the courtly portrait-painter of the seventeenth century. This was the property of Louis XIV, and the Princess, all ribbons and laces and curls, is as dainty as her frame.

Bits of carving are collected from everywhere. There is a graceful and airy flamboyant finial from Bruges, several things from Winchester, and a bit of cornice from the Throne Room at Windsor. Spanish, Italian, French, German, and Flemish wood-art are all represented. The bits of ancient furniture are sufficient to make the most contented envious. There is an exquisite inlaid table, a fifteenth-century oak cabinet so dark that it and its iron clampings just tone into each other, oaken settles, a magnificent chimney-piece from a hunting-lodge of James I, an oak chest with very early inlaid work, and a wonderful jewel-casket of Louis XVI's time with bacchante, satyrs, nymphs, and cupids dancing round it as lightly and gracefully as ever they do on Grecian vases. There are some carved wooden figures which look very plaintive with modern luggage-labels (which the exhibitors have forgotten to remove) hanging round their necks. Other curiosities are a Cinderella's slipper carved from a damson-stone and a tiny basket from a cherry-stone. Some lovely fowling-pieces inlaid with pearl and ivory in the form of grotesque figures, and a Byzantine jewel cross with the tiniest panels of carved wood let into it, are also charming specimens of art.[164]

A similarly complimentary piece was published in Westmorland's *Lakes Herald*, praising the two companies for redeeming themselves from the stain of previous allegations of inappropriate spending:

On Monday there was opened in the hall of the Worshipful Company of Carpenters an instructive collection of works in wood-carving. The City Companies of London have long been held up to public opprobrium. Their sole function, it has been said, is to arrange for the eating of many and magnificent dinners. The member of a City Livery is held by many persons to exhaust his active interest in life by the consumption of so much turtle soup and so many bottles of rare wine per annum. They are all, we are told, behind the times, and are unmindful of the responsibilities which properly belong to the trustees of important funds. The City Companies are rich. Why, it is asked, do they not do something for the crafts they represent in name and history if not in fact? The answer to this and similar questions may be found in the quiet and unostentatious work of the kind which is exemplified in the present exhibition. The organisation of this interesting collection of wood-carving is the joint work of the Carpenters' Company and the Worshipful Company of Joiners. It is the fourth exhibition of the kind, and may be considered to shew a very perceptible advance in technical and artistic skill. Much has, in fact, been done by the City Guilds to encourage the technical student in recent years. The old complaint about British shortcomings in technical skill and education ought no longer to be held. The practical effects of the improved condition of affairs are to be seen in the national trade. Even the City Companies, it would seem, are not so black as they are painted.[165]

The success of their joint exhibitions prompted the Carpenters' Company to increase the collaboration between the two companies. In the summer of 1893 they approached the Joiners and enquired whether they would 'join in some Technical Classes which [they] were instituting' at premises in Great Titchfield Street, which would become the Trades Training School.[166] The Joiners declared themselves unwilling to enter into this union, however. The Carpenters wrote in 1895 to state that they felt 'affronted in your Company not having joined them in their effort for Technical Education' and implored them to reconsider, arguing that the promotion of building trades would be greatly increased by more livery companies joining together.[167] The Carpenters bore the brunt of the financial costs of the school, providing £1,400 per annum. The Tylers' and Bricklayers' companies each provided £100 per ear, the Plasterers £37 10s, and the Wheelwrights and Painters £30 each. The Court of Assistants decided that an annual subscription of £25 would be sufficient from the Joiners.[168] Although apprenticeships still occasionally took place, by the turn of the twentieth century the method of training the next generation of joiners had changed its focus to educational schools.

Chapter 9

The World Wars and Later Twentieth Century

The First World War

Great Britain declared war on Germany on 4th August 1914, marking the formal start of a conflict which would forever change the nature of warfare. On 11th August Master Henry Newson requested permission from the Court of Assistants to donate to the Prince of Wales' National Relief Fund, which had been recently set up to 'aid the wives, families and dependents of Soldiers, Sailors, Reservists and Territorials who are on active service or who have died in the defence of their country', and to 'prevent and alleviate distress among the civil population arising out of the War'.[1] The Master's suggestion of providing a financial contribution was seconded by his deputy, and the court granted permission to donate 25 guineas.[2]

At the next court meeting on 1st September the Clerk raised the question of whether or not the Lord Mayor's Day dinner should take place as usual in November. After some discussion the court unanimously agreed that the dinner 'should not be held & that the money so saved be applied to patriotic purposes'. The deputy Master recommended that an extraordinary meeting of the Livery should be called on 6th October to ratify this decision.[3] At that meeting the motion carried, and it was agreed that the £100 usually assigned to miscellaneous charitable and patriotic causes should be primarily donated towards the war effort or charities supporting servicemen and their families.[4] It was agreed that £50 of that sum should be distributed between six charitable causes: £10 each to the Christmas Gift to the Belgian People and to Queen Mary's Royal Naval Hospital, and £5 each to the Lady Mayoress City Branch of the Red Cross, Princess Mary's Christmas Gift to Sailors and Soldiers, the City of London Russian Ambulance, and the Lord Robert Indian Soldiers' Fund. Additional grants of £5 5s each were given to the Surgical Aid Society, and the Infant Orphan Asylum Wanstead.[5] Some of the remaining money was divided between more charitable causes in January; £10 was donated to Bartholomew's Wounded Belgian Soldier Samaritan Fund, and £5 each to the Dreadnought Hospital, Queen Mary's Work for Women fund, Sir William Treloar's Cripples Home, Dr Barnardo's Homes, the Charing Cross Hospital, and the Royal Flying Corps Aid Committee.[6] Following requests for 'urgently needed' money in April, two more bequests of £5 each were sent to the Serbian Red Cross Society, and to the 25th Battalion Royal Fusiliers Frontiersmen for East Africa,[7] and £5 5s to the National Patriotic League in June.[8] These bequests totalled £110 15s, higher than the £100 fund agreed, but presumably the desire to support the war effort outweighed any necessity of sticking strictly to budget.

Discussion at the November 1914 court turned to the practical question of whether their property should be 'insured against the risk & damage that might be caused by aerial bombardment'. It was agreed that the Clerk would write to tenants Messrs Major and Field to see whether they wanted to insure Joiners' Hall, and if so, the cost would be split between them and the Company.[9] The Company had also owned property at 30 Addle Street since at least 1885,[10] and tenant Mr Jennings returned the message that he had already insured the property. Messrs Major and Field expressed their willingness to insure the Thames Street property. A premium of £25 on a policy worth £15,000 was agreed on with insurance brokers Messrs Wintle and Co of 2 Change Alley.[11] In February 1917 the tenants requested that the anti-aircraft insurance should be increased from £15,000 to £19,350. The Company repeated its commitment to covering half of the cost of the policy, but believed that the insurance should only be for £18,000.[12]

On St James' Day 1915 the Master elect Frederick Wiginton proposed that 'unless the War be terminated previously ... it would be inappropriate to hold the usual November Banquet this year' and the same amount of £100 which would have been spent on the celebration was again 'saved to Patriotic Purposes'.[13] Master Rider's final act before surrendering his chair to Master elect Wiginton on 24th August was to donate £10 of his own money 'as an addition to the fund about to be distributed for Patriotic purposes by the Company'.[14] Ultimately no November banquets were held at all during the course of the war, and instead donations of £100 were provided to the patriotic fund.

Also on St James' Day 1915 the Clerk announced to the assembled livery that four members of the Company 'had joined H.M. Forces for the War'. Harry John Butler was in the Royal Navy, Albert Henry Waters was in the East African Corps of Frontiersmen (25th Bn Fusiliers), Arthur Llewellyn Williams was in the Royal Welsh Fusiliers, and Sidney Randolph Barker was in the 3rd County of London (Machine Gun Corps). Their names were added to a Roll of Honour, demonstrating the esteem in which they were held by their remaining brethren. The four men were excused of their quarterage charge for the year, and instead the Company agreed to send each of them a guinea as a token of appreciation.[15] On St James' Day 1918 it was proposed that the freedom of the Company should automatically be presented to apprenticed sons of liverymen who had been serving in the armed forces, and discussion even turned to the possibility of elevating them all immediately to the Livery. However, the suggestion was ultimately voted down.[16]

In the summer of 1915 the question of transferring the Company's stock to the new war loan had been raised, but no agreement was reached and the matter was postponed until the next court.[17] In August the deputy Master moved that no action should be taken to transfer the stock at the present time.[18] However, the change of Master and Wardens in the autumn of that year also brought about a change in this decision. On 7th September it was reported that £100 worth of government war loans had been purchased at 4.5 per cent.[19] In October 1916, following the receipt of £37 10s profit on an investment with the Queensland National Bank in Australia, it was agreed that the money should 'be invested in Government Stock' at 6 per cent.[20] At the November court the Renter Warden reported that he had purchased £40 of exchequer bonds.[21] When a further profit of £50 was received in December a similar order was made to invest in the exchequer bonds.[22]

The largest investment, however, came in February 1917. Upon the advice of their stockbroker and Past Master Septimus Ponder, the Company agreed to convert their holdings in the 4.5 and 6 per cent loans into 'the New 5 per cent loan'. They agreed to invest an additional £500, as well as converting all previous investments.[23] However, due to heavy taxation and the constant demands on the Company's purse, by the summer of 1918 the ready money left in the Renter Warden's hands had been reduced to just £88 11s 9d. Past Master Ponder recommended that a loan of £200 should be requested from the Bank of England, secured against the war loan stock.[24]

The Interwar Years

The First World War officially ended at 11 a.m. on 11th November 1918, following the signing of the Armistice at 5.45 that morning. The Company's monthly court had taken place six days earlier, so their first meeting after the peace was on Tuesday 3rd December. The final business of that day was a question from the Renter Warden as to 'what (if any) action should be taken by the Company to celebrate the signing of peace'. After some discussion but no agreement, the Renter Warden suggested postponing any decision until the next meeting.[25] At the January court the Master and Wardens agreed to present a report on the Company's financial situation to the next court, and judge whether it would be prudent to hold a celebration or not.[26] Their investigation concluded that, although the Company's expenditure had not noticeably risen since 1914 and although they had received dividends from some investments, the drastically increased taxation on their freehold properties and their purchase of war loans had severely depleted their resources. They had invested £700 in war loans, £200 of which had been borrowed from the Bank of England. The report noted that 'although no Banquets have been held since 1914, and Comparatively on a small amount of the income thus saved has been expended on National Charities', they were in no position to throw a celebratory banquet: 'We find that as against the Cost of a Banquet (which would cost at least £250) let alone any souvenir to Commemorate the historical event, we have a decrease in income of £278, a debt to the Bank of £200 – and no accumulated balance except ... £78.' The Master and Wardens left the final decision to the Court of Assistants, but noted that if a banquet was approved they 'will have no alternative but to sell out some of the Company's Stock and still further lessen the income available for the future'.[27]

Nevertheless, at the March court a motion carried 'that it is desirable on the signing of Peace, this Company should Commemorate the event in some suitable way', but precisely what was left to the discretion of the Court of Assistants. The livery authorised the sale of 'part of the funds of the Company to provide the entertainment',[28] and ultimately in June it was voted that 'it is desirable to hold a Banquet, to which Ladies should be invited'. If it could be organised before September it would be followed by a concert, and after September by a dance. Each liveryman in attendance would be presented 'with a souvenir of the occasion' at a cost of approximately £3 per person. The Renter Warden suggested that it would be easiest to reinstate the November Lord Mayor's Day banquet and combine the occasions into a victory banquet. However, he was concerned that adding souvenirs and additional entertainment would bring the total cost to £600, and warned about 'the adverse effects of the expenditure of this amount on the finances of the Company'.[29] Ultimately, when the matter was discussed at length with the Livery on St James' Day 1919 it was decided that the ideas of victory banquet and souvenirs should be abandoned because the cost was too high.[30] However, the Assistants did agree that the November banquet should be reinstated and held at Carpenters' Hall. The date of Tuesday 4th November at 6 p.m. was agreed, although later amended to Wednesday 5th November due to the Carpenters requiring their Hall on the 4th,[31] and the Master, Wardens, and Clerk were given the task of organisation. Invitations to attend would be sent to the Masters of the other livery companies, and Past Masters of the Joiners and members of the Court of Assistants would be able to purchase extra tickets to bring additional guests. The cost of these, however, would be raised from 30s to 50s.[32]

During the peaceful years of the 1920s life was relatively quiet for the Worshipful Company of Joiners. They continued their charitable donations to various causes, for which £50 per annum was placed at the disposal of the Court of Assistants.[33] They were also unceasing in their support for the Trades Training School with annual donations of £50 and inspections twice a year. However, the war had placed a heavy burden on the country's finances, and the 1920s also saw heavy taxation as the government attempted to repay the debts it had incurred. On St James' Day 1920 the Company was informed by the Master that 'on account of the now heavy taxation it was not possible to hold the usual November Banquet without selling some of the Company's stock & thereby reducing its income'. Such a move seemed unwise, so it was agreed to forego the banquet.[34] Indeed, the outgoing Renter Warden's accounts presented to the Company the following month revealed a balance of just £43 6s 4d.[35] In light of this the new Renter Warden was authorised to sell £200 worth of 5 per cent war stock in September.[36] This was enough to carry the Company through the year, but in July 'the state of the Companys finances' made it necessary to cancel the November banquet.[37] By 1924, however, the Company's finances were sufficiently strong for them to hold the November banquet again.[38] Carpenters' Hall was fixed as the venue, and invitations were sent to the Lord Mayor, Sheriffs, and Masters of the companies associated with the Joiners through the Trades Training School. The cost of extra tickets if liverymen wished to bring a guest was 50s.[39]

The Company continued investing any profits in conversion stock during the 1920s. The Bank of England informed the Company in June 1929 that £300 of the £500 war loan they had applied for in February 1917 had matured, and the money was ready to be transferred to the Company's account.[40] This money was received just before the London Stock Exchange crash of September 1929, followed by the Wall Street Crash, which would send the world spiralling into a financial depression. The government proposed that the Company's £500 investment in the 5 per cent war loan should be transferred to the 3.5 per cent loan in July 1932.[41] Owing to the financial instability of the early 1930s, it was moved in February 1933 that the November banquet should be combined with the Ladies' banquet in March, rather than totally cancelling either event.[42] The November banquet was organised to be held again in 1934, although on a smaller scale. The only guests would be the liverymen of the Company, and invitations to other civic dignitaries of London would be confined to the Ladies' banquet.[43]

The Second World War and the Destruction of Joiners' Hall

At 11.15 p.m. on 1st September 1939 Prime Minister Neville Chamberlain announced to the nation via radio that an ultimatum issued to Germany to withdraw her troops from Poland had been ignored, and 'consequently this country is at war with Germany'. The wounds from the First World War were still keenly felt by many families in the country, and a second global conflict within their lifetimes must have seemed almost unbearable. The Company's activities were disrupted immediately. At their first wartime meeting at the Guildhall on 5th September the Clerk apologised that 'owing to the emergency' he had not been able to access his office nor any of the documents inside it, and had been forced to attend the meeting without bringing the minute book with him. He later reported that he would be depositing any Company documents in his possession into the Guildhall's vault for safekeeping. The Master then suggested that 'owing to the difficulty of transport the wearing of gowns should be dispensed with during the duration of the War', and this was agreed. Power was also granted to the Master, Wardens, and Court of Assistants 'to take any action considered by them to be necessary to protect the interests of the Company or their property during the present emergency'.[44]

Due to the increasing hostilities the Company had received a letter from the Comptroller of the Guildhall in 1939 enquiring whether 'in case of possible hostile emergency' they would prefer to have their deposited property – including the Bible, spoons, and picture – returned. If property was to remain at the Guildhall it was 'on the distinct understanding that the same may run the risk of damage or loss by any such hostile action and for this the Corporation cannot accept any responsibility'. Ultimately the decision was made to leave the property where it was.[45]

At the October meeting the precedent of cancelling the November banquet was revived, and 'the money so saved [should] be applied by the Court to patriotic purposes'.[46] The Lady Mayoress wrote to the livery companies in October asking for liverymen's wives to assist in 'making Articles required by [the] War Emergency Council' and the Red Cross.[47] The Lord Mayor shortly afterwards released an appeal for aid on behalf of the Red Cross and St John's Ambulance, and the Joiners agreed to donate 25 guineas.[48]

The November court saw a discussion about how much money should be allocated from the Company's budget for donation to patriotic causes, as had been done during the First World War. Although the sum of £100 per annum had been agreed between 1914 and 1918, in 1939 this was greatly reduced to £35 to be split amongst six charities,[49] specified in December as the Council for the Promotion of Occupational Industries amongst the Physically Handicapped, the Mansion House Justice Room poor box, the Surgical Aid Society, the Sheriffs Fund, the fund for the restoration of the organ at St Mary le Strand, and the British Sailors Society.[50] However, this resolution did not last for long, and in March a further 45 guineas was allocated for charity. Sums of 5 guineas each were sent to the Royal Hospital and Home for Incurables in Putney, the National Benevolent Institution, the Royal United Kingdom Beneficent Association, the Greater London Fund for the Blind, the Royal London Discharged Prisoners Aid Society, the Reedham Orphanage, the Dockland Settlement, the Seamens Hospital, and the Society for Ladies in Reduced Circumstances.[51]

In February 1940 the Court of Livery suggested the abandonment of the St James' Day service at St James Garlickhythe.[52] However, the following court saw a modification of the motion that the service should be held 'unless circumstances should render such a course undesirable', but the luncheon afterwards should be abandoned.[53] By May that decision had been reversed, and both the church service and the luncheon afterwards 'to which Ladies should be invited' would be provided at the Painter-Stainers' Hall.[54] The sudden death of the priest of St James Garlickhythe, however, put paid to this plan once again and the events were abandoned for 1940 once and for all.[55] In March 1941 it was moved 'that the customary Church service, and Luncheon be not held this year'. However, several Assistants objected and requested that the service should be held at St James', 'or some other alternative Church', but they lost the vote and no plans were made to celebrate St James' Day that year.[56] This was probably for the best, because the May Court of Assistants ended by a report placed on record 'that it is with regret that they learn of the damage done to St. James, Garlickhythe by enemy action, the church which their Foregathers attended as far back as 1590'.[57]

The first hint of investment in war loans comes from the court minutes of 2nd July 1940, when it was proposed that the £65 raised through livery fees should 'be invested in a Government security to be approved by the Court'.[58] At the August court a further £310 from the Company's bank account was added to the £65, and the permission of the Postmaster General was sought for an investment in National Savings certificates.[59] However, the Postmaster General refused permission in September for reasons which are unclear. Not to be dissuaded, the Company immediately decided to round their total proposed sum up to £400 and invest it in the national war bonds instead, at 2.5 per cent.[60] No further reference to the investment appeared in the court minutes until 6th February 1946. Although the money would have been redeemable on 1st July, the decision was taken to re-invest it in 3 per cent defence bonds.[61]

The First World War precedent of spending £100 per year on patriotic charities was re-adopted on 3rd September 1940, when the money was set aside 'for the purposes of Charity, Benevolence and patriotism'.[62] Again, following precedent, this sum was split into multiple small payments, rather than donating the full amount to one specific charity. Five guineas each was sent to the Royal National Lifeboat Association, the British Sailors' Society, and St Thomas' Hospital in October.[63] A further £75 allocated in March[64] was divided amongst fifteen charities, including the Surgical Aid Society, the Seamens Hospital, and the Greater London Fund for the Blind.[65]

In December 1940 the two giants used in the Lord Mayor's Day procession, Gog and Magog, which had been created by liveryman Richard Saunders in 1707,[66] were destroyed during enemy action.[67] The Sunday 29th December 1940 air raid also completely destroyed the Company's property at 30 Addle Street, which at that time comprised of a frontage of 21 feet 6 inches and depth of 42 feet, with a basement, ground, first, second, and third floors. Their surveyor, Percy Groom of Liverpool Street, reported on 30th January that he had 'with some difficulty' inspected the site, and that it 'had been entirely destroyed by enemy action'. Groom estimated that it would cost £300 to clear the site, and £6,600 to rebuild the property, and suggested that a compensation claim for £7,000 should be submitted to the government.[68]

Shortly after the outbreak of war the Guildhall announced that no meetings could be held in the building until further notice, and consequently the Joiners were obliged to find a new location for their monthly courts. In October they were able to secure the use of the Painter-Stainers' Hall at a cost of £2 2s per meeting, but expressed a preference for Girdlers' Hall in future if possible. Unfortunately Girdlers' Hall was destroyed during an air raid on Sunday 29th December 1940, and of necessity the Company was forced to temporarily return to Painter-Stainers' Hall. They did not intend to remain there, however, and the Clerk was instructed to take steps 'to obtain another Hall, if possible for future meetings'.[69] Girdlers' Hall was not the only Hall to have sustained damage during that air raid. The Clerk informed the January court that he had called upon their tenants at Joiners' Hall, Messrs Major and Field, and had been informed that 'part of the roof adjoining Friars Alley had been damaged by incendiary bombs'. They had obtained a claims form and were in the process of submitting it to the government for compensation, ahead of undertaking repairs.[70] Overtures were made to the Cutlers' Company about securing the use of their Hall for future meetings, and on 20th January they received a letter confirming that this arrangement was agreeable. The Joiners were able to lease a room for court meetings at a cost of £1 1s, and for livery meetings at £2 2s. They would also be expected to make suitable gratuities to both the Cutlers' Beadle and their hall keeper, and in return they would 'be pleased to do what [they] can to make you comfortable'.[71]

A further, and much greater, tragedy was to come. On the night of Saturday 15th May 1941 Joiners' Hall was almost entirely destroyed when a V2 bomb fell nearby. The Hall's location close to both the wharves on the Thames and Canon Street station left it particularly vulnerable, although nowhere in the city was immune to attack. The matter of clearing the site was placed in the hands of the Company's solicitors, Messrs H. H. Wells and Son, and with their surveyor Percy Groom.[72] Cutlers' Hall had also been damaged by air strikes, but nevertheless the Joiners were still permitted to hold their meetings in the building, for which they returned thanks.[73]

The loss of Joiners' Hall did not just represent the loss of the physical building; it also represented a significant loss in income. After all, their tenants could hardly be expected to pay rent for a building which had been obliterated. A committee including the Master, Wardens, and Clerk was instructed to assess the financial impact of the loss. Its report, presented to the July Court of Assistants, estimated that in August there would be a balance of £300, but that the Company's income for the following year would be £266 13s and expenditure estimated at £408 15s 8d. This would leave a deficit of £142 2s 8d. They recommended the immediate implementation of a spending freeze, including cancelling all standing orders and all court meetings. With the exception of the St James' Day meeting and the subsequent August audit, all future meetings were 'to be called at the discretion of the Master'. No more Past Master's jewels or silver medals would be awarded to outgoing Masters at the end of their tenure. The Clerk, who was already also undertaking the role of the Beadle, offered to forfeit his salary in return for just £55 per year as expenses, and the £75 allocated in March to patriotic purposes was rescinded. This report immediately passed in the Court of Assistants,[74] and was adopted by the next Court of Livery on St James' Day.[75]

With the exception of the August audit, the next court meeting did not take place until 12th December and then was only called to inform the Livery of the death of the Upper Warden and elect his successor.[76] There then followed a gap of seven months, and the next Court of Livery took place on 23rd July 1942. Messrs Wells and Son, the Company's solicitors, confirmed that the leases had been surrendered by the tenants, and that they successfully obtained the balance of rent due from Messrs Major and Field for Joiners' Hall. The court was also informed that 'the site of the Hall has been cleared by order of the Government, unfortunately the City Surveyor informed the Company, the two figures of the demi-Savages surmounting the old Gateway, crumbled to pieces on being removed'.[77]

In an attempt to ensure that the livery companies would receive the compensation they were due, a meeting was held at Mercers' Hall which representatives of all companies were requested to attend. At the meeting it was agreed that the Mercers would instruct their surveyor 'to prepare a large scale map of the City, showing plans of all war damage done to the various Livery Company's properties, in preparation for concerted action after the war'. This would not be submitted to the government until after the war, when the full extent of each company's losses was known.[78] The Company exchanged some correspondence with the Land Registry in the spring of 1943 concerning their title to the Joiners' Hall site, and what fees they would be expected to pay. The site had been valued at £11,350 in 1915, but not more recently, and ultimately the decision was made to use that estimated figure.[79] Governance of the site was transferred in trust from the ancient precedent of feoffees to the corporate body of the Company,[80] and a new deed was received from the Land Registrar by December.[81]

The Trades Training School during the World Wars

The impact of the First World War was felt almost immediately at the Trades Training School. The start of term was delayed by a month due to the confusion following the outbreak of the conflict, and the Renter Warden reported to a monthly court in December that 'the number of Students [is] considerably less than the normal, owing to a considerable number of students having enlisted'.[82] When the Company received their next report in May about the students' progress and the end of term prize-giving they were informed that

> in Consequence of the abridgement of the first term, the few attendance at the Classes during the past nine months, and the absence of some of the Students by patriotically joining the forces in defence of our Country – the examples of work submitted are few and incomplete.[83]

The report in December 1915 praised the instructors as 'thoroughly capable men' and the work being produced by the students as 'very interesting and of great merit'. Although 'owing to the war there are fewer students than usual', those who were attending the school were making excellent progress in their training.[84] The May 1916 report ended with a wish that 'after the conclusion of this terrible war the Schools will be better attended, with the result that the samples of work then shown, will be proportionate in number and satisfactory in quality'.[85] The Renter Warden noted in December that most of the students were 'elderly men', and hoped that after the war 'more young men would avail themselves of the opportunity offered by the Institution – which he considers well worth the support the Company gives'.[86]

For the academic year 1917–8 there were thirteen students signed up to attend joinery classes at the school, but attendance was described as 'rather erratic', particularly 'on occasions when there was likely to be a fear of an impending air raid'. When the Renter Warden inspected the school in November only four joinery students were present. As with the previous reports, the low attendance overall was blamed on the war, 'and the fact that as a consequence the Army takes the young men just at the age when they would be attending the classes'. The students at the school tended to specialise in one of two aspects of joinery – either handrailing or 'the comparatively new industry of propeller making' – although every aspect of the trade was available if the student wished to learn something else instead. The Renter Warden concluded his report with a note that 'a great deal of the old work of the Joiners, more especially sash making is done by machinery'. However, the 'new era of flying machines' has filled the gap left by the loss of sash making, and it was vital that the new generation of joiners learned to work with accuracy because 'lives may depend' upon their workmanship.[87]

Following the inspection of students' work which took place on Thursday 16th May 1918 a report was given to the Company that the aeroplane propellers being produced at the school were particularly worthy of praise, and indeed were described as remarkably excellent.[88] The November inspection, which took place just four days after the Armistice, noted that the joinery classes had eleven regular students. The education offered to them was 'maintaining its reputation for excellence & is keeping abreast of the times'. The report noted that one student, Corporal Luck, had been awarded the Alexander Howard prize for his construction of a model Clerget propeller.

It was hoped that the outbreak of peace would bring the enrolment of more students in the coming term, but the report suggested that the Company should 'interest the Heads of large Firms in our work, with a view of inducing them to encourage their Hands to take advantage of the great opportunities of improving themselves offered by the School'.[89] Attendance certainly had begun to improve by the time of the Renter Warden's inspection in December 1919, which noted the presence of fifteen students, fourteen of whom were young men 'who having lost most of their training through being in the Army are now trying to make up for lost time'. Now that the need for aircraft components had dropped the focus at the school was once again on traditional joinery and decorative work. The report noted that the majority of the students 'were engaged in the making of doors, sash frames, staircases & hand rails &c for ordinary domestic buildings', and others with decorations for shop fronts.[90]

Renter Warden Thomas Free, who visited in November 1920, was 'struck by the interest & energy displayed by the students', many of whom 'were ex service men, who were endeavouring to pick up what they had lost during the war'. He praised the 'very good joinery' being made in the classes, and was surprised to learn 'that the Joinery Classes of these Schools did their bit during the War in Connection with Aeroplanes, especially with Propeller Blades'. Why this should have been a surprise to him is unclear, because the Court of Assistants had been well aware of the students' activities during the course of the war thanks to earlier Renter Wardens' reports.[91]

The inspection in November 1921 discovered that the joinery classes were attended by fifty-nine students, 'which fully taxes the capacity of the accommodation and a number of students await admission'. The enrolled students ranged from 'young lads' to older ex-servicemen, and all were 'enthusiastically engaged in work' which in many cases was 'of a very high order'. The walls of the classroom were adorned with examples of joinery work created by former students, and the Renter Warden declared himself 'proud of the results of the practical efforts of the Worshipful Company of Joiners to assist the Craft'.[92]

Senior students attended on Tuesday and Thursday evenings, and juniors on Mondays and Fridays. Wednesdays featured classes on drawing which could be attended by all.[93] Classes ran from 7 p.m. to 9.30 p.m.[94] Rather than having all students working on the same item, they were actively encouraged to use their initiative and create their own designs.[95] This was noted to be 'a sound system & one calculated to keep up the interest of the student during the execution of the work'.[96] Each May the work done by the students in the school was presented in an exhibition, and prizes were distributed for superior craftsmanship. In the years following the First World War the focus at the school had been on joinery which could be used in the construction of domestic dwellings, so the prizes awarded were often for items such as handrails, staircases, and panelled doors.[97] Prizes ranged from silver and bronze medals to certificates and awards of 10s.

In spite of the high attendance at the school an emergency meeting was called by the Master of the Carpenter's Company on 5th May 1922 'because the accounts of the Titchfield St Schools showed a deficit'. The Carpenters had been obliged to invest some of their own capital to prevent it from collapsing, and a suggestion was made that the London County Council should be applied to for financial assistance. This was not popular with the livery companies, however, and general concern was raised about the LCC being able to claim a share in the school's control. Discussion then turned to the livery companies associated with the school increasing their annual contributions instead. The Master of the Plasterers stated with regret that his Company had 'reached their limit' and there 'would be little chance of their contributing more'. Similarly, Master of the Joiners Walter Phillips reported that 'although I was averse to the L.C.C. obtaining any Control of the Schools the Company were only able to maintain their present subscription at the expense of doing away with all Banquets & Entertainments & that I could hold out little hope of their being able to increase it'. Although the companies themselves appeared unable to increase their contributions, the possibility was raised of approaching individual liverymen and asking for personal subscriptions.[98] At another meeting at their Hall on 27th October the Carpenters' Company reported that the school's deficit was £3,000, and that the regular annual contributions from the associated livery companies was only £575.[99]

The Joiners themselves were not receptive to the idea of personal subscriptions, however, and when the matter was raised the Livery recommended that the Assistants should consider increasing the corporate contribution by a further £25, rather than gathering individual subscriptions.[100] Nevertheless, by December the matter had reached a crisis and the Carpenters had decided that the only way to proceed was by soliciting individual contributions.[101] The Master drafted a letter to be sent to each liveryman in January,[102] and by early March a total of £23 2s had been raised.[103] When the Renter Warden visited in November 1923 he was so impressed by the work being carried out by the students that he suggested a general invitation should be issued for members of the Livery, particularly those who had made a financial contribution, to visit the school too and inspect the work themselves.[104] Unfortunately the voluntary subscriptions provided by liverymen of the associated companies produced a far lower sum than had been hoped, and in March 1924 the Carpenters' Company announced their decision to abandon the scheme, with all subscriptions returned to the donors.[105]

The Company continued their annual donation of £50 until 1927 when they voluntarily increased the subscription to £100.[106] Their contribution towards the annual prizes was also raised from £6 to £10 in June 1929.[107] The Renter Warden's report following his inspection in November 1929 recommended that 'in future we [should] endeavour to increase our Annual payment to the Trades Training Schools, as I feel that in this way, the Company will be doing a great deal of good work, particularly in their own trade'.[108] The sum of £150 was consequently provided by the Company in 1930.[109] The Renter Warden's report from November 1933 noted that there was no longer a waiting list, although the joinery classes were almost full. This he attributed to the fact 'that so much of the ordinary joinery work is now machine made', but noted that the instruction offered at the Trades Training School 'is still considered preferable by the young men who are keen to improve their knowledge' compared with similar training offered by the LCC.[110]

It was noted that in 1936 the majority of students attending the evening classes were employed in 'machine shops by day' but they sought 'practical experience in handiwork':

> In these days, none has a knowledge of how to do hand joinery until taught at a school such as this. As a result those who take the trouble to put in 2 or even 3 nights a week, quickly rise to the top of their trade.
>
> We were informed that 90% of the students who attend the Senior Joinery class are already in that category. Further, that owing to the real revival in trade, Joiners are at a premium for all good craftsmen are engaged, and there is no unemployment. It was learnt also that men coming into the trade to-day are keen, happy, good principled workmen.[111]

In spite of this, the Company's annual subscription to the school was reduced from £150 to £100 in 1937.[112] The Director of the school stated that this was 'a matter of great regret' to him, but 'he hoped that when the Livery felt the funds of the Company permitted they would give their sympathetic consideration to restoring it to their original amount'.[113]

The outbreak of the Second World War once again disrupted the work being done at the school. The initial response was to immediately close until further notice.[114] However, a letter to the Clerk dated 4th January 1940 from the Clerk of the Carpenters' Company reported that 'on the 11th instant the War Office is sending 80 Army personnel for training at the Trades Training School'. Fifty would be trained as carpenters, twenty as blacksmiths, and ten as coppersmiths for a period of four months, and the War Office agreed to a cost of £1 per student per week. Classes in other subjects would be offered if the need arose, but for the time being those three trades would be the priority.[115] The Carpenters' Clerk wrote again on 16th February with a request that the Joiners would continue their financial support of the school because the work was 'of quite National importance', and the Renter Warden proposed that £100 should be donated immediately.[116] In a letter of thanks the Carpenters' Clerk assured the Company that 'the War Office is highly satisfied with the instruction given at the School', and that joinery was being included in the carpentry classes.[117]

When the Renter Warden went to inspect the school in November he reported that there were sixty-nine soldiers studying a six-week intensive course. He described them as 'remarkably keen on their work', and noted that 'some were making ladders, and small pieces of furniture'. A letter from the Carpenters' Clerk stated that twenty-two of the soldiers were Canadian, and that the joinery classes had been designed for skilled and semi-skilled men. He also informed the Company that 'the School has suffered superficial damage from bomb explosions' but fortunately the on-site presence of builders and craftsmen meant that repairs could be 'carried out on the spot by the trainers'.[118] The Joiners provided a further £100 for the school in February 1941,[119] but the loss of their Hall in May of that year caused them to cease their contributions for the time being. The Carpenters approached them again in July 1944, but the Clerk was instructed to state their regret that 'the present position of the Company prevented them from offering any financial assistance to the objects of the School'.[120]

After the war the government utilised the school for their training scheme, in which craftsmen were once again learning the various trade of the building industry.[121] The Master proposed in 1950 that 'the Company should renew their association with the Carpenters' Company in the work carried on at the Trades Training School', and the former annual subscription of £100 should be renewed. The motion passed unanimously.[122]

The October 1951 inspection of the school was carried out by the Master, Upper Warden, and Clerk. In his report the Master noted that over 200 students were enrolled, seventy-two of whom were taking classes in carpentry and joinery. Students attending day classes were mainly apprentices who were contracted to attend the school one day and two evenings per week for five years. The instructors were singled out for praise, because in their spare time they had set up 'a recreation room for the lads, so that they could play table tennis and darts and take their lunch in comfort'. The school was, however, 'at some disadvantage' compared with the training centres run by the LCC due to a lack of funds and materials. Nevertheless, 'the instructors clearly do their best to give the boys the most comprehensive practice possible'. The Master believed the school to be 'worthy of all encouragement' because 'it fulfils a need for many lads to obtain practice and tuition in their craft under conditions not possible on the Building Site or Workshop'.[123]

After the war the Trades Training School was renamed the Building Crafts Training School,[124] and is known today as the Building Crafts College. The Worshipful Company of Carpenters continues to be the primary sponsor of the work carried out there, and woodwork is a key part of the curriculum. The Joiners continued their annual donations of £100, and in 1975 they provided a further £25 towards the establishment of a Joiners and Ceilers Prize for Outstanding Achievement in Joinery.[125]

The Later Twentieth Century

Although the Second World War had officially ended on 2nd September 1945, the first peacetime court meeting did not take place until 6th February 1946. Early in the agenda was a communication from solicitor Mr Wells that the War Damage Commission had estimated Joiners' Hall to have been worth £28,000 and the land £10,500, but were only offering compensation of £17,500. After discussion the Company decided that this sum was inadequate and voted to hire an independent surveyor to act as a mediator with the Commission in conjunction with Mr Wells.[126] Despite multiple attempts between November and July, Wells was forced to report to the court on St James' Day 1947 that the Commission had not answered any of his letters.[127]

The Company's finances did not immediately recover after the war, and the decision from 1941 to only hold meetings on St James' Day and Audit Day, with an occasional extraordinary meeting, rather than the regular monthly meetings continued until the autumn of 1948. This was an effective way of cutting costs, although it did not dramatically improve their bank balance. The August 1946 audit revealed that the money received that year had amounted to £469 8s 4d, and that £331 18s 1d had been spent, leaving a balance of just £138 3d.[128] This was even lower in 1947, with a balance of just £104 13s 9d.[129] The situation improved somewhat on 19th January 1948 when the Clerk received a cheque for £3,641 10s 2d from the War Damage Commission as compensation for the loss of 30 Addle Street, although they continued to wait for their compensation for Joiners' Hall. The decision was made, however, to invest £3,300 of this sum in 'gilt edge securities', another term for government bonds, rather than just placing it in the bank.[130] By St James' Day the money had been invested in the 3.5 per cent war loan.[131]

By 25th July 1947, however, the Company felt sufficiently secure to debate the matter of 'reviving the annual service at St. James Garlickhythe'.[132] On Audit Day the Clerk tentatively proposed that a service could be held on 20th September. This was approved by the court, as was an instruction to organise a dinner at Tallow Chandlers' Hall for that evening. They had missed St James' Day, but after so many years of no service being held this must have been an extremely welcome return to their pre-war customs.[133]

In March 1948 the War Damage Commission provided a new proposed sum for Joiners' Hall of £37,500, which was a considerably higher offer than their initial £17,500.[134] The site itself had been valued at £10,400, and the remaining £27,100 was for the building.[135] The Company was still liable for tithes for the site in spite of the building's total destruction, and they were served with a bill for £139 10s in December of that year.[136] However, the Corporation of London ultimately wrote off the bill, a matter of 'deep satisfaction' for the Company.[137]

The Company continued to hold meetings at Cutlers' Hall after the war, although at increasing cost; room hire became 3 guineas per meeting, with a further guinea to their Beadle in fees.[138] In October 1948 the Company held discussions about how to revive their former practices. It was suggested that at least three Courts of Livery should be held each year, 'preferably in the late afternoon about 5.30pm, and to be followed by a light dinner or supper if possible'. Liveryman Captain Herbert also suggested

> that when the time come[s] for a building to be erected on the site of our old hall, the Court should very seriously consider making it a condition with the firm who takes a Building Lease that a room should be made available in the new Building for the use of the Joniers' Company for their Court Meetings and a smaller room for the use of the Clerk so that the Company's business could be conducted on its own freehold.[139]

The Company stopped using Cutlers' Hall as their meeting place at the end of 1949 when it became too expensive to continue, and instead removed to Guildhall House on Gresham Street.[140] They remained there until 1974, at which point they returned to the Guildhall itself.[141]

The Renter Warden confirmed in June 1949 that he had received £28,165 18s 3d from the War Damage Commission. Rather than leaving the money in the bank, it was agreed that 'a figure between £25,000 and £27,000' should be invested immediately, on the advice of liveryman and stockbroker Mr Tozer.[142] A total of £15,000 was invested in the Treasury's 2.5 per cent stock, which was essentially the war loan in February 1950.[143] The remaining money was divided into smaller investments. In the summer of 1951 another £5,000 was invested in the 2.5 per cent stock, to mature in 1953–4. Two sums of £2,500 each were invested in the 4 per cent consolidated stock and the 3 per cent British Transport stock, the latter of which would mature between 1968 and 1973.[144]

The Town Planning Authority notified the Company of a compulsory purchase order concerning their property at the end of 1949.[145] Another £12,100 was received from the City Corporation on 12th December 1951 for the compulsory purchase of the Upper Thames Street and Addle Street properties.[146] This meant that the idea to ask for a room in whatever building was erected on the Joiners' Hall site was null and void. Through compulsory purchase the

Company lost all interests in the site. This new sum of money was similarly invested in government bonds.

A finance committee was formed in 1950 consisting of the Master, Wardens, Clerk, and two liverymen 'to consider all matters of finance of the Company'. They would report to the Court of Assistants, but a sub-committee would also be formed 'to ask the advice of any liveryman with an expert knowledge'.[147] There was lots of money invested but this provided a limited annual income for the Company. Various attempts were made over the years to transfer stock from one fund to another to generate an extra few hundred pounds per annum, but overall the Company received low returns. The Renter Warden reported in October 1957 that 'the Company had exceeded its income by about £380 last year and that if this was allowed to go on we would be drawing on capital in a very short time'.[148] The costs of livery banquets were regularly reaching between £200 and £300 per event, with the Ladies' banquet often costing over £700. In 1973 the Committee warned the Company that 'over the past six years, expenditure had exceeded income by an average of £150 per annum'.[149]

The Worshipful Company of Painter-Stainers approached the Joiners in 1955 enquiring whether they would consider joining with them in the rebuilding of their Hall, which had also been a casualty of the Blitz.[150] After receiving an estimate of £20,000 costs, it was deemed 'impracticable at present to consider becoming associated financially with the re-building of the Painters-Stainers Hall'. However, 'the Court should ever bear in mind the desirability of having firm roots in the City once again'.[151] Carpenters' Hall had also required reconstruction, which was completed in the late 1950s,[152] and they agreed to allow the Joiners to hold their future livery dinners there at a cost of 30 guineas per event.[153] The Carpenters also offered the Joiners storage facilities in their strongroom to store their plate at £15 per annum.[154]

In 1957, after carefully consulting the charter, the Company decided to adapt its name from the Worshipful Company of Joiners to instead become Joiners and Ceilers, as specified in the 1571 document.[155] This change took time to implement and formally happened on St James' Day 1960. Indeed, it was noteworthy enough to be reported in a Birmingham newspaper:

> After having its Elizabethan charter translated from the Latin, and studied carefully, the Worshipful Company of Joiners has decided to change its name. Henceforth it will be the Company of 'Joiners and Ceilers'. The original name was 'Joiners and Ceilers or Carvers.'
>
> The Joiners' charter is, at the moment, at Guildhall. It bears a portrait of the young Elizabeth and has a border of birds, pansies, marigolds and other flowers.
>
> The Joiners and Ceilers held their annual service to-day as near to the feast of St. James as could conveniently be arranged. He is the Company's patron saint, and the procession carried not only nosegays but staves with the representation of his symbol, the cockle-shell. The apostle was adopted because London's first group of joiners and carvers were known in the fourteenth century as the Little Brethren of St. James.[156]

By the 1960s the former site of Joiners' Hall had been built over and replaced with a multi-storey car park. The Clerk was instructed to enquire whether 'the Company's arms could not be placed on the building' to demonstrate its former significance.[157] The City Corporation's architect replied stating that it would be possible 'to place on the building one of their usual design plaques stating that this was the site of Joiners' Hall, but doubted whether the Company's Arms would be incorporated'.[158] The building was repurposed into 'the Corporation of London's new Cleansing Department' in 1965, but the plaque was still permitted to be placed on it.[159] The Upper Warden reported to the Court of Assistants on 1st June that it had been affixed in place.[160] However, it stated that the earliest known date for Joiners' Hall was 1603, which this research has now pushed back to 1521.

In 1970 the Company received a letter from Michael Rayner suggesting that they 'purchase a small property in the Golden lane area with a view to acquire a small stake in the City with a view to building a small Hall', rather than continuing to hold meetings at Guildhall House.[161] However, without sufficient financial resources to commit to such a project, the Joiners declared that the 'only possible way' to acquire a new Hall would be 'to share with other smaller Companies'.[162] The matter was discussed again in late 1973, but it was once again confirmed that 'the Company has few financial resources, and certainly these are not sufficient to even start consideration of a project of this size'. Nevertheless, the matter was not entirely dismissed and a committee was instructed to pursue any potential avenues of opportunity which may present themselves.[163] Outgoing Master J. T. Lawson wrote to the liverymen of the Company in 1974 concerning the state of the Company's finances, and he drew their attention to the possibility of acquiring a new Hall:

> The immediate matter is to request your support for the church service and the luncheon following to be held this year on the 30th July. Time was, when it was possible for the Company to provide this function without charge to the Livery but now, with the dramatically reduced value of our income, which has remained static for many years, it is no longer possible for these functions to be subsidised by more than a token amount. Our Company started its life as a religious fraternity and it is altogether appropriate that the service in July should remain as one of the central functions of the Joiners year. I hope therefore that this year you will make a particular effort to attend.
>
> I have already referred obliquely to finance and this brings me on to longer term matters. The health of our Company has always depended on the active support of its members and particularly on the service of those Liverymen who are members of the Court. I have aimed during my term of office to creat a climate in which the abilities of all Liverymen can be used for the benefit of the Company, and it seems to me that this is a policy that must be pursued if the Company is to build up its strength and so endure the rigours of change which are all about us. In particular we shall need all possible help as we prepare ourselves for the tremendous task of moving back into property in the City. This will involve imagination, money, ability, and much else besides and the whole project could serve as a great stimulus for the Company.[164]

In 1976 the Company had almost £10,000 in the bank. However, this was not enough to consider purchasing or building a Hall, so the decision was taken by the Finance Committee to acquire further investments in stock.[165] By 1986 their investments had a value exceeding £100,000, although the balance in their current account was significantly lower than that.[166] By 2002 this had risen to approximately £450,000.[167]

The cost of entertainments and dining remained an ever-present problem for the Company, and concern was expressed to the Clerk by numerous Assistants and liverymen. Even though this was a problem faced by other livery companies, the Clerk noted that 'the deficit on banqueting ... over the last three years [has] varied between £2,200 and £3,200 and clearly the Company could not increase that deficit without detriment to its own finances'.[168] Nevertheless additional entertainments, such as annual golfing days, were introduced and continue to the present day.

The Company decided to establish an annual prize in joinery for students at the South East London Technical College in 1983. This would feature a shield containing the Company's arms which would be kept at the college and engraved with the names of successive prize winners, and joiners' squares with stainless steel blades to be presented to the winners themselves.[169] The following year they considered 'a more definite involvement' with the City and Guilds School through an annual subscription of £200 and a prize,[170] but ended their annual subscription to the Building Crafts Training School and instead made a donation of £500 and established an annual prize of £25, later increased to £50.[171]

St James Garlickhythe

The relationship between the Joiners' Company and the church of St James Garlickhythe was considerably strengthened after the Second World War, with the Company providing financial assistance on multiple occasions. The Master expressed concern in December 1953 over 'the condition of our Parish Church, St James, Garlickhythe, due to war damage'. The church was also suffering from an infestation of deathwatch beetle, which could cause considerable damage to wooden structural elements of old buildings.[172] After considerable discussion it was agreed that the Joiners would donate 25 guineas per year for seven years to the church's Restoration Appeal Fund.[173] In addition, a letter was sent to each liveryman recommending that they make individual donations to the fund.[174]

The Rector, Revd Foxell, approached the Company again in 1962 to say that the Painter-Stainers Company was providing the church with a painting to hang over the altar, and he wondered whether the Joiners would be able to either provide a wooden frame for it or a financial contribution towards the cost of one.[175] Ultimately the Company decided that a frame was not an appropriate gift, and a suggestion of a further donation of £125 was approved by the Court of Livery.[176] They also subscribed 25 guineas in 1968 towards a Christian Aid appeal at the church to assist members of the Commonwealth living in London,[177] and arranged an annual carol service at the church for the Company.[178] They also contributed towards the restoration of the pulpit in 1994,[179] and established an annual donation of £500.

To celebrate the approaching millennium and cement the relationship between the Company and the church, in 1999 the Joiners presented the churchwardens of St James Garlickhythe with four churchwardens' wands. They were carved in lime wood by honorary freeman Trevor Ellis, and were presented to the church on St James' Day.[180]

400th Anniversary of the Charter

The Master informed the Company at the end of 1969 that they were approaching the 400th anniversary of the grant of their charter by Elizabeth I, which would take place in 1971, and suggested that 'the Livery should seriously consider how this great event in the Company's history should be commemorated'.[181] A loyal address would be sent to Elizabeth II on 14th April to mark the occasion. The main celebration would be a service at St James Garlickhythe on 27th July conducted by the Bishop of Fulham, followed by a champagne luncheon at

Skinners' Hall. Musicians from the Guildhall School of Music were hired to play, and a selection of the Company's silver plate, in addition to the Charter and Breeches Bible, would be on display for attendees to view. A commemorative silver badge would be presented to all liverymen in attendance, with an additional gift for their ladies, and a budget of £800 was set for this event.[182] There would also be a Ladies' Banquet at Mansion House on 25th May 1971, and the Bishop of London, the Lord Mayor, and their wives were all invited to attend.[183] A total of 237 people were present, at a cost of over £1,600.[184] Lady Inglefield, wife of the former Lord Mayor of London who had served in 1967–8, wrote to the Company afterwards to express her appreciation and declare that 'it was one of the best Mansion House Banquets she had attended'.[185]

The Company's Archive

The Corporation of London approached the Company in 1949 suggesting 'that the records of this Company be deposited with them for safety and to be made available for use by students and other searchers'. They mentioned that 'many other minor and some major Companys' documents were held by them and that access within was always available on production of authority from the Clerk of the Company'. However, after some discussion the Joiners declined this offer and stated their preference to keep the Company's records in their own custody.[186]

In May 1953 the Master, Renter Warden, and Clerk paid a visit to the Guildhall to inspect 'the strong rooms where the Records of some sixty-six Livery Companies were housed under the care of the City Librarian', Raymond Smith. They saw how the records had been 'cleaned and restored by craftsmen when practically in a ruined condition'. Mr Smith asked 'for the Records of the Joiners' Company to be placed in his care', promising that they would be conserved at no cost to the Company, and that 'No body would be allowed to inspect or handle these Records without written permission signed by the Master and Clerk'. The Court of Livery voted that they would be 'failing in their duty if this offer was not accepted', and it was agreed to deposit the records as proposed.[187] The archive, consisting of 296 items, was deposited with the Guildhall Library on 11th May.[188] The Renter Warden visited the Library in November to inspect the records, and he reported to the Court of Assistants that 'they were being very well housed'. He recommended that 'as so few members of the Livery have had the opportunity of seeing the records of the Company, they should visit the Library to inspect some of the Company's treasures'.[189] Any external researcher wishing to view the Company's records would still be required to pay the Clerk a search fee of £2 2s, even though the records were no longer in the Company's hands.[190] They refused a request from the Church of Jesus Christ of Latter-day Saints to make microfilm copies of the records in 1982, but later conceded that they could copy records dated pre-1880.[191]

Although modern records remain in the hands of the Clerk, the vast majority of the Company's documentary records are still in the care of the Guildhall Library. They are now available to view free of charge, in spite of the best efforts of the Renter Warden in 1955.

Conclusion

The Worshipful Company of Joiners and Ceilers in the Twenty-first Century

The City livery companies are flourishing in the twenty-first century, with new companies regularly being formed. The Joiners remain an active Company, which believes it has two main responsibilities. The primary one is to be a livery company promoting its own craft, but it also has a duty to support and promote the City of London itself.

At the turn of the millennium the question of how craftsmen were faring in modern society was a pressing concern for the Company. Discussion in 1999 noted that 'modern society presented pressures which led to individuals working much harder with less security or leisure time. This particularly affected younger liverymen', and this was noted as a reason for the decline in people taking the livery. A number of courses of action for the Company to take from 2000 onwards were proposed 'without apparent major disagreement', including but not limited to keeping the cost of entertainments low, increasing the Company's publicity, strengthening the links with St James Garlickhythe, increasing charitable contributions, reducing the number of court meetings each year, and allowing women to take the livery.[1]

As part of this effort, Past Masters Capel, Lawson, and Stockwell proposed that the Company should 'do something active for the craft of joinery and woodcarving' through the establishment of a new sponsorship programme. This would provide financial support to 'assist people working in the fields of joinery and woodcarving when there were no other sources of funding available to them'.[2]

The most important committee within the modern Joiners' Company is the Craft Committee. This is responsible for encouraging people to take up joinery and carving, and indeed to become qualified in those crafts. This aim is supported through a charitable trust which sponsors bursaries and prizes to promote excellence. The Craft Committee is involved with the Livery Schools Link showcase every year, which provides demonstrations in Guildhall to schoolchildren to show what crafts the livery companies promote. There are hands-on activities and show-and-tell where children can find out about woodwork, hopefully providing them with an interesting new hobby which could lead to a future career. The Joiners also retain their connection with the City and Guilds Art School, and continue to support the education of wood carving there through courses including the Diploma of Historic Wood Carving and Gilding.

HRH The Duchess of Cornwall

The Company's profile was further raised by the admission of Her Royal Highness the Duchess of Cornwall as an honorary liveryman. This appointment grew out of a mutual interest in the submarine HMS *Astute*, of which the Company and the Duchess are both patrons. The Duchess was admitted during a luncheon at Apothecaries' Hall in 2011, and the Company is very proud to have this association.[3]

In 2006 liveryman James de Sausmarez became the Steward and joined the Court of Assistants. Soon thereafter the Court of Assistants bemoaned the fact that the Company did not have a military affiliation, with a preference expressed for a Royal Navy vessel. James advised that his oldest friend was a serving captain in the Royal Navy and he undertook to make enquiries and report back. His old friend put him in touch with the officer responsible for affiliations and following discussions he was offered the opportunity to affiliate with the first of the new A Class hunter killer nuclear submarines, HMS *Astute*. The Court of Assistants accepted the affiliation with enthusiasm and the Company became the first of HMS *Astute*'s affiliates. At that time HMS *Astute* was still in build at the dockyard in Barrow and this continued for a further two years. In 2008 Commander Mike Walliker was appointed the first captain of HMS *Astute* and built a close relationship between the submarine and the Company. In October 2008, Commander Walliker organised a Trafalgar Night banquet at Holker Hall, the home of Lord and Lady Cavendish, where the guest of honour was the patron of HMS *Astute*, Her Royal Highness the Duchess of Cornwall. He invited the Master of the Company to the dinner, who was unable to attend and was instead represented by the Upper Warden, James de Sausmarez. Following a very successful dinner where de Sausmarez talked with Her Royal Highness about the Company, he enjoyed a stirrup cup with Commander Walliker who suggested to him that the Company should consider inviting Her Royal Highness to be an honorary liveryman.

On taking office as Master in 2009, de Sausmarez proposed to the Court of Assistants that the Company invite both the Dean of St Paul's (the Rt Reverend Graeme Knowles) and Her Royal Highness to become honorary liverymen. The Dean promptly accepted and was duly clothed in July 2010. It took a little longer for Her Royal Highness and her office to do their due diligence but the Company was delighted to hear that she was happy to accept the honour. On Wednesday 19 October 2011, Her Royal Highness was clothed in the livery at a special meeting of the Court of Livery with James de Sausmarez standing for her as her sponsor and Clive Turrell in the Chair as Master. A celebratory lunch followed at Apothecaries' Hall where James de Sausmarez proposed the health of Her Royal Highness and she replied thanking the Company for the honour. To square the circle, now Captain Mike Walliker was clothed in the livery immediately prior to Her Royal Highness.

The craftsmen in the Company are not short of business. There is always demand for high-quality wooden furniture, even in this age of machinery and flatpack. The skills utilised by joiners need to be passed on to future generations, and the Worshipful Company of Joiners and Ceilers is determined to see this happen.

Past Master Clive Turrell had the following to say on joinery in the twenty-first century:

Throughout the ages man has used wood for all basic needs ranging from building his home, household chattels and weapons. Until the Middle Ages the skilled craftsmen who made these items were classified as carpenters. As techniques evolved and craftsmen perfected wider skills for shaping and joining wood each craft became specialised adopting new titles, ie carvers, furniture makers, shipwrights and joiners. The title of carpenter continues being related to on site works with particular emphasis on timber framed buildings, carcassing etc. These familiar names still exist today.

Through the Middle Ages and to date, methods for joining wood together have evolved. The most common joints were mortice and tenon, dovetail and half-lap. These employed the use of animal glues and pegs [dowels]. The joiner became skilled at applying these techniques to the fabrication of doors windows panelling and staircases. In addition he was able to make complex mouldings with specialist hand planes which continued to evolve.

With the advent of power, steam, internal combustion engines and electricity the amount of personal physical input reduced and allowed faster fabrication particularly with the preparation of wood from the raw material and seasoning. This led to considerable automation during the twentieth century and continues to this present day. The relatively new introduction of computer aided design and computer controlled machines has added to this process. However, to manage this, a knowledge of the basic fabrication and assembly of the components is requisite.

Today, there is still a demand for hand skills and knowledge of this complex trade. There is an increasing demand for replacement components and repairs to those which were made by hand in the past, particularly with heritage buildings. Also small quantities or 'one off' components are more effectively and economically made by the traditional hand methods but still taking advantage of mechanical equipment where it can be applied.

Many tools used by the joiner today have evolved since mediaeval times. This evolution has accelerated during the 21st century with communication nationally linking together the best of local practices. Furthermore, interaction with China and Japan has bought in new techniques and tool design. Modern glues and finishes have also contributed to this advancement.

Material sources are more and more dictated by world wide natural forest conservation. Timber today, particularly in the West, is sourced from plantation grown woods.

The future of joinery and associated careers in that trade will remain with us for a long time. Working conditions have improved since WW2 with the introduction of health and safety, management at work, control of chemical substances and dust extraction. Technological advances will continue to improve and speed up production but the basic principles of joining wood together and working the raw material will continue to apply.

Appendix A

The Company's 1572 Ordinances

To all Christian People to whom this present Writing shall come Nicholas Bacon
Knight Lord Keeper of the Greate Seale of England Robert Gatlin Knight Cheife
Justice of the Kings Bench, and James Dyer Knight Cheife Justice of the Comon
Bench send greeting in our Lord God everlasting. Whereas in a certeine Act
of Parliamt of the late most noble Prince King Henry the Seaventh holden at
Westminster in the xxvth day of January in the xixth yeare of his reigne made
and ordeined for the weale and profitt of his Subiects It was amongst other hings
ordeined established and enacted That no Master Wardens and ffellowships of
Crafts or Misteries or any of them nor any Rulers of Guyldes or ffraternityes
should take upon them to make any Acts or Ordinances nr to execute any Act
or Ordinance by them before that tyme made in disheritance or dimynycon of
the Prerogative of the King nor of other nor against the comon profitt of the
People But if the same Acts or Ordinances were examined and approved by the
Chancellor Treasurer of England or Cheife Justices of either Bench or Three of
them, or else before both the Justices of Assize in their Circuit or Progresse in
that Sheire where such Acts or Ordinances bee made upon paine of forfeiture
of fforty pounds for every tyme that they doe to the Contrary As in the said
Act more plainly doth appeare Lewes Stockett Esq. Surveyor Generall of the
Queenes Maties Workes being the Master of the Company or ffellowship of
Joyners and of Ceelers or Carvers of the Citty of London Thomas Locell Gent
and John Mason Wardens of the said Company or ffellowship with the assent
of the Assistants and of the Comunalty of the same Mistery willing and desiring
the said Act of Parliamt in all and every thinge to be observed and kept the
Twentieth day of July in the Thirteenth yeare of the reigne of our soveigne
Lady the Queenes Matie that now is exhibiting their Bill of Peticon unto us did
earnestly request that wee would examine and allow such Acts and Ordinances
as the said Mr Wardens & Assistants with the assent of the Comunalty of
the Mistery of Joyners and of Ceelers or Carvers aforesaid had upon good
deliberacon made for the Comon wealth and profitt of the said Mistery,
Whereupon they presented unto us a Booke conteining the same Statutes Acts
and Ordinances so made for the Comonweale and conservacon of the good
Estate of the said Art or Mistery of Joyners and of Ceelers or Carvers, and for
the better governmt rule and correccon of the same ffellowship and of all others
that were within their Governmt. And thereupon instantly desired us that wee
all and every the said Statutes and Ordinances would oversee examine allow and

approve, as the aforesaid Act in the said Parliamt made requireth The tenors whereof hereafter ensue.

1. Assistants

Inprimis it is ordained constituted and established that as at this present there are xii Assistants of the said Mistery or ffaculty of Joyners and of Ceelers or Carvers (that is to say) Richard Pye Richard Ridge William Phillips William Land Edmond Chapman John Christyan Henry Atkinson Ellis Marchant Thomas Granwick Gabriell Newman Dominick Richardson and Robert Sydnam, so at all tymes hereafter there shalbee xii persons chosen by the body or Comunalty of the said mistery or ffaculty of Joyners and of Ceelers or Carvers for and as Assistants of the said Mistery or ffaculty to bee assistant to the Mrs and Wardens of the said Mistery or ffaculty for the tyme being And that whensoever any of the said xii Assistants shall fortune to decease bee deprived or depart out of the Citty of London or Suburbs of the same to dwell and remaine out of the same Citty and Suburbs by the space of one whole yeare That then the Comunalty of the said Mistery or ffaculty of Joyners and of Ceelers or Carvers within xiiii dayes next after every such decease deprivacon or departure shall or may elect and choose at their Comon Hall within the Citty of London one other person as a new Assistant being one of the Society of the said Mistery or ffaculty in the place of him that shalbee so deceased deprived or departed to bee an Assistant so as there shalbee continually xii Assistants of the said Mistery or ffaculty to the said Master and Wardens.

2. Election of Mr and Wardens

Item it is ordeined and established that on the feast day of St James the Apostle next ensuing the date hereof and so yearely from thenceforth continually for ever on the said ffesst day of St James the Apostle the body or Comunalty of the said Mistery or ffaculty of Joyners and of Ceelers or Carvers for the tyme being or the more part of them from tyme to tyme and oftner if need shall so require shall at their Comon Hall elect and choose amongst the ffellowship of the said Mistery or ffaculty of Joyners and of Ceelers or Carvers one circumspect man of that Comunalty and in the same ffaculty expert Master of the said Mistery or ffaculty, and Two other men of the same ffaculty Wardens of the same Mistery or ffaculty to survey governe order and correct the same ffellowship for one yeare only then next ensuing And what person soever hee bee being a ffreeman of the said Company and Society that shalbee so elected and chosen to bee the Master or either of the Two Wardens as aforesaid and doe refuse to take upon him the same office, and to bee sworne according to the Oath of Master and Wardens hereafter expressed having no just and reasonable lett and impedimt shall forfeite to the Master Wardens and Comunalty of the said Company or ffellowship for the tyme being at every tyme so refusing ffive pounds or lesse of lawfull mony of England at the discreacon of the Mr and Two Wardens for the tyme being and Six of the said Assistants for the tyme being or the most part of the said Twelve Assistants the said Choyce to bee done according to the antient Custome or usage of the said Company The said forfeiture and mony to be converted imployed and disposed for and to the use maintennce and releife of the said ffellowship and to bee paid to the Master and Wardens of the same Company for the tyme being And if it happen the said Master or either of the said Two Wardens to decease bee deprived or depart as is aforesaid after the eleccon of them That then the said body or Comunalty or the more part of them for the tyme being to choose anew in his or their rooms which shalbee so deceased Provided alwayes that the said new Master or Wardens to bee sworne within Thirty dayes next after the feaste of the eleccon upon paine that the said old Master and Wardens residue being negligent and faulty herein or such or so many of them as shalbee negligent & faulty shall forfeite to the Master Wardens and Comunalty of the said Company or ffellowship for every such negligence ffower pounds of good and lawfull mony of England to bee paid to the Master and Wardens of the same Company for the tyme being To bee imployed to the use of the said Company or ffellowship And it is further ordered and provided that no man shalbee compelled or bounden to bee Master or Warden of the said Mistery or ffaculty or to execute the roome thereof above ffower tymes in his life.

3. For deprivacon of Officers

Item it is ordeined that if the said Master and Wardens or their Successors or so many of them as at any tume shall beare or have the said Office, and Six of the said Assistants or their successors or the most part of the said Master Wardens or Assistants that at any tyme shalbee shall thinke and agree any of the said Master Wardens or of the Assistants that now are or at any tyme hereafter shalbee to bee a notorious vitious liver in any notorious fault whereby hee shalbee an unmeet man to supply any of the said Offices or places That then the said Master and Wardens & Six Assistants or the more part of the said Master and Wardens and the said more part of the said Twelve Assistants and their successors shall and may at all tymes hereafter deprive and put out any such vicious Master Warden or Assistant from his said Office and Roome and seclude him utterly from the same Except upon his or their reformation they shall thinke good to choose him or them anew againe.

4. Auditors

Item it is ordeyned that the said Master Wardens and Comunalty or the more part of them shall yearly for the tyme being within Thirty dayes next after that new Mr and Wardens shalbee chosen choose and elect Two or more persons of the said ffellowship to bee Auditors to the intent and purpose to take and receive such Accompts and Reckonings as shalbee made or offered to bee made for or concerning any mony plate jewells goods or other things touching belonging concerning or appteining to the said Mistery or ffaculty or which shall come to belong or apperteine to the said Mistery or ffaculty.

5. For calling into the Livery

Item it is ordeined that the Master with the Wardens of the said Mistery or ffaculty or the more part of them for the tyme being and vi Assistants or the most part of the said Twelve Assistants for the tyme being as they shall need and find cause shall and may from tyme to tyme call choose and admitt into the Livery such and so many of the ffreemen of the same ffellowship as they shall thinke good meete and able thereto And that every person that shalbee so called or chosen by the aforesaid Master Wardens and Assistants or the most part of them into the Livery imediatly upon knowledge to him or them given thereof by the said Master and Wardens or any of them or by their Officer called the Beadle shall forfeite to the Master Wardens and Comunalty of the said Art or Mistery for the tyme being six shillings & eight pence of good and lawfull mony of England to bee paid to the Master and Wardens of the same Company for the tyme being to bee imployed to the use of the said Company or ffellowship And which of them soever so called or chosen that shall refuse to bee of the said

Livery they shall forfeite and pay to the use of the said Company as aforesaid ffifty three shillings and fower pence of like lawfull mony of England or lesse at the discreacon of the said Master or Wardens or the more part of them for the tyme being and of the said vi Assistants or the most part of the Twelve Assistants for the tyme being.

6. Yeomanry

Item it is ordeined that the Master Wardens and Assistants of this Company may yearly from tyme to tyme whensoever it shall please them choose some of their Company (that is to say) Two Three or more to gather the Rents forfeitures and other profitts whatsoever of the said Company Which Gatherers shalbee called Yeomen of the Company And also some of the cheifest of the said Gatherers to be called Wardens of the Yeomanry, which eleccon the said Master Wardens and Assistants or the most part of them shall yearly so make when they thinke good and shall and may leave off such eleccon when they thinke it convenient.

7. Stewards

Item it is ordeined that the Mr Wardens and the Assistants of the said ffellowship of Joyners and of Ceelers or Carvers shall at the feast of St Michaell the Archangell choose every yeare from tyme to tyme Two Three or ffower honest and meete persons of the said Company which hath not been Stewards at the said feast before to bee stewards at their Hall at the tyme of the Mayors feast and the said Stewards shall have towards the said dynner for every Master and Warden Two shillings and for every one being of the Livery Twelve pence, And whatsoever is spent more the said Stewards shall bear it on their owne charges Provided alwayes that the said Stewards shall have the pointing of the fare, and that hee or they so chosen to bee Stewards and shall refuse to bear the same shall forfeite to the said Master Wardens and Comunalty of the ffwllowship to bee paid to the Master and Wardens of the same Company or ffellowship for the tyme being to bee imploted to the use of the said Company or ffellowship the sum of fforty shillings of lawfull mony of England.

8. A monethly Court & iiii qrter dayes

Item it is ordeined that there shalbee holden monethly one Assembly or Court of this Company by the Master Wardens and Assistants of this Company there to sitt hear and determine all controversyes and debates of the same Company And it is also ordained that ffower tymes in the yeare (that is to say) on the ffirst Tuesday next after the Epiphany of our Lord God called Twelfth day also the next workday after Lowsunday the next workday after the feast day of St John Baptist and the next workday after the feast day of St Michaell the Archangell there shalbee holden in this Company ffower generall Assemblyes or Courts comonly called the ffower quarter dayes unto the which shalbee sumoned the whole body of this Company aswell forraines as others dwelling in the Suburbs of the said Citty or within Two Myles compasse of the same Citty To the intent they may have specially read unto them the Ordinances of this Company that they may the better learne to observe and keep the same, and whosoever maketh default in appearance at any of theis Quarterdays without lawfull excuse shall forfeite to the use of this Company such reasonable ffine as shalbee assessed by the Master Wardens and their Assistants or the more part of them so that it exceed not the sum of tenne shillings.

9. Silence

Item for the avoyding of confusion all men shall keep silence at the comandemt of the Master or Wardens That every mans tale or complaint may bee heard indifferently without interrupcon, and that no man being comanded to keep silence shall speake againe in that matter without Lycence firs reverently required upon paine to bee fined at the discreacon of the Master Wardens and Assistants or the most part of them being prsent So as the ffine exceed not the sum of Twenty shillings of lawfull mony of England to bee forfeited to the Master Wardens and Comunalty of the said Art or Mistery for the tyme being and to bee paid to them to bee imployed to the use of the said Company or ffellowship.

10. Disobedience to the Mr

Item it is ordeined that if any person of the said body or Comunalty or any others using or exercising the Mistery or ffaculty of Joyners and of Ceelers or Carvers within the Citty of London or within the Compasse of Two miles in or about the City of London or any of them shall hereafter bee found obstinate and disobedient against the said Master and Wardens or against any of them whereby they are letted from their exercise of any of their said Offices That then every person so being disobedient and obstinate and the same so duly proved against him by the testimony of Two honest Witnesses before the said master and Wardens or the more part of them for the tyme being and of the said vi Assistants or the most part of the said xii Assistants for the tyme being shall forfeite for every tyme so offending to the use of the said ffellowship such reasonable sums of mony as shalbee assessed upon him by the said Master and Wardens or the more part of them for the tyme being and of the said Six Assistants or the most part of the said Twelve Assistants for the tyme being so it exceed not the sum of ffive pounds of lawfull mony of England.

11. Quarteridge paying

Item it is ordeined ordered & established that every peron aswell ffreemen denizens fforeiners as Alyens strangers inhabiting or dwelling within the Citty of London or the suburbs thereof or within Two Myles compasse of the saem Citty that doth or hereafter at any tyme or tymes shall exercise use or make any thing concerning the Mistery or ffaculty of Joyners and of Ceelers or Carvers or any of them or any thing apperteining or in any wise belonging unto the said Mistery or ffaculty and doe or shall keep house and family shall contribute to the Master Wardens and Comunalty of the said Art or Mistery for the tyme being every Quarter of a yeare for his Quarteridge Six pence of mony That is Two shillings of mony by the yeare, and every Journyman at any tyme hereafter working at the same occupacon within the said Citty or within Two myles compasse thereof shall contribute to the said Mr Wardens and Comunalty for the tyme being for his or their Quarteridge Three pence of mony every Qaurter of the yeare that is Twelve pence of mony by the yeare to bee paid to the Master and Wardens of the same Company for the tyme being to bee imployed to the use of the said Company or ffellowship.

12. Search

Item it is ordeined that the Master and Wardens of the said Company or ffellowship for the tyme being from henceforth for evermore from tyme to tyme as often and when it shall seeme good unto them Three or ffower tymes in the yeare at the least shall without force enter into the houses shops sollers cellors warehouses and booths of every person working using or selling any thing or things made by Joyners and Ceelers or Carvers aswell within the Citty of London & Suburbs as within Two myles compasse of the same aswell in places priviledged and exempt as not priviledged and exempt, and aswell in faires and marketts within the said Citty and Two myles compasse of the same as elsewhere And there to view and serch all manner of Works and Wares whatsoever made by any manner of person or persons of the mistery or ffaculty aforesaid or any of them being or apperteining to the said Mistery or ffaculty or in any wise belonging whither the same bee well and workmanly wrought and of good sufficient and lawfull stuffe, and in manner and according to the Statutes of the Realme in such cases provided And whatsoever wares or stuffe shalbee found unlawfully and insufficiently wrought shalbee forfeited to the Master Wardens and Comunalty of the said Art or Mistery for the tyme being And the said Master or Wardens or the more part of them shall take bear and carry the same away unto their Comon Hall and in the prsence of the same Master and Wardens and Six of the said Assistants for the tyme being or the most part of the Master Wardens and of the said Twelve Assistants the same shalbee praized and after sold, and the mony that it shalbee sold for to goe to the use of the ffellowship of the same Mistery or ffaculty of Joyners and of Ceelers or Carvers onles upon some reasonable cause the said Master and Wardens with the said Assistants or the most part of them shall thinke meet to assasse and lesse ffine upon the offender then the valew of the same Wares amounteth unto at the discreacon of the said Master and Wardens or the most part of them for the tyme being and of the said vi Assistants or the most part of the xii Assistants for the tyme being And to take of every housholder within the said Citty Suburbs or Circuite of Two Myles of the said Citty whose wares they doe serch towards their travaile and charges once every Quarter of every yeare one penny and once every ffaire one penny of mony.

13. Assistants for the Search

Item it is ordeined that if the said Master and Wardens for the tyme being doe not call certeine of the said Assistants every Quarter of the yeare once at the least according to their old custome to goe to serch with them for the better mainteining of good wares to bee made then they shall for every Quarter so missing forfeite to the Master Wardens and Comunalty of the said Art or Mistery for the tyme being Tenne shillings of mony apeece for their default, and Bartholmew day to bee none of the said ffower serch dayes nor no other day of the same ffaire, the same mony to bee paid to the Master and Wardens of the same Company for the tyme being to bee imployed to the use of the said Company or ffellowship.

14. Educacon for Appntices

Item it is ordeined that no ffreeman of this Company shall trade teach or bring up any person or persons in the occupacon of a Joyner and Ceeler or Carver unles hee bee his owne natural Child or Children not being his Appntice bound according to the Ordinances of this Company upon paine of fforfeite such ffine not exceeding Twenty pounds of lawfull mony of England as the Master Wardens & Assistants or the most part of them shall assesse by him to bee paid therefore, the same to bee forfeited to the Master Wardens and Comunalty of the said Art or Mistery for the tyme being, and to bee paid to them to bee imployed to the use of the said Company or ffellowship And if any ffreeman of this Art or Mistery after warning to him given by the said Master or Wardens or any of them of any such Offence contrary to this Ordinance doe still keep or reteine any such person trading teaching and bringing him up in the said Art or Mistery contrary to the Ordinance That then every such offender besides the said forfeiture shall therefore suffer ffower dayes imprisonmt and longer untill the same person so trades taught and brought up bee by the said Offender either reteined as his lawfull Appntice according to the Ordinances of this Company (if by the same Ordinances hee may be so reteined) or else to bee by him utterly put away from his house trade and bringing up.

15. Every Appntice to serve 2 yeares after as a Journyman

Item it is ordeined that none Appntice made free of this Company and exercising the occupacon of a Joyner and of a Ceeler or Carver shall worke and sett up for himselfe the Joyners and Ceelers or Carvers craft with the space of Two yeares next after the tyme wherein his Appnticehood shall expire But during those Two yeares (if he worke) hee shall worke with another man allowed for an approved Workman of the said Company or ffellowship and dwell with him as his Journyman upon paine that every Offendor to the contrary shall forfeite to the Master Wardens and Comunalty of the said Art or Mistery for the tyme being, and to bee paid to them to bee imployed to the use of the said Company or ffellowship the sum of Three pounds six shillings and eight pence of lawfull mony of England.

16. Every man to make his proofe peece before &c

Item it is ordeined that no manner of Person being of the said ffellowship or any other using or exercising any of the said Arts within the Circuite aforesaid shall sett up for himselfe or reteyne or take any Servant or Appntice to worke with him untill such tyme as hee or they doe come to the Master and Wardens, and in one of the Shops of them or of any others and in the prsence of one of them or in the prsence of any others whom they the said Master and Wardens or the most part of them shall appoint to make with their owne hands some handsome peece of worke for his proofe peece whereby it may bee knowne whither hee bee a good and sufficient Workman or no And whosoever setteth up or reteineth any Servants or Appntices before hee himself bee allowed upon the making of his said proofe peece in form aforesaid to bee a Workman shall forfeite to the Master Wardens and Comunalty of the said ffellowship for every moneth so offending Twenty six shillings and eight pence and shall have his shop windowes shutt up untill such tyme as hee hath made his said proofe peece the said mony to bee paid to the Master and Wardens of the same Company for the tyme being to bee imployed to the use of the said Company or ffellowship.

17. Reteyning of Journymen

Item it is ordeined that no man of this Science or occupacon shall reteyne any Journyman to worke with him otherwise then by the whole yeare halfe yeare or quarter of a yeare unles hee present him before the Master and Wardens of the said Company or ffellowship for the tyme being at the next Court day after such retainer And then shall reteine him either in form aforesaid or otherwise as hee shalbee permitted to doe by the admission and appointmt of the said Master Wardens and Assistants or the most part of them upon paine to forfeite to the Master Wardens and Comunalty of the said Art or Mistery for the tyme being, and to bee paid to them to bee imployed to the use of the said Company or ffellowship Tenne shillings of lawfull mony of England for every such Offence.

18. Admission into the Company

Item it is ordeined that every person which shalbee admitted and sworne as a ffreeman into and of the said Art and Company taking the Oath to him apperteining shall contribute to the Master Wardens and Cominalty of the said Art or Mistery for the tyme being and to bee paid to the same Master and Wardens of the same Company for the tyme being to bee imployed to the use of the said Company or ffellowship the sum of Three shillings and fower pence of lawfull mony of England.

19. No Journyman to worke out of the Company

Item it is ordeined that no manner of person being a Journyman and free of the said Company of Joyners and of Ceelers or Carvers shall from henceforth worke with any other person using the said Art of Joyners and of Ceelers or Carvers or any of them within the Libertyes of the said Citty or Two Myles compasse thereof being not free of the said Company or ffellowship or at any tyme served as an Appntice of or to the same occupacon by the space of Seaven yeares at the least without Lycence of the Master and Wardens of the said Company or the more part of them for the tyme being and of the said vi Assistants or the most part of the said xii Assistants for the tyme being but shall work only to or with some of the said Company or ffellowship if hee may have worke and competent wages of any of the same ffellowship and Company aforesaid upon paine that every one so offending shall forfeite to the Master Wardens and Comunalty of the said Mistery or ffaculty for the tyme being Thirty three shillings and fower pence of mony or lesse at the discreacon of the said Master & Wardens or the more part of them for the tyme being and of the said vi Assistants or the most part of the said xii Assistants for the tyme being to bee paid to the Master and Wardens of the same Company for the tyme being to bee imployed to the use of the said Company or ffellowship.

20. Taking of Appntices & charges

Item it is ordeined that none of the said ffellowship take any person to bee his Appntice to abide with him above one moneth but that before the end of the same moneth if hee or they intend to keep him as his Appntice hee shall prsent him to the Master and Wardens of the said Company or ffellowship and by their knowledge to bee taken into the same occupacon as an Appntice And every person so taking any Appntices to pay for every Appntice as hee so taketh at the end of Three moneths next following the said presenting of every such Appntice Two shillings six pence of good and lawfull mony of England for the said prsenting to bee paid to the Mr and Wardens of the same Company for the tyme being to bee imployed to the use of the said Company or ffellowship, and whosoever doth not present his Appntices as is aforesaid and doth not inroll his said Appntice or Appntices within six moneths next after the ensealing of his or their Indentures shall forfeite to the said Master Wardens and Comunalty for every one of his said Appntices not so presented or enrolled iiis & iiiid of good and lawfull mony aswell for not enrolling as not presenting the same Appntices to bee imployed to the use of the said Company or ffellowship.

21. Denizons & Forraines and their Appntices

Item it is ordeined that every Stranger denizon and forraine dwelling within the City of London and the Suburbs thereof or within Two myles compasse of the same Citty aswell within places priviledged and exempt as not priviledged and exempt that doth or shall use or exercise any of the said Misteries or ffacultyes or any thing appteining thereunto shalbee contributory and bear and pay unto the Master Wardens and Comunalty of the Art or Mistery of Joyners and of Ceelers or Carvers for the tyme being to bee paid to the Master and Wardens of the same Company for the tyme being all such reasonable sums of mony as shalbee thought meete and reasonable to bee assessed upon them by the Master Wardens and Assistants of the said ffellowship or the more part of them for the tyme being aswell for the service of the Queenes Matie as for the affaires of the Citty as for any other thing and as the ffreemen of the said ffellowhip and of other Companies of the said Citty from tyme to tyme are and shalbee charged and according to their habilities And firther that no Alien using any of the said Misteries or ffaculties take or keep any more Appntices then Two at one tyme and that the same Appntices shalbee born within the Queenes dominions, and to pay to the said ffellowship for the admitting of every Appntice Two shillings and six pence of good and lawfull mony of England to bee paid to the Master and Waredns of the same Company for the tyme being to bee imployed to the use of the said Company or ffellowship as the ffreemen doe for their Appntices And every one that offendeth against this Ordinance shall pay for every tyme and every ffreeman doth pay for the like offence to the use aforesaid.

22. No Mr to have above 4 Appntices No Warden above 3 no other above 2 at one tyme

Item it is ordeined that no person or persons being free of the said Mistery or ffaculty not having been Master Warden or one of the Assistants of the said Company or ffellowship shall have at one tyme togeather above the number of Two Appntices at the most and [th]at no one that is or hath been or shalbee Warden of the said Company or ffellowship shall have at one tyme togeather above the number of Three Appntices at the most, and that no one that is hath been or shalbee Master of the said Company or ffellowship of the said Mistery or ffaculty shall have at one tyme above the number of ffower Appntices at the most, and if it happen any of the same Appntices to decease or to come out of his or their terme or termes of yeares of Appnticehood That then hee or they to take into the Roomes or places if they will so many other Appntices as is or shalbee deceased or whose termes of Appnticehood is are or shalbee determined and whatsoever hee or they bee of this said ffellowship of Joyners and of Ceelers or Carvers that shall keep any more Appntices at once then is aforesaid for him or them lymitted and expressed shall forfeite and pay for every Appntice that hee or they keep more or above the number lymitted and appointed to him or them such sums of mony for a ffine as shalbee assessed on him or them by the Master Wardens and Assistants as aforesaid of the said Company or the more part of them for tyme being so it exceed the sum of ffive pouds of lawfull mony of England Provided that it may bee lawfull notwithstanding theis Ordinances to any of the said ffellowship to take any Appntice or Appntices of the guist or setting over of any of the said Company with the assent of the Master and Wardens or the more part of them for the tyme being and of the said Six Assistants or the most part of the said xii Assistants for the tyme being above the number to him or them lymitted without any damage forfeiture or penalty.

23. Setting over of Appntices

Item it is ordeined that no person of the said Mistery or ffaculty shall from henceforth sett over any person being once bound Appntice unto any other person using any other occupacon or handecraft without the consent and agreemt of the said Master and Wardens or the more part of them for the tyme being and of the said Six Assistants or the most part of the said Twelve Assistants for the tyme being upon paine to forfeite to the said Master Wardens and Comunalty of the said Art or Mistery for the tyme being and to bee paid to the Master and Wardens of the same Company for the tyme being To bee imployed to the use of the said Company or ffellowship for every tyme hee so offendeth ffive pounds of good and lawfull mony of England or lesse at the discreacon of the said master and Wardens or the more part of them for the tyme being and of the said vi Assistants or the most part of the said xii Assistants for the tyme being.

24. For such as seek an others worke the first being unpaid
Item it is ordeined that where any of the said Company or ffellowship have or shall have taken worke to doe about any man or womans house or houses, or that any man or woman doe or shall sett any person of the said Mistery or ffaculty on worke and the same person being so in worke bee discharged before hee bee full paid or satisfied for his worke That then every other person or persons of the said ffellowship or ffaculty that shall enter into the same Worke the former Workman being not fully paid or satisfied for that hee hath done as is aforesaid shall forfeite for every such offence to the said Master Wardens and Comunalty to bee paid to them to bee imployed to the use of the said Company or ffellowship the sum of Twenty shillings of lawfull mony of England, and also to pay the former Workman for his debt which is owing him by his said Workmaster which sett him first a worke.

25. For inticing of Appntices from their Masters
Item it is ordeined that if any manner of person or persons whatsoever hee or they bee being of the said Mistery of ffaculty of Joyners and of Ceelers or Carvers that will intice or councell receive or take away any manner of person or persons being a Servant to one of the same ffellowship from their Master or Masters service before the end of the term of their service bee expired Except the Servant bee lawfully discharged of his Masters Service or have lawfull warning to depart from the service of them with whom hee was reteined shall forfeite to the Master Wardens and Comunalty of the said Art or Mistery for the tyme being to bee paid to them to bee imployed to the use of the said Company or ffellowship for every tyme so doing fforty shillings.

26. Noe Freeman to goe unto an other Company
Item it is ordeined that no manner of person being once made free of the Mistery or ffaculty of Joyners and of Ceelers or Carvers whatsoever his occupying be shall change his Trade and become free of any other ffellowship or Company without the knowledge full consent and Agreemt of the Master and of the Two Wardens and of the said Six Assistants or the most part of the said Twelve Assistants for the tyme being upon paine that every person offending that Ordinance shall forfeite and pay to the said Master Wardens and Comunalty of the said Art or Mistery for the tyme being and to bee paid to them to bee imployed to the use of the said Company or ffellowship Twenty pounds of good and lawfull mony of England or lesse at the discreacon of the Master and Wardens or the more part of them for the tyme being and of the said Six Assistants or the most part of the said Twelve Assistants for the tyme being having regard to the person so offending Except hee change his Coppy by reason of eleccon into any head Office in London.

27. Freemen or Forraines for Assembly

Item it is ordeined that none either ffreemen or fforreyner of the said Art or Craft take upon him or them to make any Privy Assembly Councell secret Conventicles or Attempts against the Master Wardens and Assistants for the tyme being for or to the violacon or breach of any good rule or order now being or hereafter to bee by them all or the most part of them had made or devised for the good Governmt of the said Company or unjustly or wrongfully to practice any thing which may bee in any wise slanderous or hurtfull to the said Master Wardens and Assistants or the rest of the Company And if any soe doe & thereof bee found faulty Then the said Master Wardens and Assistants or the most part of them for the tyme being may sett such reasonable ffines not exceeding the sum of fforty shillings of lawfull mony of England at any one tyme upon every such Offender as shalbee thought meet and convenient by the good discreacons of the said Master Wardens and Assistants or the most part of them The same ffines to bee forfeited to the Master Wardens and Comunalty of the said Art or Mistery for the tyme being to bee paid to the same Master and Wardens of the same Company for the tyme being to bee imployed to the use of the said Company or ffellowship.

28. For Indentures

Item it is ordeined that the Clark of this Company for the tyme being shall have the making of all the Indentures for any Appntices of any ffreemen or others of this Company And the same Indentures not to bee made elsewhere And for the making of every pair of the same Indentures to bee paid by the Master of every such Appntice to the said Clarke Twelve pence and not above And for the Regestring of the same, the same Masters to pay to the said Clarke six pence and not above And if any ffreeman shall make or cause to bee made any Indentures elsewhere or otherwise Then every such ffreeman to forfeite to the Master Wardens and Comunalty of the said Art or Mistery for the tyme being to be paid to the Master and Wardens of the same Company for the tyme being to bee imployed to the use of the said Company or ffellowship the sum of six shillings and eight pence of lawfull mony of England.

29. For against maintennce of Forrainers & Aliens in Shopps

Item it is ordeined that no ffreeman of the said Company shall sett up or mainteine any fforeiner alien not being his Appntice and reteined for Seaven yeares at the least to worke buy or sell as his Servant in any open Shop or Shops within the Citty of London or elsewhere within Two Miles compasse of the same upon paine of forfeiture for every such offence the sum of Three pounds of lawfull mony of England to the Master Wardens and Comunalty of the said Art of Mistery for the tyme being and to bee paid to the Master and Wardens of the same Company for the tyme being to bee imployed to the use of the said Company or ffellowship.

30. Teaching of Forraines

Item it is ordeined that no ffreemen or fforainer of the said Art or Mistery doe teach or cause to be taught from henceforth any manner of person or persons unles hee or they so to bee taught shall at and before any such teaching bee appntice or Appntices Journyman or Journymen of every such Teacher and so admitted by the said Master and Wardens of the said Art and Mistery for the tyme being upon paine that every such Teacher shall for every such Offence forfeite to the said Master Wardens and Comunalty of the said Art or Mistery for the tyme being to bee paid to the Master and Wardens of the same Company for the tyme being to bee imployed to the use of the said Company or ffellowship such ffine not exceeding the sum of Three pounds six shillings and eight pence of lawfull mony of England as the said Master Wardens and Assistants of the said Company or ffellowship or the most part of them for the tyme being shall assesse upon him or them as so offendeth this Ordinance.

31. Rs of Strangers & Forraines

Item it is ordeined that no man of this Art or Science aforesaid doe take upon him or them from henceforth to rceive into his or their Service any person or persons being fforreiner or fforreiners whatsoever they bee either alyens born or English fforreiners Except every such fforreiner shalbee within Tenne dayes next after such receiving into Service brought and presented or caused to bee presented to the Master and Wardens of the said Company for the tyme being in their Comon Hall and by them admitted so to serve upon paine that every one that shall offend in receiving of any such fforreiner contrary to the form and effect of this Ordinance shall forfeite to the Master Wardens and Comunalty of the said Art or Mistery for the tyme being and to bee paid to the Master and Wardens of the same Company for the tyme being to bee imployed to the use of the said Company or ffellowship Tenne shillings for every such offence.

32. Forreines & Aliens working

Item it is ordeined that no fforreiner and alien born at any tyme hereafter shall take in hand or worke any worke apperteining to the said Art or Mistery within the said Citty of London or any the Libertyes of the same without the Lyence of the said Master and Wardens with any person or persons other then such persons as are or then shalbee free of the said Mistery upon paine of imprisonmt, and to forfeite to the Master Wardens and Comunalty of the said Art or Mistery for the tyme being and to bee paid to the Master and Wardens of the same Company for the tyme being to bee imployed to the use of the said Company or ffellowship the sum of fforty shillings of lawfull mony of England for every tyme that such alyen born shall doe the contrary.

33. Proofe peece

Item it is ordeined that no fforreiner being an Alien born and not then having made the Proofe peece with having allowance thereof in such sort as English ffreemen of this Company ought to make and have shall worke with any of the said Art or Company Except hee bee reteyned by the whole yeare halfe yeare or quarter of the yeare upon paine that every person of the said Company or ffellowship so setting any such fforreines on worke without Lycence of the said Master Wardens and Assistants of the said Company or ffellowship or the most part of them for the tyme being shall forfeite to the Master Wardens and Comunalty of the said Art or Mistery for the tyme being and to bee paid to the Master and Wardens of the same Company for the tyme being to bee imployed to the use of the said Company or ffellowship for the first offence Three shillings and fower pence of lawfull mony of England and for the second six shillings and eight pence and for every offence after thirteene shillings and fower pence of like lawfull mony of England.

34. For Swearing

Item it is ordeined that if any man doe outrageously sweare or blaspheme the name of God That then for every such Offence hee shall forfeite to the Master

Wardens and Comunalty of the said Art or Mistery for the tyme being and to bee paid to the Master and Wardens of the same Company for the tyme being to the use of the Poor of the Company Twelve pence of lawfull mony of England And if being admonished hee should sweare againe or blaspheme That then hee shall not only pay in manner and form aforesaid for every time hee so doth Twelve pence of mony, but shall suffer imprisonmt at the discreacon of such of the said Master Wardens and Assistants or the most part of them for the tyme being and shalbee present so the imprisonmt exceed not Three dayes.

35. Marking of Wares
Item it is ordeined that no person or persons being fforreyners or Alyens of this Art or Company their wives servants or Appntices shall at any tyme hereafter sell or sett or putt to sale any wares apperteining to the said Art of Joyners and Ceelers or Carvers before the said Wares bee truly and sufficiently marked with a good and convenient marke in such sort as touching aliens is inacted by the Statute decimo quarto Henrici Octavi upon paine that every one offending this Ordinance shall forfeite to the Master Wardens and Comunalty of the said Art or Mistery for the tyme being & to bee paid to the Master and Wardens of the same Company for the tyme being to bee imployed to the use of the said Company or ffellowship the sum of Twenty shillings of lawfull mony of England for every such Offence.

36. For disobedience upon Sumons
Item it is ordeined that every person of the same Mistery or ffaculty and every other person occupying any of the said Arts within the CItty of London or the libertyes thereof or within Two Miles compasse of the same having reasonable warning by the Beadle or any other of the same ffellowship by the Assignmt and comandemt of the said Master and Wardens or any of them for the tyme being to come to any Congregacon or Assembly or any other buisnes touching any Art to bee done concerning the said Company and doth not come according as hee shalbee warned shall forfeite to the Master Wardens and Comunalty of the said Mistery or ffaculty for the first tyme six pence and for the second tyme Twelve pence, and if hee faile the third tyme hee shall forfeite Two shillings and for every tyme after Six shillings and eight pence without Redempcon to bee paid to the Master and Wardens of the same Company for the tyme being to bee imployed to the use of the same Company or ffellowship Except hee have for every tyme a lawfull excuse.

37. For Burialls
Item it is ordeined that every such person being of the Livery of Joyners and of Ceelers or Carvers that doth not come at such tyme as any of the said Livery or their wives decease and being warned and is not at the buriall or at the place where the Wardens or any of them shall appoint to meete togeather for that purpose in decent Apparell unles hee have a lawfull Excuse or have obteined leave of some of the said Master and Wardens for the tyme being for their absence shall forfeite to the said Master Wardens and Comunalty to the use aforesaid (that is to wit) every one of them so mussing without Redempcon Three shillings and fower pence And that none of them that doe come doe depart or goe away untill the Master and Wardens with the rest of the Company doe depart with them upon like paine and forfeiture, the same mony forfeited to bee paid to the Master and Wardens of the same Company for the tyme being to bee imployed to the use of the said Company or ffellowship except hee or they bee lycenced by the said Master and Wardens.

38. For Slander or evill Speech

Item it is ordeined that no manner of person of the same Company or ffellowship in any open audience or privily doe revile or misuse with evill speeches of reproach any of the same Company or ffellowship upon paine to forfeite for every tyme so doing to the Master Wardens and Comunalty of the same Art or Mistery for the tyme being Twenty shillings or lesse at the discreacon of the Master Wardens and Assistants as aforesaid for the tyme being having respect to the Offence, the same to bee paid to the Master and Wardens of the same Company for the tyme being to bee imployed to the use of the said Company or ffellowship.

39. To distraine

Item it is ordeined that if any person or persons of the said Mistery or ffaculty or any other using the same Mistery or ffaculty or any of them or any other that uttereth or selleth any kind of wares apperteining to any of the said Misteryes or ffacultyes of what degree or condicon soever hee or they bee that offendeth in any Act or Ordinance in this booke expressed and will deny or not pay such sum or sums of mony as upon him or them shalbee assessed for the same offence That then it shalbee lawfull to the Master and Wardens of the said Mistery or ffaculty or any of them for the tyme being at their will and pleasure to enter into the house shop or booth of him or them so denying or not paying such penaltys & forfeitures or sumes of mony, and there to take a distresse or distresses convenient and meete for the same sums of mony, and those distresses so taken lawfully to lead drive carry and bear away & keep to the use of the same Master Wardens & Comunalty untill the said penaltyes forfeitures or sums of mony bee paid assigning the party a tyme next after the taking of such distres to pay the same penaltyes and sums of mony and forfeitures except hee sue a Replevie for the same within Tenne dayes after the said distres taken And further if the same party at or before the same day assigned will not or doe not content and pay the said sums of mony so taxed aforesaid forfeited or assessed That then the said Master & Wardens or the more part of them for the tyme being and the said vi Assistants or the most part of the said xii Assistants for the tyme being shall have authority by theis pnts by the Oath of vi honest persons of the said Company to praize and make sale of the said distres or distresses to the full contentacon of the said forfeitures penaltyes arrearages and other the prmisses and every part and parcell thereof, & if any surplusage or Rest of mony upon the sale of the said distres or distresses doe remaine then the same to bee restored imediatly to the party or partyes from whom the same distres or distresses were taken by the Master and Wardens for the tyme being or the more part of them.

40. A Chest

Item it is ordeined that the said Company and ffellowship shall have one substantiall Chest with Three severall locks thereupon, and Three severall keys to the same which Chest shall stand in some convenient place appointed for the same wherein shalbee put all such mony plate jewells and such like treasure belonging unto the said Company or ffellowship which keys shalbee in the Custody of the said Master and Two Wardens every one of them to have a key so that they shall all Three of them in proper person go togeather to the said Chest when and as often as there shalbee an occasion to put any thing into the said Chest or to take any thing out of the same, and not one or two of them to have all the keyes neither to go alone to the said Chest about any the occasions aforesaid, but all Three Master & Wardens to goe togeather And if it happen the said Master and Wardens or any of them to bee sick or out of Towne or to have any other lawfull buisnes That then the same Master or Wardens shall appoint one of the auntients of the Assistants which hath been Master or Warden before to take his key, and in his absence for that tyme to goe and helpe to the opening of the Chest for him about the occacons aforesaid.

41. For selling of wares in the Street

Item it is ordeined that no person of the same Company nor any forraine denizon or stranger nor any other for them nor by any other meanes goe about the Streetes hawking or proferring their wares to sell from shop to shop nor in any Inne or other place within the Libertyes and franches of the Citty of London to any others then Joyners or to such as occupy the Trade of buying and selling of Joyners Ware upon paine to pay for every tyme so offending to the use of the said Company Six shillings and eight pence of good and lawfull mony of England to bee paid to the Master and Wardens of the same Company for the tyme being to bee imployed to the use of the said Company or ffellowship.

42. For Fayres & Marketts

Item it is ordeined that no person of the same ffellowship nor any others using the said Misteryes or ffacultyes shall carry to any ffayre or Market or shall send or convey any made wares concerning the said Mistery or ffaculty or any of them but only such as hee or they shall first show unto the Master and Wardens of the said Company or to one of them at the least before the carrying thereof to the intent hee or they shall utter no false or insufficient wares to the hurt or hinderance of the Queenes Maties leige People and to the dishonesting of the said ffellowship upon paine that every person so offending this Ordinance shall forfeite to the said Master Wardens & Comunalty of the said Art or Mistery for the tyme being to bee paid to the Master and Wardens of the same Company for the tyme being to bee imployed to the use of the said Company or ffellowship for every tyme Thirteene shillings and fower pence of good and lawfull mony of England or lesse at the discreacon of the said Master Wardens and Assistants of the same Company for the tyme being Provided that if any of the said Mistery or ffaculty shall before any such carrying or conveying of any wares give notice in due tyme to any of the said Master or Wardens of his said Wares so to bee carryed or conveyed and of the place where they lye to the end the said Master Wardens or Warden may (if they will) view the same And if the said Master Wardens or Warden doe not come to the same place and view the same Wares within six houres after such notice given That then any such person may lawfully carry or convey his wares to any markett or faire without any danger or penalty.

43. For executing of divers Statutes

Item whereas by severall Statutes & Ordinances made in the first yeare of king Richard the third and in the xiiiith xxith the xxiith and the xxxiith yeares of king Henry the Eighth it appeareth (amongst other things) that the Governmt of all aliens being handycrafts men and Artificers their servants and Appntices and the reteining of them and also their wares is ordered and appointed to bee within view serch and reformacon of the Wardens and others of the Company whereof they are Artificers And also that all strangers borne being Artificers should pay all such and like dutyes and charges as the subjects born in this Realme being of the same Craft or Mistery doe use to pay And also that if the said Aliens refused to pay the same Then they should incurre the penaltyes of the said Statutes and bee discharged to occupy their Art and Mistery for ever after as by the said Statutes and Ordinances more plainly appeareth It is therefore now ordeined by the said Master Wardens and Comunalty that all the said severall Statutes from tyme to tyme be duely weighed enquired of and put in Execucon amongst the Artificers of their Company of Joyners and of Ceelers or Carvers according to the purport tenor and effect of the same.

44. For the giving up of the Accompts

Item it is ordeined that within Thirty dayes next after the new Master and Wardens have taken their Oaths and charges aswell the old Master and Wardens as also all such of the said ffellowship as bear Office whereby hee or they shall meddle with Receipts or paymts of the said ffellowship or with the goods of the same ffellowship hee or they in the Comon Hall of the said ffellowship of Joyners and of Ceelers or Carvers in the pnce of the new Master and Wardens and any vi of the most auntient Assistants or the most part of the said Twelve Assistants for the tyme being shall present exhibit and make a due true and plaine Accompt examined and allowed by and under the hands of the Auditors chosen for that purpose by the same Company or ffellowship to the said new Master and Wardens and Assistants or the most part of them for the tyme being not only of all his or their Receipts and ready monyes by reason of fforfeitures and guifts to the ffellowship, and also of all Jewells plate or other goods or things whatsoever hath come to their hands to the use of the said ffellowship by reason of their Office or to the hands of any other for them by their consent but also of all manner of charges in paymts repairacons and other things with the names and specialtyes of all such as hath not paid their quarteridge forfeitures and penaltyes upon them assessed if any such shalbee, and then and there in the pnce of the aforesaid new Master and Wardens and vi Assistants at the least shall deliver their said Bookes of Accompt with the said ready monyes jewells plate and all other things as abovesaid togeather with the said Three keyes belonging unto the said Chest wherein such things were appointed to bee laid to the said new Master and Wardens And if any ready mony jewells plate or other things before specifyed by reason of the said Accompts shalbee found to bee behind due to the use aforesaid remaining unpaid or undelived or being in the hands of any of the said old Master and Wardens or in the hands of any others by their appointmt or to their use then the said person or persons being so indebted or in arrearages or having the same or any part thereof shall imediatly without delayes with one or two sufficient and able persons with him or them bind themselves in a sufficient and convenient sum of mony by his or their deed obligatory at a certeine day reasonable to bee lymitted by the said new Master and Wardens and vi of the Assistants at the least to pay and deliver unto the said new Master and Wardens within the space of Two moneths next ensuing at the furthest all such ready mony jewells plate and other things wherein hee is found in arrearages indebted or behind or the verry true vallue thereof to the said new Master and Wardens as the same shalbee valued by the Oathes taken upon a Booke before the said new Master and Wardens by such Two persons as have been Master or Wardens in the said ffellowship to bee named by the said new Master and Wardens for the tyme being so that by no colourable meanes or crafty demeanors the goods of the said ffellowship in any manner of wise bee not abused imbeziled or mispended And as often as any manner of such person will refuse or deny to accompt in manner and forme aforesaid or to enter into such Writing obligatory to bee bound as is abovesaid shall forfeite to the Master

Wardens and Comunalty of the said Art or mistery for the tyme being to bee paid to the new Master and Wardens of the same Company for the tyme being to bee imployed to the use of the said Company or ffellowship at every tyme such reasonable sums of mony and ffines as shalbee assessed by the said new Master and Wardens or the more part of them for the tyme being or of the said vi Assistants or the most part of the said Twelve Assistants for the tyme being.

45. For paymt of all Dutyes

Item it is ordeined that every person or persons whatsoever being of the said Company or ffellowship shall bear and pay such sums of mony as by the said Master Wardens and Assistants or the most part of them shalbee assessed upon him or them either for mony to bee paid to the Queenes Matie or to the Mayor of the Citty of London for the honor of the same Citty or for any other charge for the Comonwealth of this Realme and the creaditt of the same Company And whosoever refuseth to pay or upon reasonable request doth not pay according as hee is or shalbee assessed by the said Master Wardens and Assistants for the tyme being or the most part of them for any the causes aforesaid shall forfeite for every such offence to the Master Wardens and Comunalty of the said Art or Mistery for the tyme being and to bee paid to the Master Wardens and Comunalty of the same Company for the tyme being to bee imployed to the use of the said Company or ffellowship such further sum of mony or ffine not exceeding at one tyme the sum of fforty shillings of lawfull mony of England as the Master Wardens and Assistants for the tyme being or the most part of them shall agree upon and Assesse.

Oaths for the Master and Wardens

You and every of you shalbee true to our sovreigne Lady the Queene and to hir heires and successors Kings and Queenes of England yee and every of you shall endeavour yourselves the best you can justly and indifferently to execute or cause to bee executed your Offices in every respect, and all the good and lawfull Ordinances in this Booke of our Ordinances expressed without sparing any person for affeccon regard meed dread or promise of reward during the tyme yee shalbee in the same Office of your Master & Wardenship, and of all and every such goods plate jewells sums of mony or any other thing or things that by reason of your said Office shall come to any of your said hands you shall according to your Ordinances aforespecifyed make a good true and plaine Actompt or else pay such ffines as yee bee ordered to pay by our Ordinances for your not so doing, yee shall not for mallice nor for love or affeccon assesse any person or persons in a greater or lesse sum then after the quallity and quantity of his Offence after your discreacon and according to your Ordinance So helpe you God and the holy contents of that Booke.

The Oath for the Supremacy

The Oath concerning the Supremacy to bee ready by the party to bee sworne if hee can read or else to bee said by the same party after another that can read

I A: B: doe utterly testify and declare in my conscience that the Queenes highnes is the only supreme Governor of this Realme and of all other hir highnes dominions and Countryes aswell in all spirituall or eclesiasticall things as temporall and that no forreine Prince person prelate or potentate hath or ought to have any jurisdiccon power superiority preheminence or authority eclesiasticall or spirituall within this Realme And therefore I doe utterly renounce and forsake all forreine jurisdiccon power superiortyes & authorityes and doe promise that from henceforth I shall bear faith and true allegience to the Queenes highnes hir heires and lawfull successors, and to my power shall assist and defend all jurisdiccons priviledges preheminences and authorityes granted or belonging to the Queenes highnes hir heires and lawfull successors and annexed to the Imperiall Crowne of this Realme So helpe me God and by the contents of this Booke.

The Oath for the Assistants

I A: B: shall to my power mainteine keep and cause to be kept all the Ordinances rules and Statutes of this Company and shall give my best assistance advice and councell for the Comonwealth of the same, and aid and helpe the Master and Wardens of the same in all due and lawfull doings and execucon of right and justice so often as I shalbee required, if the performance of such request shall not bee to my owne greate hinderance So helpe me God and the holy contents of this Booke.

The Oath of the freedenizons

You shall swear that you shalbee good and true to our sovereigne Lady the Queene that now is and to hir heires and successors Kings and Queenes of England, the Queenes peace you shall keep to your powers and to the Master and Wardens of the Company of Joyners and of Ceelers or Carvers yee shalbee obedient and to their Successors and that none of your servants sett up no house nor shop of the said Craft of Joyners and of Ceelers or Carvers according to the Act of Parliamt made in the xiiiith and xvth yeare of our soveigne Lord King Henry the Eighth Also yee shall not make any Congregacon nor consent to any misdoers against the Queenes peace but that yee give knowledge thereof to some of the Queenes Officers for the tyme being Also the lawfull Councell of this house yee shall well and truly keep, and that yee shall not mainteine nor sett on worke no other mans servant untill that yee know that hee bee honestly departed from his Master in paien of Tenne shillings Also yee shalbee obedient to all sumons assigned by the Master and Wardens for the tyme being in paine of forfeiting for the first Offence six pence for the second Twelve pence for the Third Two shillings and for the next and every like after Six shillings and eight pence without a lawfull Excuse, the same to bee forfeited to the Master Wardens & Comunalty and to bee paid to the Master and Wardens for the tyme being to bee imployed to the use aforesaid All theis Articles yee shall well and truly keep to your power So helpe you God and the holy contents of that booke.

The Oath of Journymen & Appntices

You shalbee true to our soveigne Lady the Queene and to hir heires and successors Kings and Queenes of England, yee shalbee obedient from tyme to tyme in all matters lawfull to the Master and Wardens of your Company for the tyme being and ready to come to their lawfull sumons, except you have a lawfull excuse or else you shall pay such penaltyes as you shall forfeite by your so disobeying according to the lawfull Ordinances of your ffellowship Which Ordinances and eveyr of them to your power you shall observe and keep, all the lawfull Councell of the said ffellowship as at any tyme of Assembly shalbee lawfull in communicacon amongst your ffellowship at your comon Hall yee shall keep secret and not disclose the same to any person of the same ffellowship nor to any others and especially to any such person whom the said matter doth concerne and touch So help you God and the holy contents of that Booke.

The Oath of the Clarke

I A: B: doe sweare to bee true and faithfull to our soveigne Lady the Queene hir heires and successors Kings and Queenes of England and to the Company of Joyners and of Ceelers or Carvers all heir Councells and secrets lawfull to be concealed I shall keep secret, I shall truly without addicion diminucon or abstraccon enter into their Register all such Statutes Ordinances rules and other lawfull things as the Master Wardens and Assistants of this Company or the most part of them shall make and agree upon in open Court And in all things touching my Office I shall faithfully and truly behave my selfe towards this Company, and to the Master Wardens Officers and Rulers of the same and for the Comonwealth of the same to my power and cuning So helpe me God and the holy contents of this Booke.

The Oath of the Beadle

I A: B: doe sweare to bee faithfull and true to our soveigne Lady the Queene hir heires and successors Kings and Queenes of this Realme and to bee dilligent and attendant upon the Master and Wardens of this Company and truly and faithfully to give Sumons and Warning to every member of this Company for their appearances or for any other just cause when and as often as by the said Master and Wardens I shalbee comanded or appointed And being demaunded true and faithfull report of such my doings I shall make, and all other things apperteining to myne Office I shall duly doe and execute to the best of my power So helpe me God and the contents of this Booke.

46. Nota

Item it is ordeyned that every Assistant ffreedenizon Journyman and Appntice the Clarke and Beadle taking the Oaths aforesaid shalbee also sworn to the Oath of Supremacy above expressed in the same manner and form as the Master and Wardens bee as aforespecifyed.

47. For the Observacon of all the Orders in this Booke

Finally it is ordeined that all and every person and persons which now dwelleth or inhabiteth or hereafter shall dwell or inhabit within the Citty of London and Suburbs or within Two Myles compasse of the same aswell straingers denizons and forreines as also freemen that doe occupy any of the said Misteryes or ffacultyes of Joyners and of Ceelers or Carvers or any thing or things apperteining or in any wise belonging unto the same shall obey observe and keep all the Ordinances and rules made and written in this pnte Booke, and that aswell they as the worke made by them shalbee under the serch view and correccon of the Master and Wardens of the said Company and ffellowship of Joyners and of Ceelers or Carvers aforesaid for ever as concerning the said Mistery or ffacultyand every part thereof, and what person or persons soever hee or they bee that shall offend in any of the said Articles shall forfeite for every tyme so doing as in this said Booke is specifyed and written to the Master Wardens and Comunalty of the said Company or ffellowship, and paymt thereof shalbee made to the Master and Wardens of the same Company or ffellowship for the tyme being to bee imployed by them with the assent of vi of the Assistants or the most part of the xii Assistants of the said Company or ffellowship to the use of the said Company or ffellowship.

    All which Acts ordinances constitucons and Oaths in manner and form aforesaid aswell at the rest of the said Master Wardens Assistants and Comunalty as at the request of Edmund Chapman now Master Gabriell

Newman and Humphry Baker now Wardens of the said Company or ffellowship by the authority and virtue of the same Act of Parliamt made in the said xixth yeare of King Henry the Seaventh wee the said Lord Keeper of the greate Seale, and Lords Cheife Justices of either Bench aforesaid have seen perused read examined and fully considered, and for good lawdable and lawfull Ordinances and constitucons and Oaths wee doe accept allow and admit and by theis pnts as much as in us is or resteth ratify confirme allow and approve.

Provided alwayes and foreseene that theis Ordinances or constitucons within this Booke expressed or any of them or any part or parcell of the same in any wise extend not nor bee prejudiciall or hurtfull to the Queenes Prerogative neither to the hurt of any grant or grants by the Queenes Matie or hir noble Progenitors before tyme made to the Citty of London or any other laudable Custome used in the same Citty And in case any Article or Articles in this Book expressed seeme hereafter to the Lord Chancellor of England or Lord keeper of the greate Seale Lord Treasurer of England the Cheife Justices of the said both Benches for the tyme being or any Three of them to bee pjudiciall or hurtfull to the Queenes Maties Prerogative or to any grant by the Queenes Matie or hir noble Progenitors heretofore made to the Comunalty and Cittizens of the same City of London or any other or to any other laudable Customes above expressed or any Statutes or Lawes of this Realme That then the said Article or Articles and every of them so being pjudiciall and hurtfull as is abovesaid to bee voyd and of none effect And to bee reformed by the said Lord Chancellor Lord Keeper Lord Treasurer Cheife Justices or Thre of them for the tyme being Any thing by us the said Keeper of the greate Seale Treasurer and Two Cheife Justices in this behalfe done and made to the contrary notwithstanding.

In witnes whereof to this pnte booke wee have sett our hands and seales the ffirest day of October in the ffowerteenth yeare of the reigne of our soveigne Lady Elizabeth by the grace of God Queene of England ffrance and Ireland defendor of the faith &c.[1]

Bibliography

Secondary Literature

Books

de Acuña, Cristóbal Diatristán, *Voyages and discoveries in South-America the first up the river of Amazons to Quito in Peru, and back again to Brazil* (London: S Buckley, 1698).

Baret, John, *An Alveary or Triple Dictionary, in English, Latin, and French* (1574).

Blount, Thomas, *Glossographia* (1656).

Brewer, J. S. (Editor), *Letters and Papers, Foreign and Domestic, Henry VIII, Volume 1, 1509-1514* (London, 1920).

Brewer, J. S. (Editor), *Letters and Papers, Foreign and Domestic, Henry VIII, Volume 2, 1515-1518* (London, 1864).

Brewer, J. S. (Editor), *Letters and Papers, Foreign and Domestic, Henry VIII, Volume 3, 1519-1523* (London, 1867).

Budd, Thomas, *Good order established in Pennsilvania & New-Jersey in America being a true account of the country* (Philadelphia: William Bradford, 1685)

Butler, Sara M., *Divorce in Medieval England: From One to Two Persons in Law* (Routledge, 2013).

Carlton, Charles, *Going to the Wars: The Experience of the English Civil Wars, 1638-1651* (London: BCA, 1992).

Coles, Elisha, *An English Dictionary* (1677).

Crouch, Robert, *Royal Bargemasters: 800 Years at the Prow of Royal History* (UK: The History Press, 2019).

Defoe, Daniel, *Augusta Triumphans: Or, The Way to Make London the Most Flourishing City in the Universe* (London: 1728).

Ekwall, Eilert (Editor), 'Subsidy Roll 1292: Vintry ward', in *Two Early London Subsidy Rolls*, (1951)

Feuillerat, Albert, *Documents Relating to the Office of the Revels in the Time of Queen Elizabeth* (1908).

Firth, C. H. and Rait, R. S. (Editors), *Acts and Ordinances of the Interregnum, 1642-1660*, ed. C H Firth and R S Rait (London, 1911).

Flower, C. T. (Editor), *Calendar of Close Rolls, Henry VI: Volume 6, 1454-1461*, ed. C T Flower (London, 1947).

Gairdner, James (Editor), *Letters and Papers, Foreign and Domestic, Henry VIII, Volume 5, 1531-1532* (London, 1880).

Gairdner, James (Editor), *Letters and Papers, Foreign and Domestic, Henry VIII, Volume 6, 1533* (London, 1882).

Gairdner, James and Brodie, R. H. (Editors), *Letters and Papers, Foreign and Domestic, Henry VIII, Volume 16, 1540-1541* (London, 1898).

Gairdner, James and Brodie, R. H. (Editors), *Letters and Papers, Foreign and Domestic, Henry VIII, Volume 19, Part 1, January-July 1544* (London, 1903).

Gairdner, James and Brodie, R. H. (Editors), *Letters and Papers, Foreign and Domestic, Henry VIII, Volume 20, Part 2, August-December 1545* (London, 1907).

Gairdner, James and Brodie, R. H. (Editors), *Letters and Papers, Foreign and Domestic, Henry VIII, Volume 21, Part 1, January-August 1546* (London, 1908).

Given-Wilson, Chris; Brand, Paul; Phillips, Seymour; Ormrod, Mark; Martin, Geoffrey; Curry, Anne; and Horrox, Rosemary (Editors), *Parliament Rolls of Medieval England* (Woodbridge, 2005).

Green, Mary Anne Everett (Editor), *Calendar of State Papers Domestic: James I, 1603-1610* (London, 1857).

Gurr, Andrew and Karim-Cooper, Farah (Editors), *Moving Shakespeare Indoors: Performance and Repertoire in the Jacobean Playhouse* (Cambridge: Cambridge University Press, 2014).

Harding, Vanessa and Wright, Laura (Editors), *London Bridge: Selected Accounts and Rentals, 1381-1538* (London, 1995)

Le Hardy, William (Editor), *County of Middlesex. Calendar To the Sessions Records: New Series, Volume 1, 1612-14* (London, 1935).

Le Hardy, William (Editor), *County of Middlesex. Calendar To the Sessions Records: New Series, Volume 4, 1616-18* (London, 1941).

Henning, B. D. (Editor), *The History of Parliament: the House of Commons 1660-1690* (Boydell and Brewer, 1983)

Hill, Tracey, *Pageantry and Power: A Cultural History of the Early Modern Lord Mayor's Show, 1585-1639* (Manchester: Manchester University Press, 2011)

Holinshed, Raphael, *The firste volume of the chronicles of England, Scotlande, and Irelande* (London: John Hunne, 1577).

Huloet, Richard, *Abecedarium Anglico Latinum* (1552).

James, N. W. and James, V. A. (Editors), *The Bede Roll of the Fraternity of St Nicholas* (London, 2004).

Jones, Philip E., *The Butchers of London: A History of the Worshipful Company of Butchers of the City of London* (London: Secker & Warburg, 1976).

Jordan, W. K., *The Charities of London, 1480-1600* (Connecticut: Archon Books, 1974).

Kitching, C. J. (Editor), *London and Middlesex Chantry Certificate,1548, London Record Society Vol 16* (London, 1980).

Lane, Sidney E., *The Worshipful Company of Joiners and Ceilers or Carvers: A Chronological History* (1968).

Lindey, Laurie A., *The London Furniture Trade, 1640-1720* (PhD thesis: University of London, 2016).

Lucas, Anya and Russell, Henry, *The Livery Halls of the City of London* (Merrell, 2018).

Noorthouck, John, *A New History of London Including Westminster and Southwark* (London, 1773).

Oliver, Stefan and Croton, Guy, *Heraldry: Understanding Signs and Symbols* (London: Park Lane, 2013).

Overall, W. H. and Overall, H. C. (Editors), *Analytical Index to the Series of Records Known as the Remembrancia 1579-1664* (London, 1878).

Page, William (Editor), *A History of the County of Middlesex: Volume 2, General; Ashford, East Bedfont With Hatton, Feltham, Hampton With Hampton Wick, Hanworth, Laleham, Littleton* (London, 1911).

Palsgrave, John, *Lesclarcissement de la Langue Francoyse* (1530).

Phillips, Edward, *The New World of English Words* (1658).

Phillips, Henry Laverock, *Annals of the Worshipful Company of Joiners of the City of London* (London, 1915)

Picard, Liza, *Elizabeth's London: Everyday Life in Elizabethan London* (London: Weidenfeld & Nicolson, 2003).

Picard, Liza, *Restoration London: From Poverty to Pets, from Medicine to Magic, from Slang to Sex, from Wallpaper to Women's Rights* (London: Weidenfeld & Nicolson, 1997).

Plummer, Alfred, *The London Weaver's Company 1600-1970* (Routledge, 2013).

Raithby, John (Editor), *Statutes of the Realm: Volume 5, 1628-80* (1819).

Rider, John, *Bibliotheca Scholastica* (1589).

Sharpe, Reginald Robinson (Editor), *Calendar of Letter-books Preserved Among the Archives of the Corporation of the City of London at the Guildhall*, Vol A (London, 1899).

Sharpe, Reginald Robinson (Editor), *Calendar of Letter-books Preserved Among the Archives of the Corporation of the City of London at the Guildhall*, Vol C (London, 1901).

Sharpe, Reginald Robinson (Editor), *Calendar of Letter-books Preserved Among the Archives of the Corporation of the City of London at the Guildhall*, Vol D (London, 1902).

Sharpe, Reginald Robinson (Editor), *Calendar of Letter-books Preserved Among the Archives of the Corporation of the City of London at the Guildhall*, Vol E (London, 1903).

Sharpe, Reginald Robinson (Editor), *Calendar of Letter-books Preserved Among the Archives of the Corporation of the City of London at the Guildhall*, Vol F (London, 1904).

Sharpe, Reginald Robinson (Editor), *Calendar of Letter-books Preserved Among the Archives of the Corporation of the City of London at the Guildhall*, Vol H (London, 1907).

Sharpe, Reginald Robinson (Editor), *Calendar of Letter-books Preserved Among the Archives of the Corporation of the City of London at the Guildhall*, Vol I (London, 1909).

Sharpe, Reginald Robinson (Editor), *Calendar of Letter-books Preserved Among the Archives of the Corporation of the City of London at the Guildhall*, Vol K (London, 1911).

Sharpe, Reginald Robinson (Editor), *Calendar of Letter-books Preserved Among the Archives of the Corporation of the City of London at the Guildhall*, Vol L (London, 1912).

Sharpe, Reginald Robinson (Editor), *Calendar of Wills Proved and Enrolled in the Court of Husting, London: Part 2, 1358-1688*, (London, 1890).

Taylor, Gary and Lavagnino, John (Editors), *Thomas Middleton: The Collected Works* (Oxford: Clarendon Press, 2007).

Thomas, A. H. (Editor), *Calendar of the Plea and Memoranda Rolls of the City of London: Volume 3, 1381-1412* (London, 1932).

Thomas, Thomas, *Dictionarium Linguae Latinae et Anglicanae* (1587).

Twells, Leonard, *Twenty-Four Sermons* (London: 1743).

Ulrich, Roger B., *Roman Woodworking* (Yale: Yale University Press, 2007).

Unknown, *An Abstract or brief declaration of the present state of His Majesties revenew with the assignations and defalcations upon the same* (London: M. S., 1651).

Unknown, *Anno xi henrici vij Statuta bonu[m] publicum concerne[n]tia edita in parliamento tento apud westmonesterium xiiij die Octobris anno regni illustrissimi Domini nostri regis Henrici septimi* (1500).

Unknown, *Calendar of the Patent Rolls*, Elizabeth I, Vol 2 (London: HM Stationery Office, 1948).

Unknown, *Calendar of the Patent Rolls*, Elizabeth I, Vol 3 (London: HM Stationery Office, 1960).

Unknown, *The Kynge our souerayne lorde Henry the Seuenth* (London: Richard Pinson, 1515).

Unknown, *The Poll of the Livery-Men of the City of London at the Election for Members of Parliament* (London: 1710).

Unknown, *The Post-Office Annual Directory for 1814* (London: Critchett & Woods, 1814).

Unknown, *The Prince of Wales's National Relief Fund* (London, 1914).

Unknown, *The Proceedings at the Sessions of the Peace, and Oyer and Terminer for the City of London, and County of Middlesex*, Number VII, September 1732 (London: J Roberts, 1732).

Unknown, *The statutes prohemium Iohannis Rastell* (1527).

Veale, Elspeth M., *The English Fur Trade in the Later Middle Ages* (London, 2003).

Articles

Creasman, Pearce Paul, 'A Further Investigation of the Cairo Dahshur Boats' in *The Journal of Egyptian Archaeology*, Vol 96 (2010).

Curry, Andrew, 'The Neolithic Toolkit' in *Archaeology*, Vol 67, No 6 (Nov/Dec 2014).

Gill, Sylvia, "Of Honest Conversation and Competently Learned'. The Dissolution of the Chantries (1548) and Chantry Priests of the East and West Midlands' in *Midland History*, Vol 44, Issue 2 (2019)

Knights, Mark, 'A City Revolution: The Remodelling of the London Livery Companies in the 1680s' in *The English Historical Review*, Vol 112, No 449 (Nov 1997).

Lutkin, Jessica, 'The London Craft of Joiners, 1200-1550' in *Medieval Prosopography*, Vol 26 (2005).

Mark, Samuel E., 'Odyssey 5.234-53 and Homeric Ship Construction: A Reappraisal' in *American Journal of Archaeology*, Vol 95, No 3 (July 1991).

Rowland, Heather, 'Fighting fire with the sucking worm fire engine'; blog post published on 9 November 2016, available at https://historycollections.blogs.sas. ac.uk/2016/11/09/fighting-fire-with-the-sucking-worm-fire-engine/.

Schroeder, John J., 'War Finance in London, 1642-1646' in *The Historian*, Vol 21, No 4 (August 1959).

Unknown, 'Four Shillings in the Pound Aid 1693/4 for the City of London, City of Westminster and Metropolitan Middlesex (FSP), published online at *London Lives 1690-1800*, available via https://www.londonlives.org/static/AHDSFSP.jsp.

Unknown, 'Philip Thomas (1693/94-1762)' (Archives of Maryland (Biographical Series), 2014), available at https://msa.maryland.gov/megafile/msa/speccol/ sc3500/sc3520/001200/001246/html/01246bio.html.

Oxford Dictionary of National Biography

Breen, Kenneth. "Rodney, George Bridges, first Baron Rodney (bap. 1718, d. 1792), naval officer and politician." (2004).

Bruce, Robert J. "Boyce, William (bap. 1711, d. 1779), composer, organist, and music editor." (2004).

Ivy, Judy Crosby. "Constable, John (1776–1837), landscape painter and draughtsman." (2004).

Mercer, M. J. "Clark, Richard (1739–1831), lawyer and chamberlain of London." (2004).

Newman, John. "Jones, Inigo (1573–1652), architect and theatre designer." (2004).

Seaward, Paul. "Charles II (1630–1685), king of England, Scotland, and Ireland." (2004).

Sheldon, R. D. "Barbon, Nicholas (1637/1640–1698/9), builder and economist." (2004).

Stacey, Robert C., "Brito, Ranulf [Ranulf le Breton] (d. 1246), administrator and ecclesiastic." *(2004)*.

Thomas, Peter D. G. "Wilkes, John (1725–1797), politician." (2004).

Primary Sources

The British Library
8248.bb.29(7).
General Reference Collection 514.k.27.
General Reference Collection 522.m.9.
General Reference Collection 522.m.13.(1.).

British Museum
Banks, 70.89.
Heal, 70.94.

College of Arms
Harvey's Grants, I.C.B. 101.
Vincent 157 or 178, Old Grants 2.

Guildhall Library
MS00818/001
MS4810/001.
MS8038.
MS8039.
MS8041/001.
MS8041/002.
MS8041/003.
MS8042/005.
MS8046/001.
MS8046/002.
MS8046/003.
MS8046/004.
MS8046/005.
MS8046/006.

MS8046/007.
MS8046/008.
MS8046/009.
MS8046/010.
MS8046/011.
MS8046/012.
MS8046/013.
MS8046/014.
MS8046/015.
MS8046/016.
MS8046/017.
MS8046/018.
MS8046/019.
MS8046/020.
MS8046/021.
MS8046/022.
MS8046/023.
MS8046/024.
MS8046/025.
MS8047/001.
MS8055/001.
MS8055/002.
MS8055/004.
MS8056.
MS8058.
MS8059.
MS8060.
MS8062.
MS8063/1.
MS8063/10.
MS8063/14.
MS8063/20.
MS8063/23.
MS8063/24.
MS8063/36.
MS8064/2.
MS8064/5.
MS8064/7.
MS8064/9.
MS8064/11.
MS8064/15.
MS8064/27.
MS8064/31.
MS8064/46.
MS8065/01.
MS8065/02.
MS8065/03.
MS8065/10.
MS8065/11.
MS8065/12.
MS8065/17.
MS8065/18.

MS8065/19.
MS8065/25.
MS8065/29.
MS8065/31.
MS8065/36.
MS8070.
MS9052/48/131.

Huntingdonshire Archives
HP24/3/5.

London Metropolitan Archives
COL/CA/01/01/019/046/4.
Microfilm X109/142.
WJ/SP/1737/04/006.

The National Archives
ADM 106/515/378.
ADM 106/541/99.
ADM 106/553/145.
ADM 106/626/40.
ADM 106/690/12.
ADM 106/703/4.
ADM 106/709/34.
ADM 106/724/24.
ADM 106/724/36.
ADM 106/732/29.
ADM 106/775/31.
ADM 106/835/41.
ADM 106/866/10.
ADM 106/887/7.
ADM 106/943/91.
AO 1/2411/1-4.
AO 1/2412/6-8.
C 1/209/46.
C 1/239/56.
C 241/117/293.
C 241/121/182.
C 241/128/330.
C 241/131/16.
C 241/157/4.
C 241/179/106.
C 231/180/71.
E 115/77/32.
E 115/339/65.
E 115/346/74.
E 115/355/155.
E 115/375/83.
E 351/3202-3212.
IR 1/15.
IR 1/19.
PROB 6/66.

PROB 11/11/130.
PROB 11/61/171.
PROB 11/73/71.
PROB 11/80/513.
PROB 11/100/133.
PROB 11/102/171.
PROB 11/443/126.
PROB 11/456/191.
PROB 11/601/360.
PROB 11/639/267.
PROB 11/664/231.
PROB 11/742/243.
PROB 11/812/172.
PROB 11/845/427.
PROB 11/952/61.
PROB 11/1010/332.
RG 6/328.
RG 6/330.
RG 6/331.
RG 6/495.
RG 6/496.
RG 6/673.
RG 6/1098.
RG09/72/15/26.
SC 8/117/5826.
SP 14/128.
SP 16/222.
SP 18/71.
SP 44/335.

Newspapers

The Antiquary, Vol 1, June 1905.
Bell's Weekly Messenger, No 820, Sunday 22nd December 1811.
The Birmingham Post, No 31755, Wednesday 27th July 1960.
The British Architect, 10th July 1885.
The Chester Chronicle, No 35, Monday 25th December 1775.
Country Journal or The Craftsman, Issue 182, 27th December 1729.
Coventry Evening Telegraph, Vol LXVIII, No 10511, Thursday 15th January 1925.
Daily Journal, Issue 3003, 21st August 1730.
The Daily Register of Commerce and Intelligence, Vol 1, Issue 257, 6th November 1760.
The Daily Telegraph, No 15928, Tuesday 23rd January 1906.
The Derby Mercury, Vol XXXVI, No 1874, Friday 18th March 1768.
The Evening News and Southern Daily Mail, Issue 11511, Tuesday 28th July 1914.
The Examiner, No 3611, Saturday 14th April 1877.
The Furniture Gazette, 7th October 1876.
The Furniture Gazette, 17th February 1877.
The Furniture Gazette, 22nd September 1877.
The Furniture Gazette, 6th December 1884.
Gazetteer and New Daily Advertiser, No 12177, Monday 14th March 1768.
General Advertiser, Issue 4138, 24th March 1748.
The Globe, No 32832, Thursday 23rd August 1900.
Jackson's Oxford Journal, No 777, Saturday 19th March 1768.

The Kentish Gazette, No 351, Tuesday 1st October 1771.

The Lakes Herald, No 874, Friday 30th October 1896.

Leicester Daily Post, No 9059, Thursday 9th October 1913.

London City Press, Vol IV, No 162, Saturday 4th August 1860.

London City Press, Vol IV, No 166, Saturday 1st September 1860.

London City Press, Vol IV, No 177, Saturday 17th November 1860.

London City Press, No 459, Saturday 10th March 1866.

London City Press, No 746, Saturday 5th August 1871.

London Daily News, No 4188, Saturday 15th October 1859.

London Daily Post and General Advertiser, Issue 2627, Wednesday 23rd March 1743.

The London Evening Post, Issue 125, 24th to 26th September 1728.

The London Evening Post, Issue 2909, 26th to 28th June 1746.

The London Evening Post, Issue 3933, 11th to 15th January 1753.

The London Evening Post, Issue 4618, 11th to 14th June 1757.

London Evening Standard, No 11148, Saturday 5th May 1860.

The London Gazette, Issue 9056, 7th May 1751.

The London Gazette, Issue 9068, 18th June 1751.

The Manchester Mercury, No 1107, Tuesday 22nd September 1772.

Mercurius Pragmaticus, Issue 24, 25th September to 2nd October 1649.

Morning Chronicle, Issue 28079, Tuesday 23rd December 1856.

The Morning Post, No 20870, Friday 10th November 1837.

The Morning Post, No 34103, Friday 14th October 1881.

The Northampton Mercury, Vol LV, No 35, Monday 7th November 1774.

The Public Advertiser, Issue 6483, Monday 28th July 1755.

The Public Advertiser, Issue 7058, Friday 10th June 1757.

The Public Ledger and Daily Advertiser, Vol LII, No 16031, Wednesday 1st April 1812.

The Reading Mercury, No 508, Monday 7th October 1771.

The Salisbury and Winchester Journal, Vol LXXVI, No 3906, Monday 23rd December 1811.

St James's Gazette, Vol XXXIII, No 5095, Wednesday 28th October 1896.

The Times, Issue 9909, Friday 9th August 1816.

The Times, Issue 11364, Thursday 11th October 1821.

The Times, Issue 16606, Friday 22nd December 1837.

The Times, Issue 48066, Saturday 6th August 1938.

The Times, 20th October 2011.

Volunteer Service Gazette and Military Dispatch, Vol X, No 478, Saturday 19th December 1868.

Volunteer Service Gazette and Military Dispatch, Vol X, No 521, Saturday 16th October 1869.

Weekly Journal or Saturday's Post, 7th November 1719.

Western Times, Issue 20234, Monday 11th May 1914.

British and Irish Furniture Makers Online

British and Irish Furniture Makers Online; entry for 'Astell, John (1659)', available at https://bifmo.history.ac.uk/entry/astell-john-1659.

British and Irish Furniture Makers Online; entry for 'Astell, John (1666)', available at https://bifmo.history.ac.uk/entry/astell-john-1666.

British and Irish Furniture Makers Online; entry for 'Astell, William (1688)', available at https://bifmo.history.ac.uk/entry/astell-william-1688.

British and Irish Furniture Makers Online; entry for 'Astell, William (1695)', available at https://bifmo.history.ac.uk/entry/astell-william-1695.

British and Irish Furniture Makers Online; entry for 'Farish, Timothy (1718)', available at https://bifmo.history.ac.uk/entry/farish-timothy-1718.

British and Irish Furniture Makers Online; entry for 'Hope, Richard (1719)', available at https://bifmo.history.ac.uk/entry/hope-richard-1719.

British and Irish Furniture Makers Online; entry for 'Ince, William', available at https://bifmo.history.ac.uk/entry/ince-william.

British and Irish Furniture Makers Online; entry for 'Mayhew, John and Ince, William (1736-1811)', available at https://bifmo.history.ac.uk/entry/mayhew-john-and-ince-william-1736-1811.

British and Irish Furniture Makers Online; entry for 'Kidder, Edward (1691)', available at https://bifmo.history.ac.uk/entry/kidder-edward-1691.

British and Irish Furniture Makers Online; entry for 'Lyall, John (1717)', available at https://bifmo.history.ac.uk/entry/lyall-john-1717.

British and Irish Furniture Makers Online; entry for 'Munt, Humphrey (1654)', available at https://bifmo.history.ac.uk/entry/munt-humphrey-1654.

British and Irish Furniture Makers Online; entry for 'Munt, Humphrey (1663)', available at https://bifmo.history.ac.uk/entry/munt-humphrey-1663.

British and Irish Furniture Makers Online; keyword search results for 'Munt', available at https://bifmo.history.ac.uk/find-people?keywords=munt&name=&active_from=&active_to=&place=&occupation=&source=All.

British and Irish Furniture Makers Online; entry for 'Rand, Walter (1654)', available at https://bifmo.history.ac.uk/entry/rand-walter-1654.

British and Irish Furniture Makers Online; entry for 'Rogers, John (1679)', available at https://bifmo.history.ac.uk/entry/rogers-john-1679.

British and Irish Furniture Makers Online; entry for 'Seagood, Henry (1709)', available at https://bifmo.history.ac.uk/entry/seagood-henry-1709.

British and Irish Furniture Makers Online; entry for 'Seagood, Henry (1718)', available at https://bifmo.history.ac.uk/entry/seagood-henry-1718.

British and Irish Furniture Makers Online; entry for 'Smyth, Richard (1647)', available at https://bifmo.history.ac.uk/entry/smyth-richard-1647.

British and Irish Furniture Makers Online; entry for 'Smith, Richard (1655)', available at https://bifmo.history.ac.uk/entry/smith-richard-1655-0.

British and Irish Furniture Makers Online; entry for 'Spelsworth, Samuel (1657)', available at https://bifmo.history.ac.uk/entry/spelsworth-samuell-1657.

Miscellaneous

Boyd's Inhabitants of London, available via www.findmypast.co.uk.

Boyd's London Burials transcribed at www.findmypast.co.uk.

Boyd's Marriage Index transcribed at www.findmypast.co.uk.

Catalogue description of 'Badge', Museum of London, available via https://collections.museumoflondon.org.uk/online/object/131016.html.

Catalogue description of 'Badge', Museum of London, available via https://collections.museumoflondon.org.uk/online/object/131021.html

Catalogue description of 'William Frisbe tankard: Joiners' Company tankard', Museum of London, available via https://collections.museumoflondon.org.uk/online/object/112518.html.

Catalogue description of 'Master's chair of the Joiners' Company', Victoria and Albert Museum, available via http://collections.vam.ac.uk/item/O59056/masters-chair-of-the-joiners-armchair-newman-edward/.

Catalogue for *An Auction of Coins, Tokens, Historical Medals, Cabinets and Books* sold in September 2016, available at https://www.dnw.co.uk/media/auction_catalogues/Coins%2021%20Sep%2016.pdf.

Bibliography

Greater London Burial Index transcribed at www.findmypast.co.uk.

London Apprenticeship Abstracts 1442-1850, available via www.findmypast.co.uk.

London and Surrey Marriage Bonds and Allegations digitised by www.ancestry.co.uk.

New York Passenger Lists digitised at www.ancestry.co.uk.

The Proceedings of the Old Bailey, reference t17320906-21, 6th September 1732, p. 9, available via

https://www.oldbaileyonline.org/browse.jsp?id=t17320906-21&div=t17320906-21&terms=henry_seagood#highlight.

Samuel Pepys, *The Diary of Samuel Pepys*, transcribed online at https://www.pepysdiary.com/diary/1666/09/.

St Andrew, Holborn parish register digitised by www.ancestry.co.uk.

St Augustine, Watling Street parish register digitised by www.ancestry.co.uk.

St Bartholomew the Great parish register digitised by www.ancestry.co.uk.

St Dunstan and All Saints, Stepney parish registers digitised by www.ancestry.co.uk.

St Dunstan in the West parish register digitised by www.ancestry.co.uk.

St Mary the Virgin, Stone parish register index available via www.findmypast.co.uk.

St Michael, Cornhill parish register digitised by www.ancestry.co.uk.

Westminster Poor Law and Parish Administration records available at www.findmypast.co.uk.

Endnotes

Introduction: What Is a Joiner?

1. Thomas Thomas, *Dictionarium Linguae Latinae et Anglicanae* (1587).
2. Definition of "joiner, n.". OED Online, accessed September 2020.
3. John Baret, *An Alveary or Triple Dictionary, in English, Latin, and French* (1574).
4. John Rider, *Bibliotheca Scholastica* (1589).
5. Thomas Blount, *Glossographia* (1656); Edward Phillips, *The New World of English Words* (1658); Elisha Coles, *An English Dictionary* (1677).
6. John Palsgrave, *Lesclarcissement de la Langue Francoyse* (1530).
7. *The Furniture Gazette*, 7th October 1876, pp. 213-4.
8. Guildhall Library MS8046/023, unfoliated; entry dated 7th February 1939.
9. A square or rectangular hole is carved into one piece of wood, and a tenon or projecting piece on another piece of wood is slotted into it. It is a simple but extremely strong technique.
10. Andrew Curry, 'The Neolithic Toolkit' in *Archaeology*, Vol 67, No 6 (Nov/Dec 2014), pp. 38-41.
11. Pearce Paul Creasman, 'A Further Investigation of the Cairo Dahshur Boats' in *The Journal of Egyptian Archaeology*, Vol 96 (2010), pp. 101-23.
12. Samuel E. Mark, 'Odyssey 5.234-53 and Homeric Ship Construction: A Reappraisal' in *American Journal of Archaeology*, Vol 95, No 3 (July 1991), pp. 441-5.
13. Roger B. Ulrich, *Roman Woodworking* (Yale: Yale University Press, 2007), pp. 59-71.
14. Cristóbal Diatristán de Acuña, *Voyages and discoveries in South-America the first up the river of Amazons to Quito in Peru, and back again to Brazil* (London: S Buckley, 1698), Chapter XXXIX, pp. 90-1; EEBO Wing / V746.
15. Thomas Budd, *Good order established in Pennsilvania & New-Jersey in America being a true account of the country* (Philadelphia: William Bradford, 1685), p. 14; EEBO Wing (2nd ed., 1994) / B5358.
16. *The Furniture Gazette*, 17th February 1877, p. 90.
17. *The Furniture Gazette*, 22nd September 1877, p. 215.

Chapter 1: The Origins of the Company

1. Henry Laverock Phillips, *Annals of the Worshipful Company of Joiners of the City of London* (London, 1915), p. 2.

2. Jessica Lutkin, 'The London Craft of Joiners, 1200-1550' in *Medieval Prosopography*, Vol 26 (2005), pp. 129-64 (p. 141).

3. Ibid, p. 141.

4. Ibid, p. 129.

5. Ibid, p. 142.

6. Ibid, p. 146.

7. Ibid, p. 143.

8. Phillips, *Annals*, p. 4.

9. C. J. Kitching (Editor), 'Introduction' in *London and Middlesex Chantry Certificate, 1548*, London Record Society Vol 16 (London, 1980), pp. ix-xxxiv.

10. Sylvia Gill, "Of Honest Conversation and Competently Learned'. The Dissolution of the Chantries (1548) and Chantry Priests of the East and West Midlands' in *Midland History*, Vol 44, Issue 2 (2019), pp. 205-221.

11. 'Chantry Certificate, 1548: Corporations and Companies of the City', in Kitching, *Chantry Certificate*, pp. 81-95; the Joiners are number 197.

12. "Chantry Certificate, 1548: City of London," in Kitching, *Chantry Certificate*, pp. 1-60; St James Garlickhythe is number 16. 'Introduction' in Kitching, *Chantry Certificate*, pp.ix-xxxiv.

13. GL MS8063/14 and MS8063/20.

14. Lutkin, 'Joiners', p. 136; Reginald Robinson Sharpe (Editor), *Calendar of Letter-books Preserved Among the Archives of the Corporation of the City of London at the Guildhall*, Vol F (London, 1904), pp. 277-8.

15. Raphael Holinshed, *The firste volume of the chronicles of England, Scotlande, and Irelande* (London: John Hunne, 1577), p. 655; EEBO STC (2nd ed) / 13568b.

16. Robert C. Stacey, "Brito, Ranulf [Ranulf le Breton] (d. 1246), administrator and ecclesiastic.", ODNB (2004).

17. Eilert Ekwall (Editor), 'Subsidy Roll 1292: Vintry ward', in *Two Early London Subsidy Rolls*, (1951), pp. 181-186.

18. Sharpe, *Letter-books*, Vol C (1901), p. 245.

19. Ibid, pp. 182-3.

20. Sharpe, *Letter-books*, Vol D (1902), p. 44.

21. Ibid, p. 83.

22. Lutkin, 'Joiners', p. 137 citing Ekwall, *Subsidy Rolls*, pp. 227, 233.

23. A form of bail.

24. Sharpe, *Letter-books*, Vol D, p. 83.

25. Sharpe, *Letter-books*, Vol E (1903), p. 82.

26. Ibid, pp. 165, 167.

27. Ibid, pp. 198, 205.

28. Sharpe, *Letter-books*, Vol F, pp. 255-6.

29. The National Archives C 241/117/293.

30. TNA C 241/128/330.

31. TNA C 241/121/182.

32. TNA C 241/131/16.

33. TNA C 241/157/4.

34. TNA C 231/180/71.

35. TNA C 241/179/106.

36. Lutkin, 'Joiners', p. 147.

37. Robert Louthe died in the winter of 1401, and in his will he bequeathed land and tenements in the parish of St James Garlickhythe to his son; Reginald Robinson Sharpe (Editor), *Calendar of Wills Proved and Enrolled in the Court of Husting, London: Part 2, 1358-1688*, (London, 1890), p. 351.

38. Sharpe, *Letter-books*, Vol H (1907), pp. 41-3.

39. 'Calendar - Roll A 25: 1381-83', in A. H. Thomas (Editor), *Calendar of the Plea and Memoranda Rolls of the City of London: Volume 3, 1381-1412*, ed. A H Thomas (London, 1932), pp. 1-35.

40. 'Bridge House Weekly Payments Book 1(2): Account for 1420-1', in Vanessa Harding and Laura Wright (Editors), *London Bridge: Selected Accounts and Rentals, 1381-1538* (London, 1995), pp. 65-113.

41. Sharpe, *Letter-books*, Vol H, p. 13.

42. Sharpe, *Letter-books*, Vol A (1899), p. 150.

43. Ibid, p. 174.

44. Ibid, p. 208.

45. Sharpe, *Letter-books*, Vol I (1909), pp. 146-157.

46. Ibid, pp. 167-175.

47. Ibid, pp. 206-219.

48. Sharpe, *Letter-books*, Vol L (1912), p. 30.

49. Ibid, p. 53.

50. Ibid, p. 77.

51. Ibid, p. 98.

52. Ibid, p. 144.

53. Sharpe, *Letter-books*, Vol K (1911), pp. 248-269.

54. Lutkin, 'Joiners', p. 147.

55. Sharpe, *Calendar of Wills*, Part 2, pp. 425-429.

56. Sharpe, *Letter-books*, Vol L, pp. 61-2.

57. Sharpe, *Calendar of Wills*, Part 2, p. 548.

58. TNA SC 8/117/5826.

59. C. T. Flower (Editor), *Calendar of Close Rolls, Henry VI: Volume 6, 1454-1461*, ed. C T Flower (London, 1947), pp. 106-115.

60. *Anno xi henrici vij Statuta bonu[m] publicum concerne[n]tia edita in parliamento tento apud westmonesterium xiiij die Octobris anno regni illustrissimi Domini nostri regis Henrici septimi* (1500); EEBO STC (2nd ed,) / 9352; 'Henry VII: October 1495', in Chris Given-Wilson, Paul Brand, Seymour Phillips, Mark Ormrod, Geoffrey Martin, Anne Curry and Rosemary Horrox (Editors), *Parliament Rolls of Medieval England* (Woodbridge, 2005).

61. *The statutes prohemium Iohannis Rastell* (1527); EEBO STC (2nd ed.) / 9518.

62. J. S. Brewer (Editor) *Letters and Papers, Foreign and Domestic, Henry VIII, Volume 3, 1519-1523* (London, 1867), pp. 616-631.

63. GL MS8046/005, unfoliated; entry dated 23rd February 1724/5.

64. *The Kynge our souerayne lorde Henry the Seuenth* (London: Richard Pinson, 1515); EEBO STC / 1752:44.

65. Brewer, *Letters and Papers Henry VIII*, Vol 1 (1920), pp. 369-377.

66. Ibid, pp. 1212-1222, 1485-1503.

67. Brewer, *Letters and Papers Henry VIII*, Vol 3, pp. 1533-1539.

68. James Gairdner and R. H. Brodie (Editors), *Letters and Papers, Foreign and Domestic, Henry VIII, Volume 16, 1540-1541* (London, 1898), pp. 178-210.

69. Gairdner and Brodie, *Letters and Papers*, Vol 19, Part 1 (1903), pp. 358-388.

70. Gairdner and Brodie, *Letters and Papers*, Vol 20, Part 2 (1907), pp. 301-330.

71. Gairdner and Brodie, *Letters and Papers*, Vol 21, Part 1 (1908), pp. 749-785.

72. Brewer, *Letters and Papers Henry VIII*, Vol 2 (1864), pp. 1490-1518.

73. Brewer, *Letters and Papers Henry VIII*, Vol 3, pp. 231-249.

74. James Gairdner (Editor), *Letters and Papers, Foreign and Domestic, Henry VIII, Volume 5, 1531-1532* (London, 1880), pp. 440-459.

75. Ibid, pp. 619-636.

76. Gairdner, *Letters and Papers*, Vol 6 (1882), pp. 2-16.

Chapter 2: The Company's Charters and Ordinances

1. Phillips, *Annals*, p. 7; Sidney E. Lane, *The Worshipful Company of Joiners and Ceilers or Carvers: A Chronological History* (1968), p. 21.
2. *Calendar of the Patent Rolls*, Elizabeth I, Vol 2 (London: HM Stationery Office, 1948), p. 518.
3. The Calendar of Patent Rolls gives the date as 11th March 1564, but Stockett's accounts containing a copy of the patent give the date 11th December.
4. *Calendar of the Patent Rolls*, Elizabeth I, Vol 3 (London: HM Stationery Office, 1960), p. 85.
5. TNA E 115/375/83; E 115/339/65; E 115/346/74; E 115/355/155.
6. TNA E 351/3202-3212; AO 1/2411/1-4; AO 1/2412/6-8.
7. TNA AO 1/2411/1.
8. Ibid.
9. William Page (Editor), *A History of the County of Middlesex: Volume 2, General; Ashford, East Bedfont With Hatton, Feltham, Hampton With Hampton Wick, Hanworth, Laleham, Littleton* (London, 1911), pp. 319-324.
10. This was calculated using The National Archives' Currency Converter: 1270-2017 using the 1560 option.
11. Ibid.
12. Albert Feuillerat, *Documents Relating to the Office of the Revels in the Time of Queen Elizabeth* (1908), p. 447.
13. Ibid, p. 452.
14. TNA AO 1/2411/3.
15. LMA COL/CA/01/01/019/046/4; Microfilm X109/142.
16. GL MS8041/001, unfoliated, account dated 31st August 1640 to 19th August 1641.
17. St Dunstan in the West parish register digitised by www.ancestry.co.uk.
18. TNA PROB 11/61/171.
19. GL MS8063/24.
20. GL MS8046/024, unfoliated; entry dated 5th March 1957.
21. GL MS8059, pp. 5-8; This translation appears to have been reproduced in *Minute of the Court of Assistants of the Joiners' Company, under date 4th October, 1865* (London: 1868); BL 8248.bb.29(7). The original 1571 charter can be found in GL MS8056.
22. This transcription was created by combining documents GL MS8039, College of Arms, Vincent 157 or 178, Old Grants 2, f. 556r, and College of Arms, Harvey's Grants, I.C.B. 101, f. 106v. The description of the arms in MS8039 is badly damaged and cannot be read with clarity.
23. Stefan Oliver and Guy Croton, *Heraldry: Understanding Signs and Symbols* (London: Park Lane, 2013), pp. 46, 50, 52, 68-9, 77, 150-1, 158-63.
24. See the website of the Worshipful Company of Carpenters.
25. See the website of the Worshipful Company of Clockmakers.
26. GL MS8039.
27. *The Derby Mercury*, Vol XXXVI, No 1874, Friday 18th March 1768, p. 3.
28. *Jackson's Oxford Journal*, No 777, Saturday 19th March 1768, p. 1.
29. *The Globe*, No 32832, Thursday 23rd August 1900, p. 6.
30. GL MS8046/013, unfoliated; entry dated 3rd February 1829.
31. Ibid; 11th January 1831.
32. GL MS8046/014, unfoliated; entry dated 1st February 1842.
33. Ibid; 11th February 1842.
34. Ibid; 1st March 1842.
35. *The Globe*, No 32832, Thursday 23rd August 1900, p. 6.

36. GL MS8046/023, unfoliated; entry dated 2nd October 1934.

37. Ibid; 7th May 1935.

38. GL MS8059, pp. 58-9.

39. GL MS8038; a copy of this also appears in GL MS8059, pp. 60-72.

40. GL MS8046/001, unfoliated; accounts dated 3rd September 1633 to 8th August 1634.

41. W. H. Overall and H. C. Overall (Editors), *Analytical Index to the Series of Records Known as the Remembrancia 1579-1664* (London, 1878), pp. 466-470.

42. This was calculated using The National Archives' Currency Converter: 1270-2017 using the 1630 option.

43. GL MS8041/001, unfoliated.

44. GL MS8046/001, unfoliated; accounts dated 25th August 1638 to 2nd September 1639.

45. Ibid; 31st August 1640 to 19th August 1641.

46. John J. Schroeder, 'War Finance in London, 1642-1646' in *The Historian*, Vol 21, No 4 (August 1959), pp. 356-71 (p. 360).

47. GL MS8046/001, unfoliated; accounts dated 19th August 1641 to 1st August 1642.

48. TNA SP 29/6, f. 224r.

49. GL MS8046/001, unfoliated; accounts dated 22nd August 1642 to 1st August 1643.

50. John J Schroeder, 'War Finance in London, 1642-1646' in *The Historian*, Vol 21, No 4 (August 1959), pp. 356-71 (p. 361).

51. This figure was provided using TNA's Currency Converter using the 1650 option.

52. GL MS8046/001, unfoliated.

53. C. H. Firth and R. S. Rait (Editors), *Acts and Ordinances of the Interregnum, 1642-1660*, ed. C H Firth and R S Rait (London, 1911), p. 2.

54. Charles Carlton, *Going to the Wars: The Experience of the English Civil Wars, 1638-1651* (London: BCA, 1992), pp. 202-7.

55. *Mercurius Pragmaticus*, Issue 24, 25th September – 2nd October 1649; EEBO Thomason / 88:E.575[3].

56. GL MS8046/001, unfoliated.

57. Ibid; 6th September 1659 to 6th September 1660.

58. John Raithby (Editor), *Statutes of the Realm: Volume 5, 1628-80* (1819), pp. 207-225.

59. GL MS8046/001, unfoliated; accounts dated 6th September 1660 to 26th September 1661.

60. Laurie A. Lindey, *The London Furniture Trade, 1640-1720* (PhD thesis: University of London, 2016) p. 108.

61. GL MS8046/001, unfoliated; entries dated 6th May 1684 and 5th August 1684.

62. Paul Seaward, "Charles II (1630–1685), king of England, Scotland, and Ireland." ODNB (2004).

63. Mark Knights, 'A City Revolution: The Remodelling of the London Livery Companies in the 1680s' in *The English Historical Review*, Vol 112, No 449 (Nov 1997), pp. 1141-78 (pp. 1152-3).

64. GL MS8046/001, unfoliated; entry dated 24th February 1684/5.

65. Ibid; 27th February 1684/5.

66. TNA SP 44/335, p. 512.

67. GL MS8046/001, unfoliated; entries dated 3rd March 1684/5, 6th March 1684/5.

68. Ibid; 7th April 1685.

69. Ibid; 5th May 1685.

70. GL MS8070; a note at the bottom of the final page states that this document was 'Translated from the Copy in the Town Clerks office Guildhall' in 1854.

71. GL MS8046/002, unfoliated; entry dated 28th May 1685.

72. Ibid; 25th July 1685.
73. Ibid; 6th October 1685.
74. Ibid; 12th January 1685/6.
75. Ibid; 11th October 1687.
76. Ibid; 20th October 1687.
77. Ibid; 26th October 1687.
78. Ibid; 27th October 1687.
79. Ibid; 24th October 1687.
80. Ibid; 29th October 1687.
81. Ibid; 8th November 1687.
82. Ibid; 8th November 1687.
83. Ibid; 8th May 1688, 12th June 1688.
84. Ibid; 8th July 1688.
85. Ibid; 14th February 1687/8.
86. Ibid; 5th February 1688/9.
87. Ibid; 8th October 1688, 10th October 1688.
88. Ibid; 8th October 1688.
89. Ibid; 15th July 1690, 18th July 1690, 25th July 1690, 5th August 1690.
90. GL MS8046/005, unfoliated; entry dated 14th April 1724.
91. Ibid; 5th May 1724.
92. Ibid; 2nd June 1724.
93. Ibid; 24th June 1724.
94. Ibid; 22nd September 1724.
95. Ibid; these ordinances were copied into the entry for 26th July 1725.
96. GL MS8046/007, unfoliated; entry dated 12th January 1738/9.
97. Ibid; 16th April 1740.
98. GL MS8058.

Chapter 3: Joiners' Hall

1. GL MS8063/1.
2. *The Times*, Issue 48066, Saturday 6th August 1938, p. 13.
3. GL MS8064/2.
4. GL MS8064/7.
5. Brewer, *Letters and Papers Henry VIII*, Vol 1, pp. 1212-1222.
6. GL MS8064/5.
7. 'Chantry Certificate, 1548: Corporations and Companies of the City', in Kitching, *Chantry Certificate*, pp. 81-95; the Joiners are number 197.
8. GL MS8064/9.
9. GL MS8064/11.
10. GL MS8064/15.
11. GL MS8063/23.
12. GL MS8063/24.
13. Brewer, *Letters and Papers Henry VIII*, Vol 3, pp. 616-631.
14. GL MS8059, pp. 9-57.
15. However, the text of these copies does differ slightly to the 'official' copy presented to the Company which is now at the Guildhall.
16. Richard Huloet, *Abecedarium Anglico Latinum* (1552).
17. College of Arms, Harvey's Grants, I.C.B. 101, f. 106r; this was actually the back of the document originally but the way it has been bound means that this is the recto side of the folio, rather than the verso.

18. When Henry Laverock Phillips was conducting his research for the first published history of the Company he photographed both of the inventories, and in 1910 the photographs were pasted into a scrapbook which survived in the Company's archive; GL MS8062, p. 73.

19. GL MS8041/001, unfoliated; inventory written immediately before the 1642-3 account; A second, incomplete copy of this inventory, just listing the items in the kitchen and the parlour, was entered into the book immediately before the 1644-5 account.

20. GL MS8041/001, unfoliated; inventory written immediately before the 1645-6 account.

21. Ibid; 17th August 1654 to 20th August 1655.

22. Ibid; 1st September 1656 to 14th September 1657.

23. Ibid; 14th September 1657 to 17th August 1658.

24. GL MS8065/10.

25. GL MS8041/001, unfoliated, account dated 4th September 1665 to 30th September 1666.

26. Ibid; 4th September 1665 to 30th September 1666.

27. Samuel Pepys, *The Diary of Samuel Pepys*, transcribed online at https://www.pepysdiary.com/diary/1666/09/.

28. GL MS8046/001, unfoliated; entries dated 15th August 1682 and 5th August 1684.

29. GL MS8046/005, unfoliated, entry dated 23rd February 1724/5.

30. GL MS8041/001, unfoliated; inventory written immediately before the 1645-6 account.

31. Ibid; 4th September 1665 to 30th September 1666.

32. Ibid; 30th September 1666 to 7th October 1667.

33. This was calculated using The National Archives' Currency Converter: 1270-2017 using the 1670 option.

34. GL MS8041/001, unfoliated; account dated 7th October 1667 to 7th September 1668.

35. Ibid; 7th September 1668 to 20th September 1669.

36. GL MS8046/002, unfoliated; entry dated 3 March 1695/6.

37. Ibid; 6 July 1697.

38. Ibid; 5 June 1694.

39. Heather Rowland, 'Fighting fire with the sucking worm fire engine'; blog post published on 9 November 2016, available at https://historycollections.blogs.sas.ac.uk/2016/11/09/fighting-fire-with-the-sucking-worm-fire-engine/ (accessed 9 August 2019).

40. GL MS8046/002, unfoliated; entry dated 16 May 1694.

41. John P. Ferris, 'PARSONS, John (1639-1717), of Well Close Square, Ratcliffe, Mdx. and The Priory, Reigate, Surr.' in B. D. Henning (Editor), *The History of Parliament: the House of Commons 1660-1690* (Boydell and Brewer, 1983); R. D. Sheldon, "Barbon, Nicholas (1637/1640–1698/9), builder and economist." ODNB (2004).

42. GL MS8046/002, unfoliated; entries dated 4 April 1693, 2 May 1693.

43. Ibid; 3 March 1695/6.

44. Ibid; 1 May 1694.

45. Ibid; 30 April 1694.

46. Ibid; 18 May 1694.

47. Ibid; 5 June 1694, 26 June 1694.

48. Ibid; 4 September 1694.

49. Ibid; 2nd April 1695.

50. GL MS8046/003, unfoliated; entry dated 5th July 1698.

51. GL MS8046/002, unfoliated; entry dated 2 October 1694.

52. Ibid; 3 July 1694.

53. Ibid; 27 November 1694, 15th January 1694/5, 5th February 1694/5, 6th March 1694/5.

54. Ibid; 15th January 1694/5.

55. Ibid; 5th August 1695.

56. Ibid; 15th January 1694/5.

57. Ibid; 15th January 1694/5.

58. Ibid; 15th January 1694/5.

59. Ibid; 22nd August 1695.

60. GL MS8046/003, unfoliated; entry dated 5th April 1698.

61. Ibid; 5th July 1698.

62. GL MS8041/001, unfoliated; account from August 1621 to August 1622.

63. Ibid; August 1649 to August 1650.

64. Ibid; 12th April 1681.

65. GL MS8046/002, unfoliated; entry dated 26th October 1687.

66. GL MS8046/001, unfoliated; entry dated 22nd May 1683.

67. GL MS8046/002, unfoliated; entry dated 29th December 1687.

68. Ibid; 29th December 1687.

69. Ibid; 7th August 1688.

70. GL MS8046/009, unfoliated; entry dated 6th June 1758.

71. GL MS8046/007, unfoliated; entry dated 6th May 1735.

72. Ibid; 3rd June 1735.

73. Ibid; 1st July 1735.

74. Ibid; 5th July 1735.

75. Ibid; 5th August 1735.

76. Ibid; 29th August 1735.

77. GL MS8041/002, unfoliated; accounts dated 24th August 1735 to 23rd August 1736.

78. GL MS8046/007, unfoliated; entry dated 7th October 1735.

79. Ibid; 4th November 1735.

80. Ibid; 3rd February 1735/6.

81. Ibid; 12th November 1735.

82. Ibid; 13th January 1735/6.

83. Ibid; 26th February 1735/6.

84. Ibid; 10th February 1736/7.

85. Ibid; 5th April 1737.

86. John Noorthouck, *A New History of London Including Westminster and Southwark* (London, 1773), pp. 612-614.

87. GL MS8046/009, unfoliated; entry dated 5th February 1754.

88. Ibid; 3rd June 1755.

89. Ibid; 5th August 1755.

90. Ibid; 1st July 1755.

91. Ibid; 2nd September 1755.

92. Ibid; 7th February 1758.

93. Ibid; 2nd December 1760.

94. Ibid; 4th August 1761.

95. Ibid; 4th November 1763.

96. GL MS8046/010, unfoliated; entry dated 3rd December 1771.

97. Ibid; 7th May 1771.

98. Ibid; 20th June 1771.

99. Ibid; 6th August 1771.

100. Ibid; 7th September 1773.
101. Ibid; 7th December 1773.
102. Ibid; 7th January 1772.
103. Ibid; 3rd March 1772.
104. Ibid; 2nd March 1779.
105. Ibid; 5th September 1780.
106. GL MS8065/01.
107. GL MS8063/24.
108. GL MS8065/02.
109. GL MS8065/03.
110. GL MS8060, unfoliated.
111. GL MS8064/27.
112. GL MS8065/11.
113. GL MS8065/17.
114. GL MS8063/36.
115. GL MS8065/12.
116. GL MS8046/001, unfoliated; entry dated 4th March 1683/4; GL MS8065/15.
117. GL MS8046/002, unfoliated; entry dated 2nd March 1685/6.
118. GL MS8065/18.
119. GL MS8046/002, unfoliated; entry dated 24th May 1694.
120. Ibid; 5th February 1705/6.
121. GL MS8046/004, unfoliated; entry dated 14th April 1713.
122. GL MS8065/19.
123. GL MS8065/25.
124. GL MS8046/010, unfoliated; entry dated 7th April 1772.
125. Ibid; 5th May 1772.
126. Ibid; 25th July 1772.
127. *The Manchester Mercury*, No 1107, Tuesday 22nd September 1772, p. 2.
128. GL MS8046/010, unfoliated; entries dated 3rd May 1774 and 10th May 1774.
129. Ibid; 7th June 1774.
130. Ibid; 5th July 1774.
131. *The Chester Chronicle*, No 35, Monday 25th December 1775, p. 3.
132. Judy Crosby Ivy, "Constable, John (1776–1837), landscape painter and draughtsman." ODNB (2004).
133. GL MS8046/010, unfoliated; entry dated 15th February 1775.
134. Ibid; 21st March 1775.
135. Ibid; 4th April 1775.
136. Ibid; 2nd May 1775.
137. Ibid; 9th May 1775.
138. Ibid; 24th August 1775.
139. Ibid; 5th September 1775.
140. Ibid; 4th June 1776, 2nd July 1776.
141. Ibid; 10th September 1776, 8th October 1776.
142. Ibid; 15th November 1776.
143. Ibid; 7th March 1775.
144. Ibid; 4th March 1777, 12th March 1777.
145. Ibid; 2nd November 1779.
146. GL MS8065/29.
147. GL MS8046/012, unfoliated; entry dated 4th October 1799.
148. Ibid; 11th November 1799.
149. Ibid; 19th November 1799.
150. GL MS8065/31.

151. GL MS8046/012, unfoliated; entry dated 21st January 1800.
152. Ibid; 12th December 1799.
153. Ibid; 17th December 1799.
154. Ibid; 21st January 1800.
155. Ibid; 21st January 1800.
156. Ibid; 21st January 1800.
157. Ibid; 4th February 1800.
158. Ibid; 4th March 1800.
159. Ibid; 14th March 1800.
160. Ibid; 18th March 1800.
161. Ibid; 25th March 1800.
162. Ibid; 1st April 1800.
163. GL MS8046/022, p. 324; entry dated 6th September 1927.
164. GL MS8046/012, unfoliated; entry dated 6th May 1800.
165. GL MS8041/003, unfoliated; accounts dated 24th August 1799 to 24th August 1800.
166. GL MS8046/012, unfoliated; entry dated 1st July 1800.
167. Ibid; 25th July 1800.
168. Ibid; 23rd August 1800.
169. Ibid; 7th October 1800.
170. Ibid; 13th January 1801.
171. Ibid; 2nd June 1801.
172. Ibid; 10th April 1804.
173. Ibid; 2nd April 1805.
174. *The Public Ledger and Daily Advertiser*, Vol LII, No 16031, Wednesday 1st April 1812, p. 4.
175. GL MS8046/012, unfoliated; entry dated 24th August 1807.
176. Ibid; 2nd February 1808.
177. Ibid; 21st March 1808.
178. *Bell's Weekly Messenger*, No 820, Sunday 22nd December 1811, p. 6.
179. *The Salisbury and Winchester Journal*, Vol LXXVI, No 3906, Monday 23rd December 1811, p. 3.
180. GL MS8046/012, unfoliated; entry dated 20th December 1811.
181. Ibid; 14th January 1812.
182. Ibid; 16th January 1812.
183. Ibid; 25th February 1812.
184. Ibid; 3rd March 1812.
185. Ibid; 19th May 1812; this contains a useful summary of the interactions.
186. Ibid; 25th May 1812.
187. GL MS8064/46.
188. GL MS8046/012, unfoliated; entry dated 5th October 1813.
189. Ibid; 1st February 1814.
190. Ibid; 1st March 1814.
191. *The Times*, Issue 9909, Friday 9th August 1816, p. 3.
192. *The Times,* Issue 11364, Thursday 11th October 1821, p. 4.
193. GL MS8046/013, unfoliated; entry dated 5th February 1822.
194. Ibid; 6th April 1824.
195. Ibid; 2nd February 1830.
196. *The Times*, Issue 16606, Friday 22nd December 1837, p. 2.
197. *Morning Chronicle*, Issue 28079, Tuesday 23rd December 1856. P. 6.
198. GL MS8046/013, unfoliated; entry dated 7th June 1831.
199. GL MS8046/014, unfoliated; entry dated 6th July 1847.

200. Ibid; 5th October 1847.
201. Ibid; 7th December 1847.
202. Ibid; 14th December 1847.
203. Ibid; 11th January 1848.
204. Ibid; 5th December 1848.
205. Ibid; 11th January 1848.
206. Ibid; 7th March 1848.
207. Ibid; 24th August 1848.
208. Ibid; 1st May 1849.
209. Ibid; 1st March 1853.
210. Ibid; 5th April 1853.
211. Ibid; 7th June 1853.
212. Ibid; 7th February 1854.
213. Ibid; 4th April 1854.
214. Ibid; 13th April 1854.
215. Ibid; 6th June 1854.
216. GL MS8046/015, unfoliated; entry dated 4th March 1856.
217. Ibid; 11th March 1856.
218. GL MS8065/36.
219. GL MS8046/016, unfoliated; entry dated 3rd March 1874.
220. GL MS8046/017, unfoliated; entry dated 18th April 1882.
221. GL MS8046/016, unfoliated; entry dated 3rd March 1874.
222. Ibid; 7th April 1874.
223. Ibid; 1st September 1874.
224. Ibid; 6th October 1874; MS8046/017, unfoliated; entry dated 4th April 1882.
225. GL MS8046/017, unfoliated; entry dated 4th April 1882.
226. Ibid; 18th April 1882.
227. Ibid; 4th May 1882.
228. Ibid; 6th June 1882.
229. Ibid; 1st August 1882, 3rd October 1882.
230. Ibid; 3rd October 1882.
231. Ibid; 27th February 1883.
232. Ibid; 4th March 1884.
233. Ibid; 7th April 1885.
234. Ibid; 6th October 1885.

Chapter 4: The Company's Members

1. GL MS8059, pp. 9-57.
2. Document still held by the Worshipful Company of Joiners and Ceilers.
3. GL MS8046/001, unfoliated; entry dated 15th August 1682.
4. Ibid; 9th September 1684.
5. GL MS8046/002, unfoliated; entry dated 1st February 1686/7.
6. Ibid; 7th November 1693.
7. GL MS8046/004, unfoliated; entry dated 7th February 1715/6.
8. GL MS8059, pp. 9-57.
9. Lindey, *London Furniture Trade*, pp. 99-100.
10. Ibid, p. 120.
11. TNA SP 16/222, f. 84r.
12. St Andrew, Holborn parish register digitised by www.ancestry.co.uk.
13. LMA WJ/SP/1737/04/006.

14. *The Examiner*, No 3611, Saturday 14th April 1877, p. 10.
15. GL MS8046/022, p. 199; entry dated 8th January 1924.
16. Ibid, p. 491; 5th July 1932.
17. GL MS8046/003, unfoliated; entry dated 3rd March 1701/2.
18. Ibid; 2nd March 1702/3.
19. GL MS8059.
20. Ibid.
21. Ibid.
22. TNA PROB 11/80/513.
23. TNA PROB 11/100/133.
24. TNA PROB 11/102/171.
25. GL MS8046/022, p. 163; entry dated 6th February 1923.
26. GL MS8046/024, unfoliated; entry dated 3rd July 1956.
27. GL MS8046/010, unfoliated; entry dated 10th March 1768.
28. GL MS8046/005, unfoliated; entry dated 23rd February 1724/5.
29. *The Furniture Gazette*, 6th December 1884, p. 467.
30. GL MS8046/015, unfoliated; entry dated 6th August 1867.
31. John Newman, "Jones, Inigo (1573–1652), architect and theatre designer." ODNB (2004).
32. GL MS8059.
33. GL MS8046/002, unfoliated; entry dated 27th September 1688.
34. GL MS8046/005, unfoliated; these ordinances were copied into the entry for 26th July 1725.
35. GL MS8058.
36. GL MS8046/009, unfoliated; entry dated 6th December 1763.
37. GL MS8046/012, unfoliated; entry dated 29th September 1813.
38. GL MS8046/014, unfoliated; entry dated 12th October 1837.
39. Ibid; 7th September 1841.
40. GL MS8046/022, p. 191; entry dated 2nd October 1923.
41. Ibid; 2nd September 1924.
42. GL MS8046/001, unfoliated; entry dated 15th August 1682; Gary Taylor and John Lavagnino (Editors), *Thomas Middleton: The Collected Works* (Oxford: Clarendon Press, 2007), p. 1254; Elspeth M. Veale, *The English Fur Trade in the Later Middle Ages* (London, 2003), pp. 133-155.
43. GL MS8059.
44. GL MS8046/013, unfoliated; report dated 5th June 1834.
45. GL MS8046/004, unfoliated; entry dated 7th September 1708.
46. Ibid; 5th June 1716.
47. GL MS8046/005, unfoliated; entry dated 23rd February 1724/5.
48. *Gazetteer and New Daily Advertiser*, No 12177, Monday 14th March 1768, p. 4.
49. GL MS8046/010, unfoliated; entry dated 9th November 1771.
50. Ibid; 25th July 1780, 24th August 1780.
51. GL MS8046/013, unfoliated; entry dated 25th July 1827.
52. *The Furniture Gazette*, 6th December 1884, p. 467.
53. GL MS8046/017, unfoliated; entry dated 2nd August 1887.
54. GL MS8046/022, p. 144; entry dated 25th July 1922.
55. Ibid, p. 167; entry dated 28th March 1923.
56. Ibid, p. 311; entry dated 7th June 1927.
57. Ibid, p. 217; entry dated 5th August 1924.
58. Ibid, p. 437; 3rd March 1931.
59. GL MS8046/023, unfoliated; entry dated 5th October 1948.
60. GL MS8046/025, unfoliated; entry dated 3rd April 1973.

61. Ibid; 3rd May 1973.
62. GL MS8046/006, unfoliated; entry dated 6th February 1732/3.
63. GL MS8046/003, unfoliated; 14th January 1706/7.
64. GL MS8046/008, unfoliated; 10th January 1748/9.
65. GL MS8046/014, unfoliated; entry dated 7th August 1849.
66. GL MS8046/001, unfoliated; entry dated 7th April 1685.
67. GL MS8046/002, unfoliated; entry dated 30th December 1689.
68. GL MS8041/001, unfoliated, account dated 4th December 1637 to 20th August 1638.
69. GL MS8047/001, unfoliated; entry dated 7th October 1662.
70. GL MS8046/002, unfoliated; entry dated 25th July 1688.
71. Ibid; 4th September 1688.
72. Ibid; 6th August 1689, 5th August 1690, 1st August 1693.
73. Ibid; 21st October 1689.
74. Ibid; 15th July 1690.
75. Ibid; 24th October 1690.
76. Ibid; 22nd September 1692.
77. Ibid; 6th August 1695.
78. British and Irish Furniture Makers Online; entry for 'Kidder, Edward (1691)', available at https://bifmo.history.ac.uk/entry/kidder-edward-1691.
79. GL MS8046/002, unfoliated; entry dated 7th December 1697.
80. GL MS8046/003, unfoliated; entry dated 9th September 1701.
81. Ibid; 18th October 1706.
82. GL MS8046/004, unfoliated; entry dated 21st August 1715.
83. GL MS8046/005, unfoliated; entry dated 7th December 1725.
84. GL MS8046/007, unfoliated; entry dated 4th December 1739.
85. British and Irish Furniture Makers Online; entry for 'Farish, Timothy (1718)', available at https://bifmo.history.ac.uk/entry/farish-timothy-1718.
86. British and Irish Furniture Makers Online; entry for 'Lyall, John (1717)', available at https://bifmo.history.ac.uk/entry/lyall-john-1717; entry for 'Hope, Richard (1719)', available at https://bifmo.history.ac.uk/entry/hope-richard-1719.
87. GL MS8046/007, unfoliated; entries dated 25th July 1740 and 3rd September 1743.
88. Leonard Twells, *Twenty-Four Sermons* (London: 1743), p. xvii.
89. GL MS8046/009, unfoliated; entry dated 3rd April 1759.
90. TNA PROB 11/845/427.
91. GL MS8046/009, unfoliated; entry dated 5th August 1760.
92. Ibid; 7th August 1764.
93. GL MS8046/010, unfoliated; entry dated 5th November 1771.
94. Ibid; 3rd December 1771.
95. Ibid; 7th December 1779.
96. GL MS8046/011, unfoliated; entry dated 6th September 1796.
97. GL MS8046/002, unfoliated; entries dated 13th April 1686, 5th October 1686, and 11th January 1686/7.
98. GL MS8059.
99. GL MS8046/013, unfoliated; report dated 5th June 1834.
100. GL MS8046/022, p. 324; entry dated 6th September 1927.
101. Ibid; 1st November 1927.
102. GL MS8046/002, unfoliated; entry dated 8th October 1685.
103. Ibid; 1st March 1686/7.
104. Ibid; 13th September 1692.
105. GL MS8041/003, unfoliated; accounts dated 24th August 1781 to 24th August 1782.

106. GL MS8046/007, unfoliated; entry dated 7th December 1736.
107. GL MS8041/001, unfoliated, account dated 17th August 1654 to 20th August 1655.
108. Ibid; 7th August 1658 to 6th September 1659.
109. GL MS8047/001, unfoliated; entry dated 5th May 1662.
110. Ibid; 1st December 1662.
111. Ibid; 2nd February 1662/3.
112. Ibid; 6th October 1663.
113. Ibid; 7th November 1663.
114. Ibid; 7th December 1663.
115. Ibid; 15th September 1664.
116. British and Irish Furniture Makers Online; entry for 'Spelsworth, Samuel (1657)', available at https://bifmo.history.ac.uk/entry/spelsworth-samuell-1657.
117. Boyd's Inhabitants of London, available via www.findmypast.co.uk.
118. GL MS8046/001, unfoliated; entries dated 4th March 1681/2 and 4th April 1682.
119. British and Irish Furniture Makers Online; entry for 'Rogers, John (1679)', available at https://bifmo.history.ac.uk/entry/rogers-john-1679.
120. GL MS8046/001, unfoliated; entry dated 8th April 1684.
121. GL MS8046/002, unfoliated; entry dated 12th December 1692.
122. GL MS8046/003, unfoliated; entry dated 4th March 1700/1.
123. GL MS8046/002, unfoliated; entry dated 7th February 1692/3.
124. GL MS8046/003, unfoliated; entry dated 3rd April 1705.
125. Ibid; 8th January 1705/6.
126. GL MS8046/005, unfoliated; entry dated 8th January 1722/3.
127. Ibid; 5th February 1722/3.
128. GL MS8046/002, unfoliated; entry dated 4th April 1693.
129. Ibid; 10th January 1693/4.
130. GL MS8046/004, unfoliated; entry dated 25th July 1712.
131. Ibid; 25th July 1713.
132. GL MS8046/005, unfoliated; entry dated 7th August 1722.
133. Ibid; 8th January 1722/3, 24th January 1722/3, 5th February 1722/3.
134. *London Daily Post and General Advertiser*, Issue 2627, Wednesday 23rd March 1743, p. 2.
135. *The London Evening Post*, Issue 2909, 26th to 28th June 1746, p. 3.
136. Robert J. Bruce, "Boyce, William (bap. 1711, d. 1779), composer, organist, and music editor." ODNB (2004).
137. GL MS8046/009, unfoliated; entry dated 25th July 1755.
138. Document still held by the Worshipful Company of Joiners and Ceilers; minutes dated 1st April 1999.
139. GL MS8046/008, unfoliated; entry dated 5th December 1752.
140. Ibid; 9th January 1753.
141. Ibid; 11th January 1753.
142. *The London Evening Post*, Issue 3933, 11th to 15th January 1753, p. 1.
143. GL MS8046/008, unfoliated; entry dated 6th February 1753.
144. GL MS8046/009, unfoliated; entry dated 4th December 1753.
145. Ibid; 25th July 1755.
146. *The Public Advertiser*, Issue 6483, Monday 28th July 1755, p. 1.
147. Greater London Burial Index transcribed at www.findmypast.co.uk.
148. GL MS8046/009, unfoliated; entry dated 7th June 1757.
149. *The Public Advertiser*, Issue 7058, Friday 10th June 1757, p. 1.
150. GL MS8046/009, unfoliated; entry dated 10th June 1757.
151. *The London Evening Post*, Issue 4618, 11th to 14th June 1757, p. 4.

152. GL MS8046/010, unfoliated; entry dated 12th April 1770.

153. Ibid; 26th April 1770.

154. Ibid; 26th July 1779.

155. Ibid; 9th August 1779.

156. Ibid; 8th January 1782.

157. Ibid; 6th February 1782.

158. Ibid; 7th February 1782.

159. GL MS8046/012, unfoliated; entry dated 9th April 1806.

160. Ibid; 2nd June 1812.

161. Ibid; 29th September 1815.

162. GL MS8046/013, unfoliated; entry dated 29th September 1819.

163. Ibid; 26th October 1819.

164. Ibid; 14th January 1823.

165. Ibid; 4th March 1823. Lambun was sometimes incorrectly referred to in the court minutes as James Lamburn.

166. Ibid; 14th January 1834, 4th February 1834.

167. Ibid; 4th February 1834.

168. Ibid; 4th March 1834.

169. GL MS8046/015, unfoliated; entry dated 25th July 1854.

170. GL MS8046/016, unfoliated; entry dated 5th June 1877.

171. Ibid; 25th July 1877.

172. Ibid; 4th June 1878.

173. Ibid; 25th July 1878.

174. GL MS8046/019, unfoliated; entries dated 6th July 1897, 26th July 1897.

175. GL MS8046/022, unfoliated; entry dated 5th March 1918.

176. Ibid; 9th April 1918.

177. GL MS8059.

178. GL MS8046/013, unfoliated; report dated 5th June 1834.

179. GL MS8046/002, unfoliated; entry dated 15th October 1696.

180. GL MS8046/022, p. 306; entry dated 5th April 1927.

181. GL MS8046/002, unfoliated; entry dated 1st October 1689.

182. Ibid; November 1688.

183. Ibid; 11th December 1688.

184. Ibid; 7th May 1689.

185. Ibid; 7th January 1695/6.

186. Ibid; 3rd March 1695/6.

187. GL MS8046/003, unfoliated; entry dated 7th May 1700.

188. Ibid; 12th January 1702/3, 11th January 1703/4, 9th January 1704/5, 8th January 1705/6.

189. Ibid; 1st April 1707.

190. TNA PROB 11/601/360.

191. GL MS8046/005, unfoliated; entry dated 2nd March 1724/5.

192. Ibid; 4th March 1724/5.

193. Ibid; 26th July 1725.

194. Ibid; 10th July 1728.

195. Ibid; 25th July 1728.

196. GL MS8046/008, unfoliated; entry dated 4th September 1750.

197. GL MS8046/009, unfoliated; entry dated 3rd October 1753.

198. Ibid; 8th January 1754.

199. Ibid; 15th January 1754.

200. Ibid; 25th July 1763.

201. GL MS8046/011, unfoliated; entry dated 23rd July 1787.

202. Ibid; 25th July 1787.
203. GL MS8046/012, unfoliated; entry dated 25th July 1817.
204. GL MS8046/013, unfoliated; entry dated 12th January 1819.
205. Ibid; 16th February 1819.
206. Ibid; 2nd December 1828.
207. Ibid; 5th October 1819.
208. Ibid; 16th December 1828.
209. Ibid; 13th January 1829.
210. Ibid; 18th March 1829.
211. Ibid; 25th July 1831.
212. Ibid; dated 18th March 1829.
213. Ibid; 16th April 1829.
214. Ibid; 5th May 1829.
215. Ibid; 25th July 1837.
216. Ibid; 24th August 1837.
217. GL MS8046/014, unfoliated; entry dated 5th September 1837.
218. Ibid; 5th September 1837.
219. Ibid; 12th September 1837.
220. Ibid; 3rd October 1837.
221. Ibid; 3rd April 1838.
222. Ibid; 1st May 1838.
223. Ibid; 6th April 1841.
224. Ibid; 6th July 1841.
225. Ibid; 26th July 1841.
226. Ibid; 2nd December 1851.
227. Ibid; 7th January 1852.
228. Ibid; 13th January 1852.
229. Ibid; 7th January 1852, 26th July 1852; the entry from January stated a salary of £40 but this was raised on St James' Day to £60.
230. Ibid; 6th December 1853.
231. Ibid; 7th February 1715/6.
232. GL MS8046/014, unfoliated; entry dated 2nd July 1844.
233. GL MS8046/022, p. 147; entry dated 1st August 1922.
234. GL MS8046/001, unfoliated; entry dated 15th August 1682.
235. Taylor and Lavagnino, *Thomas Middleton,* p. 1254.
236. GL MS8047/001, unfoliated; entry dated 2nd December 1661.
237. GL MS8046/001, unfoliated; entry dated 15th August 1682.
238. GL MS8046/002, unfoliated; entry dated 5th May 1691.
239. GL MS8046/007, unfoliated; entry dated 3rd October 1738.
240. TNA RG 6/330, p. 604.
241. GL MS8059.
242. GL MS8046/013, unfoliated; report dated 5th June 1834.
243. GL MS8046/003, unfoliated; entry dated 6th December 1698.
244. GL MS8046/007, unfoliated; entries dated 31st July 1738, 16th August 1738, 11th September 1739.
245. Ibid; 26th July 1742.
246. GL MS8046/010, unfoliated; entry dated 14th April 1778.
247. Ibid; 16th June 1781.
248. GL MS8046/012, unfoliated; entry dated 19th September 1815.
249. GL MS8046/013, unfoliated; entry dated 25th July 1821.
250. Ibid; 25th July 1831.
251. Ibid; 1st October 1833.

252. GL MS8046/021, unfoliated; entry dated 11th January 1916 .
253. GL MS8046/022, p. 410; entry dated 1st April 1930.
254. Document still held by the Worshipful Company of Joiners and Ceilers; minutes dated 25th August 1987, 1st December 1987.
255. GL MS8059.
256. GL MS8046/013, unfoliated; report dated 5th June 1834.
257. GL MS8046/001, unfoliated; entry dated 7th March 1663/4.
258. GL MS8046/002, unfoliated; entry dated 1st October 1689.
259. Ibid; 13th June 1693.
260. Ibid; 4th July 1693.
261. GL MS8046/009, unfoliated; entry dated 25th July 1759.
262. Ibid; 25th July 1758.
263. Ibid; 7th August 1759.
264. Ibid; 11th September 1759.
265. Ibid; 2nd October 1759.
266. Ibid; 15th October 1759.
267. GL MS8046/007, unfoliated; entry dated 1st July 1735.
268. GL MS8046/022, p. 280; entry dated 26th July 1926.
269. GL MS8046/013, unfoliated; report dated 5th June 1834.
270. Ibid; 7th Octobeer 1828.
271. GL MS8046/015, unfoliated; entries dated 6th March 1860; 29th March 1860.
272. Ibid; 10th May 1860.
273. Ibid; 4th December 1860.
274. Ibid; 5th March 1861.
275. Ibid; 24th January 1865.
276. GL MS8046/023, unfoliated; entry dated 23rd August 1946.
277. Document still held by the Worshipful Company of Joiners and Ceilers; minutes dated 7th July 1981.
278. GL MS8046/001, unfoliated; entry dated 15th August 1682.
279. Ibid; 8th April 1684.
280. Ibid; 21st August 1684.
281. GL MS8046/002, unfoliated; entries dated 20th August 1691, 1st September 1691, 6th October 1691, 13th October 1691, 1st December 1691.
282. Ibid; 8th January 1694/5.
283. GL MS8046/004, unfoliated; entry dated 25th July 1712; MS8046/005, unfoliated; entry dated 4th March 1724/5.
284. TNA PROB 11/664/231.
285. GL MS8046/005, unfoliated; entry dated 2nd July 1728.
286. GL MS8046/005, unfoliated; entry dated 25th July 1728.
287. *The London Evening Post*, Issue 125, 24th to 26th September 1728, p. 1.
288. Daniel Defoe, *Augusta Triumphans: Or, The Way to Make London the Most Flourishing City in the Universe* (London: 1728), pp. 61-3.
289. GL MS8046/010, unfoliated; entry dated 13th October 1780.
290. Ibid; 9th January 1781.
291. Ibid; 3rd April 1781.
292. Ibid; 2nd July 1782.
293. Ibid; 13th October 1780.
294. Ibid; 6th February 1781.
295. Ibid; 11th March 1776.
296. Ibid; 7th October 1777.
297. M. J. Mercer, "Clark, Richard (1739–1831), lawyer and chamberlain of London." ODNB (2004).

298. GL MS8046/011, unfoliated; entry dated 3rd October 1784.

299. GL MS8041/003, unfoliated; accounts dated 24th August 1781 to 24th August 1782.

300. Kenneth Breen, "Rodney, George Bridges, first Baron Rodney (bap. 1718, d. 1792), naval officer and politician." ODNB (2004).

301. GL MS8046/022, p. 194; entry dated 6th November 1923.

302. Lindey, *London Furniture Trade*, p. 85.

303. Brewer, *Letters and Papers Henry VIII*, Vol 3, pp. 616-631.

304. Page, *County of Middlesex*, pp. 139-141.

305. TNA SP 14/128, ff. 81r:v.

306. TNA SP 18/71, f. 56.

307. Raithby, *Statutes*, pp. 603-612.

308. GL MS8046/002, unfoliated; entry dated 5th June 1694.

309. Ibid; 19th October 1694; a printed copy of this act can be found at EEBO Wing / L2861F.

310. GL MS4810/001, f. 15r.

311. TNA PROB 11/73/71.

312. GL MS8064/31.

313. Boyd's Marriage Index transcribed at www.findmypast.co.uk.

314. Westminster Poor Law and Parish Administration records available at www.findmypast.co.uk.

315. Mary Anne Everett Green (Editor), *Calendar of State Papers Domestic: James I, 1603-1610* (London, 1857), pp. 64-90.

316. TNA E 115/77/32.

317. Green, *State Papers Domestic: James I*, pp. 495-507.

318. Robert Crouch, *Royal Bargemasters: 800 Years at the Prow of Royal History* (UK: The History Press, 2019).

319. William Le Hardy (Editor), *County of Middlesex. Calendar To the Sessions Records: New Series, Volume 1, 1612-14* (London, 1935), pp. 370-400.

320. Le Hardy, *Middlesex Sessions*, Vol 4 (1941), pp. 85-6.

321. Oliver Jones, 'Documentary evidence for an indoor Jacobean theatre' in Andrew Gurr and Farah Karim-Cooper (Editors), *Moving Shakespeare Indoors: Performance and Repertoire in the Jacobean Playhouse* (Cambridge: Cambridge University Press, 2014), pp. 65-78 (p. 76).

322. *An Abstract or brief declaration of the present state of His Majesties revenew with the assignations and defalcations upon the same* (London: M. S., 1651), p. 63; EEBO Wing (2nd ed, 1994) / A148; this was a reprint.

323. Boyd's London Burials transcribed at www.findmypast.co.uk.

Chapter 5: The Women of the Joiners' Company

1. GL MS8064/2.

2. Philip E. Jones, *The Butchers of London: A History of the Worshipful Company of Butchers of the City of London* (London: Secker & Warburg, 1976), pp. 11, 26, 76, 143.

3. N. W. James and V. A. James (Editors), *The Bede Roll of the Fraternity of St Nicholas* (London, 2004), pp. 98-107.

4. TNA PROB 11/11/130.

5. TNA C 1/209/46.

6. Sara M. Butler, *Divorce in Medieval England: From One to Two Persons in Law* (Routledge, 2013), p. 36.

7. TNA C 1/239/56.
8. GL MS8064/5-8.
9. GL MS8063/10.
10. 'Chantry Certificate, 1548: Corporations and Companies of the City', in Kitching, *Chantry Certificate*, pp. 81-95; the Joiners are number 197.
11. GL MS8046/002, unfoliated; entries dated 2nd October 1688, 2nd December 1690, 9th June 1691, 6th October 1691.
12. GL MS8046/001, unfoliated; entries dated 12th April 1681, 6th September 1681, 10th January 1681/2, 1st August 1682; MS8046/002, unfoliated; entries dated 3rd November 1685, 5th October 1686, 3rd April 1688.
13. GL MS8046/002, unfoliated; entries dated 7th January 1689/90, 1st July 1690.
14. GL MS8046/009, unfoliated; entry dated 8th October 1756.
15. GL MS8046/012, unfoliated; entry dated 3rd August 1813.
16. Ibid; 10th January 1815.
17. Ibid; 4th April 1815.
18. GL MS8046/014, unfoliated; entry dated 2nd April 1844.
19. Ibid; 4th November 1845.
20. Ibid; 25th July 1850.
21. GL MS8046/015, unfoliated; entry dated 25th July 1856.
22. GL MS8046/021, unfoliated; entry dated 6th July 1915.
23. Ibid; 10th August 1915.
24. GL MS8046/022, p. 325; entry dated 4th October 1927.
25. GL MS8046/003, unfoliated; entry dated 7th March 1703/4.
26. GL MS8046/005, unfoliated; entry dated 8th January 1722/3.
27. GL MS8046/003, unfoliated; entry dated 6th November 1705.
28. GL MS8046/013, unfoliated; entry dated 5th August 1834.
29. GL MS8046/014, unfoliated; entry dated 7th April 1846.
30. New York Passenger Lists digitised at www.ancestry.co.uk.
31. GL MS8046/014, unfoliated; entry dated 5th June 1849.
32. Ibid; 7th June 1853.
33. He was Master for the year 1659-60.
34. GL MS8046/001, unfoliated; entries dated 7th January 1661/2, 2nd February 1661/2.
35. GL MS8046/006, unfoliated; entry dated 1st April 1735; MS8046/007, unfoliated; entry dated 9th September 1735.
36. GL MS8046/008, unfoliated; entry dated 12th November 1745.
37. GL MS8046/002, unfoliated; entries dated 7th October 1690, 5th December 1693.
38. GL MS8046/002, unfoliated; entry dated 6th March 1692/3; MS8046/004, unfoliated; entry dated 9th September 1718.
39. GL MS8046/002, unfoliated; entry dated 5th April 1698; MS8046/003, unfoliated; entry dated 4th July 1704; MS8046/004, unfoliated; entry dated 6th September 1720.
40. GL MS8046/011, unfoliated; entry dated 4th March 1788.
41. GL MS8046/002, unfoliated; entry dated 7th April 1691.
42. Ibid; 5th May 1696.
43. Ibid; 9th September 1690, 4th November 1690, 7th November 1693, 3rd July 1694.
44. British and Irish Furniture Makers Online; entry for 'Rand, Walter (1654)', available at https://bifmo.history.ac.uk/entry/rand-walter-1654.
45. Boyd's Inhabitants of London; available via www.findmypast.co.uk.
46. St Michael, Cornhill parish register digitised by www.ancestry.co.uk.
47. St Augustine, Watling Street parish register digitised by www.ancestry.co.uk.
48. GL MS8046/001, unfoliated; entry dated 1st August 1682.

49. GL MS8046/003, unfoliated; entry dated 5th March 1705/6.
50. GL MS8046/006, unfoliated; entry dated 3rd September 1734.
51. GL MS8055/001, unfoliated.
52. British Museum Banks, 70.89 and Heal, 70.94.
53. TNA IR 1/14, f. 99.
54. GL MS8046/008, unfoliated; entry dated 2nd December 1746.
55. TNA IR 1/15, p. 203.
56. TNA RG 6/328, p. 332.
57. TNA RG 6/331, p. 596.
58. TNA RG 6/496, p. 325.
59. TNA RG 6/496, p. 594.
60. TNA RG 6/328, p. 349.
61. TNA RG 6/673, f. 7r.
62. *Country Journal or The Craftsman*, Issue 182, 27th December 1729, p. 2.
63. TNA RG 6/673, f. 46v.
64. *Daily Journal*, Issue 3003, 21st August 1730, p. 3.
65. TNA PROB 11/639/267.
66. TNA RG 6/1098, p. 325.
67. TNA RG 6/330, p. 488.
68. TNA RG 6/495, p. 529.
69. Unknown, 'Philip Thomas (1693/94-1762)' (Archives of Maryland (Biographical Series), 2014), available at https://msa.maryland.gov/megafile/msa/speccol/sc3500/sc3520/001200/001246/html/01246bio.html.
70. GL MS8046/008, unfoliated; entry dated 2nd December 1746.
71. GL MS8055/002.
72. GL MS8046/010, unfoliated; entry dated 4th May 1773.
73. GL MS8046/012, unfoliated; entry dated 1st December 1812.
74. GL MS8046/002, unfoliated; entry dated 14th July 1691.
75. British and Irish Furniture Makers Online; entry for 'Munt, Humphrey (1654)', available at https://bifmo.history.ac.uk/entry/munt-humphrey-1654; entry for 'Munt, Humphrey (1663)', available at https://bifmo.history.ac.uk/entry/munt-humphrey-1663.
76. Catalogue for *An Auction of Coins, Tokens, Historical Medals, Cabinets and Books* sold in September 2016, available at https://www.dnw.co.uk/media/auction_catalogues/Coins%2021%20Sep%2016.pdf.
77. Boyd's Marriage Index transcribed at www.findmypast.co.uk.
78. British and Irish Furniture Makers Online; keyword search results for 'Munt', available at https://bifmo.history.ac.uk/find-people?keywords=munt&name=&active_from=&active_to=&place=&occupation=&source=All.
79. TNA PROB 6/66, p. 13.
80. London Apprenticeship Abstracts 1442-1850, available via www.findmypast.co.uk.
81. GL MS8046/006, unfoliated; entry dated 4th February 1734/5.
82. GL MS8046/012, unfoliated; entry dated 4th October 1803.
83. GL MS8055/004.
84. *The Post-Office Annual Directory for 1814* (London: Critchett & Woods, 1814), p. 10.
85. GL MS8055/001.
86. British and Irish Furniture Makers Online; entry for 'Seagood, Henry (1709)', available at https://bifmo.history.ac.uk/entry/seagood-henry-1709.

87. British and Irish Furniture Makers Online; entry for 'Seagood, Henry (1718)', available at https://bifmo.history.ac.uk/entry/seagood-henry-1718.
88. St Bartholomew the Great parish register digitised by www.ancestry.co.uk.
89. *The Proceedings at the Sessions of the Peace, and Oyer and Terminer for the City of London, and County of Middlesex*, Number VII, September 1732 (London: J Roberts, 1732), p. 181.
90. *The Proceedings of the Old Bailey*, reference t17320906-21, 6th September 1732, p. 9, available via https://www.oldbaileyonline.org/browse.jsp?id=t17320906-21&div=t17320906-21&terms=henry_seagood#highlight.
91. GL MS9052/48/131.
92. *The London Gazette*, Issue 9056, 7th May 1751, p, 4.
93. *The London Gazette*, Issue 9068, 18th June 1751, p. 4.
94. GL MS8046/008, unfoliated; entries dated 7th August 1744, 7th July 1747.
95. TNA PROB 11/952/61.
96. TNA IR 1/19, p. 132.
97. TNA PROB 11/1010/332.
98. GL MS8055/001, unfoliated.
99. St Mary the Virgin, Stone parish register index available via www.findmypast.co.uk.
100. TNA PROB 11/742/243.
101. *General Advertiser*, Issue 4138, 24th March 1748, p. 3.
102. British and Irish Furniture Makers Online; entry for 'Ince, William', available at https://bifmo.history.ac.uk/entry/ince-william; entry for 'Mayhew, John and Ince, William (1736-1811)', available at https://bifmo.history.ac.uk/entry/mayhew-john-and-ince-william-1736-1811.
103. GL MS8046/002, unfoliated; entries dated 24th October 1687, 19th August 1689
104. GL MS8046/017, unfoliated; entry dated 3rd June 1884.
105. GL MS8046/015, unfoliated; entry dated 19th May 1857.
106. Ibid; 7th June 1859.
107. GL MS8046/016, unfoliated; entry dated 6th July 1880.
108. *The Examiner*, No 3611, Saturday 14th April 1877, p. 11.
109. GL MS8046/022, p. 304; entry dated 29th March 1927.
110. Ibid, p. 310; 12th May 1927.
111. Ibid, p. 332; 6th December 1927.
112. Ibid, p. 335; 3rd January 1928.
113. Ibid, p. 368; 9th January 1929.
114. Ibid, p. 401; 3rd December 1929.
115. Ibid, p. 434; 6th January 1931.
116. Ibid, p. 484; 5th April 1932, 7th February 1933.
117. GL MS8046/023, unfoliated; entry dated 5th March 1935.
118. Ibid; 7th April 1936, 9th June 1936.
119. Ibid; 25th July 1949.
120. Ibid; 22nd February 1950.
121. Ibid; 30th January 1951.
122. Ibid; 10th April 1951.
123. Unknown, 'Four Shillings in the Pound Aid 1693/4 for the City of London, City of Westminster and Metropolitan Middlesex (FSP), published online at *London Lives 1690-1800*, available via https://www.londonlives.org/static/AHDSFSP.jsp.
124. GL MS8046/002, unfoliated; entry dated 23rd August 1693.
125. Ibid; 2nd April 1695.
126. Ibid; 20th August 1696.

127. Ibid; 4th December 1694.
128. Ibid; 8th January 1694/5.
129. Ibid; 15th January 1694/5.
130. Ibid; 7th April 1696, 27th April 1697; St Dunstan and All Saints, Stepney parish registers digitised by www.ancestry.co.uk.
131. TNA PROB 11/456/191.
132. GL MS8046/003, unfoliated; entry dated 6th August 1700.
133. GL MS8046/008, unfoliated; entries dated 2nd August 1743, 6th September 1743, 6th December 1743.
134. TNA PROB 11/812/172.
135. GL MS8046/002, unfoliated; entry dated 2nd July 1695.
136. GL MS8046/008, unfoliated; entry dated 6th December 1746.
137. Ibid; 6th November 1750.
138. GL MS8046/009, unfoliated; entry dated 6th May 1760.
139. GL MS8046/007, unfoliated; entry dated 3rd May 1743.
140. GL MS8046/008, unfoliated; entry dated 5th March 1744/5.
141. Ibid; 18th November 1746.
142. GL MS8046/002, unfoliated; entry dated 4th August 1691.
143. Ibid; 10th November 1692.
144. Ibid; 1st August 1693.
145. GL MS8046/004, unfoliated; entry dated 14th July 1713; MS8046/005, unfoliated; entry dated 4th February 1728/9.
146. GL MS8046/006, unfoliated; entry dated 7th January 1734/5.
147. Ibid; 4th March 1734/5.
148. Document still held by the Worshipful Company of Joiners and Ceilers; Joiners' Company Membership Committee report, 2001.
149. Ibid; minutes dated 6th June 2002, 2nd July 2002.
150. Ibid; minutes dated 1st April 2003.
151. Ibid; minutes dated 16th November 2004.

Chapter 6: The Company's Calendar

1. GL MS8059.
2. GL MS8046/002, unfoliated; entry dated 10th January 1693/4; MS8046/008, unfoliated; entry dated 2nd October 1750.
3. GL MS8046/003, unfoliated; entry dated 7th June 1698.
4. GL MS8046/001, unfoliated; entry dated 5th September 1682.
5. Ibid; 3rd February 1684/5.
6. GL MS8047/001, unfoliated; entry dated 2nd December 1661.
7. GL MS8046/003, unfoliated; entry dated 4th September 1705.
8. GL MS8046/002, unfoliated; entry dated 7th November 1693.
9. GL MS8046/008, unfoliated; entry dated 2nd October 1750.
10. GL MS8046/009, unfoliated; entry dated 30th August 1757.
11. GL MS8046/010, unfoliated; entries dated 10th February 1769, 3rd April 1770.
12. Ibid; 2nd October 1770.
13. Ibid; 4th May 1779.
14. GL MS8046/023, unfoliated; entry dated 20th October 1949.
15. GL MS8046/025, unfoliated; entry dated 5th November 1974.
16. GL MS8059.
17. GL MS8046/014, unfoliated; entry dated 26th July 1852.
18. GL MS8046/002, unfoliated; entry dated 8th July 1688.

19. GL MS8046/008, unfoliated; entry dated 3rd April 1750.
20. GL MS8059.
21. GL MS8038; a copy of this also appears in GL MS8059, pp. 60-72.
22. GL MS8041/001, unfoliated; accounts dated 15th August 1621 to 9th September 1622.
23. GL MS8046/001, unfoliated; entries dated 2nd February 1662/3, 4th November 1679, 5th August 1690, 2nd August 1692, 9th June 1696, 4th August 1696, 7th June 1698.
24. Ibid; 2nd May 1664.
25. Ibid; 9th June 1726.
26. GL MS8041/002, unfoliated; accounts dated 24th August 1739 to 22nd August 1740.
27. GL MS8046/008, unfoliated; entry dated 7th July 1747.
28. GL MS8046/002, unfoliated; entries dated 25th July 1688, 2nd December 1690.
29. GL MS8046/003, unfoliated; entry dated 14th January 1706/7.
30. Ibid; 4th February 1706/7.
31. GL MS8046/007, unfoliated; entry dated 5th September 1732.
32. Ibid; 6th May 1735, 3rd June 1735.
33. Ibid; 9th September 1735.
34. GL MS8046/008, unfoliated; entry dated 7th July 1747.
35. *The Examiner*, No 3611, Saturday 14th April 1877, p. 10; See Lindey, *Furniture Trade* for further discussion about the decline of guilds during the eighteenth and nineteenth centuries.
36. GL MS8063/10.
37. GL MS4810/001, f. 5r.
38. GL MS8063/24.
39. GL MS00818/001, f. 6r.
40. Ibid; f. 123v.
41. GL MS8046/002, unfoliated; entries dated 5th October 1686, 6th March 1687/8; MS8046/005, unfoliated; entry dated 7th November 1727.
42. GL MS8046/022, p. 408; entry dated 26th March 1930.
43. Ibid, p. 439; 30th March 1931.
44. Ibid, p. 441; 14th April 1931.
45. Ibid, p. 452; 28th July 1931.
46. GL MS8046/023, unfoliated; entry dated 6th May 1941.
47. GL MS8063/24.
48. GL MS8059.
49. GL MS8063/24.
50. GL MS8046/012, unfoliated; entry dated 25th July 1800.
51. Ibid; 7th July 1801.
52. Ibid; 2nd July 1805.
53. Ibid; 1st July 1806.
54. *London City Press*, Vol IV, No 162, Saturday 4th August 1860, p. 4.
55. 1861 census; TNA RG09/72/15/26.
56. *London City Press*, Vol IV, No 166, Saturday 1st September 1860, p. 4.
57. *London City Press*, Vol IV, No 177, Saturday 17th November 1860, p. 4.
58. GL MS8059.
59. GL MS8046/001, unfoliated; entry dated 7th September 1663; GL MS8046/002, unfoliated; entries dated 3rd August 1686, 2nd August 1687.
60. GL MS8046/010, unfoliated; entry dated 25th July 1780.
61. GL MS8046/005, unfoliated; entry dated 23rd August 1726.
62. GL MS8046/013, unfoliated; entry dated 2nd December 1828.

63. Ibid; 1st October 1833.
64. Ibid; 5th June 1834.
65. GL MS8046/024, unfoliated; entry dated 1st February 1955.
66. GL MS8046/002, unfoliated; entry dated 19th August 1689.
67. GL MS8046/008, unfoliated; entry dated 5th September 1749.
68. GL MS8046/009, unfoliated; entry dated 5th August 1755.
69. Ibid; 6th September 1763.
70. Ibid; 4th October 1763.
71. GL MS8046/012, unfoliated; entry dated 23rd August 1806.
72. GL MS8046/015, unfoliated; entry dated 4th September 1860.
73. GL MS8046/003, unfoliated; entry dated 14th October 1702.
74. GL MS8046/009, unfoliated; entry dated 12th January 1762.
75. GL MS8046/003, unfoliated; entry dated 18th October 1706.
76. GL MS8046/005, unfoliated; entry dated 7th November 1727; MS8046/008, unfoliated; entry dated 6th December 1748.
77. GL MS8046/002, unfoliated; entries dated 6th November 1688 and 12th November 1689.
78. Ibid; 3rd June 1690.
79. Ibid; 1st December 1691, 5th April 1698.
80. GL MS8046/003, unfoliated; entry dated 7th February 1698/9.
81. GL MS8046/005, unfoliated; entry dated 1st October 1728.
82. GL MS8046/004, unfoliated; entry dated 3rd August 1708.
83. Ibid; 6th October 1719.
84. GL MS8046/006, unfoliated; entry dated 2nd November 1731.
85. Ibid; 3rd December 1734.
86. Ibid; 5th November 1734, 7th January 1734/5.
87. GL MS8046/007, unfoliated; entries dated 6th April 1742, 3rd May 1743; MS8046/008, entries dated 6th November 1744, 5th March 1744/5, 18th November 1746, 6th December 1748.
88. GL MS8046/008, unfoliated; entry dated 3rd November 1747.
89. GL MS8046/009, unfoliated; entry dated 4th December 1753.
90. Ibid; 3rd December 1754.
91. Ibid; 4th November 1755.
92. Ibid; 13th January 1756.
93. Ibid; 1st December 1761.
94. GL MS8046/010, unfoliated; entry dated 6th December 1768.
95. Ibid; 5th December 1769.
96. Phillips, *Annals*, p. 70.
97. GL MS8046/002, unfoliated; entry dated 11th October 1686.
98. Ibid; 27th October 1687.
99. *Weekly Journal or Saturday's Post*, 7th November 1719, p. 291.
100. GL MS8046/009, unfoliated; entry dated 13th January 1756.
101. Ibid; 1st February 1763.
102. GL MS8046/006, unfoliated; entry dated 7th December 1731.
103. Ibid; 7th November 1732.
104. Ibid; 5th December 1732.
105. GL MS8046/009, unfoliated; entry dated 4th November 1760.
106. *The Daily Register of Commerce and Intelligence*, Vol 1, Issue 257, 6th November 1760, p. 1027.
107. GL MS8046/012, unfoliated; entry dated 22nd September 1814.
108. GL MS8046/013, unfoliated; entry dated 25th July 1823.
109. *The Morning Post*, No 20870, Friday 10th November 1837, p. 1.

110. GL MS8046/014, unfoliated; entry dated 19th October 1837.
111. Ibid; 28th October 1837.
112. Ibid; 2nd November 1837.
113. The following year Payne requested that this letter should be removed from the record.
114. GL MS8046/015, unfoliated; entry dated 7th November 1854. Richardson wrote in 1859 to request that his letter be removed from the record.
115. GL MS8046/024, unfoliated; entry dated 26th August 1963.
116. Document still held by the Worshipful Company of Joiners and Ceilers.
117. GL MS8046/022, unfoliated; entry dated 2nd September 1919.
118. GL MS8046/024, unfoliated; entry dated 3rd January 1956.

Chapter 7: The Company's Goods

1. GL MS8046/017, unfoliated; entry dated 18th May 1886.
2. GL MS8046/012, unfoliated; entry dated 12th December 1799.
3. GL MS8046/013, unfoliated; entry dated 13th January 1818.
4. Ibid; 3rd October 1826.
5. Ibid; 13th January 1829.
6. GL MS8046/015, unfoliated; entry dated 3rd March 1868.
7. Ibid; 5th May 1868.
8. Ibid; 6th October 1868.
9. Ibid; 1st December 1868.
10. GL MS8046/016, unfoliated; entry dated 24th August 1880.
11. GL MS8046/017, unfoliated; entry dated 12th January 1886.
12. GL MS8046/018, unfoliated; entry dated 5th September 1893.
13. Ibid; 3rd October 1893.
14. Ibid; 9th August 1894.
15. GL MS8046/021, unfoliated; entry dated 24th August 1915.
16. Ibid; 14th August 1917.
17. GL MS8046/022, unfoliated; entry dated 25th August 1919.
18. Ibid; 2nd September 1919.
19. Ibid; 4th November 1919.
20. GL MS8046/023, unfoliated; entry dated 7th December 1937.
21. Ibid; 4th January 1938.
22. Ibid; 7th November 1939.
23. GL MS8046/024, unfoliated; entry dated 1st March 1960.
24. Ibid; 3rd May 1960.
25. Document still held by the Worshipful Company of Joiners and Ceilers; minutes dated 12th March 1991.
26. GL MS8046/009, unfoliated; entry dated 1st October 1754.
27. Ibid; 12th November 1754.
28. GL MS8041/002, unfoliated; accounts from 22 August 1754 to August 1755.
29. Catalogue description of 'Master's chair of the Joiners' Company', Victoria and Albert Museum, available via http://collections.vam.ac.uk/item/O59056/masters-chair-of-the-joiners-armchair-newman-edward/.
30. GL MS8046/013, unfoliated; entry dated 2nd October 1827.
31. GL MS8046/014, unfoliated; entry dated 3rd March 1852.
32. GL MS8046/015, unfoliated; entry dated 14th January 1868.
33. GL MS8046/016, unfoliated; entry dated 2nd March 1880.
34. GL MS8046/020, unfoliated; entry dated 1st December 1903.

35. GL MS8046/020, unfoliated; entry dated 5th September 1905.

36. GL MS8046/020, unfoliated; entry dated 3rd October 1905.

37. *The Daily Telegraph*, No 15928, Tuesday 23rd January 1906, p. 6.

38. GL MS8046/021, unfoliated; entry dated 7th March 1916.

39. GL MS8046/022, p. 57; entry dated 25th August 1919.

40. Ibid, p. 117; 24th August 1921.

41. Ibid, p. 139; 6th June 1922.

42. Ibid, p. 223; 2nd September 1924.

43. *Coventry Evening Telegraph*, Vol LXVIII, No 10511, Thursday 15th January 1925, p. 4.

44. GL MS8046/022, pp. 272-3; entry dated 6th July 1926.

45. Ibid, p. 287; 7th September 1926.

46. Ibid, p. 307; 3rd May 1927.

47. GL MS8046/023, unfoliated; entry dated 4th February 1936.

48. Ibid; 3rd June 1941.

49. Ibid; 15th December 1949.

50. Ibid; 20th February 1951.

51. GL MS8046/024, unfoliated; entry dated 17th March 1960; Document still held by the Worshipful Company of Joiners and Ceilers; minutes dated 4th May 1999.

52. GL MS8041/001, unfoliated; account dated 28th August 1655 to 21st August 1656.

53. Ibid; inventory written immediately before the 1642-3 account.

54. Ibid; inventory written immediately before the 1645-6 account.

55. GL MS8046/014, unfoliated; entry dated 6th April 1852.

56. GL MS8046/023, unfoliated; entry dated 6th June 1939.

57. *The Antiquary*, Vol 1, June 1905, p. 231.

58. Document still held by the Worshipful Company of Joiners and Ceilers; minutes dated 8th November 1988.

59. GL MS8046/025, unfoliated; entries dated 25th March 1970.

60. I did contact the Museum of London asking for any acquisition notes they may hold about this item but due to the closures caused by COVID-19 it was not possible for the staff to retrieve this information.

61. Catalogue description of 'William Frisbe tankard: Joiners' Company tankard', Museum of London, available via https://collections.museumoflondon.org.uk/online/object/112518.html.

62. GL MS8041/001.

63. Boyd's Inhabitants of London, entry 39483, available via www.findmypast.co.uk.

64. Boyd's Marriage Index transcribed at www.findmypast.co.uk.

65. Boyd's Inhabitants of London, entry 48758, available via www.findmypast.co.uk.

66. British and Irish Furniture Makers Online; entry for 'Smyth, Richard (1647)', available at https://bifmo.history.ac.uk/entry/smyth-richard-1647; entry for 'Smith, Richard (1655)', available at https://bifmo.history.ac.uk/entry/smith-richard-1655-0.

67. GL MS8041/001, unfoliated; accounts dated 20th August 1646 to 17th August 1647.

68. GL MS8047/001, unfoliated; entry dated 7th October 1662.

69. GL MS8046/008, unfoliated; entry dated 2nd October 1750.

70. GL MS8046/012, unfoliated; entry dated 12th December 1799.

71. GL MS8046/014, unfoliated; entry dated 24th August 1838.

72. GL MS8046/016, unfoliated; entry dated 2nd March 1880.

73. *Western Times*, Issue 20234, Monday 11th May 1914, p. 4.

74. *The Evening News and Southern Daily Mail*, Issue 11511, Tuesday 28th July 1914, p. 8.

75. GL MS8046/023, unfoliated; entry dated 7th March 1933.
76. Ibid; 23rd August 1935.
77. Ibid; 28th March 1952.
78. GL MS8046/024, unfoliated; entry dated 12th October 1954.
79. Ibid; 5th February 1963.
80. Ibid; 1st December 1964.
81. GL MS8046/025, unfoliated; entry dated 1st June 1976.
82. Ibid; 25th August 1969.
83. Ibid; 7th July 1970.
84. Ibid; 25th March 1976.
85. Ibid; 7th December 1976.
86. Ibid; 1st March 1977.
87. Ibid; 5th April 1977.
88. Ibid; 7th February 1978.
89. Ibid; 9th October 1979, 6th November 1979.
90. GL MS8042/005, p. 187.
91. GL MS8046/025, unfoliated; entry dated 5th February 1980.
92. Ibid; 25th March 1980.
93. Ibid; 6th May 1980.
94. Document still held by the Worshipful Company of Joiners and Ceilers; minutes dated 7th December 1982.
95. GL MS8046/025, unfoliated; entry dated 3rd June 1980.
96. Document still held by the Worshipful Company of Joiners and Ceilers; minutes dated 7th December 1982.
97. GL MS8046/016, unfoliated; entry dated 5th September 1876.
98. GL MS8046/017, unfoliated; entry dated 3rd April 1883.
99. Ibid; 5th June 1883.
100. GL MS8046/023, unfoliated; entry dated 26th March 1935.
101. Ibid; 2nd July 1935.
102. Ibid; 4th June 1935.
103. Ibid; 2nd July 1935.
104. GL MS8046/024, unfoliated; entry dated 24th August 1966.
105. Ibid; 4th October 1966.
106. Document still held by the Worshipful Company of Joiners and Ceilers; minutes dated 11th June 1991.
107. Ibid; letter dated 25th February 1991.
108. Ibid; minutes dated 4th February 1992, 3rd November 1992.
109. See the website of the Worshipful Company of Tylers and Bricklayers; Alfred Plummer, *The London Weaver's Company 1600-1970* (Routledge, 2013), p. 119.
110. GL MS8041/001, unfoliated, account dated 22nd September 1650 to 16th September 1651.
111. Ibid; 9th August 1639 to 3rd August 1640.
112. Ibid; 28th August 1655 to 21st August 1656.
113. Ibid; 17th August 1658 to 6th September 1659.
114. Ibid; 26th September 1661 to 25th September 1662.
115. Ibid; 26th September 1662 to 19th September 1663, 19th September 1663 to 15th September 1664.
116. Ibid; 7th October 1667 to 7th September 1668.
117. GL MS8046/022, p. 375; entry dated 27th March 1929.
118. Ibid, p. 275; 1st June 1926.
119. Ibid, p. 301; 1st March 1927.

120. Ibid, p. 303; 29th March 1927.
121. Ibid, pp. 377-8; 9th April 1929.
122. GL MS8046/024, unfoliated; entry dated 3rd May 1960.
123. Ibid; 30th August 1960.
124. Ibid; 3rd October 1961.
125. Ibid; 4th December 1962.
126. Ibid; 3rd November 1964.
127. Ibid; 7th March 1967.
128. GL MS8046/015, unfoliated; entry dated 25th July 1866; GL MS8046/016, unfoliated; entry dated 1st March 1870.
129. GL MS8046/016, unfoliated; entry dated 29th March 1870.
130. Ibid; 5th April 1870.
131. Ibid; 25th July 1870.
132. Ibid; 3rd October 1871.
133. GL MS8046/017, unfoliated; entry dated 1st November 1881.
134. Ibid; 2nd October 1883.
135. GL MS8046/024, unfoliated; entry dated 6th September 1955.
136. Ibid; 29th March 1961.
137. GL MS8046/021, unfoliated; entry dated 1st September 1914.
138. GL MS8046/022, p. 368; entry dated 8th January 1929.
139. GL MS8046/023, unfoliated; entry dated 4th July 1933.
140. GL MS8046/022, p. 104; entry dated 3rd May 1921.
141. GL MS8046/023, unfoliated; entry dated 11th August 1936.
142. GL MS8046/022, p. 415; entry dated 1st July 1930.
143. GL MS8046/025, unfoliated; entry dated 4th March 1975.
144. GL MS8046/024, unfoliated; entry dated 18th March 1964.
145. GL MS8046/025, unfoliated; entries dated 2nd April 1968, 7th May 1968.
146. Ibid; 4th June 1968.
147. Ibid; 3rd December 1968.
148. Document still held by the Worshipful Company of Joiners and Ceilers; minutes dated 25th August 1987.
149. GL MS8046/014, unfoliated; entry dated 3rd April 1838.
150. GL MS8046/016, unfoliated; entry dated 17th March 1876.
151. GL MS8046/015, unfoliated; entry dated 6th September 1859.
152. Ibid; 6th October 1863.
153. *Leicester Daily Post*, No 9059, Thursday 9th October 1913, p. 5.
154. Catalogue description of 'Badge', Museum of London, available via https://collections.museumoflondon.org.uk/online/object/131021.html.
155. Catalogue description of 'Badge', Museum of London, available via https://collections.museumoflondon.org.uk/online/object/131016.html.
156. GL MS8046/024, unfoliated; entry dated 4th July 1967.
157. Ibid; 25th July 1967.
158. GL MS8046/025, unfoliated; entry dated 25th October 1978.

Chapter 8: Eighteenth- and Nineteenth-century Finance and Politics

1. British and Irish Furniture Makers Online; entry for 'Astell, John (1659)', available at https://bifmo.history.ac.uk/entry/astell-john-1659.
2. British and Irish Furniture Makers Online; entry for 'Astell, John (1666)', available at https://bifmo.history.ac.uk/entry/astell-john-1666.
3. Lindey, *Furniture Trade*, p. 149.

4. British and Irish Furniture Makers Online; entry for 'Astell, William (1688)', available at https://bifmo.history.ac.uk/entry/astell-william-1688.
5. British and Irish Furniture Makers Online; entry for 'Astell, William (1695)', available at https://bifmo.history.ac.uk/entry/astell-william-1695.
6. GL MS8046/002, unfoliated; entry dated 8th October 1697.
7. *The Poll of the Livery-Men of the City of London at the Election for Members of Parliament* (London: 1710), p. 95.
8. TNA PROB 11/443/126.
9. TNA ADM 106/515/378.
10. TNA ADM 106/541/99; ADM 106/553/145.
11. The National Archives' Discovery catalogue states that there are over 700 letters concerning Astell in the ADM series relating to his Navy contract.
12. TNA ADM 106/887/7.
13. TNA ADM 106/626/40; ADM 106/703/4; ADM 106/943/91;
14. TNA ADM 106/724/24; ADM 106/835/41.
15. TNA ADM 106/709/34; ADM 106/690/12; ADM 106/724/36; ADM 106/732/29; ADM 106/775/31; ADM 106/866/10.
16. London and Surrey Marriage Bonds and Allegations digitised by www.ancestry.co.uk.
17. Huntingdonshire Archives, HP24/3/5.
18. GL MS8046/004, unfoliated; entry dated 15th July 1720.
19. Ibid; 13th September 1720.
20. BL General Reference Collection 514.k.27, item 19.
21. BL General Reference Collection 514.k.27, items 16 and 17.
22. BL General Reference Collection 522.m.9.
23. This was calculated using The National Archives' Currency Converter: 1270-2017 using the 1720 option.
24. BL General Reference Collection 522.m.9.
25. BL General Reference Collection 514.k.27.(1.).
26. BL General Reference Collection 522.m.13.(1.).
27. GL MS8046/005, unfoliated; entries dated 1st May 1722, 5th June 1722; GL MS8041/002, unfoliated; account dated 24th August 1721 to 24th August 1722.
28. GL MS8046/005, unfoliated; entries dated 5th February 1722/3 and 5th March 1722/3.
29. Ibid; 14th April 1724, 14th July 1724.
30. GL MS8046/007, unfoliated; entry dated 26th February 1735/6.
31. GL MS8046/005, unfoliated; entries dated 1st September 1724 and 6th October 1724.
32. GL MS8046/006, unfoliated; entry dated 12th January 1730/1.
33. GL MS8046/005, unfoliated; entry dated 7th September 1725.
34. Ibid; 7th September 1731, 2nd November 1731.
35. GL MS8046/006, unfoliated; entries dated 4th September 1733, 2nd October 1733, and 6th November 1733.
36. GL MS8041/002, unfoliated; entry dated 19th February 1734.
37. This was calculated using The National Archives' Currency Converter: 1270-2017 using the 1730 option.
38. GL MS8046/007, unfoliated; entries dated 7th October 1735, 12th November 1735.
39. Ibid; 26th February 1735/6.
40. Ibid; 10th February 1736/7.
41. Ibid; 5th April 1737.
42. Ibid; 24th August 1737.
43. Ibid; 7th February 1737/8, 21st February 1737/8.

44. GL MS8055/001, unfoliated; list of Court of Assistants, 1737-8.
45. GL MS8046/007, unfoliated; entry dated 7th February 1737/8.
46. GL MS8046/008, unfoliated; entry dated 23rd August 1751.
47. Ibid; 22nd August 1745.
48. Ibid; 24th August 1752.
49. GL MS8046/009, unfoliated; entry dated 4th February 1755.
50. Ibid; 4th March 1755.
51. Ibid; 24th August 1759.
52. Ibid; 7th February 1764.
53. Ibid; 4th December 1764.
54. Ibid; 8th January 1765.
55. Ibid; 2nd April 1765.
56. GL MS8046/010, unfoliated; entry dated 7th May 1765.
57. Ibid; 22nd August 1765.
58. Ibid; 3rd March 1767.
59. Ibid; 7th April 1767.
60. Ibid; 5th May 1767.
61. Ibid; 2nd June 1767.
62. Ibid; 7th July 1767, 26th July 1767.
63. Ibid; 4th August 1767.
64. Ibid; 1st September 1767.
65. Ibid; 24th August 1767.
66. Ibid; 6th October 1767.
67. Ibid; 3rd November 1767.
68. Ibid; 1st December 1767.
69. Ibid; 12th January 1768.
70. Ibid; 7th June 1768.
71. Ibid; 6th September 1768.
72. Ibid; 4th October 1768.
73. Ibid; 1st November 1768.
74. Ibid; 6th December 1768.
75. Ibid; 3rd April 1770.
76. Ibid; 4th September 1770.
77. Peter D. G. Thomas, "Wilkes, John (1725–1797), politician." ODNB (2004).
78. GL MS8046/010, unfoliated; entry dated 10th March 1768.
79. *Gazetteer and New Daily Advertiser*, No 12177, Monday 14th March 1768, p. 4.
80. Ibid.
81. Thomas, "Wilkes".
82. GL MS8046/010, unfoliated; entry dated 25th July 1770.
83. Ibid; 24th August 1770.
84. Ibid; 4th September 1770.
85. Ibid; 18th September 1770, 21st September 1770, 25th September 1770, 28th September 1770, 29th September 1770.
86. Ibid; 2nd October 1770.
87. Ibid; 6th November 1770.
88. Ibid; 4th December 1770.
89. Ibid; 8th January 1771.
90. Ibid; 5th February 1771, 5th March 1771, 9th April 1771.
91. Ibid; 7th May 1771.
92. Ibid; 4th June 1771, 2nd July 1771.
93. Ibid; 9th July 1771.
94. Ibid; 25th July 1771, 6th August 1771.

95. Ibid; 24th August 1771.
96. *The Kentish Gazette*, No 351, Tuesday 1st October 1771, p. 3.
97. *The Reading Mercury*, No 508, Monday 7th October 1771, p. 3.
98. GL MS8046/010, unfoliated; entries dated 18th October 1774, 25th October 1774.
99. Ibid; 6th December 1774.
100. Ibid; 15th February 1775.
101. Ibid; 18th October 1774.
102. Ibid; 18th October 1774.
103. Ibid; 25th October 1774.
104. *The Northampton Mercury*, Vol LV, No 35, Monday 7th November 1774, p. 3.
105. GL MS8046/010, unfoliated; entry dated 6th December 1774.
106. Ibid; 4th April 1775.
107. Ibid; 21st November 1781.
108. Document still held by the Worshipful Company of Joiners and Ceilers; minutes dated 1st October 1985.
109. Ibid; minutes dated 24th August 1988.
110. GL MS8046/010, unfoliated; entry dated 9th November 1771.
111. Ibid; 28th January 1772.
112. Ibid; 4th February 1772.
113. Ibid; 8th August 1772.
114. Ibid; 24th August 1772.
115. Ibid; 27th November 1772.
116. Ibid; 27th November 1772.
117. Ibid; 20th November 1772.
118. Ibid; 11th October 1773.
119. GL MS8046/013, unfoliated; entry dated 23rd August 1817.
120. GL MS8046/014, unfoliated; entry dated 14th August 1838.
121. Ibid; 2nd July 1839.
122. Ibid; 25th July 1839.
123. Ibid; 15th August 1843.
124. Ibid; 7th April 1840.
125. Ibid; 2nd February 1841.
126. Ibid; 3rd June 1845.
127. *London Evening Standard*, No 11148, Saturday 5th May 1860, p. 4.
128. *London City Press*, No 459, Saturday 10th March 1866, p. 5.
129. GL MS8046/014, unfoliated; entry dated 31st January 1844.
130. Ibid; 14th January 1845.
131. Ibid; 4th February 1845.
132. Ibid; 4th March 1845.
133. Ibid; 25th July 1845.
134. Ibid; 7th October 1845.
135. Ibid; 6th April 1847.
136. Ibid; 25th July 1850.
137. Ibid; 1st October 1850.
138. Ibid; 7th October 1851, 2nd November 1852.
139. Lane, *Joiners*, p. 26.
140. GL MS8046/015, unfoliated; entry dated 4th April 1861.
141. GL MS8046/016, unfoliated; entry dated 2nd April 1880.
142. GL MS8046/015, unfoliated; entry dated 29th March 1864.
143. *London Daily News*, No 4188, Saturday 15th October 1859, p. 6.
144. *Volunteer Service Gazette and Military Dispatch*, Vol X, No 478, Saturday 19th December 1868, pp. 3-4.

145. *Volunteer Service Gazette and Military Dispatch*, Vol X, No 521, Saturday 16th October 1869, p. 2.
146. *The Examiner*, No 3611, Saturday 14th April 1877, p. 11.
147. GL MS8046/016, unfoliated; entry dated 29th March 1870.
148. Ibid; 5th April 1870.
149. Ibid; 6th December 1870.
150. Ibid; 7th February 1871.
151. Ibid; 7th March 1871.
152. *London City Press*, No 746, Saturday 5th August 1871, p. 3.
153. GL MS8046/016, unfoliated; entry dated 25th July 1872; 25th July 1873.
154. Ibid; 25th July 1874.
155. Ibid; 3rd December 1878.
156. Ibid; 5th February 1872.
157. Ibid; 5th August 1873.
158. GL MS8046/017, unfoliated; entry dated 24th August 1883.
159. Ibid; 4th March 1884.
160. *The Morning Post*, No 34103, Friday 14th October 1881, p. 5.
161. GL MS8046/017, unfoliated; entry dated 25th July 1883.
162. Ibid; 7th August 1883.
163. *The British Architect*, 10th July 1885, p. 16.
164. *St James's Gazette*, Vol XXXIII, No 5095, Wednesday 28th October 1896, p. 4.
165. *The Lakes Herald*, No 874, Friday 30th October 1896, p. 2.
166. GL MS8046/018, unfoliated; entry dated 1st August 1893.
167. Ibid; 6th August 1895.
168. GL MS8046/019, unfoliated; entry dated 3rd September 1895.

Chapter 9: The World Wars and Later Twentieth Century

1. *The Prince of Wales's National Relief Fund* (London, 1914), digitised by the Wellcome Collection, available at https://wellcomecollection.org/works/f5fn33k8.
2. GL MS8046/021, unfoliated; entry dated 11th August 1914.
3. Ibid; 1st September 1914.
4. Ibid; 6th October 1914.
5. Ibid; 3rd November 1914.
6. Ibid; 12th January 1915.
7. Ibid; 13th April 1915.
8. Ibid; 1st June 1915.
9. Ibid; 3rd November 1914.
10. GL MS8046/023, unfoliated; entry dated 4th February 1941.
11. GL MS8046/021, unfoliated; entry dated 1st December 1914.
12. Ibid; 6th February 1917.
13. Ibid; 26th July 1915.
14. Ibid; 24th August 1915.
15. Ibid; 26th July 1915.
16. GL MS8046/022, unfoliated; entry dated 25th July 1918.
17. GL MS8046/021, unfoliated; entry dated 6th July 1915.
18. Ibid; 10th August 1915.
19. Ibid; 7th September 1915.
20. Ibid; 3rd October 1916.
21. Ibid; 7th November 1916.

22. Ibid; 5th December 1916.
23. Ibid; 6th February 1917.
24. GL MS8046/022, p. 12; entry dated 2nd July 1918.
25. Ibid, p. 30; 3rd December 1918.
26. Ibid, p. 31; 7th January 1919.
27. Ibid, pp. 33-34; 4th February 1919.
28. Ibid, p. 38; 31st March 1919.
29. Ibid, p. 46; 3rd June 1919.
30. Ibid, p. 52; 25th July 1919.
31. Ibid, p. 62; 8th October 1919.
32. Ibid, p. 58; 2nd September 1919.
33. Ibid, p. 255; 27th July 1925.
34. Ibid, p. 83; 26th July 1920.
35. Ibid, p. 86; 24th August 1920.
36. Ibid, p. 88; 7th September 1920.
37. Ibid, p. 113; 25th July 1921.
38. Ibid, p. 216; 25th July 1924.
39. Ibid, p. 222; 2nd September 1924.
40. Ibid, p. 383; 4th June 1929.
41. Ibid, p. 491; 5th July 1932.
42. GL MS8046/023, unfoliated; entry dated 7th February 1933.
43. Ibid; 24th October 1934.
44. Ibid; 5th September 1939.
45. Ibid; 6th June 1939.
46. Ibid; 3rd October 1939.
47. Ibid; 17th October 1939.
48. Ibid; 7th November 1939.
49. Ibid; 7th November 1939.
50. Ibid; 5th December 1939.
51. Ibid; 5th March 1940.
52. Ibid; 6th February 1940.
53. Ibid; 19th March 1940.
54. Ibid; 7th May 1940.
55. Ibid; 2nd July 1940.
56. Ibid; 25th March 1941.
57. Ibid; 6th May 1941.
58. Ibid; 2nd July 1940.
59. Ibid; 6th August 1940.
60. Ibid; 4th September 1940.
61. Ibid; 6th February 1946.
62. Ibid; 3rd September 1940.
63. Ibid; 1st October 1940.
64. Ibid; 4th March 1941.
65. Ibid; 1st April 1941.
66. Lane, *Joiners*, p. 36.
67. GL MS8046/023, unfoliated; entry dated 7th January 1941.
68. Ibid; 4th February 1941.
69. Ibid; 7th January 1941.
70. Ibid; 7th January 1941.
71. Ibid; 4th February 1941.
72. Ibid; 3rd June 1941.
73. Ibid; 3rd June 1941.

74. Ibid; 1st July 1941.

75. Ibid; 25th July 1941.

76. Ibid; 12th December 1941.

77. Ibid; 23rd July 1942.

78. Ibid; 23rd July 1942.

79. Ibid; 19th April 1943.

80. Ibid; 29th July 1943, 24th August 1943.

81. Ibid; 16th December 1943.

82. GL MS8046/021, unfoliated; entry dated 1st December 1914.

83. Ibid; 1st June 1915.

84. Ibid; 7th December 1915.

85. Ibid; 6th June 1916.

86. Ibid; 5th December 1916.

87. Ibid; 4th December 1917.

88. GL MS8046/022, pp. 9-10; entry dated 4th June 1918.

89. Ibid, pp. 27-28; 3rd December 1918.

90. Ibid, p. 68; 2nd December 1919.

91. Ibid, p. 94; 14th December 1920.

92. Ibid, p. 124; 6th December 1921.

93. Ibid, p. 195; 4th December 1923.

94. GL MS8046/023, unfoliated; entry dated 5th December 1933.

95. GL MS8046/022, p. 159; entry dated 9th January 1923.

96. Ibid, p. 196; 4th December 1923.

97. Ibid, pp. 78-79; 1st June 1920; p. 138; 6th June 1922.

98. Ibid, pp. 139-40; 6th June 1922.

99. Ibid, p. 154; 7th November 1922.

100. Ibid, p. 145; 25th July 1922.

101. Ibid, p. 157; 5th December 1922.

102. Ibid, p. 160; 9th January 1923.

103. Ibid, p. 165; 6th March 1923.

104. Ibid, p. 196; Ibid 4th December 1923.

105. Ibid, p. 204; 28th March 1924.

106. Ibid, p. 303; 29th March 1927.

107. Ibid, pp. 381-2; 4th June 1929.

108. Ibid, p. 400; 3rd December 1929.

109. Ibid, p. 407; 26th March 1930.

110. GL MS8046/023, unfoliated; entry dated 5th December 1933.

111. Ibid; 2nd February 1937.

112. Ibid; 24th March 1937.

113. Ibid; 7th December 1937.

114. Ibid; 3rd October 1939.

115. Ibid; 6th February 1940.

116. Ibid; 5th March 1940.

117. Ibid; 25th July 1940.

118. Ibid; 3rd December 1940.

119. Ibid; 4th February 1941.

120. Ibid; 31st July 1944.

121. Ibid; 25th July 1946.

122. Ibid; 17th May 1950, 25th July 1950.

123. Ibid; 20th December 1951.

124. GL MS8046/024, unfoliated; entry dated 25th July 1952.

125. GL MS8046/025, unfoliated; entries dated 4th March 1975, 25th July 1975.

126. GL MS8046/023, unfoliated; entry dated 6th February 1946.
127. Ibid; 25th July 1947.
128. Ibid; 23rd August 1946.
129. Ibid; 25th August 1947.
130. Ibid; 2nd March 1948.
131. Ibid; 26th July 1948.
132. Ibid; 25th July 1947.
133. Ibid; 25th August 1947.
134. Ibid; 2nd March 1948.
135. Ibid; 19th May 1949.
136. Ibid; 7th December 1948.
137. Ibid; 1st February 1949.
138. Ibid; 8th September 1949.
139. Ibid; 5th October 1948.
140. Ibid; 20th October 1949.
141. GL MS8046/025, unfoliated; entry dated 5th November 1974.
142. GL MS8046/023, unfoliated; entry dated 2nd June 1949.
143. Ibid; 22nd February 1950.
144. Ibid; 28th August 1951.
145. Ibid; 20th October 1949.
146. Ibid; 20th December 1951.
147. Ibid; 17th October 1950.
148. GL MS8046/024, unfoliated; entry dated 25th October 1957.
149. GL MS8046/025, unfoliated; entry dated 6th February 1973.
150. GL MS8046/024, unfoliated; entry dated 24th August 1955.
151. Ibid; 6th September 1955.
152. Ibid; 2nd June 1959.
153. Ibid; 24th August 1959.
154. Ibid; 7th March 1961.
155. Ibid; 5th November 1957.
156. *The Birmingham Post,* No 31755, Wednesday 27th July 1960, p. 6.
157. GL MS8046/024, unfoliated; entry dated 7th May 1963.
158. Ibid; 11th June 1963.
159. Ibid; 6th April 1965.
160. Ibid; 1st June 1965.
161. GL MS8046/025, unfoliated; entry dated 3rd November 1970.
162. Ibid; 2nd February 1971.
163. Ibid; 5th February 1974.
164. Ibid; 25th July 1974.
165. Ibid; 2nd March 1976.
166. Document still held by the Worshipful Company of Joiners and Ceilers; minutes dated 6th May 1986.
167. Ibid; minutes dated 2nd July 2002.
168. Ibid; minutes dated 2nd February 1988.
169. Ibid; minutes dated 3rd May 1983, 14th June 1983.
170. Ibid; minutes dated 3rd April 1984, 4th February 1986.
171. Ibid; minutes dated 5th March 1985, 7th November 1991.
172. GL MS8046/024, unfoliated; entry dated 16th December 1953.
173. Ibid; 2nd March 1954.
174. Ibid; 15th April 1954.
175. Ibid; 25th July 1962.
176. Ibid; 2nd October 1962, 30th October 1962.

177. GL MS8046/025, unfoliated; entry dated 25th July 1968.
178. Document still held by the Worshipful Company of Joiners and Ceilers; minutes dated 3rd November 1987.
179. Ibid; minutes dated 8th November 1994.
180. Ibid; minutes dated 5th May 1998, 2nd February 1999.
181. GL MS8046/025, unfoliated; entries dated 29th October 1969.
182. Ibid; 2nd February 1971, 3rd March 1971.
183. Ibid; 1st December 1970.
184. Ibid; 6th July 1971.
185. Ibid; 8th June 1971.
186. GL MS8046/023, unfoliated; entry dated 25th August 1949.
187. GL MS8046/024, unfoliated; entry dated 12th May 1953.
188. Ibid; 24th August 1953.
189. Ibid; 11th November 1953.
190. Ibid; 5th April 1955.
191. Document still held by the Worshipful Company of Joiners and Ceilers; minutes dated 1st June 1982, 6th May 1986.

Conclusion: The Worshipful Company of Joiners and Ceilers in the Twenty-first Century

1. Ibid; minutes dated 6th July 1999.
2. Ibid; minutes dated 2nd March 1999.
3. *The Times*, 20th October 2011, p. 64.

Appendix A: The Company's 1572 Ordinances

1. GL MS8059, pp. 9-57.